Genetic Control of Environmental Pollutants

BASIC LIFE SCIENCES

Alexander Hollaender, General Editor

Associated Universities, Inc., Washington, D.C.

A Continuation Order Plan is available for this series. A continuation order will bring delivery of each new
volume immediately upon publication. Volumes are billed only upon actual shipment. For further information
please contact the publisher.

Genetic Control of Environmental Pollutants

Edited by

Gilbert S. Omenn

University of Washington
Seattle, Washington

and

Alexander Hollaender

Associated Universities, Inc.
Washington, D.C.

Associate Editors

A. M. Chakrabarty, Morris Levin, Eugene Nester,
and Gordon H. Orians

Technical Editor

Claire M. Wilson

PLENUM PRESS • NEW YORK AND LONDON

Library of Congress Cataloging in Publication Data

Main entry under title:

Genetic control of environmental pollutants.

(Basic life sciences; v. 28)
"Proceedings of a conference. . . held July 31–August 3, 1983, in Seattle, Washington"—Verso t.p.
Includes bibliographical references and index.
1. Genetic engineering—Congresses. 2. Pollution—Congresses. I. Omenn, Gilbert S. II. Hollaender, Alexander, 1898–   . III. Series.
TP248.6.G45   1984   628.5   83-26942
ISBN 0-306-41624-7

Proceedings of a conference on Genetic Control of Environmental Pollutants, held July 31–August 3, 1983, in Seattle, Washington.

This material is based upon work supported in part by the Department of the Navy (Grant N00014-83-G-0022 issued by the office of the Naval Research), National Science Foundation (Grant OIR-08218327), U.S. Department of Energy (Grant DE-FG06-83ER), Environmental Protection Agency (Contract 79-D-X0856), and National Institute of Environmental Health Science (Contract 1Y01-ES3010600).

Any opinions, findings, and conclusions or recommendations expressed in this publication are those of the authors and do not necessarily reflect the views of the above-mentioned agencies, nor does mention of trade names or commercial products constitute endorsement or recommendation for use.

The U.S. Government has a royalty-free license throughout the world in all copyrightable material contained herein.

DEDICATION

Robert W. Day   J. Thomas Grayston

Tom Grayston and Bob Day were Vice-President for Health
Sciences and Dean of the School of Public Health and Community
Medicine, respectively, at the University of Washington during the
time this Conference was organized. They are Gil Omenn's predeces-
sors as Dean of Public Health and leading figures in their field.

We share their view that the field of Public Health is much
enriched by substantial collaborations with laboratory scientists,
ecologists, engineers, physicians, and policy researchers. The
challenges of protecting people from natural and man-made hazards in
the modern environment require just the kind of multidisciplinary,
multi-sector efforts as are represented in this Conference and in
this volume.

THE EDITORS

CONTENTS

DIVERSE CAPABILITIES OF MICROORGANISMS

POSTERS

WELCOME AND INTRODUCTION

Gilbert S. Omenn

Dean, Public Health and Community Medicine
University of Washington
Seattle, Washington 98195

On behalf of the University of Washington, the City of Seattle, the sponsors and donors, and my co-organizers, I am delighted to welcome all of you to this Conference on Genetic Control of Environmental Pollutants. My only regret is that Dr. Alexander Hollaender, who has inspired so many of us as young scientists and stimulated so many trail-blazing conferences in environmental sciences and in genetic engineering, is ill and was unable to make the trip to Seattle. He sends his warm good wishes for an outstanding meeting and a fine volume.

The purpose of this Conference is to identify and assess strategies for more effectively and safely managing wastes and toxic substances in the environment, in part through use of genetically engineered microorganisms. There is a sense of desperation in our society that modern technologies have introduced a bewildering array of potential hazards to human health and to our environment. There is an accompanying sense of frustration that our prodigious basic research capabilities and our technological ingenuity have not yielded practical ways to control many pollutants and waste streams, or—better still—to convert them to useful products. This Conference is dedicated to the notion that biological scientists and engineers really can join forces with both traditional and newly emerging techniques to make substantial progress in controlling environmental pollution and do so safely with thoughtful anticipation of potential consequences.

This Conference is one of many research and policy-oriented meetings in the exciting area of biotechnology that we call genetic engineering. Others, including the series edited by Hollaender and colleagues and published by Plenum Press, have dealt with applica-

1

tions in basic biology, development of vaccines for humans and animals, production of agricultural and industrial chemicals, or modifications of plants. This Conference is the first devoted to the
many facets of genetic engineering applications for control of environmental pollutants.

We have a rich mix of molecular geneticists, microbial ecologists, applied microbiologists, industrial engineers, environmental
health specialists, economists, and managers from academia, industry, government, and environmental agencies. Our format of lec-
tures, discussions, poster sessions, and roundtables is designed to
foster communication that bridges these quite separate fields. We
will note some remarkable, manipulable, and useful properties of
Nature. We will learn about the current state of management of several classes of wastes. We will seek some consensus about the kinds
of environmental problems for which early application of microbial
organisms with special degradative capabilities might be most promising and most appropriate. Finally, we will try to anticipate some
of the problems that might arise in going from laboratory schemes
and small-scale experiments to field trials and industrial and environmental applications.

At this point I want to note with considerable appreciation the
financial support for this Conference and participation in the meeting from the following federal agencies: Department of Energy, Environmental Protection Agency, National Science Foundation, National
Toxicology Program (National Institute for Environmental Health Sciences), and Office of Naval Research; from the following corporate
donors: 3M Company, Procter & Gamble, Shell, and Texaco; and from
the sponsoring institutions: the Department of Environmental
Health, School of Public Health & Community Medicine, and Institute
for Environmental Studies at the University of Washington and the
Council for Research Planning in Biological Sciences, Inc., Washington, D.C.

Finally, I want to thank Ms. Virginia Daigle, our Conference
Coordinator and our entire group of staff and students from the
Department of Environmental Health for their dedication, effectiveness, and cheerfulness throughout the whole Conference. Thanks also
to Ms. Claire Wilson, Dr. Hollaender's editor at the Council, and
her production assistants, Ms. Carol von Dohlen and Mr. Barry
Epstein, for promptly producing this Volume.

MICROBIAL BIODEGRADATION OF 2,4,5-TRICHLOROPHENOXYACETIC

ACID AND CHLOROPHENOLS

J. S. Karns, J. J. Kilbane, D. K. Chatterjee,
and A. M. Chakrabarty

Department of Microbiology and Immunology
University of Illinois at Chicago
Health Sciences Center
Chicago, Illinois 60612

INTRODUCTION

Maintaining the carbon, nitrogen, and sulfur balances in the environment is one of the main tasks of microorganisms in nature; microorganisms degrade most compounds so that their basic elements can be recycled. However, naturally occurring chlorinated hydrocarbons are rather rare (25). Chlorinated synthetic chemicals such as PCBs, dichloro-diphenyl-trichloro-ethane (DDT), and 2,4,5-T, generally are degraded only slowly (20,23,24), mostly through co-oxidative metabolism (1,23). The persistence of these compounds is thought to be due to a lack of the ability of microbial cells to derive their energy and cellular constituents from the oxidative metabolism of these compounds (1). Persistence of chemicals in nature will amplify our pollution problems as time progresses, so that even what seems like an insignificant amount of a given chemical, if applied repeatedly, will accumulate until its environmental impact is felt.

There is a need for the development of microbial technology for the removal of toxic, persistent chemicals from the environment. In many cases, there are chemical methods that allow the rapid degradation of various toxic chemicals (2,26). Such methods can, however, be applied only at the source, and not after the release of the chemicals in the environment. There is thus no technology for the purification of contaminated soil, and the only available means at our disposal to deal with such problems is to evacuate and fence off the contaminated areas (as in Seveso, Italy and Love Canal, New York, see Ref. 24).

The perceived problems for the development of a microbial technology for the enhanced biodegradation of toxic chemicals are many.
The three major problems are (i) the presence of innumerable carbon
sources in the soil that might be utilized in preference to the toxic chemicals and (ii) competition by the indigenous microflora for
available minerals, growth factors, and the like, which may not allow the proliferation of the desired microorganisms. However, the
most important problem undoubtedly is (iii) the inability of most
natural microflora to degrade some of the highly chlorinated compounds at an appreciable rate. Most often, the co-oxidative metabolic rates are too low to allow significant biodegradation, resulting in an accumulation of toxic chemical in the environment. In
this paper we describe the development of a specific bacterial
strain that can utilize a recalcitrant compound such as 2,4,5-trich-
lorophenoxyacetic acid (2,4,5-T) as a sole source of carbon and
energy, and which can also dechlorinate a variety of chlorophenols.
Additionally, such a strain is shown to be highly effective in removing large quantities of 2,4,5-T from contaminated soil, thereby
allowing the growth of plants that are normally sensitive to the
presence of small quantities of 2,4,5-T.

Role of Plasmids in the Dissimilation of Chlorinated Compounds

It is known that plasmids play a major role in the biodegradation of a variety of complex organic compounds (4). Recently, the
involvement of plasmids in the dissimilation of some mono- or di-
chloro organic compounds has been described (5,22). A list of some
plasmids is given in Tab. 1. However, although a number of plasmids
have been implicated in the dissimilation of chlorinated compounds,
only a few such as pAC25, pWR1, and pAC31 are known to allow complete dechlorination of the compounds. The biochemistry of chlorobenzoate degradation, as specified by pAC25, demonstrates the operation of a modified ortho pathway in the conversion of chlorobenzoate
or chlorocatechol to maleylacetic acid (5). Several new enzymes,
with or without substantial activity towards the nonchlorinated parents, are known to be involved in such a pathway.

The evolution of a chlorobenzoate degradative plasmid such as
pAC25 specifying a number of new enzymes having maximal activity towards the chlorinated substrates, raises the interesting question as
to how new degradative functions evolve in nature. There are several lines of evidence that suggest that plasmids interact with one
another to greatly extend the substrate range of plasmid-specified
enzymes. This was initially demonstrated by Knackmuss and his colleagues (13) who showed that growth in a chemostat of their 3-chlor-
obenzoate degrading Pseudomonas species B13 with 4-chloro- or 3,5-
dichlorobenzoate allowed emergence of strains capable of degrading
these compounds, only when other Pseudomonas strains harboring the
TOL plasmid were introduced into the chemostat. We have demonstrated that under such conditions, a part of the TOL plasmid (the 39
kilobase pair TOL segment) undergoes transposition on the chromosome

Table 1. List of plasmids encoding degradation of some chlorinated
          compounds.

Plasmid	Degradative pathway	Molecular size (Mdal)	Reference
pUO1	Fluoroacetate	43	Kawasaki et al (1981)[a]
pAC21	p-chlorobiphenyl	65	Kamp and Chakrabarty (1979)[b]
pKF1	p-chlorobiphenyl	53	see ref. 12
pJP2	2,4-D	36	Don and Pemberton (1981)[c]
pJP4	2,4-D	52	Don and Pemberton (1981)[c]
	3-chlorobenzoate		
pWR1 (pB13)	3-chlorobenzoate	72	see ref. 13; Chatterjee and Chakrabarty (1982)[d]
pAC25	3-chlorobenzoate	76	Chatterjee and Chakrabarty (1983)[d]
pAC31	3,5-Dichlorobenzoate	72	see ref. 7
No designation	2,6-Dichlorotoluene	63	Vandenbergh et al (1981)[e]

a) Agri. Biol. Chem. 45: 1477-1481;
b) Plasmids of Medical, Environmental and Commercial Importance (K.N.
    Timmis and A. Puhler, eds), Elsevier/North-Holland Biomedical Press,
    Amsterdam;
c) J. Bacteriol. 145: 681-686;
d) J. Bacteriol. 153: 532-534;
e) Appl. Environ. Microbiol. 42: 737-739.

to provide the broad substrate specific benzoate oxygenase function
that is necessary for the conversion of chlorinated benzoates to the
corresponding chlorocatechols (7). Since growth with 3,5-dichloro-
benzoate needs participation of additional enzymes capable of dechlorinating the chlorolactone and chloromaleyl acetic acid, a segment of TOL containing the replication/incompatibility genes and a
segment of the chlorobenzoate plasmid pAC27 are recombined to give
rise to a separate plasmid, which then undergoes mutational divergence to generate new enzymatic activities for the dechlorination of
the chlorinated intermediates. Thus, plasmids appear to play a vi-
tal role in nature as carriers of duplicated genes for their ultimate mutational divergence to generate new degradative functions.

The strong homology demonstrated by the chlorobenzoate degradative plasmid pAC25 with other naturally occurring plasmids such as
TOL, SAL, or the antibiotic resistance plasmid pAC30 had previously
been inferred to be due to recruitment of plasmid genes by various
replicons to generate new degradative plasmids (3,17). In addition,

we have also demonstrated that several plasmids may be involved in
the total degradation of a synthetic chlorinated compound, although
individually each plasmid may be ineffective in allowing such degradation (12).   These examples reinforce our concept that plasmids
and their gene products interact in nature to allow effective degradation of complex organic compounds.

Other useful information emerging from the studies of degradative plasmids relates to the extent of clustering of degradative
genes on such plasmids.   In the case of xylene or toluene degradation encoded by the TOL plasmid, the genes are known to be clustered
in two operons, and the products of such genes are regulated under
positive control (11,14).   Similarly, the naphthalene to salicylate
or the salicylate degradative genes are tightly clustered, and are
regulated as operons (27).   How are the genes encoding degradation
of a synthetic compound such as chlorobenzoate likely to occur?   We
have recently constructed a physical map of the chlorobenzoate degradative plasmid pAC27 (Fig. 1) and demonstrated that the degradative genes are clustered within a single EcoR1-fragment of the plasmid (6).   Similar to the TOL plasmid, where the promoter sequences
appear to be different from those of _Escherichia coli_ plasmid genes
and are not recognized in the enteric bacteria (4,14), the cloned
chlorobenzoate degradative genes, when transferred to _E. coli_, are
not expressed (6).   The specificity of plasmid promoter sequences in
Pseudomonas may help explain why in spite of the transmissible nature of such plasmids, pseudomonads are the predominant scavengers
in nature.

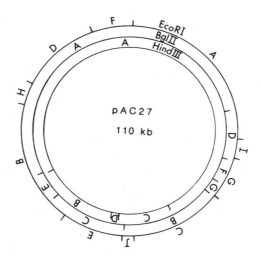

Fig. 1.   A restriction map of the chlorobenzoate degradative plas-
          mid pAC27 with _EcoR_1, _Bgl_ II, and _Hind_ III.

Development of a Strain Capable of Utilizing 2,4,5-T

The similarity in the clustering of chlorobenzoate degradative genes, inducibility of the gene products, and the homology of such genes with those of SAL and TOL appear to indicate that degradative genes evolve primarily by recruitment of analogous genes from other plasmids or chromosomes, followed by mutational divergence and recombinational processes to allow the block of genes to be expressed as a unit. However, the entire process of genetic assortment may take considerable time, and one is likely to find a lack of clustering of the genes or a relaxed mode of regulation of the gene products in a newly evolved pathway. Based on the premise that plasmids evolve by recruitment of genes from other plasmids or from the chromosome, and new genetic functions are acquired through mutational divergence of genes specifying analogous biological functions (4), we have developed laboratory culture conditions which have yielded a strain Pseudomonas cepacia AC1100 that can utilize 2,4,5-T as a sole source of carbon and energy (17,19). The steps involved in the development of this microorganism have been detailed elsewhere (4) and will not be repeated here.

Dehalogenation

Most work concerning bacterial dehalogenation of synthetic chemicals has primarily focused on chlorinated molecules, and relatively little is known about the biodegradability of fluorinated, brominated, and iodinated molecules, particularly aromatic molecules. If the escalation in the number and amounts of synthetic chemicals produced continues, as it has in recent decades, then it seems certain that we will be confronted by an even larger array of halogenated products in the environment than we have currently. The AC1100 resting cell suspensions are known to be capable of oxidizing and dechlorinating a number of chlorophenols (15). Our data concerning dehalogenation (Tab. 2) show that different halogen atoms on analogous molecules can lead to different efficiencies of dehalogenation. These limited studies suggest that halogen atoms are removed in decreasing order Fl > Cl > Br > I, consistent with the general literature information on dehalogenation of halogenated aromatic molecules. Reineke and Knackmuss reached similar conclusions in studies of dioxygenation of halogenated benzoic acids (21). The implications of this work are that other halogenated compounds can be considered similarly biodegradable. It may be necessary to develop in bacteria degradative capabilities with efficient dehalogenating systems tailor-made for each halogen; this is particularly true for deiodination.

Regulation

The regulation of the dehalogenating functions of AC1100 has been partially elucidated (16). The enzyme(s) for the conversion of

Table 2.   Dehalogenation by __Pseudomonas__ __cepacia__ strain AC1100.

Substrate[a]	%Halogen Release[b]
2,4,5-Trichlorophenoxyacetic acid	83
2,4-Dichlorophenol	85
2,4-Dibromophenol	60
2,4,5-Trichlorophenol	67
2,4,6-Trichlorophenol	53
2,4,6-Tribromophenol	80
2,4,6-Triiodophenol	0
2,3,5,6-Tetrachlorophenol	28
2,3,5,6-Tetrafluorophenol	100
Pentachlorophenol	94
Pentabromophenol	34
Pentafluorophenol	94

Each result is an average of at least two experiments in which AC1100 was grown with 2,4,5-T, harvested and washed by centrifugation, and resting cell suspensions at A540 1.0 were prepared and monitored for 24 hours.

    a.   Each substrate was present at 0.1mM.

    b.   Halogen release was measured using ion selective electrodes (Orion Research 94 series).

2,4,5-T to 2,4,5-trichlorophenol (2,4,5-TCP) are constitutive, but the enzymes needed for 2,4,5-TCP degradation are inducible. Also, 2,4,5-TCP (or some metabolite), but not pentachlorophenol (PCP), can serve as an inducer.

The AC1100 is capable of growing with 2,4,5-TCP as a sole source of carbon and energy when 2,4,5-TCP is infused into the culture at low levels (25 µg/ml) so that it never reaches toxic concentrations. In contrast, when AC1100 was cultured in a medium containing succinate plus 1 mg/ml 2,4,5-T, large (and toxic) amounts of 2,4,5-TCP accumulated. Also, AC1100 grown in 2,4,5-T rapidly and completely dechlorinated PCP and produced no intermediate or by-product from PCP, indicating complete degradation; however, AC1100 could not grow with PCP as a sole source of carbon and energy.

Resting cell suspensions of AC1100 grown on alternate carbon sources such as succinate, glucose, or lactate were incapable of de-chlorinating 2,4,5-TCP or PCP over a 5-hour period. However, resting cell suspensions prepared from AC1100 grown on lactate plus 0.1 mM PCP dechlorinated 2,4,5-TCP after a 1-hour lag, even though they could not dechlorinate PCP (Fig. 2). The appearance of 2,4,5-TCP dechlorination activity in these resting cell suspensions was completely prevented by the presence of chlorampenicol (Fig. 2)

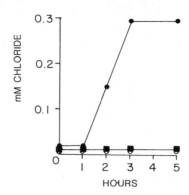

Fig. 2.   Dechlorination of 2,4,5-TCP (●) and PCP (■) by resting
           cell suspensions of AC1100 grown of lactate plus 0.1 mM
           PCP. Resting cell suspensions were prepared from washed
           exponential phase cells and adjusted to a turbidity of 1.0
           at 540 nm as measured Spectronic 20. (O) TCP dechlorina-
           tion in a resting cell suspension to which chloramphenicol
           was added to 1 mg/ml prior to the addition of 2,4,5-TCP.
           Chlorophenols were added to a final concentration of
           0.1 mM to initiate the experiment. Dechlorination was
           measured using an Orion 94-17 chloride selective electrode
           and an Orion double junction reference electrode.

indicating that de novo protein synthesis was required for dechlorination to occur. The same results were obtained when 0.1 mM
2,4,5-TCP was used instead of PCP during growth or when glucose or
succinate replace lactate as the primary carbon source.

     Preincubation with 2,4,5-TCP of resting cell suspensions of
AC1100 grown on succinate plus PCP eliminated the lag in the appearance of 2,4,5-TCP dechlorination and even resulted in measurable
PCP dechlorination (Fig. 3). Preincubation with PCP neither eliminated the lag in 2,4,5-TCP dechlorination nor caused PCP dechlorination. These findings support the conclusions that the enzymes for
2,4,5-TCP degradation and those involved in PCP degradation are inducible and that 2,4,5-TCP (or some intermediate in the degradation
of 2,4,5-TCP) is an inducer. Indeed, AC1100 cells grown with
2,4,5-TCP as a sole source of carbon and energy were capable of dechlorinating PCP as well as 2,4,5-TCP at rates comparable to those
seen in 2,4,5-T grown AC1100 (16).

     The accumulation of 2,4,5-TCP in cultures of AC1100 grown in
the presence of succinate plus 2,4,5-T suggested that while synthesis of the enzymes for 2,4,5-TCP dechlorination was repressed during
the growth in the presence of an alternate carbon source, the first
step in 2,4,5-T degradation, that is the enzymatic conversion of

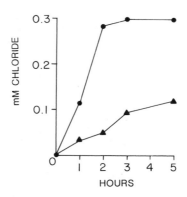

Fig. 3.   Dechlorination of 2,4,5-TCP (●) and PCP (▲) by resting
           cell suspensions of AC1100 grown on succinate plus 0.1 mM
           PCP that were preincubated 1.5 hr with 2,4,5-TCP prior to
           washing and again resuspending in buffer. At T=0
           2,4,5-TCP or PCP was added to 0.1 mM and dechlorination
           was monitored as described in the legend to Fig. 2.

2,4,5-T to 2,4,5-TCP, was constitutively expressed. Resting cells
of succinate grown AC1100 converted 2,4,5-T to 2,4,5-TCP (Tab. 3)
even in the presence of chloramphenicol, confirming that this enzyme
system is synthesized constitutively. It is also apparent that one
or all of these intitial steps of 2,4,5-T metabolism is also the
rate limiting factor in 2,4,5-T degradation by AC1100. The rate of
2,4,5-T dechlorination in resting cells of 2,4,5-T grown AC1100
(Tab. 4) and the rate of conversion of 2,4,5-T to 2,4,5-TCP in resting cells of succinate grown AC1100 (Tab. 3) were dependent upon the

Table 3.   Conversion of 2,4,5-T to 2,4,5-TCP by succinate grown
            AC1100.

mM 2,4,5-T	μmoles TCP formed/ml/h
3	0.158
1	0.080
0.5	0.036
0.1	0.010
1 + 1mg/ml Chloramphenicol	0.080

Resting cell suspensions of turbidity 1.0 at 540 nm (as measured in a Spectronic
20) were prepared from washed log phase AC1100 grown in a basal salt medium
(BSM) containing succinate. Chloramphenicol when added was added as a 300
mg/ml stock dissolved in methanol so that the final concentration was 1 mg/ml.
2,4,5-TCP accumulation in the supernatant fluids was monitored by high-performance liquid chromatography on a Perkin-Elmer HS-3 C18 column with a solvent
system of 60% acetonitrile in phosphoric acid, final pH 3.

intitial concentration of 2,4,5-T present. The rate of 2,4,5-T
dechlorination only approached the rate of dechlorination of 0.1 mM
TCP when the 2,4,5-T concentration is 20-fold higher (Tab. 4).
Thus, it appears that the strain has evolved an interesting method
for regulation of 2,4,5-T metabolism during growth on 2,4,5-T as a
sole source of carbon. The relatively slow rate of 2,4,5-T uptake
and/or conversion of 2,4,5-T to 2,4,5-TCP combined with the relatively fast and efficient dechlorination (degradation) system for
2,4,5-TCP assures that the cell will not accumulate any appreciable
(and possibly toxic) quantities of 2,4,5-TCP during growth on
2,4,5-T when the 2,4,5-T concentration does not exceed 6 mM.

When we examined the ability of resting cells of succinate
grown AC1100 to convert 2,4,5-T to 2,4,5-TCP, we noticed that after
about 3 hours of incubation the level of 2,4,5-TCP in the supernatant began to drop and that chloride ion was eventually released
(Fig. 4). Thus, in the presence of 2,4,5-T, resting cells of succinate grown AC1100 were able to induce the 2,4,5-TCP metabolizing
enzymes while as described previously (Fig. 2) the same resting
cells would not induce these enzymes in response to 2,4,5-TCP. This
suggested one of two possibilities for the induction of these enzymes in succinate grown AC1100: (a) that 2,4,5-T is a more potent
inducer of the 2,4,5-TCP metabolic enzymes, or (b) that there is a
difference in the ability of endogenously generated 2,4,5-TCP and
exogenously supplied 2,4,5-TCP to induce the 2,4,5-TCP metabolic
systems in succinate grown AC1100. Experiments with a mutant strain
DK60, a 2,4,5-T$^-$, 2,4,5-TCP$^+$ derivative of AC1100, indicated that
the second possibility was correct. Resting cells of succinate plus
2,4,5-T grown DK60 were not capable of dechlorinating 2,4,5-TCP over
a 5-hour period when resting cells of succinate plus 2,4,5-TCP over
a 5-hour perid. When resting cells of succinate plus 2,4,5-TCP
grown DK60 were preincubated for 2 hours with 2,4,5-TCP, there was

Table 4.   Effect of concentration of 2,4,5-T on the rate of dechlor-
           ination.

mM 2,4,5-T	Dechlorination rate (μmoles Cl$^-$ released/ml/hr)
2	0.38
1	0.15
0.5	0.06
0.2	0.015
0.1	0.01
0.1mM 2,4,5-TCP	0.39

Resting cell suspensions of exponential phase 2,4,5-T grown AC1100 were prepared and chloride ion release was measured as described in the legend to Fig.
2. Total chloride release from 2,4,5-T was monitored over 3 hours and was
linear over this period.

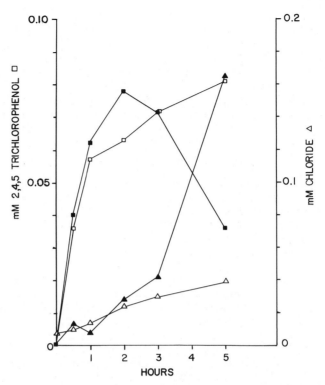

Fig. 4.   Conversion of 2,4,5-T to 2,4,5-TCP by resting cell suspen-
           sions of succinate grown on AC1100. A washed resting cell
           suspension of exponential phase AC1100 grown on basal
           salts medium (BSM)-succinate was incubated with 1 mM
           2,4,5-T. At the times indicated aliquots were removed and
           the concentration of 2,4,5-TCP in the supernatant fluids
           was measured by HPLC as described in Tab. 3. Chloride ion
           release was measured as described in the legend to Fig. 2.
           (■) 2,4,5-TCP concentration in resting cell suspension;
           (□) 2,4,5-TCP concentration in resting cell suspension to
           which chloramphenicol was added 15 min prior to the addi-
           tion of 2,4,5-T.; (▲) free chloride ion in resting cell
           suspension; (Δ) free chloride ion in resting cell suspen-
           sion to which chloramphenicol was added.

no lag in the dechlorination of 2,4,5-TCP by these cells (Fig. 5);
however, when the same resting cell suspension was preincubated for
2 hours with 2,4,5-T and subsequently exposed to 2,4,5-TCP there was
an initial lag in the appearance of 2,4,5-TCP dechlorination (Fig.
5) indicating that 2,4,5-TCP was an inducer of 2,4,5-TCP metabolism
and that 2,4,5-T itself was incapable of inducing the 2,4,5-TCP metabolic systems.

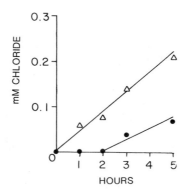

Fig. 5.   Dechlorination of 2,4,5-TCP by resting cell suspensions of
           mutant strain DK60 that had been preincubated for 2 hr
           with either 0.1 mM 2,4,5-TCP (Δ) or 1 mM 2,4,5-T (●).
           Strain DK60 was grown to mid-exponential phase in BSM con-
           taining succinate plus 0.1 mM 2,4,5-TCP. The cells were
           harvested by centrifugation, washed once and resuspended
           in buffer. 2,4,5-TCP was added to 0.1 mM in one flask and
           2,4,5-T was added to 0.1 mM in another flask. The suspen-
           sions were incubated for 2 hr at 30°C with shaking after
           which the cells were collected by centrifugation, washed
           twice, and resuspended in buffer. At T=0, 2,4,5-TCP was
           added to 0.1 mM and chloride ion release was measured as
           described in the legend to Fig. 2.

     Thus, in strain AC1100 grown on carbon sources other than
2,4,5-T, there is a difference in the ability of 2,4,5-TCP to induce
its own dechlorination mechanisms depending on whether it is encountered inside or outside the cell. This also raises interesting
questions about the role of the chlorophenols in AC1100 growing on
succinate, glucose, or lactate, plus either TCP or PCP. We have
shown that the 2,4,5-TCP dechlorinating system is induced only after
the resting cell suspensions are prepared (Fig. 2) and only after
fresh 2,4,5-TCP is added in the absence of alternate carbon sources.
Pentachlorophenol itself cannot induce any dechlorination
mechanisms, yet growth in succinate plus PCP somehow preinduces the
cells so that they are capable of being induced when exposed to
2,4,5-TCP. These results, plus the ability of endogenously generated 2,4,5-TCP to induce dechlorination when exogenously supplied
2,4,5-TCP will not, indicates that when growing on alternate carbon
sources, the presence of low levels of chlorophenol alters the permeability of the cells to 2,4,5-TCP after growth has terminated.
The effect of PCP on AC1100 grown on succinate is transitory since,
as shown in Fig. 6, when an actively growing culture of AC1100 in
succinate plus 0.1 mM PCP is washed and transferred to a medium containing succinate alone for 1.5 generations, there is a substantial

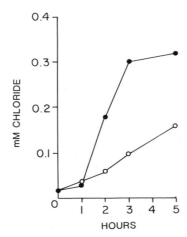

Fig. 6.   Effect of removal of PCP from a culture of AC1100 growing
           on succinate plus 0.1 mM PCP on the ability to induce
           2,4,5-TCP dechlorination in resting cell suspensions. A
           mid-exponential phase culture of AC1100 growing in BSM
           containing succinate plus 0.1 mM PCP was harvested by cen-
           trifugation. One-half of the cells were resuspended in
           500 ml BSM succinate plus 0.1 mM PCP while the other half
           were resuspended in 500 ml BSM containing only succinate.
           After 6 hr both cultures were harvested and the cells were
           used to make resting cell suspensions. 2,4,5-TCP was ad-
           ded to 0.1 mM at T=0 and free chloride ion in the super-
           natant fluids of the suspensions was measured as described
           in the legend to Fig. 2. (●) chloride release by succin-
           ate plus PCP grown AC1100; (O) chloride release by AC1100
           that were transferred to growth in the absence of PCP.

difference in the ability to dechlorinate 2,4,5-TCP confirming that
PCP alters the cells ability to induce 2,4,5-TCP metabolism rather
than select for mutant organisms in which dechlorination is continuously expressed.

     Since AC1100 is acutely susceptible to poisoning itself when
exposed to 2,4,5-T plus an alternate carbon source, the potentially
dangerous 2,4,5-T metabolic pathway seems to be incompletely or in-
efficiently regulated. However, when the method by which this bacterium was isolated is considered a possible explanation for the
evolution of such a mode of regulation can be formulated. Pseudomonas cepacia AC1100 was developed in the laboratory using a chemostat, as described previously (17,19). When the chemostat was
switched over to 2,4,5-T as the sole source of carbon and energy it
was acting as a continuous enrichment culture and breeding ground
for bacteria with the ability to rapidly metabolize 2,4,5-T and

derive carbon and energy from it. Thus, as the genetic information
necessary for the complete degradation of 2,4,5-T was evolving,
growth on 2,4,5-T alone was the only selective pressure present.
There was no selective pressure on this organism to evolve an effective means of regulating the 2,4,5-T degradative pathway in the
presence of alternate carbon sources. We feel that the manner by
which the 2,4,5-T degradative pathway is regulated reflects the
"evolutionary youth" of this organism.

Degradation of 2,4,5-T in Soil

     AC1100 is not only effective in degrading 2,4,5-T in liquid
culture and on plates but can also degrade 2,4,5-T in contaminated
soil (8,18). Since 2,4,5-T is an herbicide it is most commonly
found in the environment in soil, and concentrations as high as
20,000 µg of 2,4,5-T per gram of soil have been found in soil samples from parts of Vietnam as well as some U.S. Air Force bases
where Agent Orange was stored (28). We have previously shown that
after six AC1100 treatments greater than 90% of 2,4,5-T originally
present at 20,000 µg per gram of soil.was degraded (18). Moreover,
soil contaminated with as much as 5,000 µg of 2,4,5-T per gram of
soil has been successfully detoxified by AC1100 treatment such that
plants sensitive to as little as 10 µg of 2,4,5-T per gram of soil
could grow. This point is more clearly demonstrated in Fig. 7 where
panel A shows the sensitivity of plant growth (lettuce and alyssum)
to low amounts of 2,4,5-T, and panel B shows that the ability of
contaminated soil to support plant growth can be restored by AC1100
treatment.

     A very close agreement on the 2,4,5-T level in soil was consis-
tently obtained between physical and biological assays. Figure 7
also illustrates that while AC1100 is effective in removing 2,4,5-T
from soil, AC1100-treated soil is never able to support plant growth
quite as well as uncontaminated soil. Apparently, 2 to 10 µg of
2,4,5-T per gram of soil, or a breakdown product, remains in the
soil, perhaps because some 2,4,5-T becomes bound irreversibly to
soil particles and is unavailable for microbial degradation.

     This persistence of low amounts of some toxic substance in soil
despite AC1100 treatment suggests a possible problem with the microbial degradation of pollutants found at extremely low concentrations. For example, a concentration of one part per million of a
chemical so potent as 2,3,7,8-tetrachlorodibenzo-p-dioxin (TCDD)
constitutes a biohazard but may be so dilute as to escape effective
degradation, even though a tailor-made TCDD degrading microorganism
is developed in the laboratory. We have shown that AC1100 possesses
an inducible 2,4,5-T degradative pathway and that the presence of
abundant alternative carbon sources suppresses that induction. Even
though we have demonstrated that the 2,4,5-T degradative pathway of
AC1100 can be induced in contaminated soil and that 2,4,5-T can sup-

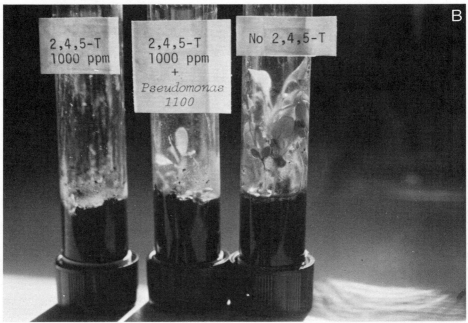

port the proliferation of AC1100 in soil, these experiments involved concentrations of 2,4,5-T at 1,000 parts per million. If a TCDD degrading strain could be isolated in the laboratory, its environmental usefulness might be limited because the presence of other carbon sources in the soil could be abundant relative to the TCDD concentration and induction of the TCDD degradative pathway might be suppressed. Moreover, since extremely dilute TCDD concentration would fail to support appreciable growth, the half-life of a TCDD degrading strain in soil might be quite brief if it fails to compete successfully with indigenous microflora for limiting nutrients.

     In addition to documenting the effectiveness of AC1100 to degrade 2,4,5-T in soil we also investigated the ability of AC1100 to survive in soil and the impact on indigenous microorganisms caused by the addition of 2,4,5-T and/or AC1100 to soil. Studies by Chatterjee et al. (8) suggested that AC1100 could not only survive but could flourish in soil. Those experiments indicated that while growth of AC1100 in soil is possible, it is highly, if not exclusively, dependent upon the presence of 2,4,5-T in the soil. In uncontaminated soil or immediately after degradation of 2,4,5-T in soil, the titer of AC1100 was seen to plummet; however, those experiments titered AC1100 by quantitating colony forming units on 2,4,5-T agar. Early investigations of AC1100 showed a high rate of loss of 2,4,5-T degradation ability upon growth in the absence of 2,4,5-T so that in soil lacking 2,4,5-T the titer of AC1100 could be

←——

Fig. 7.   Plant growth in 2,4,5-T contaminated soil with and without AC1100 treatment.

           (A) 20 g samples of soil were placed in glass beakers and contaminated with 2,4,5-T at the following concentrations: 0, 1, 10, and 50 µg of 2,4,5-T/g soil. Six lettuce (Lactuca sativa) and six alyssum (Alyssum spinosum) seeds were then planted in each beaker. All four beakers were kept watered on a sunny windowsill for three weeks and then photographed. Note that as little as 10 µg of 2,4,5-T/g soil causes a nearly complete inhibition of plant growth.

           (B) Three soil samples were prepared: to the first sample 1 mg 2,4,5-T/g soil was added, to the second 1 mg 2,4,5-T/g soil and 10^7 AC1100/g soil was added, while no additions were made to the third sample. All three soils were then hydrated to 20% of their dry weight and incubated at 30°C for two weeks. Inoculations with seeds was done as described in (A).

significantly higher than indicated by the number of bacteria capable of growth on 2,4,5-T agar. To accurately determine the survival of AC1100 in soil a spontaneous mutant of AC1100 resistant to
nalidixic acid (Nal) was isolated and used to inoculate uncontaminated soil or soil contaminated with 750 µg of 2,4,5-T/g soil. The
concentration of AC1100 in soil as measured either by Nal^r or
$2,4,5-T^+$ colony forming units gave consistent results and is highly
dependent upon the presence of 2,4,5-T in the soil (18).

When AC1100 Nal^r was added to soil lacking 2,4,5-T, the titer
of AC1100 (measured as CFU on 2,4,5-T agar and on Nal nutrient agar)
fell from 10^7 cells per gram of soil to undetectable levels within 8
weeks (data not shown). Subsequent addition of 2,4,5-T to the soil
led to the reappearance, after a 2-week lag, of colonies on $2,4,5-T^r$
agar. Moreover, when single colonies of Nal^r bacteria isolated from
the soil were tested, occasionally $2,4,5-T^-$ colonies were found
(especially if the soil lacked 2,4,5-T) indicating that the 2,4,5-T
degradation ability of AC1100 is unstable as previously shown (19);
however, when $2,4,5-T^+$ single colonies were tested all were found to
be Nal^r. This result suggests that whereas AC1100 is capable of
utilizing 2,4,5-T in soil as a growth substrate, it is unable to
transfer this ability to other soil bacteria. Furthermore, in the
absence of 2,4,5-T AC1100 must compete with indigenous microorganisms for nutrients in soil and is able to maintain only an extremely
dilute population.

The effect of 2,4,5-T and AC1100 on indigenous soil bacteria
was tested by plating extracts from appropriate soil samples onto
nutrient agar. By this test no appreciable effect on the number or
on the various kinds of bacteria in soil was observed by the addition of either 1 mg of 2,4,5-T per gram of soil or 10^7 AC1100 cells
per gram of soil (data not shown). The titer of indigenous bacterial flora in the soil was about 2×10^8 cells per gram of soil, so
that 10^7 AC1100 cells per gram of soil represented about 5% of the
total soil microflora.

SUMMARY

We have succeeded in isolating a pure culture of Pseudomonas
cepacia, AC1100, from a chemostat enrichment culture experiment that
is capable of growing on 2,4,5-trichlorophenoxyacetic acid as its
sole source of carbon and energy. AC1100 is not only capable of degrading 2,4,5-T but is also able to completely or partially dehalo-
genate a wide variety of halophenols. The regulation of the dehalogenating ability of AC1100 has been investigated which demonstrates
that the enzyme(s) which allow the conversion of 2,4,5-T to 2,4,5-
TCP are constitutive, while the enzymes that allow the degradation
of 2,4,5-TCP are inducible by 2,4,5-TCP (or some metabolite of
2,4,5-TCP) but not by 2,4,5-T or other halophenols which can serve

as substrates. Moreover, the 2,4,5-TCP degradative pathway is repressed by the presence of an abundant alternative carbon source. The detailed pathway of 2,4,5-T degradation by AC1100 is currently under study.

Although field tests have yet to be conducted, laboratory experiments have demonstrated rapid and complete degradation of 2,4,5-T from contaminated soil. Soil previously contaminated with as much as 5,000 µg of 2,4,5-T/g of soil could be detoxified by AC1100 treatment, allowing the growth of plants sensitive to less than 10 µg 2,4,5-T/g of soil. Moreover soil contaminated with as much as 20,000 µg of 2,4,5-T/g of soil showed greater than 90% degradation after six weekly AC1100 treatments. After 2,4,5-T has been substantially degraded in contaminated soil the titer of AC1100 rapidly falls to nearly undetectable levels, which indicates that no serious ecological disturbance is likely to result from the application of AC1100. It appears possible that the treatment of contaminated areas with appropriate microorganisms may allow essentially a total restoration of the original soil condition.

ACKNOWLEDGEMENTS

This research was supported by collaborative agreement CR809666-01-0 with the U.S. Environmental Protection Agency, by a Reproductive Hazards in the Workplace Grant 15-2 from the March of Dimes Birth Defects Foundation, and in part by grant PCM 81-13558 from the National Science Foundation. J.S.K. and J.J.K. acknowledge the support of National Research Service Awards 1F 32ES 05189 and 5F 32GM 08885, respectively, from the National Institutes of Health. We thank Mr. David Crowe and Mr. Douglas Fuhrer for expert technical assistance.

REFERENCES

1. Alexander, M. (1981) Biodegradation of chemicals of environmental concern. Science 211:132-138.
2. Ayers, D.C. (1981) Destruction of polychlorodibenzo-p-dioxins. Nature 290:323-324.
3. Bayley, S.A., D.W. Morris, and P. Broda (1979) The relationship of degradative and resistance plasmids of Pseudomonas belonging to the same incompatability group. Nature 280:338-339.
4. Chakrabarty, A.M., J.S. Karns, J.J. Kilbane, and D.K. Chatterjee (1983) Selective evolution of genes for enhanced degradation of persistent, toxic chemicals. In Genetic Manipulation: Impact on Man and Society, W. Arber, W.J. Peacock, K. Illmensee, and P. Starlinger, eds. ICSU Press, Miami (in press).
5. Chatterjee, D.K., S.T. Kellogg, S. Hamada, and A.M. Chakrabarty

(1981) A plasmid specifying total degradation of 3-chloroben-
zoate by a modified ortho pathway. J. Bacteriol. 146:639-646.

6. Chatterjee, D.K., and A.M. Chakrabarty (1983) Restriction map-
    ping of chlorobenzoate degradative plasmid and molecular clon-
    ing of degradative genes. Gene (in press).

7. Chatterjee, D.K., and A.M. Chakrabarty (1982) Genetic rear-
    rangements in plasmids specifying total degradation of chlorin-
    ated benzoic acids. Mol. Gen. Genet. 188:279-285.

8. Chatterjee, D.K., J.J. Kilbane, and A.M. Chakrabarty (1982)
    Biodegradation of 2,4,5-trichlorophenoxyacetic acid in soil by
    a pure culture of Pseudomonas cepacia. Appl. Environ. Micro-
    biol. 44:514-516.

9. Cookson, C., (1979) Emergency ban on 2,4,5-T in US. Nature
    278:108-109.

10. Firestone, D. (1978) The 2,3,7,8-tetrachlorodibenzo-para-dioxin
    problem: A review. In Chlorinated Phenoxy Acids and their
    Dioxins, C. Ramel, ed. Ecological Bulletin, Stockholm, pp.
    39-52.

11. Franklin, F.C.H., M. Bagdasarian, M.M. Bagdasarian, and K.N.
    Timmis (1981) Molecular and functional analysis of the TOL
    plasmid pWWO from Pseudomonas putida and cloning of genes for
    the entire regulated aromatic ring meta cleavage pathway.
    Proc. Natl. Acad. Sci., U.S.A. 78:7458-7462.

12. Furakawa, K., and A.M. Chakrabarty (1982) Involvement of plas-
    mids in total degradation of chlorinated biphenyls. Appl.
    Environ. Microbiol. 44:619-626.

13. Hartmann, J., W. Reineke, and H.J. Knackmuss (1979) Metabolism
    of 3-chloro, 4-chloro and 3,5-dichlorobenzoate by a pseudo-
    monad. Appl. Environ. Microbiol. 37:421-428.

14. Inouye, S., A. Nakazawa, and T. Nakazawa (1983) Molecular clon-
    ing of regulatory gene xylR and operator-promoter regions of
    the xylABC and xylDEGF operons of the TOL plasmid. J. Bact.
    155:1192-1199.

15. Karns, J.S., J.J. Kilbane, S. Duttagupta, and A.M. Chakrabarty
    (1983) Metabolism of halophenols by a 2,4,5-trichlorophenoxy-
    acetic acid degrading Pseudomonas cepacia. Appl. Environ. Mi-
    crobiol. (in press).

16. Karns, J.S., S. Duttagupta, and A.M. Chakrabarty (1983) Regula-
    tion of 2,4,5-trichlorophenoxyacetic acid and chlorophenol
    metabolism in Pseudomonas cepacia AC1100. Appl. Environ.
    Microbiol. (in press).

17. Kellogg, S.T., D.K. Chatterjee, and A.M. Chakrabarty (1981)
    Plasmid assisted molecular breeding - new technique for en-
    hanced biodegradation of persistent toxic chemicals. Science
    214:1133-1135.

18. Kilbane, J.J., D.K. Chatterjee, and A.M. Chakrabarty (1983) De-
    toxification of 2,4,5-trichlorophenoxyacetic acid from contami-
    nated soil by Pseudomonas cepacia. Appl. Environ. Microbiol.
    45:1697-1700.

19. Kilbane, J.J., D.K. Chatterjee, J.S. Karns, S.T. Kellogg, and

A.M. Chakrabarty (1982) Biodegradation of 2,4,5-trichlorophenoxyacetic acid by a pure culture of Pseudomonas cepacia. Appl. Environ. Microbiol. 44:72-78.

20. McCall, P.J., S.A. Vrona, and S.S. Kelley (1981) Fate of uniformly carbon-14 ring labeled 2,4,5-trichlorophenoxyacetic acid and 3,4-dichlorophenoxyacetic acid. J. Agric. Food Chem. 29:100-107.

21. Reineke, W., and H.J. Knackmuss (1978) Chemical structure and biodegradability of dehalogenated aromatic compounds: Substituent effects of 1,2-dioxygenation of benzoic acid. Biochim. Biophys. Acta 542:412-423.

22. Reineke, W., S.W. Wessels, M.A. Rubio, J. Lattorre, U. Schwien, E. Schmidt, M. Schlomann, and H.J. Knackmuss (1982) Degradation of monochlorinated aromatics following transfer of genes encoding chlorocatechol catabolism. FEMS Microbiol. Lett. 14:291-294.

23. Rosenberg, A., and M.J. Alexander (1980) 2,4,5-Trichlorophenoxyacetic acid (2,4,5-T) decomposition in tropical soil and its co-metabolism by bacteria in vitro. J. Agric. Food Chem. 28:705-709.

24. Schneider, M.J. (1979) Persistent Poisons: Chemical Pollutants in the Environment. The New York Academy of Sciences, New York.

25. Siuda, J.F., and J.F. DeBernardis (1973) Naturally occurring halogenated organic compounds. Lloydia 36:197-243.

26. Walsh, J. (1977) Seveso: The questions persist where dioxin created a wasteland. Science 197:1064-1067.

27. Yen, K.M., and I.C. Gunsalus (1982) Plasmid gene organization: Naphthalene/salicylate oxidation. Proc. Natl. Acad. Sci., U.S.A. 79:874-878.

28. Young, A.L., C.E. Thalken, and E.W. Ward (1975) Tech. Report AFATL-TR-75-142, U.S. Air Force Armament Lab; pp. 1-126.

BACTERIAL TRANSFORMATIONS OF AND

RESISTANCES TO HEAVY METALS

Simon Silver and Tapan K. Misra

Biology Department
Washington University
St. Louis, Missouri 63130

ABSTRACT

Bacteria carry out chemical transformations of heavy metals. These transformations (including oxidation, reduction, methylation, and demethylation) are sometimes byproducts of normal metabolism and confer no known advantage upon the organism responsible. Sometimes, however, the transformations constitute a mechanism of resistance. Many species of bacteria have genes that control resistances to specific toxic heavy metals. These resistances often are determined by extrachromosomal DNA molecules (plasmids). The same mechanisms of resistance occur in bacteria from soil, water, industrial waste, and clinical sources. The mechanism of mercury and organomercurial resistance is the enzymatic detoxification of the mercurials into volatile species (methane, ethane, metallic Hg^0) which are rapidly lost from the environment. Cadmium and arsenate resistances are due to reduced net accumulation of these toxic materials. Efficient efflux pumps cause the rapid excretion of Cd^{2+} and AsO_4^{3-}. The mechanisms of arsenite and of antimony resistance, usually found associated with arsenate resistance, are not known. Silver resistance is due to lowered affinity of the cells for Ag^+, which can be complexed with extracellular halides, thiols, or organic compounds. Sensitivity is due to binding of Ag^+ more effectively to cells than to Cl^-.

INTRODUCTION

Bacterial cells divide the Periodic Table into three classes. Some elements are necessary for intracellular metabolism (67); some elements are not used generally within the cell, but abound in natural environments and can be coupled to extracellular structural or

23

regulatory functions; finally, some elements have no useful biological function (69,79). Potassium and phosphorus are examples of the
first class; calcium and chlorine are not needed at all for most
bacteria; and arsenic, mercury, and cadmium are examples of toxic
elements without biological utility. This report will deal with
toxic elements and their compounds. In some cases, such as mercury
and arsenic, microbes can transform elements from relatively less
toxic inorganic ions into relatively more toxic methylated forms.
The same or other microbes can degrade organometallic compounds
(15,79); oxidation and reduction by microbial enzymes also affect
the bioavailability and toxicity of heavy metals. It is crucial to
understand the interactions of microbes with heavy metals in order
to follow the pathways and transformations of heavy metals in the
environment, and to design interventions that will reduce pollution.

Free-living bacterial cells have evolved resistance mechanisms
to cope with heavy metal pollution. These resistance mechanisms are
highly specific. The genes determining the resistance mechanisms
occur on small nonchromosomal DNA molecules called plasmids. These
resistance plasmids also have genes controlling resistance to most
known antibiotics. We have reviewed this subject periodically
(e.g., 68-70, 79) most recently in Ref. 70.

MERCURY AND MERCURIAL TRANSFORMATIONS AND RESISTANCES

The mercury cycle (Fig. 1) is the best known case of microbial
metabolism affecting the chemical form of a heavy metal. Microbial
activity is associated with mercury methylation, demethylation (15),
and oxidation and reduction of inorganic mercury. I will deal first
with the transformations from highly toxic methylmercury (found in
fish) to less toxic ionic Hg^{2+} (the predominant form in seawater) to
least toxic Hg^0. Both of these transformations are carried out by
enzymes governed by bacterial resistance plasmids and transposons
(moveable DNA sequences) and not by the more usual (chromosomal)
genes. Without the plasmid genes, the cells remain mercury sensitive. Then we will address microbial oxidation and methylation of
mercury.

The earliest studies of enzymatic detoxification of Hg^{2+} were
with a multiply drug-resistant Escherichia coli (37) and with a soil
pseudomonad (21,84). The frequency of Hg^{2+} resistance among clinical isolates can be over 50% (44,45,92). Recently, mercuric- and
organomercurial-resistant strains with very similar properties have
been found in a wide variety of bacterial species from soil, water,

$$CH_3Hg^+ \rightleftharpoons Hg^{2+} \rightleftharpoons Hg^0$$

Fig. 1.   Environmental transformations of mercury.

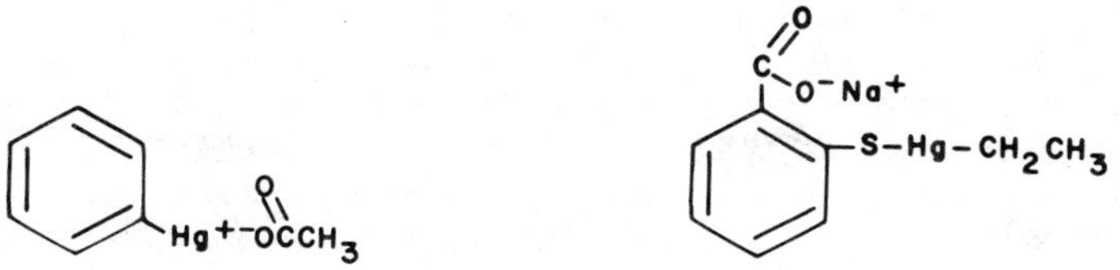

PHENYLMERCURIC
ACETATE

ETHYLMERCURITHIOSALICYLATE
(THIMEROSAL; THIOMERSOL;
MERTHIOLATE)

Fig. 2.   Structures of phenylmercuric acetate and thimerosal: or-
           ganomercurials that are degraded by plasmid-determined en-
           zymes.

and marine environments (20,34,52,53,61,83). Mercuric-resistant microorganisms are found in much higher frequencies in polluted waters
than in nearby cleaner waters (48).

     Bacteria with plasmids showed a small number of patterns of re-
sistance to organomercurials (65,90):   (a) In E. coli about 96% of
the mercuric-resistance plasmids also controlled resistance to the
organomercurials merbromin and fluorescein mercuric acetate, but to
no other tested organomercurial. The other 4% determined additional
resistances to phenylmercuric acetate (an important agricultural

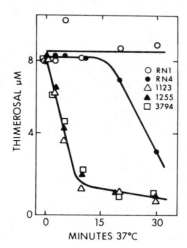

Fig. 3.   Detoxification of (loss of mercury from) thimerosal by a
           plasmid-less sensitive strain (RN1), by a thimerosal-sen-
           sitive plasmid-containing strain (RN4) and by new thimer-
           osal-resistant isolates (1123, 1255, and 3794) (from Ref.
           70).

chemical) and thimerosal (available as an antiseptic at any drug
store) (65; Fig. 2). (b) The plasmids in Pseudomonas aeruginosa also fell into two classes with regard to resistance to organomercurials (12). However, about 50% fell into each class. All Pseudomonas
plasmids controlled resistance to p-hydroxymercuribenzoate and some
Pseudomonas plasmids showed additional resistance to methylmercuric
and ethylmercuric compounds (12,90). (c) Initially a single pattern
was reported with S. aureus plasmids (88,90). This pattern is different from those with the gram-negative bacteria because S. aureus
plasmids control resistances to phenylmercuric acetate, p-hydroxymercuribenzoate, and fluorescein mercuric acetate, but not to thimerosal or to merbromin. Recently, the first thimerosal-resistant S.
aureus were found (60). These new clinical isolates volatilize mercury more rapidly from thimerosal (Fig. 3) than do the previous S.
aureus strains. Of course, the sensitive strain without a plasmid
cannot volatilize mercury from thimerosal at all (Fig. 3). The new
strains also showed activity for thimerosal as an inducer of synthesis of this mercuric detoxification system, which is only made after
exposure to low levels of Hg^{2+} or organomercurials (60,88). The
limited number of patterns of resistance can be understood in terms
of the biochemistry of the enzymes involved.

Since this is a publication relating to environmental pollutants, it is worth emphasizing that mercurial-detoxifying mercurial-
resistant strains have been found in every type of bacteria tested.
These include soil and marine bacteria [Bacillus (34,61), Pseudomonas, (12), and Mycobacterium (J. O. Falkinham, personal communica-
tion], mineral-leaching Thiobacillus (53,54), and even antibiotic-
producing Streptomyces (S. Silver, unpublished data).

Genetics of Mercurial Resistance

Inorganic mercuric ion and organomercurial resistance is always
determined by an inducible "operon" structure of closely linked
genes (16,47,90). The genes have been recently analyzed by transposon mutagenesis (16,49) and by direct DNA sequencing (11; T. K.
Misra and N.L. Brown, unpublished results). Figure 4 is our current
picture of the map for the operon from plasmid R100 cloned into the
small vector plasmid pBR322 (49; T. K. Misra et al., unpublished results). The operon consists of a series of genes, in order: merR,
the gene for a small diffusible positively acting regulatory protein; then an operator promoter sequence as the site of binding of
the merR polypeptide and of initiation of messenger RNA synthesis;
then $merT_2$,the gene for a membrane protein responsible for movement
of the Hg^{2+} from outside the cell to its intracellular site of detoxification (16,47); then merC, a newly discovered gene (49) without a clearly known function at the moment; then merA, the large
gene for the subunit of the mercuric reductase enzyme (see below);
and finally, merD, another newly discovered gene (49) of unknown
function. It is even unclear at present whether the merD gene

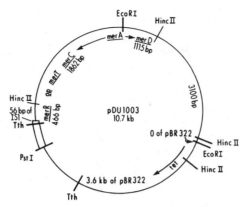

Fig. 4.   The genetic and physical maps of the mercuric resistance
           operon cloned into a small vector plasmid (data from Ref.
           49 and newer unpublished experiments). EcoRI, HincII,
           PstI, and TthlllI represent the sites of cleavage by these
           restriction endonuclease enzymes. IS1 is the remnant of
           insertion sequence 1 originating from plasmid R100 and tet
           is the determinant of tetracycline resistance from plasmid
           pBR322. The mercuric operon genes are described in the
           text. pb, base pairs; kb, kilobase pairs.

extends beyond the HincII restriction endonuclease cut site or stops
before that point. From the DNA sequencing information, biologically interesting insights are coming for the structures and functions
of these genes. The operon from transposon Tn501 has been sequenced
in Bristol, England by N. L. Brown and co-workers (11; unpublished
data), and the very similar sequence from plasmid R100 is being determined in our laboratory in St. Louis by T. K. Misra et al. The
sequences of these two systems, which originated in microbes as evolutionarily distant as Pseudomonas (Tn501) and Shigella (R100), show
approximately 80% base identity. Of the 20% differences, about 80%
of these are in third "wobble" positions in codons and do not result
in amino acid changes.

     Figure 5 shows an example of this yet tentative analysis for
the merR regulatory protein. Both the Tn501 and the R100 polypeptides are 60 amino acids long and have an abundance of positively
charged amino acids (mainly arginine). Of the 25 base pair changes
in the 180 base pair gene (marked with "ticks" in Fig. 5), only 6
result in changes of amino acids. One of these, interestingly, results in the change from a single cysteine in the Tn501 polypeptide
to two cysteines for the comparable R100 polypeptide. This seems
important for a protein that must interact with the inducer compound
Hg^{2+}. The results in Fig. 5 and our additional analysis should be
considered tentative, as we do not expect the sequencing to be

```
          ✓         ✓    ✓
Tn501  MET ARG ALA ARG SER ALA ILE PHE SER ARG
R100    .   .   .   .   .   .   .   .   .   .

                           ✓         ✓
Tn501  THR SER LEU SER LEU CYS SER ALA ARG LEU
R100    .   .   .   .   .   .   .   .   .   .

           ✓           ✓            ✓   ✓
Tn501  LEU ALA SER SER GLN TRP VAL PRO SER SER
R100    .   .   .   .   .   .   .   .   .   .

               ✓              ✓           ✓
Tn501  SER ARG SER SER SER ALA ILE SER SER ARG
R100    .   .  ASN  .   .   .   .   .   .   .

           ✓            ✓   ✓
Tn501  LEU LYS PRO SER ARG TRP ALA ASP PHE THR
R100    .  ASN  .   .   .  CYS  .   .   .   .

       ✓  ✓✓        ✓  ✓✓✓  ✓          ✓
Tn501  LYS ARG THR ARG VAL THR SER ALA SER PRO
R100  ASN PHE  .   .  THR  .   .   .   .   .
```

Fig. 5.   The amino acid sequences of the merR polypeptides from
           plasmid R100 and transposon Tn501 as deduced from DNA se-
           quence analysis. The sequences are identical (as indi-
           cated with dots in the R100 lines) except for the six
           changes indicated. The 25 base pair differences between
           the two genes are indicated by "ticks" above the amino
           acids corresponding to the codons (T. K. Misra and N. L.
           Brown, unpublished data).

complete before publication date of this monograph and we expect to
find a small number of errors (perhaps 3 to 5) in our current sequences. However, we feel fairly confident with the merR sequence
which has been independently determined in the two laboratories.

Enzymatic Mechanism of Mercurial Detoxification

     Hg^{2+} resistance in bacteria results from enzymatic detoxifica-
tion of mercury compounds. The mercury is volatilized (37,78,84) as
metallic Hg^0 and the enzyme responsible is called mercuric reductase
(Fig. 6).

     Several organomercurials are also enzymatically detoxified to
volatile compounds (Figs. 3 and 6). Benzene is produced from phen-
ylmercury, methane from methylmercury, and ethane from ethylmercury.
The enzymes responsible for cleaving the Hg-C bond are organomercurial lyases. Tezuka and Tonomura (81,82) separated two small soluble
lyase enzymes from a Pseudomonas strain. Both have molecular
weights of about 19,000. One enzyme cleaved phenylmercuric acetate,
p-hydroxymercuribenzoate and methylmercury, while the other enzyme
cleaved only phenylmercuric acetate and p- hydroxymercuribenzoate
(81,82). With an organomercurial-resistant E. coli, there was no
evidence for cleavage of p-hydroxymercuribenzoate (90), and Schottel
(64) was unable to separate the two lyases. Nevertheless, kinetic

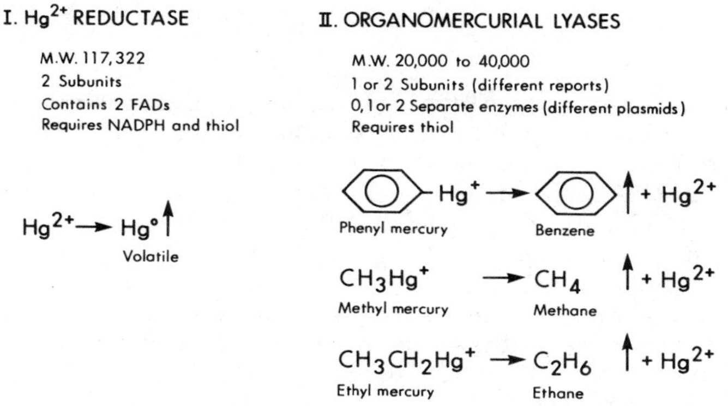

I. Hg^{2+} REDUCTASE

M.W. 117,322
2 Subunits
Contains 2 FADs
Requires NADPH and thiol

II. ORGANOMERCURIAL LYASES

M.W. 20,000 to 40,000
1 or 2 Subunits (different reports)
0, 1 or 2 Separate enzymes (different plasmids)
Requires thiol

Hg^{2+} → Hg°↑
Volatile

Phenyl mercury → Benzene ↑ + Hg^{2+}

CH$_3$Hg$^+$ → CH$_4$ ↑ + Hg^{2+}
Methyl mercury   Methane

CH$_3$CH$_2$Hg$^+$ → C$_2$H$_6$ ↑ + Hg^{2+}
Ethyl mercury   Ethane

Fig. 6.   Enzymatic pathways of mercury and organomercurial resistance.

analysis indicated that there were two enzymes active toward phenyl-mercuric acetate and only one active toward methyl- and ethylmerc-ury. The general properties of the enzymes from the soil pseudo-monad and E. coli were similar, except that the E. coli organomer-curial lyases had a somewhat greater molecular weight (64).

Mercuric reductase has been studied in greater detail (17,23, 35,64). We once thought the enzyme was strictly NADPH-dependent, but it now appears that some mercuric reductases can utilize either

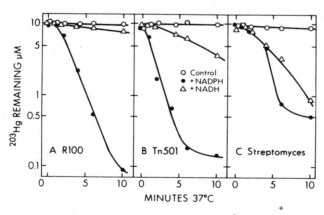

Fig. 7.   Volatilization of mercury from Hg^{2+} by enzyme preparations from cells bearing (A) plasmid R100, (B) transposon Tn501, or (C) a new Streptomyces strain. Conditions were as given by Schottel (64) except 25 µM NAD(P)H was added with 10 µM ^{203}Hg^{2+} (S. Silver, unpublished experiment).

NADPH or NADH (e.g., the Streptomyces strain in Fig. 7).

Characterization of the mercuric reductase enzyme (17) has shown it to be similar to a class of NAD(P)H-dependent FAD-containing flavoproteins including glutathione reductase and lipoamide dehydrogenase (91). These enzymes have a reaction sequence starting with (a) NAD(P)H-reducing enzyme-bound FAD to $FADH_2$. Next, (b) $FADH_2$ reduces the disulfide bond between two neighboring cysteines in the enzyme active site. Finally, (c) Hg^{2+} is bound to the two cysteine SH groups, and (d) Hg^{2+} is reduced to Hg^0 (17). The structure and partial amino acid sequences of E. coli, yeast, and human glutathione reductase and of E. coli and pig lipoamide dehydrogenase are known (38,91). One can identify the location and sequence of the mercuric reductase gene from the DNA sequence analysis (11). Mercuric reductase contains a 15 amino acid sequence which is essentially identical to sequences at the active sites of glutathione reductase and lipoamide dehydrogenase (38,91) (Fig. 8) and which contains the active cystine. This is the first application of DNA sequencing technology to studies of heavy metal resistances. It provides a suggestion of the source from which enzymes able to detoxify heavy metals might have arisen: enzymes of normal cellular metabolism.

The subunit structure of the mercuric reductase enzyme from various sources is currently under reevaluation. Furukawa and Tonomura (22) reported that the enzyme from a soil pseudomonad had a molecular weight of about 65,000. Schottel (64) reported that the enzyme from plasmid R831 which originated in Serratia was a trimer of 170,000 daltons containing identical monomer subunits, each approximately the size of the Pseudomonas enzyme. Each subunit contained a single bound FAD, for a total of three FADs per 170,000 molecular weight. We obtained similar evidence for a trimeric structure for

Hg^{2+} Reductase Tn501

THR ILE GLY GLY THR CYS VAL ASN VAL GLY CYS VAL PRO SER LYS
                    L_____J

Glutathione Reductase

LEU GLY GLY THR CYS VAL ASN VAL GLY CYS VAL PRO LYS
                L_____J

Lipoamide Dehydrogenase

THR LEU GLY GLY VAL CYS LEU ASN VAL GLY CYS ILE PRO SER LYS
                    L_____J

Fig. 8.   The active site amino acid sequences of Pseudomonas mercuric reductase, human red blood cell glutathione reductase, and E. coli lipoamide dehydrogenase (11,38,91).

mercuric reductase from a variant of plasmid R100 by both gel fil-
tration and electrophoresis through gels of differing porosity (73;
T. G. Kinscherf and S. Silver, unpublished data). Yet, Rinderle et
al. (63) found a gel filtration/denatured gel electrophoresis mobility ratio consistent with a dimeric enzyme for another variant of
plasmid R100, and Fox and Walsh (17) reported that the molecular
weight of another mercuric reductase (from transposon Tn501) was
about 125,000, and the enzyme appeared to be dimeric. We have confirmed the dimeric structure of the mercuric reductase of Tn501.

Antibodies were prepared against purified mercuric reductases
coded by two plasmids in E. coli (73). Reductases obtained from all
but one different gram-negative source reacted with these antibodies, as shown by inhibition of enzyme activity and by formation of
precipitin bands on double-diffusion gels. The enzymes fell into
two major subclasses, based on only partial immunological identity.
The prototype of the first enzyme class is coded by transposon Tn501
(4). This enzyme class also includes mercuric reductases governed
by a variety of plasmids found in clinical, soil, and marine bacteria. One strong conclusion from studies of plasmid-determined mercuric resistance is that the same system appears widely in bacterial
isolates from diverse environments. Newer Hg^{2+} - (and in one case
phenylmercuric-) resistance transposons from soil microbes showed
different patterns of digestion by DNA restriction endonucleases
(61).

The second immunological subgroup of gram-negative mercuric reductases has as its prototype the enzyme coded for by plasmid R100.
It is with R100 that the genetic structure of the mercuric resistance operon is being studied in detail (16,47,49). This subgroup
includes enzymes from a wide variety of sources including the enzyme
determined by a second Pseudomonas mercury transposon Tn502 (73; V.
Stanisich, personal communication). All of the mercuric reductases
from gram-negative bacteria were immunologically related, with the
single exception of the enzyme from Thiobacillus ferrooxidans (54).
The antibodies prepared against the two classes of gram-negative enzymes did not cross react with mercuric reductases from S. aureus
strains and marine and soil bacilli. These enzymes from gram-
positive sources showed otherwise similar functional requirements to
those from the gram-negative bacteria (73,88); yet they are immunologically distinct.

To summarize briefly the current understanding of plasmid-
determined mercuric and organomercurial resistances: (a) They occur
widely in all bacterial types tested and are the best understood of
all plasmid-coded heavy metal resistances. (b) Resistance is due to
enzymatic detoxification of the mercurials to volatile compounds of
lesser toxicity. (c) The enzymes responsible (mercuric reductases
and organomercurial lyases) have been purified and are being characterized. (d) The newer tools of DNA cloning and sequencing are being applied to these systems.

Oxidation and Methylation of Mercury

Much less is known about the oxidation of Hg^0 to Hg^{2+} and the subsequent methylation of Hg^{2+} to CH_3Hg^+ and $(CH_3)_2Hg$ than is known about the reverse processes. However, microbial activities have been implicated in both reactions. Since most atmospheric mercury is Hg^0 and most aqueous mercury (in the rivers, lakes, and seas) is Hg^{2+} (see review in Ref. 79 for original references), how is the geochemical mercury cycle maintained? A wide range of bacteria can oxidize Hg^0 to Hg^{2+} (32). The bacteria that oxidize Hg^0 do not (in general) carry out the further conversion of Hg^{2+} to methylmercury (32). The ubiquitous enzyme catalase (found in animal tissues and bacteria) can oxidize Hg^0 to Hg^{2+} and is probably responsible for the rapid conversion of inhaled mercury vapor into ionic mercury in the blood (26). There appears to be general agreement that Hg^{2+} can be methylated abiotically and extracellularly by methylcobalamin (vitamin B12) (10,40,93). Cobalamin is synthesized only by micro-bial cells and is either excreted or released on cell lysis. Other bacteria (such as E. coli) and cells of higher organisms (plants and animals, all of which require this vitamin for growth) can accumu-late cobalamin and methylate it enzymatically (93) to provide for methyl transfer reactions. Many common bacteria carry out mercury methylation (87), presumably by this means. Mercury can be methyl-ated by microbial activities in such environments as river sludge (29) and human feces (15). Both bacteria and fungi can methylate mercury (87). Although only the methylcobalamin-dependent process has been studied in detail (93), there are reasons [such as lack of dependency upon added cobalamin with some but not with other baceria (87)] to question whether a second biologically important methyl do-nation process may exist. This is a topic where further work is needed (10). It is also unclear as to whether all of the methylmer-cury found in fish and in man arose initially by methylation by mi-crobes growing in intestines and on gills (as suggested in Ref. 79), or whether mammalian enzymes also function to produce methylmercury.

ARSENIC AND ANTIMONY RESISTANCES

Arsenic and antimony resistances are governed by plasmids that also code for antibiotic and other heavy metal resistances (30,51, 76). Arsenate, arsenite, and antimony(III) resistances are coded for by an inducible operon-like system in both S. aureus and E. coli (71). Each of the three ions induces all three resistances. In E. coli, Bi(III) is a gratuitous inducer of arsenate resistance, even though the plasmid system does not confer Bi(III) resistance. S. aureus has a genetically separate plasmid-mediated Bi(III) resis-tance determinant (50,51) of unknown mechanism.

The mechanism of arsenate resistance is a reduced accumula-tion of arsenate by induced resistant cells. Arsenate is normally

accumulated via the cellular phosphate transport systems, of which
many bacteria appear to have two (Fig. 9). The distinction between
arsenate and arsenite resistance was shown initially by finding that
phosphate did not protect against arsenite inhibition of growth
(71). Genetic studies have also demonstrated that the arsenate resistance gene is different from, but closely linked to, the arsenite
resistance gene. Arsenite and antimony resistances may be determined by separate genes (50). The presence of the resistance plasmid does not alter the kinetic parameters of the cellular phosphate
transport systems; even the K_i for arsenate as a competitive inhibitor of phosphate transport (Fig. 9) is unchanged. This finding,
along with direct evidence for plasmid-governed energy-dependent efflux of arsenate, indicated that the block on net uptake of arsenate
resulted from rapid efflux. The energy dependence of the efflux
process was shown by its sensitivity to "uncouplers" and ionophore
antibiotics such as nigericin and monensin (72). Hg^{2+} also inhibited the efflux system, and the Hg^{2+} inhibition was readily reversed
by mercaptoethanol (72). Mobley and Rosen (43) demonstrated that
glucose but not succinate could energize arsenate efflux in an E.
coli strain that could not synthesize ATP from respiratory substrates. Although all of these data are indirect, AsO_4^{3-} efflux appears to directly involve an ATPase-linked transport system (Fig. 9).

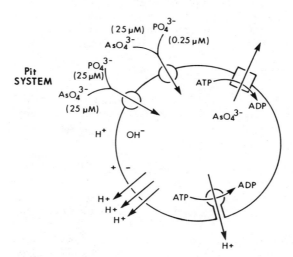

Pst SYSTEM

Fig. 9.   The phosphate (arsenate) transport systems and the arse-
         nate efflux system of E. coli. 0.25 μM or 25 μM, where
         indicated, is the K_m (for PO_4^{3-}) or the K_i (for AsO_4^{3-} as
         a competitive inhibitor of PO_4^{3-} transport) for the Pit
         (Pi transport) and Pst (Phosphate specific transport)
         phosphate transport systems.

An interesting question about the arsenate efflux system concerns its specificity. Arsenate generally functions as a phosphate analogue and is accumulated by bacteria via phosphate transport systems (67). The arsenate-resistance efflux system should not excrete phosphate, since the cells would then become phosphate starved, a situation no more advantageous than being arsenate inhibited! A basic conclusion from our work on arsenate (and also on Cd^{2+} resistance; see below) is that toxic heavy metals often get into cells by means of transport systems for normally required nutrients (67,79). Energy-dependent efflux systems functioning as resistance mechanisms must be highly specific for the toxic anion or cation to prevent loss of the required nutrient.

The mechanism(s) of plasmid-determined arsenite and antimony resistances are not known. Arsenite is not oxidized to the less toxic arsenate by plasmid-bearing E. coli or S. aureus (71), although Alcaligenes strains bave been isolated that do have an inducible arsenite oxidizing system (55,58). Arsenicals and antimonials are toxic by virtue of inhibiting thiol-containing enzymes (1). Plasmid-containing resistant cells did not excrete soluble thiol compounds into the medium (71). The absence of "detoxification" (measured by experiments inoculating sensitive cells into medium "preconditioned" by growth of resistant cells) eliminates all other mechanisms involving changes in extracellular chemical states. It is possible that arsenite resistance (like arsenate resistance; above) results from a change in cell membrane transport. Arima and Beppu (3,5) isolated an arsenite resistant Pseudomonas pseudomallei which had an inducible decrease in the energy-dependent accumulation of arsenite. No further work has been done on this system.

Oxidation and Methylation of Arsenic

Oxidation and methylation of arsenic compounds by microbes was known well before the modern era of molecular genetics. Arsenite-resistant bacteria capable of oxidizing the more toxic arsenite ion to somewhat less toxic arsenate were first isolated from cattle-dipping tanks in South Africa in 1918 and later in Australia (reviewed in Ref. 79). Similar strains have appeared over the years and these arsenite-oxidizing strains contain an inducible soluble arsenite dehydrogenase enzyme (55,58,79). There is no evidence of involvement of plasmids in the oxidation of arsenite by these bacteria.

Fungal growth producing a garlic-like smell of methylarsine was first found in moldly wallpaper in the 1940s (reviewed in Ref. 40, 79). The process of methyl donation requires CH_3-cobalamin, as does the methylation of Hg^{2+} (40). An enzymatic reaction sequence of (a) reduction of AsO_4^{3-} to AsO_3^{3-}, (b) methylation by methylcobalamin of arsenite to $CH_3AsO_3^{2-}$, followed by (c) methylation to $(CH_3)_2AsO_2^{-}$, and then followed by (d) reduction to $(CH_3)_2AsH$ (dimethylarsine) was

postulated (40) and later directly demonstrated (14,59). The volatile arsenic compound found was entirely dimethylarsine. Clearly
this sequence is a more complex one than the abiotic methylation of
of Hg^{2+} by methylcobalamin. However, under some conditions, the entire volatile methylation product of Hg^{2+} was $(CH_3)_2Hg$ (36). It is
not possible at present to tell how different or how similar the
methylation of different heavy metals and metalloids is at the biochemical level (10,40,93).

CADMIUM AND ZINC RESISTANCE

     Plasmid-determined cadmium resistance has been found only in S.
aureus (51). In some collections, Cd^{2+} resistance is the most common S. aureus plasmid resistance, more common than mercury or penicillin resistance (44). Gram-negative cells without plasmids are
just as resistant to Cd^{2+} as are staphylococci with plasmids (45),
probably because of relatively reduced Cd^{2+} uptake. However, there
are occasional gram-negative bacteria that are sensitive or even
"hypersensitive" to Cd^{2+} (52; T. Barkay, unpublished data). The basis of Cd^{2+} sensitivity and resistance in other bacterial species is
not known. There is no evidence, however, for chemical transformations associated with resistance.

     In staphylococci, Cd^{2+} is accumulated by a membrane transport
system utilizing the cross-membrane electrical potential (57,86,89)
(Fig. 10). This uptake system is highly specific for Cd^{2+} and Mn^{2+}
with respective K_m's of 10 μM and 16 μM in whole cells (89) and
0.2 μM and 0.95 μM in membrane vesicles (57).

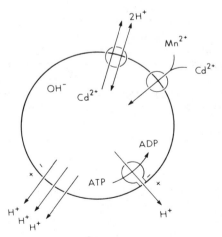

Fig. 10. Model for Cd^{2+} uptake and efflux systems.

Two separate plasmid genes are responsible for the Cd^{2+} resistance of S. aureus strains (50,51) (Fig. 11). The cadA and cadB genes confer, respectively, a large and a small increase in Cd^{2+} resistance (Fig.11). When both genes are present, the effect of cadA masks the cadB gene effect; cadA$^+$ cadB$^+$ strains are no more resistant than are cadA$^-$ cadB$^-$ strains. Both genes confer increased Zn^{2+} resistance (Fig. 11). This and the genetic linkage of Cd^{2+} and Zn^{2+} resistance (57) indicate that the cadA and cadB genes are also responsible for Zn^{2+} resistance.

Cd^{2+} resistance is due to lessened accumulation of Cd^{2+} by resistant cells (86,89). The cadA gene product causes this lessened Cd^{2+} accumulation (57,89) (Fig. 12). A plasmid-encoded efflux system rapidly excretes Cd^{2+} from resistant cells (Fig. 13). Although not directly demonstrated, it seems plausible that the cadA gene product might also cause Zn^{2+} efflux. However, the presence of the cadA$^+$ gene neither reduces Mn^{2+} uptake nor causes rapid efflux of accumulated Mn^{2+} (57). CadA$^+$ resistant strains possess this efflux system, but sensitive cells and cadB$^+$ resistant strains do not (74).

The cadA-encoded efflux system is energy dependent. Cd^{2+} efflux was abolished by dinitrophenol and at low temperature (Fig. 13). Inhibitor studies indicate that the efflux system is a $Cd^{2+}/2H^+$ exchange system (Fig. 10), analogous to the tetracycline efflux system (42) responsible for plasmid-mediated resistance to that antibiotic.

We do not know the mechanism of cadB gene function. Our clues at the moment include the significant resistance to Zn^{2+} conferred by cadB (Fig. 11) and an inducible Cd^{2+} binding activity governed by this gene (74). This binding activity is not energy-dependent. We hypothesize that it might be due to a membrane component analogous to metallothionein, the small Cd^{2+}-binding protein made by both mammals and microbes. This is no more than a working hypothesis at this time. When seeking Cd^{2+}-resistant mutants of mammalian cells, Corrigan and Huang (13) found what appeared to be transport mutants that accumulate less Cd^{2+} and more Zn^{2+} than wild-type cells. Whether the metallothionein studies or mammalian transport studies will provide a basis for understanding cadB resistance is an open question.

SILVER RESISTANCE

Microbial silver toxicity is found in situations of industrial pollution, especially associated with the use of photographic film. In hospitals, silver salts are preferred antimicrobial agents for burns (18,19). It is thus not surprising that silver-resistant bacteria have been found in urban and industial polluted sites (77) or

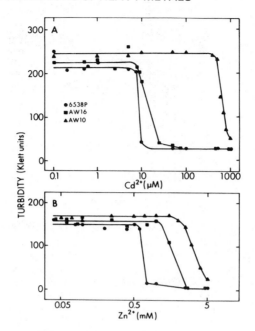

Fig. 11. Cd^{2+} and Zn^{2+} resistance of strains with and without plasmids. Overnight cultures were diluted 1:200 into broth
containing varying concentrations of (A) $CdCl_2$ or (B)
$ZnSO_4$. Culture turbidities were measured after 7 h of
growth at 37°C. Strains 6538P (sensitive), AW10 (cadA$^+$-
resistant) and AW16 (cadB$^+$-resistant) (from Ref. 57).

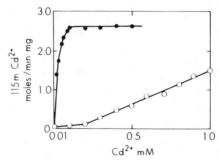

Fig. 12. Cd^{2+} uptake by sensitive and by resistant S. aureus. Initial rate of accumulation of $^{115m}Cd^{2+}$ by a resistant plasmid-containing strain (o) and its sensitive plasmidless
variant (•) (86).

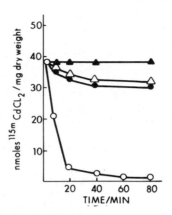

Fig. 13. Retention of $^{115m}Cd^{2+}$ by cadmium-resistant S. aureus. The
cell suspensions were pre-incubated with 1 mM $^{115m}Cd^{2+}$ for
10 min at 37°C. Cells were washed free of Cd^{2+}, and then
$^{115m}Cd^{2+}$ efflux was assayed. o, control cells at 37°C; ▲,
cells at 4°C; Δ, cells with 10 mM dinitrophenol; and ●,
cells with 100 μM dicyclohexylcarbodiimide (85).

that silver-resistant bacteria (2,9,31) and silver resistance plasmids (41) have been described. The plasmid-determined resistance is
very great, and the ratio of minimum-inhibitory Ag^+ concentrations
(resistant:sensitive) can be greater than 100:1 (70,74). The level
of resistance is strongly dependent upon available halide ions;
without Cl^-, there was relatively little difference between cells
with or without resistance plasmids (74). Br^- and I^- protected both
sensitive and resistant cells at concentrations far below those used
for Cl^-. Both sensitive and resistant cells bind Ag^+ tightly and
are killed by effects on cell respiration and other cell surface
functions (8,66). Once bound extracellularly, Ag^+ enters the cell
and is found in high speed centrifugal supernatant fractions
(Silver, unpublished data). Our current hypothesis is that the sensitive cells bind Ag^+ so tightly that they extract it from AgCl and
other bound forms, whereas cells with resistance plasmids do not
compete successfully with Ag^+-halide precipitates for Ag^+.

OTHER HEAVY METAL RESISTANCES

     There are several other plasmid heavy metal resistances (75,
77,79), but nothing today is known about the mechanisms of resistance to bismuth, boron, cobalt, lead, nickel, or tellurium ions.
Chromate resistance in a pseudomonad isolated from river sediment is
due to reduction of toxic Cr(VI) to less toxic Cr(III) and this resistance appears to be plasmid determined (7). Cupric ion resistance has been found both with plasmids in E. coli (33,80) and in S.
aureus (25), but no studies have been reported on the mechanism of
this resistance.

Methylation of Other Heavy Metals

In addition to arsenic and mercury, chemical or biogenic methylation reactions have been reported for palladium, thallium, sele-
nium, lead, platinum, gold, tin, chromium, and sulfur (10,62,93).
Tin-resistant bacteria were isolated from polluted areas of Chesapeake Bay (27). These bacteria were also resistant to dimethyltin.
Bacteria from Chesapeake Bay were able to synthesize dimethyl- and
trimethyltin (28), as was previously proposed during a general discussion of methylcobalamin-dependent methylation (93). It is not
known whether the bacteria resistant to methyltin synthesize or degrade methyltin. Resistance may (as in the case of mercury) be unrelated to the ability to synthesize these organometallic compounds.
Once methylated by biological processes, abiotic transmethylation
reactions occur (10) and heavy metal compounds can be destroyed
abiotically by oxidation (56).

Over the last 13 years, our laboratory has been studying the
mechanisms and genetics of plasmid-mediated heavy metal resistances.
In the frequent absence of any obvious source of direct selection,
one may ask why these resistances occur with such high frequencies.
Selective agents in hospitals and "normal human" environments are
only beginning to be examined. It has been suggested that heavy
metal resistances may have been selected in earlier times, and that
they are merely carried along today "for a free ride" with selection
for antibiotic resistances. We doubt that there is such a thing as
"a free ride" as far as these determinants are concerned. For example, in Tokyo in the late 1970s, both heavy metal resistances and
antibiotic resistances were found with high frequencies in E. coli
isolated from hospital patients, whereas heavy metal resistance
plasmids without antibiotic resistance determinants were found in E.
coli from an industrially polluted suburban river (46). Selection
occurs for resistances to both types of agents in the hospital, but
only that for toxic heavy metals in the river environment. Radford,
et al. (61) found Hg^{2+}-resistant microbes in agricultural soil with
no known human mercurial input. In such settings, the frequency of
resistant microbes may be very low, but it may come into much greater quantitative prominence after industrial or agricultural pollution (21,52,77,83). This situation may be closely analogous to that
with antibiotic-resistance plasmids which are found in low frequencies in antibiotic-virgin populations (24,39), but which become dominant with extensive human use of antibiotics.

POTENTIAL APPLICATIONS IN ENVIRONMENTAL
MONITORING AND POLLUTION CONTROL

The "take home message" for this presentation is that transformations of toxic heavy metals that occur on a global scale are generally brought about by microorganisms. Considerations of human
health problems must take into account the chemical forms of heavy
metals available. Specific microbial strains and frequencies of

resistances to toxic heavy metals in environmental populations of microbes could be useful biomonitors of heavy metal pollution and as a means of pollution control. Microbes might be utilized to convert more toxic forms of heavy metals into less toxic forms (perhaps the mercury cycle); or other microbes might be fooled into accumulating heavy metals in order to clean up sources of concern. For example, there are preliminary reports of the use of microbes to bioaccumulate silver (from Eastman Kodak Company) and low level waste uranium (Oak Ridge National Laboratory). There are proposals but no real evidence for the use of cadmium accumulating microbes to clean up both marine and sediment pollution problems. In both cases, understanding of the basic biochemical and genetic bases for microbial resistances to heavy metals and microbial transformations of these materials is essential for rational planning.

ACKNOWLEDGEMENTS

    The work in our laboratory on these topics over the last decade has been contributed to by many talented people whose names often appear as coauthors in the References section. Support has been provided most recently by National Science Foundation Grant PCM 82-05592 and by U.S. Public Health Service Grant AI15672.

REFERENCES

1. Albert, A. (1973) Arsenicals, antimonials and mercurials. In Selective Toxicity, Fifth Edition, Chapman and Hall, London, pp. 392-397.

2. Annear, D.I., B.J. Mee, and M. Bailey (1976) Instability and linkage of silver resistance, lactose fermentation and colony structure in Enterobacter cloacae from burn wounds. J. Clin. Path. 29:441-443.

3. Arima, K., and M. Beppu (1964) Induction and mechanisms of arsenite resistance in Pseudomonas pseudomallei. J. Bacteriol. 88:143-150.

4. Bennett, P.M., J. Grinsted, C.L. Choi, and M.H. Richmond (1978) Characterization of Tn501, a transposon determining resistance to mercuric ions. Mol. Gen. Genet. 159:101-106.

5. Beppu, M., and K. Arima (1964) Decreased permeability as the mechanism of arsenite resistance in Pseudomonas pseudomallei. J. Bacteriol. 88:151-157.

6. Bisogni, Jr., J.J. (1979) Kinetics of methylmercury formation and decomposition in aquatic environments. In The Biogeochemistry of Mercury in the Environment, J.O. Nriagu, ed. Elsevier/North Holland Press, Amsterdam, pp. 221-230.

7. Bopp, L.H., A.M. Chakrabarty, and H.L. Ehrlich (1983) Plasmid-determined resistance to Cr(VI) and reduction of Cr(VI) to Cr(III). J. Bacteriol. 155:1105-1109.

8. Bragg, P.D., and D.J. Rainnie (1974) The effect of silver ions on the respiratory chain of Escherichia coli. Can. J. Microbiol. 20:883–889.

9. Bridges, K., A. Kidson, E.J.L. Lowbury, and M.D. Wilkins (1979) Gentamicin- and silver-resistant Pseudomonas in a burns unit. Brit. Med. J. 1:446–449.

10. Brinkman, F.E., G.J. Olson, and W.P. Iverson (1982) The production and fate of volatile molecular species in the environment: Metals and metalloids. In Atmospheric Chemistry. Dahlem Konferenzen, E.D. Goldberg, ed. Springer-Verlag, Berlin, pp. 231–249.

11. Brown, N.L., S.J. Ford, R.D. Pridmore, and D.C. Fritzinger (1983) Nucleotide sequence of a gene from the Pseudomonas transposon Tn501 encoding mercuric reductase. Biochemistry 22:4089–4095.

12. Clark, D.L., A.A. Weiss, and S. Silver (1977) Mercury and organomercurial resistance determined by plasmids in Pseudomonas. J. Bacteriol. 132:186–196.

13. Corrigan, A.J., and P.C. Huang (1981) Cellular uptake of cadmium and zinc. Biol. Trace Element Res. 3:197–216.

14. Cullen, W.R., B.C. McBride, and A.W. Pickett (1979) The transformation of arsenicals by Candida humicola. Can. J. Microbiol. 25:1201–1205.

15. Edwards, T., and B.C. McBride (1975) Biosynthesis and degradation of methylmercury in human faeces. Nature 253:462–463.

16. Foster, T.J., H. Nakahara, A.A. Weiss, and S. Silver (1979) Transposon A-generated mutations in the mercuric resistance genes of plasmid R100-1. J. Bacteriol. 140:167–181.

17. Fox, B., and C.T. Walsh (1982) Mercuric reductase: Purification and characterization of a transposon-encoded flavoprotein containing an oxidation-reduction active sulfide. J. Biol. Chem. 257:2498–2503.

18. Fox, Jr., C.L. (1968) Silver sulfadiazine. A new topical for Pseudomonas in burns. Arch. Surg. 96:184–188.

19. Fox, Jr., C.L., and S.M. Modak (1974) Mechanism of silver sulfadiazine action on burn wound infections.. Antimicrob. Agents Chemother. 5:582–588.

20. Friello, D.A., and A.M. Chakrabarty (1980) Transposable mercury resistance in Pseudomonas putida. In Plasmids and Transposons: Environmental Effects and Maintenance Mechanisms, C. Suttard and K.R. Rozee, eds. Academic Press, New York, pp. 249–260.

21. Furukawa, K., T. Suzuki, and K. Tonomura (1969) Decomposition of organic mercurial compounds by mercury-resistant bacteria. Agric. Biol. Chem. 33:128–130.

22. Furukawa, K., and K. Tonomura (1971) Enzyme system involved in the decomposition of phenyl mercuric acetate by mercury-resistant Pseudomonas. Agric. Biol. Chem. 35:604–610.

23. Furukawa, K., and K. Tonomura (1972) Metallic mercury-releasing enzyme in mercury-resistant Pseudomonas. Agric. Biol. Chem. 36:217–226.

24. Gardner, P., D.H. Smith, H. Beer, and R.C. Moellering, Jr. (1969) Recovery of resistance (R) factors from a drug-free community. Lancet 2:774-776.
25. Groves, D.J., and F.E. Young (1975) Epidemiology of antibiotic and heavy metal resistance in bacteria: Resistance patterns in Staphylococci isolated from populations not known to be exposed to heavy metals. Antimicrob. Agents Chemother. 7:614-621.
26. Halbach, S., and T.W. Clarkson (1978) Enzymatic oxidation of mercury vapor by erythrocytes. Biochim. Biophys. Acta 523:522-531.
27. Hallas, L.E., and J.J. Cooney (1981) Tin and tin-resistant microorganisms in Chesapeake Bay. Appl. Env. Microbiol. 41:446-471.
28. Hallas, L.E., J.C. Means, and J.J. Cooney (1982) Methylation of tin by estuarine microorganisms. Science 215:1505-1507.
29. Hamdy, M.K., and O.R. Noyes (1975) Formation of methylmercury by bacteria. Appl. Microbiol. 30:424-432.
30. Hedges, R.W., and S. Baumberg (1973) Resistance to arsenic compounds conferred by a plasmid transmissable between strains of Escherichia coli. J. Bacteriol. 115:459-460.
31. Hendry, A.T., and I.O. Stewart (1979) Silver-resistant enterobacteriaceae from hospital patients. Can. J. Microbiol. 25:915-921.
32. Holm, H.W., and M.F. Cox (1975) Transformation of elemental mercury by bacteria. Appl. Microbiol. 29:491-494.
33. Ishihara, M., Y. Kamio, and Y. Terawaki (1978) Cupric ion resistance as a new marker of a temperature sensitive R plasmid, Rts1 in Escherichia coli. Biochem. Biophys. Res. Comm. 82:74-80.
34. Izaki, K. (1981) Enzymatic reduction of mercurous and mercuric ions in Bacillus cereus. Can. J. Microbiol. 27:192-197.
35. Izaki, K., Y. Tashiro, and T. Funaba (1974) Mechanism of mercuric chloride resistance in microorganisms. III. Purification and properties of a mercuric ion reducing enzyme from Escherichia coli bearing R factor. J. Biochem. 75:591-599.
36. Jensen, S., and A. Jernelöv (1969) Biological methylation of mercury in aquatic organisms. Nature 223:753-754.
37. Komura, I., T. Funaba, and K. Izaki (1971) Mechanism of mercuric chloride resistance in microorganisms. II. NADPH-dependent reduction of mercuric chloride and vaporization of mercury from mercuric chloride by a multiple drug resistant strain of Escherichia coli. J. Biochem. 70:895-901.
38. Krauth-Siegel, R.L., R. Blatterspiel, M. Saleh, E. Schiltz, R.H. Schirmer, and R. Untucht-Grau (1982) Glutathione reductase from human erythrocytes. The sequences of the NADPH domain and of the interface domain. Eur. J. Biochem. 121:259-267.
39. Maré, I.J. (1968) Incidence of R factors among gram negative bacteria in drug-free human and animal communities. Nature 220:1046-1047.
40. McBride, B.C., and T.L. Edwards (1977) Role of the methanogenic

bacteria in the alkylation of arsenic and mercury. In ERDA
Symposium Series #42, pp. 1-19.

41. McHugh, G.L., R.C. Moellering, C.C. Hopkins, and M.N. Schwartz
     (1975) Salmonella typhimurium resistant to silver nitrate,
     chloramphenicol, and ampicillin. Lancet 1:235-240.

42. McMurry, L., R.E. Petrucci, Jr., and S.B. Levy (1980) Active
     efflux of tetracycline encoded by four genetically different
     tetracycline resistance determinants in Escherichia coli.
     Proc. Natl. Acad. Sci., USA 77:3974-3977.

43. Mobley, H.L.T., and B.P. Rosen (1982) Energetics of plasmid-
     mediated arsenate resistance in Escherichia coli. Proc. Natl.
     Acad. Sci., USA 79:6119-6122.

44. Nakahara, H., T. Ishikawa, Y. Sarai, and I. Kondo (1977) Dis-
     tribution of resistances to metals and antibiotics of
     Staphylococcal strains in Japan. Zentralb. Bakteriol.
     Parasitenkd. Infektionskr. Hyg. 1 Abt. Orig. A 237:470-476.

45. Nakahara, H., T. Ishikawa, Y. Sarai, I. Kondo, H. Kozukue, and
     S. Silver (1977) Linkage of mercury, cadmium, and arsenate and
     drug resistance in clinical isolates of Pseudomonas aeruginosa.
     Appl. Envir. Microbiol. 33:975-976.

46. Nakahara, H., and H. Kozukue (1982) Volatilization of mercury
     determined by plasmids in E. coli isolated from an aquatic en-
     vironment. In Drug Resistance in Bacteria: Genetics, Bio-
     chemistry, and Molecular Biology, S. Mitsuhashi, ed. Japanese
     Scientific Societies Press, Tokyo, pp. 337-340.

47. Nakahara, H., S. Silver, T. Miki, and R.H. Rownd (1979) Hyper-
     sensitivity to Hg^{2+} and hyperbinding activity associated with
     cloned fragments of the mercurial resistance operon of plasmid
     NR1. J. Bacteriol. 140:161-166.

48. Nelson, Jr., J.D., and R.R. Colwell (1975) The ecology of mer-
     cury-resistant bacteria in Chesapeake Bay. Microb. Ecol.
     1:191-218.

49. NiBhriain, N., S. Silver, and T.J. Foster (1983) Tn5 insertion
     mutations in the mercuric ion resistance genes derived from
     plasmid R100. J. Bacteriol. 155:690-703.

50. Novick, R.P., E. Murphy, T.J. Gryczan, E. Baron, and I. Edelman
     (1979) Penicillinase plasmids of Staphylococcus aureus: Re-
     striction-deletion maps. Plasmid 2:109-129.

51. Novick, R.P., and C. Roth (1968) Plasmid-linked resistance to
     inorganic salts in Staphylococcus aureus. J. Bacteriol.
     95:1335-1342.

52. Olson, B.H., T. Barkay, and R.R. Colwell (1979) Role of plas-
     mids in mercury transformation by bacteria isolated from aquat-
     ic environment. Appl. Env. Microbiol. 38:478-485.

53. Olson, G.J., W.P. Iverson, and F.E. Brinckman (1981) Volatiliz-
     ation of mercury by Thiobacillus ferrooxidans. Current Micro-
     biol. 5:115-118.

54. Olson, G.J., F.D. Porter, J. Rubinstein, and S. Silver (1982)
     Mercuric reductase enzyme from a mercury-volatilizing strain of
     Thiobacillus ferrooxidans. J. Bacteriol. 151:1230-1236.

55. Osborne, F.H., and H.L. Ehrlich (1976) Oxidation of arsenite by a soil isolate of Alcaligenes. J. Appl. Bacteriol. 41:295-305.
56. Parris, G.E., and F.E. Brinckman (1976) Reactions which relate to environmental mobility of arsenic and antimony. II. Oxidation of trimethylarsine and trimethylstibine. Env. Sci. Technol. 10:1128-1134.
57. Perry, R.D., and S. Silver (1982) Cadmium and manganese transport in Staphylococcus aureus membrane vesicles. J. Bacteriol. 150:973-976.
58. Phillips, S.E., and M.L. Taylor (1976) Oxidation of arsenite to arsenate by Alcaligenes faecalis. Appl. Env. Microbiol. 32:392-399.
59. Pickett, A.W., B.C. McBride. W.R. Cullen, and H. Manji (1981) The reduction of trimethylarsine by Candida humicola. Can. J. Microbiol. 27:773-778.
60. Porter, F.D., C. Ong, S. Silver, and H. Nakahara (1982) Selection for mercurial resistance in hospital settings. Antimicrob. Agents Chemother. 22:852-858.
61. Radford, A.J., J. Oliver, W.J. Kelly, and D.C. Reanney (1981) Translocatable resistance to mercuric and phenylmercuric ions in soil bacteria. J. Bacteriol. 147:1110-1112.
62. Ridley, W.P., L.J. Dizikes, and J.M. Wood (1977) Biomethylation of toxic elements in the environment. Science 197:329-332.
63. Rinderle, S.J., J.E. Booth, and J.W. Williams (1983) Mercuric reductase from R-plasmid NR1: Characterization and mechanistic study. Biochem. 22:869-876.
64. Schottel, J.L. (1978) The mercuric and organomercurial detoxifying enzymes from a plasmid-bearing strain of Escherichia coli. J. Biol. Chem. 253:4341-4349.
65. Schottel, J., A. Mandal, D. Clark, S. Silver, and R.W. Hedges (1974) Volatilisation of mercury and organomercurials determined by inducible R-factor systems in enteric bacteria. Nature 251:335-337.
66. Schreurs, W.J.A., and H. Rosenberg (1982) Effect of silver ions on transport and retention of phosphate by Escherichia coli. J. Bacteriol. 152:7-13.
67. Silver, S. (1978) Transport of cations and anions. In Bacterial Transport, B.P. Rosen, ed. Marcel Dekker, Inc., New York, pp. 221-324.
68. Silver, S. (1981) Mechanisms of bacterial resistances to toxic heavy metals: Arsenic, antimony, silver, cadmium and mercury. In Environmental Speciation and Monitoring Needs for Trace Metal-Containing Substances from Energy-Related Processes, F.E. Brinckman and R.H. Fish, eds. Special Publ. 618. National Bureau of Standards, Washington, D.C., pp. 301-314.
69. Silver, S. (1981) Mechanisms of plasmid-determined heavy metal resistances. In Molecular Biology, Pathogenicity and Ecology of Bacterial Plasmids, S.B. Levy, R.C. Clowes, and E.L. Koenig, eds. Plenum Press, New York, pp. 179-189.

70. Silver, S. (1983) Bacterial transformations of and resistances to heavy metals. In Changing Metal Cycles and Human Health, Dahlem Konferenzen, J.O. Nriagu, ed. Springer-Verlag, Berlin (in press).

71. Silver, S., K. Budd, K.M. Leahy, W.V. Shaw, K. Hammond, R.P. Novick, G.R. Willsky, M.H. Malamy, and H. Rosenberg (1981) Inducible plasmid-determined resistance to arsenate, arsenite and antimony(III) in Escherichia coli and Staphylococcus aureus. J. Bacteriol. 146:983-996.

72. Silver, S., and D. Keach (1982) Energy-dependent arsenate efflux: The mechanism of plasmid-mediated resistance. Proc. Natl. Acad. Sci., USA, 79:6114-6118.

73. Silver, S., and T.G. Kinscherf (1982) Genetic and biochemical bases for microbial transformations and detoxification of mercury and mercurial compounds. In Biodegradation and Detoxification of Environmental Pollutants, A.M. Chakrabarty, ed. CRC Press, Boca Raton, FL, pp. 85-103.

74. Silver, S., R.D. Perry, Z. Tynecka, and T.G. Kinscherf (1982) Mechanisms of bacterial resistances to the toxic heavy metals antimony, arsenic, mercury and silver. In Drug Resistance in Bacteria: Genetics, Biochemistry, and Molecular Biology, S. Mitsuhashi, ed. Japan Scientific Societies Press, Tokyo, pp. 347-361.

75. Smith, D.H. (1967) R factors mediate resistances to mercury, nickel, and cobalt. Science 156:1114-1116.

76. Smith, H.W. (1978) Arsenic resistance in Enterobacteria: Its transmission by conjugation and by phage. J. Gen. Microbiol. 109:49-56.

77. Summers, A.O., G.A. Jacoby, M.N. Swartz, G. McHugh, and L. Sutton (1978) Metal cation and oxyanion resistances in plasmids of gram-negative bacteria. In Microbiology 1978, D. Schlessinger, ed. American Society for Microbiology, Washington, D.C., pp. 128-131.

78. Summers, A.O., and S. Silver (1972) Mercury resistance in a plasmid-bearing strain of Escherichia coli. J. Bacteriol. 112:1128-1136.

79. Summers, A.O., and S. Silver (1978) Microbial transformation of metals. Ann. Rev. Microbiol. 32:637-672.

80. Tetaz, T.J., and R.K.J. Luke (1983) Plasmid-controlled resistance to copper in Escherichia coli. J. Bacteriol. 154:1263-1268.

81. Tezuka, T., and K. Tonomura (1976) Purification and properties of an enzyme catalyzing the splitting of carbon-mercury linkages from mercury-resistant Pseudomonas K-62 strain. I. Splitting enzyme 1. J. Biochem. 80:79-87.

82. Tezuka, T., and K. Tonomura (1978) Purification and properties of a second enzyme catalyzing the splitting of carbon-mercury linkages from mercury-resistant Pseudomonas K-62. J. Bacteriol. 135:138-143.

83. Timoney, J.F., J. Port, J. Giles, and J. Spanier (1978) Heavy-metal and antibiotic resistance in the bacterial flora of sediments of New York Bight. Appl. Env. Microbiol. 36:465–472.
84. Tonomura, K., and F. Kanzaki (1969) The reductive decomposition of organic mercurials by cell-free extract of a mercury-resistant pseudomonad. Biochim. Biophys. Acta 184:227–229.
85. Tynecka, Z., Z. Gos, and J. Zajac (1981) Energy-dependent efflux of cadmium coded by a plasmid resistance determinant in Staphylococcus aureus. J. Bacteriol. 147:313–319.
86. Tynecka, Z., Z. Gos, and J. Zajac (1981) Reduced cadmium transport determined by a resistance plasmid in Staphylococcus aureus. J. Bacteriol. 147:305–312.
87. Vonk, J.W., and A.K. Sijpesteijn (1973) Studies on the methylation of mercuric chloride by pure cultures of bacteria and fungi. Anton. vanLeeuwenhoek J. Microbiol. Serol. 39:505–513.
88. Weiss, A.A., S.D. Murphy, and S. Silver (1977) Mercury and organomercurial resistances determined by plasmids in Staphylococcus aureus. J. Bacteriol. 132:197–208.
89. Weiss, A.A., S. Silver, and T.G. Kinscherf (1978) Cation transport alteration associated with plasmid-determined resistance to cadmium in Staphylococcus aureus. Antimicrob. Agents Chemother. 14:856–865.
90. Weiss, A.A., J.L. Schottel, D.L. Clark, R.G. Beller, and S. Silver (1978) Mercury and organomercurial resistance with enteric, staphylococcal, and pseudomonad plasmids. In Microbiology 1978, D. Schlessinger, ed. American Society for Microbiology, Washington, D.C., pp. 121–124.
91. Williams, Jr., C.H., L.D. Arscott, and G.E. Schulz (1982) Amino acid sequence homology between pig heart lipoamide dehydrogenase and human erythrocyte glutathione reductase. Proc. Natl. Acad. Sci., USA 79:2199–2201.
92. Witte, W., N. Van Dip, and R. Hummel (1980) Resistenz gegen quecksilber und cadmium bei Staphylococcus aureus unterschiedlicher okologischer herkunft. Z. Allg. Mikrobiol. 20:517–521.
93. Wood, J.M., A. Cheh, L.J. Dizikes, W.P. Ridley, S. Rakow, and J.R. Lakowicz (1978) Mechanisms for the biomethylation of metals and metalloids. Fed. Proc. 37:16–21.

THE IDENTIFICATION AND CLONING OF GENES ENCODING HALOAROMATIC CATABOLIC ENZYMES AND THE CONSTRUCTION OF HYBRID PATHWAYS FOR SUBSTRATE MINERALIZATION

A. J. Weightman, R. H. Don, P. R. Lehrbach,
and K. N. Timmis

Département de Biochimie Médicale
Centre Médicale Universitaire
9, avenue de Champel
1211 Geneva 4, Switzerland

INTRODUCTION

Halogenated organic compounds constitute one of the largest groups of environmental pollutants and have achieved notoriety as a result of their widespread use despite concerns regarding their toxicity, bioconcentration, and persistence in the biosphere. Government legislation resulting in termination of production of some halogenated aromatics, for example, 2,2-bis (4-chlorophenyl)-1,1,1-trichloroethane (DDT) and the polychlorinated biphenyls (PCBs), has not alleviated problems related to these banned chemicals. According to data presented by Hutzinger and Veerkamp (49), further contamination of the environment may be threatened by PCBs occupying landfills where 22% of total production in the U.S.A. for domestic use since 1929 has been deposited. These authors also suggested that up to 63% of total production is likely still to be present in the environment.

The sources of industrially produced halogenated organic compounds are numerous and fall into the following categories: herbicides, insecticides, fungicides, synthetic intermediates, solvents, plasticizers, and flame retardants. Table 1 lists the major groups of halogenated herbicides and indicates the variety of compounds which may be found in just one of the categories mentioned above. In 1979, the U.S. Environmental Protection Agency (54) cited seventy haloorganic compounds, of which all but seven were chlorinated, in

Table 1. Representative groups of commonly used herbicides.

Group	Example	Structure
Benzoic acid herbicides	TCB 2,3,6-Trichlorobenzoate	
Phenols	PCP Pentachlorophenol	
Diphenyl ethers	CNP p-Nitrophenyl-2,4,6-trichlorophenylether	
Pyridine based	PICLORAM 4-Amino-3,5,6-trichloropicolinic acid	
Phenoxyalkanoic acids	245T 2,4,5-Trichlorophenoxyacetate	
s-Triazines	ATRAZINE 2-Chloro-4-ethylamino-6-isopropylamino-s-triazine	
Substituted ureas	DIURON 3-(3,4-Dichlorophenyl)-1,1-dimethylurea	
Chloroacetamides	PROPACHLOR 2-Chloro-N-isopropyl-acetanilide	
Chlorinated alkanoic acids	DALAPON 2,2-Dichloropropionate	$H_3C \cdot CCl_2 \cdot COOH$

their list of 129 "priority pollutants." The list shows very clearly that production and discharge into the environment of halogenated aliphatic substances presents as much of a problem to industrialized countries as that posed by haloaromatic pollutants. For example, production of the solvent, synthetic intermediate, and "priority pollutant" ethylene dichloride (1,2-dichloroethane) in the U.S.A. during 1978 was about 5.2 million metric tonnes. Vinyl chloride, another "priority pollutant," is used in the production of polyvinyl chloride, and production in the U.S.A. for the same year reportedly total 3.5 million tonnes.

Another factor which should be considered in discussing haloorganic pollutants is the diversity of toxic compounds in formulations of industrial products. This problem relates to many herbicides, which are commercially available, but is highlighted by analyses of

PCBs, toxaphene (formulation of chlorinated terpenes), polychloro-
terphenyls, and polychloroquaterphenyls, formulations of which can
contain from 10^2 up to 10^5 different isomers.

The ability of microorganisms to metabolize haloaromatic and
haloaliphatic compounds has been subject to a good deal of research
effort. There is little doubt that microbial involvement in the
transformation of these compounds is an important factor in determining the fate of many of these compounds in the environment
(13,52). Naturally occurring halogenated compounds are not uncommon
and might well be of importance in the adaptation of microorganisms
to utilize halogenated xenobiotic compounds. Suida and DeBernadis
(95) identified more than 200 halogenated natural products of which
more than 75% were chlorinated. Although this list was by no means
complete, almost all of the chlorinated hydrocarbons were fungal
metabolites, and the majority of brominated products came from marine environments where the relative abundance of bromine is greater
than that of all other halogens except chlorine. Despite the limitations now apparent in Gale's original proposition of "microbial
infallibility" (1,2), reports of the biodegradation of compounds
formerly classified as recalcitrant (e.g., pentachlorophenol and
2,4,5-trichlorophenoxyacetate) have led to a general reappraisal of
the potential for adaption existing in microorganisms. Since
Reineke and Knackmuss' original report of construction of a catabolic pathway for the mineralization of 4-chlorobenzoate in Pseudomonas
sp. B13 (75) by introduction of the TOL-plasmid, encoding enzymes
catalyzing degradation of toluene, xylenes, toluates, and related
aromatic hydrocarbons (65,101,102), into that strain, several authors have described similar experiments in which the range of substrates utilized by bacterial isolates has been extended. These
findings and the potential for construction of microbial strains
which can be degrade environmental pollutants in situ will be discussed towards the end of this chapter.

MICROBIAL CATABOLISM OF HALOGENATED HYDROCARBONS

The difficulties of assessing biodegradability of halogenated
organic compounds in terms of chemical reactivity have been noted by
Dagley (21). The relative stabilities of bonds between carbon and
halogen atoms, as reflected in bond energies which decrease with decreasing electronegativity of the halogen substituent, give only a
poor indication of the relative resistances to microbial attack of
compounds containing different halogens bonded to either aliphatic
or aromatic carbon skeletons. Substrate analogues containing the
most electronegative halogen or fluorine are substrates for several
microbial enzymes which cannot convert chlorinated or brominated
analogues. Electronegativity does seem to be important in determining the activity of ring-cleavage enzymes (pyrocatechases) and,
presumably other dioxygenases, with substrates where the enzymes

catalyze electrophilic attack by molecular oxygen (21,62). Correlation between the deactivation of the aromatic nucleus as a result of
increase in the number of electron-withdrawing halogen substituents,
and reduction in rates of dioxygenase catalyzed conversion was apparent in the enzymes studied by Knackmuss' group (26,73,74).

    The plethora of papers in the literature which detail aspects
of halogenated hydrocarbon biodegradation belies the fact that few
catabolic pathways for these substrates have been elucidated. The
pathways of 2,4-dichlorophenoxyacetate (2,4-D) and fluoro- and
chlorobenzoate catabolism are best understood and are detailed in
Figs. 1 and 2. Detailed discussion of the catabolic pathways falls
outside the scope of this paper but features pertaining to the genetic studies described below should be outlined. The convergence
of 2,4-D and chlorobenzoate pathway is shown in Fig. 1 to occur at
chlorocatechol (11,33,41,62) and the mineralization of this intermediate is effected by a modified ortho-pathway in which dehalogenation is a fortuitous reaction catalyzed by cycloisomerase II (cis,
cis-chloro-muconate lactonizing enzyme) which attacks unsubstituted
and chloro-cis, cis-muconates as substrates (10,42,62,87,97). The
products of this reaction are chlorolactones (4-chloro- and 5-
chloro-4-carboxymethylbut-2-en-4-olide) which are unstable and spontaneously eliminate chloride to regenerate the diene chromophore
forming diene-lactones (trans- and cis-4-carboxymethylenebut-2-en-4-
olide). The diene-lactones are both substrates for hydrolase II, an
enzyme catalyzing their conversion to maleylacetate (83).

    The archetypal β-ketoadipate (ortho-) pathway is induced during
growth on benzoate and on substrates which are metabolized via this
compound in a variety of soil bacteria (90), and is compared with
the modified ortho-pathway in Fig. 1. This pathway operates in
Pseudomonas sp. B13 but can only process unsubstituted and, to a
limited extent, fluorinated catechols (84). Thus, catechol is converted to β-ketoadipate via 4-carboxymethylbut-3-en-4-olide which is
a substrate for hydrolase I. As can be seen in Fig. 2, two different routes have been proposed for the mineralization of chloromal-
eylacetate, an intermediate derived from 3,4-dichlorocatechol catabolism (15,28), although it seems likely that unsubstituted maleylacetate is converted to β-ketoadipate by a reductase (16).

    The modified ortho-pathway illustrates some important points
with regard to the metabolism of halogenated hydrocarbons. The importance of broad-specificity enzymes was exemplified by comparison
of enzyme from strain B13's chlorocatechol pathway with isofunctional enzymes from the β-ketoadipate pathway, the latter being highly
specific for their substrates (69). Methyl-substituted catechols
are catabolized by the chlorocatechol pathway, though only as far
as methyl-substituted lactones, which are not substrates for hydrolase II (63). Critical steps in haloaromatic catabolism have been

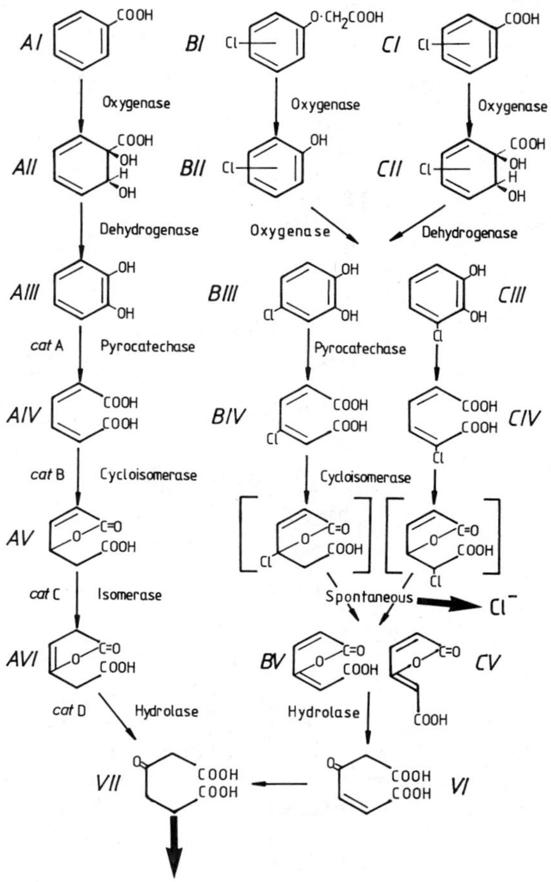

Fig. 1.   Converging ortho-ring cleavage pathways for the catabolism
of: benzoate (AI), chlorophenoxyacetates (BI) and chlorobenzoates (CI) and channeling of these substrates into
central metabolism via β-ketoadipic acid. The following
intermediates are marked: 3,5-cyclohexadiene-1,2-diol-1-
carboxylic acid or DHB (AII), chlorophenol (BII), chloro-
DHB (CII), catechol (AIII), 4-chlorocatechol (BIII), 3-
chlorocatechol (CIII), cis,cis-muconic acid (AIV), 3-
chloro-cis,cis-muconic acid (BIV), 2-chloro-cis,cis-
muconic acid (CIV), 4-carboxylmethylbut-2-en-4-olide (AV),
4-carboxymethylbut-3-en-4-olide (AVI), cis-4-carboxymeth-
ylenebut-2-en-4-olide (BV), trans-4-carboxymethylenebut-2-
en-4-olide (CV), maleylacetic acid (VI), β-ketoadipic acid
(VII).   Enzymes catalyzing the conversions are indicated.
Intermediates in parentheses are unstable and spontaneously dechlorinate.

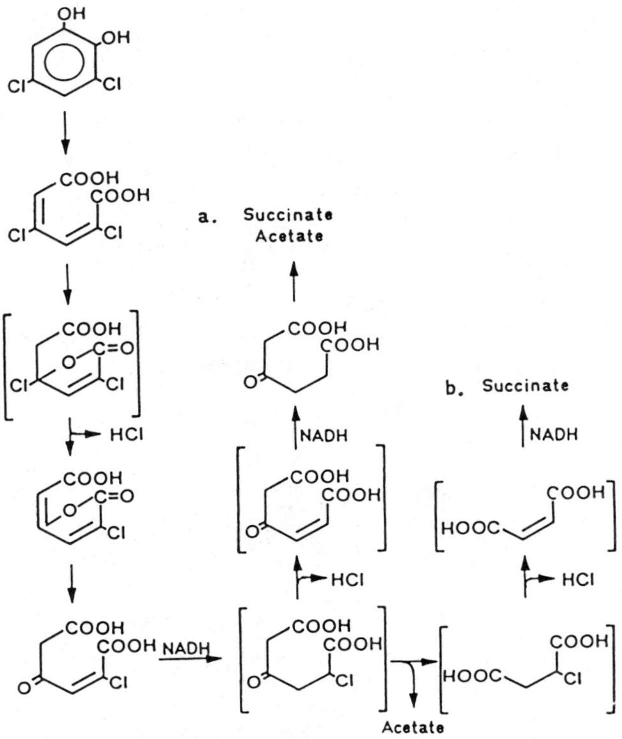

Fig. 2.   Conversion of 3,5-dichlorocatechol to intermediates of
          central metabolism via a modified ortho-cleavage pathway.
          Alternative routes proposed by (a) Chapman (15) and (b)
          Duxbury et al. (28) for the conversion of chloromaleylace-
          tic acid to succinate and acetate.

identified as the ring-cleaving pyrocatechase II, dechlorinating cycloisomerase II and hydrolase II; the latter is an enzyme unique to
halocatechol catabolism having no activity with β-ketoadipate enol-
lactone substrate of hydrolase I of the β-ketoadipate pathway (62).

     Dehalogenation of haloaromatic compounds before ring-cleavage
has been demonstrated in the microbial catabolism of several different substrates and seems to proceed via regioselective hydroxylation
(32).   For example, pseudomonads degrade 2-fluorobenzoate via catechol, fluoride elimination occurring as a result of attack by benzoate 1,2-dioxygenase which labilizes the fluorine substituent by
catalyzing the formation of an unstable intermediate, 2-fluoro-1,2-
dihydro-1,2-dihydroxybenzoate (2-fluoroDHB).   Other dehalogenating
"hydroxylases" have been proposed by Lingens and his colleagues to

account for catabolism by <u>Pseudomonas</u> spp., <u>Nocardia</u> sp., and
<u>Arthrobacter</u> sp., of <u>para</u>-substituted haloaromatic substrates via
unsubstituted substrates for ring-cleavage enzymes (53,58,59,60,80).
Mechanisms for hydroxylase catalyzed dehalogenations of aromatic
substrates have been discussed by Guroff et al., (44) - the "NIH
shift" mechanisms - and Husain et al., (48).

   Studies of halogenated aliphatic metabolism in microorganisms
have been largely confined to elucidation of mechanisms for enzymatic dehalogenation and mineralization of short chain, usually β-sub-
stituted, chlorinated, and brominated alkanoic acids (43,67,89,100).
Leisinger and his colleagues have suggested that dehalogenation of
dichloromethane by <u>Pseudomonas</u> sp. DM1 is effected by an alkanoic
acid dehalogenase upon conversion of the substrate by other broad
specificity enzymes (94). Bartinicki and Castro (7) examined the
reaction catalyzed by a partially purified enzyme from <u>Flavobac-
terium</u> sp. This enzyme showed activity with α-haloepoxides (catalyzing a transhalogenation) and dehalogenation of 3-bromo-2-butanol
isomers which involved stereospecific <u>trans</u>- elimination of Br⁻ resulting in epoxide formation. Direct involvement of the methane
monooxygenase system in dehalogenation of haloaliphatic compounds
has been demonstrated by Dalton's group (20,92,93), but these compounds cannot be utilized as the sole carbon and energy sources by
methylotrophs.

   Few of the organisms described in this section have been genetically characterized. Two recently developed and powerful genetic
techniques facilitate such characterization of catabolic and other
phenotypes: transposon mutagenesis and gene cloning. The construction of broad host range plasmid cloning vectors and their use in
soil bacteria has been reviewed elsewhere (5). Transposon mutagenesis is described in the following section.

TRANSPOSON MUTAGENESIS

   The importance of transposons in generating easily detected,
non-leaky and ordinarily polar mutation by insertion into DNA target
site has been recognized for several years (61) and has been applied
to the genetic analysis of <u>E</u>. <u>coli</u> and related bacteria with great
effect. Organisms harboring transposon insertions can be selected
by expression of antibiotic (Tn<u>1</u>, Tn<u>3</u>, Tn<u>5</u>, Tn<u>7</u>, Tn<u>9</u>, Tn<u>10</u>, etc.) or
mercury (Tn<u>501</u>) resistance and in some cases can be used to generate
deletion mutations in genes of interest (9). The insertion specificity of many transposons is sufficiently low to allow them to be
used as mutagens and insertionally inactivated genes can be detected
either directly in an assay for the gene product or indirectly by
complementation analysis.

   Furthermore, transposon insertions can be mapped relative to
restriction endonuclease cleavage sites close to the target DNA by

restriction enzyme cleavage analysis. Until recently, the use of
transposon mutagenesis has been precluded in many genetically uncharacterized bacteria because of the absence of suitable broad host
range transposon donors. In some cases it has been possible to
transfer and select for genes of interest in E. coli and to mutagenize in this host. Franklin et al. (37) were able to perform transposon Tn5 mutagenesis on pWWO-141, a TOL-plasmid derivative, in this
way. Other more specific and less direct methods for obtaining
transposon insertions have been developed, often with the aid of
host-specific bacteriophages, and as a result are not generally
useful.

     Methods of transposon mutagenesis have been reviewed recently
by Foster (36). In many cases these methods are direct and allow
mutagenesis of genes in their natural host, an important factor when
gene expression is to be considered. In addition, several transposon donors based on replicons linked to broad host range transfer
functions have been developed and can be used for the mutagenesis of
uncharacterized bacteria. The mechanisms of transposition from a
donor to a recipient or target replicon requires replication of a
transposon, and transposons in the donor and target DNA sequences
must be segregated, in most cases, to enable detection of the transposition event by selection of transposon encoded antibiotic or
metal resistance. Methods of transposon mutagenesis from a variety
of transposon donors are described below.

Transposition from a "Suicide" Donor Replicon

     Two different types of "suicide" transposon donors have been
described. These are: 1) transposons on narrow host range replicons linked to broad host range transfer functions, and 2) transposons on broad host range, conjugative plasmid derivatives in which
plasmid replication/maintenance is affected by insertion of the bacteriophage Mu.

     An example of the first type is the colicin plasmid pLG221
(ColIb drd-1 cib::Tn5), which is derepressed (drd-1) for conjugal
transfer (12) and which contains Tn5 (encoding resistance to kanamycin and neomycin) inserted into the gene encoding colicin Ib
(cib). Boulnois et al. (12) found that pLG221 could be transferred
by conjugation from E. coli to Pseudomonas spp., but that it was
unable to replicate in transconjugants. The inability of the transposon donor to replicate means that it is eliminated from the recipient population after transfer and allows selection of transconjugants in which transposition of Tn5 to other stable replicons (plasmids or chromosome) has occurred. Other ColIb plasmid derivatives
containing Tn3 (encoding ampicillin resistance) and Tn10 (encoding
tetracycline resistance) have been constructed. Another example of
a narrow host range replicon which can transfer into a nonpermissive

host is phage PI which has been used to construct a "suicide" transposon Tn5 donor for the mutagenesis of Myxococcus xanthus (64).

An extremely useful system for transposon mutagenesis has been
described by Simon et al. (88) who first constructed a recA E. coli
"donor strain" which contained an RP4 plasmid derivative, RP4-2
(=RP4Δbla aphA::Tn7 tet::Mu) in the chromosome. Plasmid pSUP2021
([pBR325-Mob]::Tn5) was constructed from the narrow host range non-
conjugative plasmid, pBR325 containing the cloned oriT gene (origin
of transfer, and designated the mobilization or Mob-site) of RP4 and
a Tn5 insertion. The plasmid was mobilized at high frequencies by
the "donor strain" into the host range of RP4 but the pBR325 replicon was not active outside E. coli and related organisms. A similar
plasmid, pSUP5011 (pBR325-Mob::Tn5) was constructed by cloning the
Mob-site into Tn5 at a position which did not affect expression of
transposition functions or resistance genes (Km^r, Nm^r). Transposition mutagenesis with this second "suicide" transposon donor should,
the authors suggest, allow target DNA sequences to be mobilized with
RP4-4 (a Km^s derivative of RP4).

Two "suicide" transposon donors have been described in which a
broad host range plasmid (eg., RP4, RK2), containing a mutation
inactivating replication, was linked to a narrow host range replicon, such colicin plasmid ColE1. Examples of chimeric plasmids of
this type containing transposons are pAS8Rep-1 (=pAS8Tc^{s}rep-1::Tn7),
a derivative of the RP4-ColE1 hybrid pAS8 which displayed ColE1
dependent replication and maintenance (81), and pRKTV14 ([RK2-
ColE1]::Tn7::Tn5) (B.A. Finette and D.T. Gibson. Abstr. Annu. Meet.
Am. Soc. Microbiology, 1983. H127, p. 127). The broad host range
of these RP4/RK2 derived plasmids was reflected in their ability to
transfer by conjugation from E. coli to Pseudomonas sp. and Brode-
tella pertussis.

Two other "suicide" transposon donors, based on temperature-
sensitive plasmid RP4 replicons, have been described (45,46,78).
These plasmids contain Tn1 (encoding ampicillin resistance) and are
unable to replicate in hosts which are maintained at a nonpermissive
temperature (42° C).

The instability of the second type of "suicide" transposon
donor is introduced as a result of the insertion of Mu into these
plasmids and seems to be caused by host specified restriction directed towards Mu sequences, and some unidentified function coded by
Mu (22,98). Beringer et al. (8) constructed an IncP1 plasmid containing Mu and Tn5 designated pJB4JI (pPH1JI::Mu::Tn5) which was
transferred to Rhizobium spp. but which was not maintained in this
host. Consequently, they were able to detect transposition of Tn5
in recipients. This plasmid has also been used to mutagenize Caulo-
bacter crescentus (31). Two other similar plasmids, pGV5010

(RP4::Mucts61 [::T7] bla aphA tet) and pSP601 (R751::Tn5::Tn1::
Tn1771::Muc⁺) have been used by other groups to carry out transposon
mutagenesis of different genera (14,22,96,98; A. Puhler, personal
communication).

Transposition by Conjugal Transfer

        Three methods have been used to mutagenize conjugal plasmids
with transposons encoding selectable resistance markers. Firstly,
transposition of transposons located on the donor organism's chromosome to conjugal plasmids can be detected by appropriate selection
on the transconjugant population. Secondly, transposon mutagenesis
of the conjugal plasmid may be effected by transposition from a non-
conjugative nonmobilizable plasmid. Thirdly, transposition from a
low transfer-frequency conjugative plasmid donor to another conjugative plasmid which transfers at higher frequencies may be detected
in transconjugants if the difference between the frequencies of
transfer of the two plasmids and the transposition frequency are
high enough. The first two methods are commonly used in E. coli.
Transposon mutagenesis of pJP4 (a plasmid encoding enzymes for the
degradation of chlorinated phenoxyacetates and chlorobenzoate) by
Tn5 inserted into the chromosome of A. eutrophus JMP134 has been
used to obtain Tn5 (Km^r) in the plasmid after transfer to and selection in A. eutrophus JMP222. An example of the third method was
described in the mutagenesis of the CAM-OCT plasmid (encoding
enzymes catalyzing the catabolism of camphor and alkanes) which was
found to lower the frequency of transfer of plasmid RP4::Tn7 (Tn7
encodes resistance to trimethoprim and streptomycin) in P. aeruginosa, thus enabling the selection of CAM-OCT::Tn7 derivatives from
donor strains containing both plasmids (34).

Transposition from Low Copy Number Plasmid Donor to High Copy Number
Plasmid Target

        Such a transposition event can be detected in cases where the
resultant cellular increase in number of transposon of resistance
genes causes an increased resistance to antibiotic (i.e., a gene
dosage effect) (6,85).

Transposition from a Donor Replicon to Target DNA Detected by
Introduction of and Selection for an Incompatible Replicon

        Plasmids which are classified within the same incompatibility
(Inc) group cannot be maintained in the same host cell. Chromosomal
insertions of Tn7 have been obtained in Caulobacter crescentus by
transferring the wild type RP4 plasmid into a strain containing an
incompatible RP4 derivative, RP4 aphA::Tn7 (Tn7 insertion inactivated Km resistance gene), and selecting for the maintenance of RP4
and Tn7 (30,31).

In our laboratory, the use of "suicide" transposon donors, particularly pLG221 and pSUP2021, has proved most successful in the mutagenesis of catabolic functions in uncharacterized soil bacteria. Transposon Tn5 mutagenesis of bacteria able to utilize halobenzoates and chlorophenoxyacetates, and analysis of mutant phenotypes is described in the next section.

GENETICS OF HALOGENATED HYDROCARBON CATABOLISM

Détailed study of the genetic basis of aromatic hydrocarbon ca-tabolism has, until recently, been limited to pathways in which the enzymes are almost all plasmid-encoded. It is not surprising, therefore, that the TOL-plasmid and the NAH-plasmid (e.g., NAH7, en-coding enzymes catalyzing the dissimilation of naphthalene and sali-cylate, 27) have been best characterized in this respect (37,38,82, 103,104). These two catabolic plasmids have additional advantages in that they are relatively small, are self transmissible to hosts such as E. coli, and are easily purified.

Pemberton's group was the first to report the isolation of a plasmid associated with catabolism of a halogenated organic compound (71). Fisher et al. (35) presented evidence for the involvement of plasmid pJP1 in the degradation of 2,4-D by Alcaligenes paradoxus JMP116. Subsequently, Pemberton et al. (70) and Don and Pemberton (25) isolated six plasmids which they found to be associated with the same phenotype. All the plasmids were transferred into A. eu-trophus JMP222 (cured of the plasmid and ability to utilize 2,4-D, 2-methyl-4-chlorophenoxyacetate, 4-chlorophenoxyacetate and 3-chlor-obenzoate) from the uncharacterized soil bacteria in which they were originally found. In the isogenic background, two classes of cata-bolic plasmids were distinguished on the basis of incompatibility grouping, plasmid-associated mercury resistance, molecular weight and host-range. One of these plasmids, pJP4, is described in more detail below.

Plasmid involvement in the biodegradation of other haloaromatic substrates by a variety of bacteria has been suggested by several groups. In almost every case, however, there has been no unequivo-cal demonstration of any plasmid-encoded catabolic enzymes. The ca-tabolism of 3-chlorobenzoate has been shown to be a transmissible phenotype (19,77) and to be associated with plasmid DNA in Pseudo-monas sp. B13 (pWR1) and Pseudomonas putida (pAC25). Extensive ho-mology between these two plasmids was shown by Chatterjee and Chakrabarty (18). Plasmid pWR1 has been transferred and maintained in other Pseudomonas species and A. eutrophus by selection of recip-ients capable of utilizing 3-chlorobenzoate as the sole carbon and energy source. Until insertion mutations in catabolic genes have been mapped the possibility that pWR1 serves to mobilize catabolic

genes located on the chromosome or on some larger, undetected plasmid cannot be excluded. The plasmid pWR1 is isolated in only very
low yields from batch cultures growing on 3-chlorobenzoate regard-
less of the genetic background and, in our hands, no plasmid DNA can
be obtained from batch cultures grown on complex media. Chemostat
cultures utilizing 3-chlorobenzoate as growth limiting carbon source
have been used for the isolation of much greater yields of plasmid,
although this technique has proved successful only in steady-state
cultures obtained at dilution rates below 0.05 hr^{-1} (i.e., culture
doubling time, t_d = 14 hr). Analysis of culture supernatants indicated that >99% of the carbon source was utilized and dechlorinated
by Pseudomonas sp. B13 under these conditions. It seems reasonable
to suppose that high plasmid yields resulted from increased copy
number of pWR1 and that in mimicking a deceleration/stationary batch
growth phase the effect could be triggered in continuous-flow cultures.

     Transposon Tn5 mutagenesis of Pseudomonas sp. B13 (pWR1) and P.
putida PaW340 (pWR1), [a transconjugant from a mating between B13
and PaW340 (Sm^r trp) selected on plates containing 3-chlorobenzoate,
streptomycin and tryptophan] with the "suicide" transposon donor
pLG221 has resulted in the isolation of mutants unable to grow on
the chloroaromatic substrate. The mutants were purified from a mem-
brane-filter mating mixture of E. coli ED2196(pLG221) and the chlorobenzoate utilizer incubated at 30° C on nutrient agar for 6-8hr.
Mutagenized recipients were selected by plating the mix onto an appropriate selective medium (Km included at 20-100 µg ml^{-1}) so as to
give approximately 100 colonies per plate (Km^r transconjugants were
selected at a frequency of 10^{-7} per donor cell). Where selected,
auxotrophs of PaW340(pWR1) represented about 2-3% of all the Km^r mutants isolated and 0.5-1.0% of transconjugants receiving Tn5 were
defective in 3-chlorobenzoate catabolism. Mapping of the Tn5 insertions is being carried out and will facilitate distinction between chromosomally-encoded and plasmid-encoded catabolic functions.

     The mutant phenotypes have been distinguished on the basis of
the accumulation of different pathway intermediates during 3-chloro-
benzoate catabolism. Such compounds were detected by spectrophoto-
metric and thin-layer chromatographic analyses of supenatant fluids
from bacterial cultures containing 3-chlorobenzoate and a second
carbon source (e.g., acetate). Mutations in most of the genes
encoding enzymes catalyzing 3-chlorobenzoate catabolic functions
have been identified in this way (M.P. Weishaar, A.J. Weightman, W.
Reineke, and K.N. Timmis. Abstracts for poster sessions of Conference on Genetic Control of Environmental Pollutants). These different Tn5 insertions are currently being mapped.

Genetic Analysis of Chlorophenoxyacetate Catabolism by Alcaligenes eutrophus

     The isolation of A. eutrophus JMP134 (pJP4) has been out-
lined above. The plasmid in strain JMP134 was shown to be closely

associated with the catabolism of 2,4-D, 3-chlorobenzoate, 2-methyl-
4-chlorophenoxyacetate (MCPA) and 4-chlorophenoxyacetate (4CPA) (24,
A.J. Weightman and R.H. Don, unpublished observations). The analysis of haloaromatic substrate catabolism in JMP134 has involved
transposon Tn5 mutagenesis of the strain using two methods which are
represented in Fig. 3. The "suicide" vector pLG221 was used to introduce Tn5 insertions into the plasmid and chromosome of JMP134 by
the same method as described for Pseudomonas sp. B13. These insertion mutants were screened and phenotypes of those defective in haloaromatic catabolism were determined with respect to intermediate
accumulation. In addition, Tn5 mutants of JMP134 containing the
transposon inserted into the chromosome and able to grow on the haloaromatic substrates were used to mutagenize pJP4, and were detected
by cotransfer of Km^r into A. eutrophus JMP222 (a Sm^r cured derivative of JMP134) upon conjugal transfer of pJP4 into this recipient.
High frequencies of insertion in catabolic genes were obtained by
the second method, reflecting the inactivation of catabolic functions tions encoded by plasmid pJP4. Mutants were again analyzed to
determine phenotype, and insertions into the plasmid were mapped
using restriction endonucleases for which the sites in Tn5 were
known (79).

       Figure 4 shows the restriction enzyme digest obtained with
wild-type pJP4, and compares this pattern with three Tn5 insertion

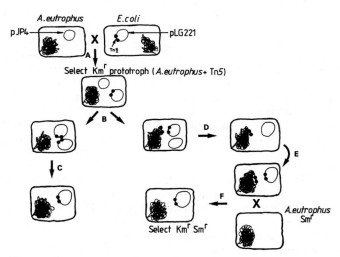

Fig. 3.   Schematic representation of transposon Tn5 mutagenesis of
           A. eutrophus JMP134 (pJP4) to generate Tn5 insertions in
           plasmid and chromosomal DNA (steps A and B) with subse-
           quent loss of the transposon donor (step C and D). Trans-
           position mutagenesis of pJP4 from the chromosome of A.
           eutrophus by conjugal transfer of mutated plasmid DNA is
           illustrated in steps E and F.

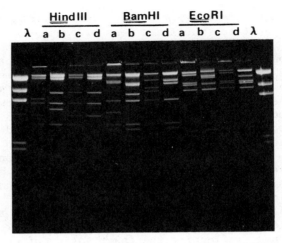

Fig. 4.   Electrophoretic separation of HindIII, BamHI, and EcoRI
           restriction endonuclease generated fragments of plasmids
           pJP4 (track d), pJP4::Tn5-104, 24D⁻, 3CB⁻ (track c) pJP4::
           Tn5-150, 240⁺, 3CB⁺ (track b) and pJP4::Tn5-110, 24D⁻,
           3CB⁺ (track a) on a 0.7% agarose gel. The tracks marked λ
           contain HindIII digested bacteriophage λ as a marker.
           Transposon Tn5 insertion are found in the following re-
           striction endonuclease fragments: EcoRI-B, BamHI-C,
           HindIII-G (pJP4::Tn5-104); EcoRI-C, BamHI-B, HindIII-E
           (pJP4::Tn5-150); EcoRI-B, BamHI-C, HindIII-C (pJP4::Tn5-
           110).

derivatives, one of which was unaffected in haloaromatic catabolism
(24D⁺3CB⁺) and two of which represent each of the other major phenotypes obtained from transposon mutagenesis: those in which the upper pathway of chlorophenoxyacetate catabolism (i.e., conversion of
substrate to chlorocatechol, see Fig. 2) was inactivated (24D⁻3CB⁻)
and those which did not express the full chlorocatechol pathway and
were therefore unable to utilize any chloroaromatics (24D⁻3CB⁻). In
two 24D⁻3CB⁻ mutants the degradative functions had been deleted from
pJP4. Deletions of this type were obtained at high frequency in
conjugal transfer of pJP4 from JMP134 into Pseudomonas putida after
Hgʳ selection in the recipient. Other deletion mutants occurred at
a frequency of about 0.5 when ability to utilize 3-chlorobenzoate
was selected in the same recipients to obtain conjugal transfer of
pJP4. The physical and functional maps of pJP4 based on results
from Tn5 mutagenesis are represented in Fig. 5. Transposon insertion inactivating haloaromatic catabolism were all found to map
within the BamHI-C fragment, and Tn5 insertions causing accumulation
of chlorocatechols from 2,4-D and 3-chlorobenzoate mapped into the
1.6 kb HindIII-G fragment.

The 24D⁻ 3CB⁺ A. eutrophus JMP222 mutants carrying pJP4::Tn5
derivative plasmids were all found to accumulate 2,4-dichlorophenol
when grown in media containing 2,4-D, presumably as a result of inactivation of the gene encoding the chlorophenol oxygenase of the
chlorophenoxyacetate upper pathway (11). Cell-free extracts from
cultures of these mutants induced with 2,4-D exhibited very low pyrocatechase activities compared with the activity induced in A. eutrophus JMP134(pJP4) during growth on 2,4-D. No mutations affecting
the conversion of chlorophenoxyacetates to their corresponding
chlorophenols (side-chain cleaving oxygenase, gene A product) (41)
were isolated, which was a surprising result since the cured derivatives of A. eutrophus JMP134(pJP4) are unable to catabolize 2,4-D.
Further transposition mutagenesis, possibly using a different transposon might result in the identification of the A gene. Mutants accumulating chlorocatechols, chloromuconates, and diene-lactones
could be readily distinguished, and Tn5 insertions in them were
mapped in DNA sequences marked C, D, and E, respectively (Fig. 5).
A fifth class of Tn5 insertion mutants requires further definition with respect to product accumulation and was shown to occupy
the region between sequences E and B. Polar effects of Tn5 insertions on catabolic genes have not thus far been examined, although
substrates for assaying pyrocatechase II, cycloisomerase II, and

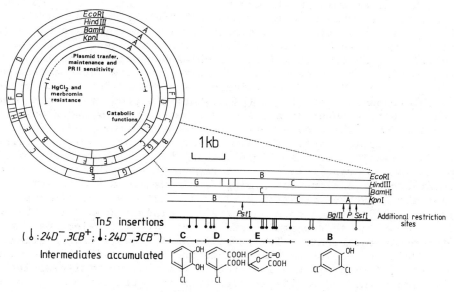

Fig. 5.   Physical and functional map of the plasmid pJP4. Restriction endonuclease sites are indicated as are digest fragments generated by treatment with enzymes EcoRI, HindIII,
BamHI, and KpnI. See text for details.

hydrolase II are being synthesized for this purpose and, thus, to
facilitate analysis of transcription of degradative genes and analysis of their regulation.

Mutagenesis of JMP134(pJP4) directly with pLG221 resulted in
the isolation of another class of mutants with the phenotype
24D$^+$3CB$^-$. Tn5 insertions in these mutants were not found in pJP4
and were therefore assumed to be located in the chromosome of A. eutrophus. Additional evidence for the location of genes encoding enzymes converting 3-chlorobenzoate to chlorocatechols was obtained by
complementation analysis. Conjugal transfer of pJP4::Tn5-4 (a Km^r
24D$^-$3CB$^+$ derivative of pJP4) into P. putida strains harboring mutations in genes encoding benzoate 1,2-dioxygenase (PaW94) and DHB-
dehydrogenase (BACS 2.1) with selection for Km^r recipients did not
result in complementation of these two mutations (recipients were
unable to grow on benzoate) nor could 3CB$^+$ transconjugants be selected from these matings.

Cloning of Restriction Fragments of pJP4 and pWR1

The broad host range plasmid cloning vector pKT231 (3,4,5) constructed from the RSF1010 replicon (Fig. 6), was used to construct
gene banks of plasmids pJP4 and pWR1. The HindIII-G fragment of
pJP4 (Fig. 5), ligated into the unique HindIII site of pKT231 (producing hybrid plasmid pKJ11) was first cloned into E. coli ED8654
and was subsequently used to transform KT2442 (P. putida PaW85
Rif^r). The cloned fragment was stably maintained in this host and
expressed pyrocatechase II activity sufficiently well to prevent accumulation of chlorocatechol from 3-chlorobenzoate catabolism by
chromosomally encoded benzoate 1,2-dioxygenase and DHB-dehydrogenase
in this strain. No chloride release was detected in the conversion
of 3-chlorobenzoate by KT2442 (pKJ11) and the product which accumulated in culture supernatants showed a peak at 264nm and 278nm upon
acidification. These data were consistent with the production of a
chloro-cis,cis muconate. The clustering of chloroaromatic catabolism inactivating Tn5 insertions within the EcoR1-B fragment of pJP4
implied an important role for this region in the biodegradation of
halocatechols. A clone containing EcoRI fragments B,E,F, and I, was
isolated after transformation of E. coli ED8654 with a ligation mixture of EcoRI digested pJP4 and pKT231. Plasmid R64drd-11 (68) was
used to mobilize this plasmid (pKJ15) into KT2442, selecting for Km^r
prototrophic recipients. The plasmid pKJ15 transferred efficiently
into KT2442 and was stably maintained in 17 out of the 20 recipients
from which plasmid DNA was isolated by the boiling mini-prep method
(47). The 17 KT2442(pKJ15) strains thus isolated could all grow on
3-chlorobenzoate but not on 2,4-D. The three spontaneous deletion
derivatives of pKJ15 found in KT2442 did not enable the recipient to
utilize either substrate as the sole carbon and energy source. The
minimum fragment size of pJP4 required for conversion of KT2442 to
the 3CB$^+$ phenotype is under investigation.

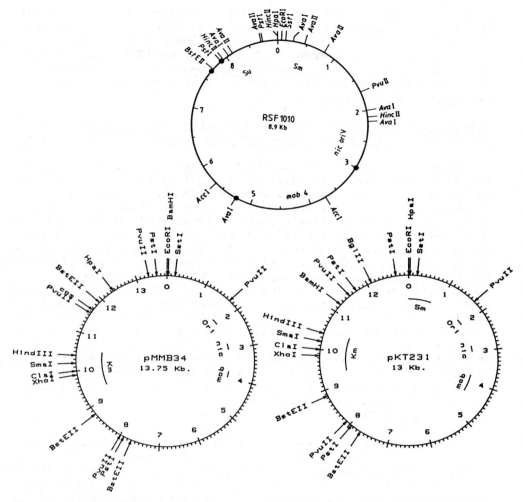

Fig. 6.   Plasmid cloning vector pKT231 and cosmid pMMB34 derived
from plasmid RSF1010.· Abbreviations: Su, Sm, Km, resistance to sulphonamide, streptomycin, and kanamycin, respectively; mob, nic, ori, determinants for plasmid mobilization, relaxation nick site, and origin of vegetative
replication, respectively. Closed circles represent RNA
polymerase binding sites (see text and refs. 3,4,5,39).

    In an attempt to detect fragments of plasmid pWR1 containing
catabolic genes, restriction digest fragments of the plasmid were
transferred from agarose gels onto nitrocellulose filters and hy-
bridized with two nick-translated ^{32}P-labelled DNA probes, pJP4 and
pKJ11. No homology between pWR1 and these latter two plasmids was
detected under hybridization conditions of high stringency (filters

were washed under conditions allowing ± 1% mismatch). This result
was unexpected in view of the similarities that have been observed
in the chlorocatechol pathway enzymes of JMP134 and B13 (H.J. Knackmuss, personal communication). Experiments are now being carried
out to determine if the genome of Pseudomonas sp. B13 contains any
DNA sequences which are homologous to those from pJP4 encoded modified ortho-pathway enzymes.

Strategy for the Genetic Analysis of Uncharacterized Bacteria Capable of Utilizing 2,4,5-T as the Sole Carbon and Energy Source

Several different bacteria have been isolated in this laboratory which are capable of utilizing 2,4,5-T as the sole carbon and
energy source. These bacteria were purified from mixed cultures
selected by conventional enrichment techniques involving the incubation and subculture of liquid cultures inoculated with soil samples.
Three soils were used, two of which had no history of 2,4,5-T contamination and one garden soil that had been exposed to low concentrations of 2,4,5-T when sprayed with an herbicide formulation containing this compound. All three soils were ultimately enriched for
2,4,5-T utilizers. A pre-enrichment of the soils for other haloaromatic substrate utilizers with 3-chlorobenzoate, 2,4-D and MCPA reduced the lag phase in subsequent 2,4,5-T enrichment cultures. The
mixed cultures were not analyzed in detail but degraded 2,4,5-T at
faster rates than the pure cultures so far examined. Growth rates
of about $0.12 \ hr^{-1}$ was obtained with mixed batch cultures utilizing
2-5 mM-2,4,5-T as sole carbon and energy source, whereas growth
rates of the three pure cultures on 2 mM-2,4,5-T fell in the range
$0.04 \ hr^{-1}$ (strains 11C and 83A2) to $0.06 \ hr^{-1}$ (41A2). In all cases
>95% of organically bound chlorine was mineralized.

Four plasmids have been detected in strain 83A2 ranging in size
from about 2 kb to approximately 30 kb, and strain 11C contained 2
plasmids. The instability of the $245T^+$ phenotype of 83A2 in the absence of selection was not associated with the loss of any of the
identified plasmid species since all four were stably maintained in
$245T^-$ mutants.

The "suicide" transposon donor pLG221 was used to mutagenize
the more stable strain, 11C, and about 2-3% of Km^r mutants were
found to be defective in 2,4,5-T and 2,4-D catabolism. Plasmid DNA
isolated from three of these $245T^-$ $24D^-$ mutants was not found to
contain Tn5 sequences (based on fragmentation of the plasmids after
XhoI and HindIII restriction digests). It seems reasonable to assume that some if not all of the genes encoding 2,4,5-T associated
catabolic functions in this strain are present on the chromosome or
on some undetected plasmid.

The strategy being adopted to isolate genes associated with
2,4,5-T degradation in strain 11C involves obtaining a gene library

from the genomic DNA of this strain by cloning into the broad host range cosmid vector pMMB34 (Fig. 6) (39). This gene library will be screened by colony hybridization for DNA sequences which show homology with radioactively labeled probes containing cloned sequences known to be involved in 2,4,5-T catabolism. The probes will be obtained from the Tn5 insertion mutants already isolated which are presumed to contain the transposon inserted in or close to genes of interest. Sequences from these genes may be cloned by digesting genomic DNA with an enzyme which does not cut Tn5 (e.g., EcoRI) and ligating into a suitable cloning vector (e.g., pBR322). The transposon plus flanking sequences may be isolated by transformation of E. coli with the ligation mix and selection for Tn5 (Km^r) in the vector.

CONSTRUCTION OF CATABOLIC PATHWAYS FOR THE MINERALIZATION OF HALOORGANIC COMPOUNDS

Kellogg et al. (55) described a procedure in which they enriched for 2,4,5-T utilizing organisms by a process that they called "plasmid-assisted molecular breeding." It involved the mixing in a chemostat of samples from various waste-dumping sites with laboratory bacterial strains harboring a variety of catabolic plasmids. That "prolonged incubation" of waste-dumping site samples in enrichment flasks containing 2,4,5-T did not result in the isolation of organisms capable of utilizing this substrate whereas the chemostat experiment did (after 8-10 months of continuous-flow culture with control of substrate concentrations) suggested to the authors that the 2,4,5-T degrading microorganisms which were subsequently purified (56,57) arose as a result of uncharacterized interactions between plasmids introduced into the chemostat culture. Since the two types of experiment are not strictly comparable, the results presented do not provide unambiguous evidence of "molecular breeding." In fact, it seems more likely that the 2,4,5-T utilizer was isolated as the result of a successful enrichment carried out in a chemostat where organisms from the waste dump site samples were actively growing and continuously exposed to aromatic substrates for hundreds of generations.

Reineke and Knackmuss introduced the idea of constructing catabolic pathways for the mineralization of haloaromatic substrates (75). These authors isolated a transconjugant able to grow on 4-chlorobenzoate (4CB) from a mating between P. putida PaW1 (containing the TOL-plasmid, pWWO) and Pseudomonas sp. B13, the 3-chlorobenzoate utilizer. It was suggested that the transconjugant strain, WR241 had acquired the ability to utilize 4CB essentially as a result of the recruitment to toluate 1,2-dioxygenase activity encoded by the TOL-plasmid which had been transferred into Pseudomonas sp. B13. This enzyme was able to catalyze the conversion of 4-chlorobenzoate to 4-chlorodihydro-1,2-dihydroxybenzoate (4-chloroDHB),

whereas the isofunctional enzyme, benzoate 1,2-dioxygenase, produced
by Pseudomonas sp. B13 could not catalyze this reaction. The 4-
chloroDHB could be converted to 4-chlorocatechol by dehydrogenases
encoded by either Pseudomonas sp. B13 or the TOL-plasmid. Mineralization of 4-chlorocatechol was effected by the modified ortho-ring
cleavage pathway in strain B13. Acquisition of the gene (xylD) encoding toluate 1,2-dioxygenase by strain B13 also facilitated the
isolation of mutants capable of utilizing 3,5-dichlorobenzoate
(35DCB) as the sole source of carbon and energy (76). Again, recruitment of the broad specificity TOL-plasmid catabolic functions
by the chlorocatechol ortho-cleavage pathway of strain B13 was implicated in construction of a pathway for 35DCB dissimilation.

Other authors have described similar constructions producing
bacteria capable of utilizing chlorobenzoates (17,99), chlorobiphe-
nyls (40), chlorophenols (86), chlorotoluates, and chloronapthalenes
(T. Lui and P.J. Chapman (1983) Abstr. Annu. Meet. Am. Soc. Microbiology. K211, p. 212). In all cases so far described, genes present on naturally occurring conjugative plasmids have been exploited,
and, where examined, expression of the desired phenotype required
mutations in host and/or introduced DNA sequences (17,50,51,72).

The use of cloned catabolic genes allows a better defined approach to pathway construction and introduces the possibility of
controlling the expression of specific enzymes. The strategy of
linking broad specificity upper pathway enzymes, capable of catalyzing transformations of halogenated substrate analogues, with a modified ortho-ring cleavage pathway for dissimilation of halocatechols
thus generated seems to be generally applicable to construction of
mineralization pathways for mono- and dihalogenated aromatic substrates (Fig. 7). In a reconstruction of Reineke and Knackmuss' experiment described above, the xylD (toluate 1,2-dioxygenase), xylL
(DHB dehydrogenase) and xylS (regulatory) genes from the TOL-plasmid
were introduced into B13 on the hybrid plasmid pPL403 (Fig. 8).
Although 4CB$^+$ transconjugants were isolated after mobilization of
pPL403, acquisition of the hybrid plasmid per se was not sufficient
to produce this phenotype. The additional mutation(s) which was
required (selected at a frequency of about 10^{-3}) did not result in
detectable structural alterations to pPL403 and did not allow 4CB$^-$
transconjugants to grow on 35DCB.

A chlorosalicylate-utilizing organism was constructed using the
same rationale as described above. Salicylate hydroxylase encoded
by the plasmid NAH7 catalyzes the conversion of all three isomers of
chlorosalicylate and unsubstituted salicylate to corresponding
catechols (J. Zeyer, unpublished observations). The gene (nahG)
encoding this enzyme was isolated and used to construct plasmid
pPL300 by ligation of EcoRI cut pBR322 nahG with the broad host
range plasmid vector, pKT231, digested with the same enzyme (Fig.
9). The resultant hybrid plasmid could replicate and be expressed
in Pseudomonas spp., and after isolation in E. coli was mobilized to

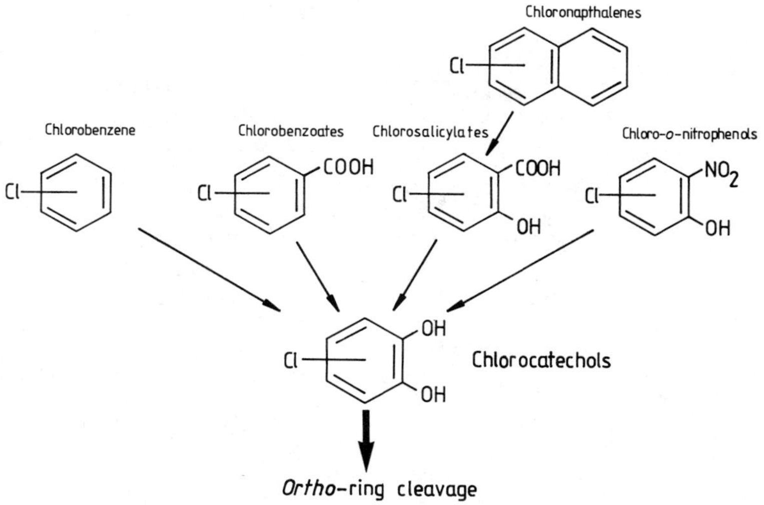

Fig. 7.   Strategy for the construction of pathways for the catabolism of various haloaromatic compounds. See text for
details.

P. putida mt-2 KT2442, where salicylate-utilizing (SAL^+) transconjugants were selected at a frequency of 2 x 10^{-4} per recipient cell.
Screening of the plasmid DNA in transconjugants showed that deletion
of a 1.6 kb fragment of DNA from pPL300 occurred in 3/5 transconjugants and was associated with loss of kanamycin and tetracycline
resistances as well as expression of higher uninduced levels of
salicylate hydroxylase. This deleted plasmid, pPL300-1, was transferred into Pseudomonas sp. B13 and transconjugants selected on
salicylate were all found to be capable of utilizing 3-chloro, 4-
chloro-, and 5-chlorosalicylates as sole carbon and energy sources.
Mineralization of chlorosalicylate therefore required only the recruitment of a broad specificity salicylate hydroxylase by a strain
capable of catabolizing chlorocatechols.

    A bacterium, designated strain SB100, isolated from the soil
after enrichment culture with 2-methylnaphthalene was capable of
utilizing this substrate as sole carbon and energy source, and catabolic genes derived from it were used to construct a chloronaphthalene degrading strain. Initially, it was found that strain SB100
was able to catabolize 1-chloro- and 2-chloronaphthalenes to corres-
pondingly substituted catechol and muconate-semialdehyde, respectively. Substituted and unsubstituted naphthalene catabolism was associated with an 80 kb conjugative plasmid (pSB100) and extensive
homology was found between catabolic genes of the NAH7 plasmid and
pSB100 (S. Bas and P.R. Lehrbach, unpublished observation). Preliminary evidence suggested that the naphthalene pathway enzymes induced in strain SB100 had similar activities to those encoded by

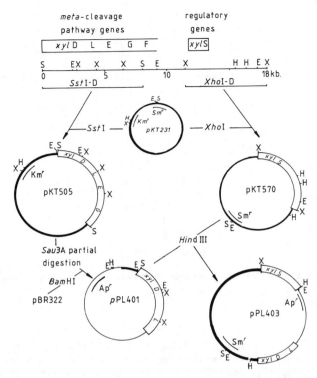

Fig. 8.   Genealogy of the recombinant plasmid containing xylD and
           xylL genes. Abbreviations: X, H, S, and E, cleavage
           sites for restriction endonucleases XhoI, HindIII, SstI,
           and SmaI, respectively; Km^r, Ap^r, Sm^r, determinants for
           resistance to kanamycin, ampicillin, and streptomycin,
           respectively. The genes xylD, xylL and xylS from the TOL
           plasmid, pWWO, encoding toluate 1,2-dioxygenase, DHB–dehy-
           drogenase, and the lower pathway regulatory protein,
           respectively; kb, kilobase pair.

NAH7 but that the two catabolic pathways differed with respect to
regulation. Plasmid pSB100 was transferred by conjugation into
strain KT2442 (pKJ15), which contained genes encoding critical enzymes of the chlorocatechol pathway cloned from degradative plasmid
pJP4, and transconjugants were selected on naphthalene. The ability
of transconjugants to utilize 2-chloronaphthalene as a growth substrate was tested and was found to require further mutations(s), the
nature of which is at present unknown. That the NAH7 plasmid could
not be used in the same way to construct a chloronaphthalene–utiliz
ing strain demonstrated an important difference between this plasmid
and pSB100. Mineralization of 2-chloronaphthalene was also shown to
require the presence of plasmid pKJ15, indicating that the pSB100

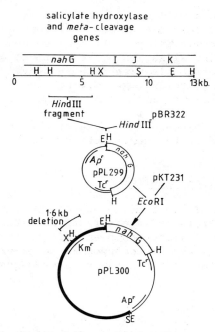

Fig. 9.   Genealogy of the recombinant plasmid containing the nahG
           gene. Abbreviations: Tc^r, determinant for resistance to
           tetracyline, nahG, NAH plasmid gene encoding salicylate
           hydroxylase. See also legend to Fig. 8.

upper pathway genes were active in the conversion of 2-chloronaph-
thalene to chlorocatechol and that this intermediate was a substrate
for the modified ortho-cleavage pathway encoded by pKJ15.

     An isopropylbenzene-utilizing bacterium was isolated in this
laboratory and has been shown to contain a plasmid which encodes enzymes catalyzing the conversion of this substrate to isobutanoate
(29). The upper pathway genes were shown to encode broad specificity enzymes capable of converting chlorobenzene to chlorocatechol
and were cloned after inactivation of meta-ring cleavage activity by
Tn5 insertion into the plasmid gene encoding the catechol 2,3-dioxy-
genase (Tn5-encoded kanamycin resistance located the catabolic genes
on the plasmid). A strategy is being developed to link these upper
pathway genes with the cloned chlorocatechol pathway genes so as to
facilitate the isolation of a catabolic pathway for chlorobenzene
dissimilation.

     The importance of transport functions in pathway construction
is illustrated in the following example. 2-Nitrophenol induces in

Pseudomonas sp. strain ONP1 an enzyme which catalyzes the transformation of the substrate and 4-chloro-2-nitrophenol to catechol and
4-chlorocatechol, respectively. Attempts to construct a pathway for
chloronitrophenol mineralization by recruitment of this activity to
the chlorocatechol _ortho_-cleavage pathway proved unsuccessful because the chlorosubstrate analogue was not a substrate for 2-nitro-
phenol induced uptake system.

In summarizing this section, some of the main factors which
should be considered in the construction of catabolic pathways are
listed.

Identification and Cloning of Genes

Having considered biochemical aspects pertaining to the mineralization of a substrate of interest the investigator needs to be
able to identify and isolate genes encoding the activities which are
to be recruited. The use of transposons to generate mutations in
catabolic pathways facilitates a simultaneous genetic and biochemical analysis.

Gene Expression

The expression of genes cloned from uncharacterized soil bacteria is likely to require that they be transferred, after cloning,
into a closely related strain. To achieve this object broad host
range cloning vectors capable of replicating in, say, _Pseudomonas_
and related genera must be used (5,23,66). In addition, expression
of catabolic and transport genes has to be quantitatively commensurate with growth on the substrate. One important advantage of _in
vitro_ over _in vivo_ techniques may be seen in constructions where the
rate-limiting catabolic step is too slow to allow growth of the
host. If cloned genes are used for the construction, then genetic
manipulation can effect the elevated expression of growth-rate limiting enzymes. Another advantage of the _in vitro_ techniques is that
they allow the possibility of constructing hybrid pathways in which
catabolic genes are placed under the control of constitutive promoters; thus an enzyme may be recruited for a pathway even if the
pathway substrate and intermediates do not induce its expression _in
vivo_.

Stability of Cloned Genes in the Bacterial Host

From the point of view of genetic analysis it is important that
constructions be stable with respect to vector, cloned, and host
DNA sequences. Under certain conditions, however, it may be useful
to construct catabolic pathways which, as a result of the presence
of genes encoding transfer functions, can be easily disseminated
throughout a natural, but essentially contained, microbial population as might be present in, say, a waste treatment reactor.

Stability of the Bacterial Host

The stability of bacteria receiving genes encoding catabolic enzymes, from whatever source, is unlikely to be affected by the expression of these genes. However, the integrity of the host cell envelope could be adversely affected as a result of high level expression of genes encoding membrane-bound enzymes and transport proteins.

Inhibitory Effects of Substrate and Pathway Intermediates

Intracellular accumulation of many halogenated organic compounds by many different genera leads to growth inhibition. It is important, therefore, that in the construction of haloorganic catabolic pathways consideration to be given to inhibitory effects of the compounds, whether as substrates or presumptive intermediates, upon pathway enzymes and upon the general metabolism of the host microorganism.

CONCLUDING REMARKS

The prospects for the construction of catabolic pathways to effect mineralization/detoxification of haloorganic substrates are encouraging, despite the fact that techniques to realize these objectives have only recently been developed.

As described above, transposon mutagenesis is a technique which offers the investigator the potential to rapidly analyze the genetics and biochemistry of a catabolic pathway by uncharacterized soil bacteria. Bacteria which can utilize PCBs (Chakrabarty, personal communication), pentachlorophenol (91) and 2,4,5-T as sole carbon and energy sources have recently been isolated in several laboratories. Alongside other utilizers of halogenated hydrocarbons, these organisms will provide the genetic material from which various constructions can be made. Other potential sources of catabolic genes, such as extreme and anaerobic environments, are as yet relatively undeveloped, but could be important from at least two points of view: firstly, so that diversification of aerobic an mesophilic catabolism currently available to the geneticist may be achieved, and secondly, so that engineered organisms may be introduced into these environments.

The utility of constructed organisms in dealing with problems related to environmental pollution outside the laboratory has yet to be tested. It is difficult not to be optimistic about the prospects for the successful reintroduction of genetically engineered microorganisms into the ecosystems from which they were isolated, but any optimism should be guarded in view of the natural barriers which obviously exist and which are discussed at length by other contributors to this volume.

SUMMARY

     This paper reviews the genetic basis of haloaromatic biodegra-
dation by bacteria, with a focus on the genetic analysis of Alcaligenes eutrophus JMP134, an organism which can utilize 3-chloroben-
zoate, 2,4-dichlorophenoxyacetate (2,4-D) and related compounds as
sole carbon and energy sources, and Pseudomonas sp. B13, a chlorobenzoate degrader. The involvement of transmissible plasmids pJP4
and pWR1, isolated from strains JMP134 and B13, respectively, in
chloroaromatic mineralization has been examined, and restriction
fragments of both plasmids have been cloned on the broad host range
plasmid vector pKT231. Transposon Tn5 mutagenesis of these and
other soil isolates enriched in and purified from mixed cultures
utilizing 2,4,5-trichlorophenoxyacetate (2,4,5-T) as sole carbon and
energy source, has been carried out using a "suicide" transposon
donor, pLG221 (ColIbdrd-1::Tn5). Mapping of Tn5 insertions in mutants which accumulate pathway intermediates has facilitated the
identification and cloning of genes encoding chlorocatechol 1,2-
dioxygenase, and other key enzymes in haloaromatic catabolism.
There are good prospects for the genetic construction of hybrid haloaromatic catabolic pathways by combining genes encoding broad specificity enzymes, capable of transforming halogenated analogues of
their natural substrates, with genes for halocatechol degradation.

ACKNOWLEDGEMENTS

     We are very grateful to Sylvette Bas, Josef Zeyer, Richard
Eaton and Graham Boulnois for kindly providing us with results prior
to their publication. We thank Professor H-J. Knackmuss and Dr. W.
Reineke for extremely stimulating and helpful discussions. Work
carried out in the authors' laboratory was supported by grants from
the Bundesministerium für Forschung und Technologie (grant 0384219
to K. N. T. and H-J. Knackmuss) and Transgéne SA (to K. N. T.). A.
J. W. gratefully acknowledges receipt of a postdoctoral fellowship
from the Royal Society of Great Britain.

REFERENCES

1. Alexander, M. (1965) Biodegradation: Problems of molecular re-
   calcitrance and microbial fallibility. Adv. in Appl. Microbiol. 7:35-76.
2. Alexander, M. (1981) Biodegradation of chemicals of environmental concern. Science 211:132-138.
3. Bagdasarian M., M.M. Bagdasarian, R. Lurz, A. Nordheim, J.
   Frey, and K.N. Timmis (1982) Molecular and functional analysis
   of the broad host range plasmid RSF1010 and construction of
   vectors for gene cloning in Gram-negative bacteria. In Drug
   Resistance in Bacteria. Genetics, Biochemistry and Molecular

Biology, S. Mitsuhashi, ed. Thieme-Stratton Inc., New York, pp. 183-197.

4. Bagdasarian, M., R. Lurz, B. Rückert, F.C.H. Franklin, M.M. Bagdasarian, J. Frey, and K.N. Timmis (1981) Specific purpose plasmid cloning vectors. II. Broad host range, high copy number, RSF1010-derived vectors, and host-vector system for gene cloning in Pseudomonas. Gene 16:237-247.

5. Bagdasarian, M., and K.N. Timmis (1982) Host:vector systems for gene cloning in Pseudomonas. Current Topics in Microbiology and Immunology 96:47-67.

6. Barth, P.T., L. Tobin, and G.S. Sharpe (1981) Development of broad host-range plasmid vectors. In Molecular Biology, Pathogenicity and Ecology of Bacteria Plasmids, S.B. Levy, R.C. Clowes, and E.L. Koenig, eds. Plenum Press, New York, pp. 439-448.

7. Bartinicki, E.W., and C.E. Castro (1969) Biodehalogenation. The pathway for transhalogenation and the stereochemistry of epoxide formation from halohydrins. Biochemistry 8:4677-4680.

8. Beringer, J.W., J.L. Beynon, A.V. Buchanan-Wollaston, and A.W.B. Johnston (1978) Transfer of the drug-resistance transposon Tn5 to Rhizobium. Nature (London) 276:633-634.

9. Bochner, B.R., H-C. Huang, G.L. Schieven, and B.N. Ames (1980) Positive selection for loss of tetracycline resistance. J. Bact. 143:926-933.

10. Bollag, J.M., G.G. Briggs, J.E. Dawson, and M. Alexander (1968) 2,4-D metabolism. Enzymatic degradation of chlorocatechols. J. Agri. & Food Chem. 16:829-833.

11. Bollag, J.M., C.S. Helling, and M. Alexander (1968) 2,4-D metabolism. Enzymatic hydroxylation of chlorinated phenols. J. Agri. & Food Chem. 16:826-828.

12. Boulnois, G.J. (1981) Colicin Ib does not cause plasmid-promoted abortive phage infection of Escherichia coli K-12. Mol. Gen. Genet. 182:508-510.

13. Bourquin, A.W., and P.H. Pritchard (1979) Proceedings of the Workshop: Microbial Degradation of Pollutants in Marine Environments. U.S. Environmental Protection Agency, Washington, D.C.

14. Cen, Y., G.L. Bender, M.J. Trinick, N.A. Morrison, K.F. Scott, P.M. Gresshoff, J. Shine, and B.F. Rolfe (1982) Transposon mutagenesis in Rhizobia which can modulate both legumes and the nonlegume Parasponia. Appl. Envir. Microbiol. 43:233-236.

15. Chapman, P.J. (1979) Degradation mechanisms. In Proceedings of the Workshop: Microbial Degradation of Pollutants in Marine Environments, A.W. Bourquin and P.H. Pritchard, eds. U.S. Environmental Protection Agency, Washington, D.C., pp. 28-66.

16. Chapman, P.J., and D.W. Ribbons (1976) Metabolism of resorcinylic compounds by bacteria: Alternative pathways for resorcinol catabolism in Pseudomonas putida. J. Bact. 125:985-998.

17. Chatterjee, D.K., and A.M. Chakrabarty (1982) Genetic rearrangements in plasmids specifying total degradation of chlorin-

ated benzoic acids. Mol. Gen. Genet. 188:279–285.

18. Chatterjee, D.K., and A.M. Chakrabarty (1983) Genetic homology between independently isolated chlorobenzoate-degradative plasmids. J. Bact. 153:532–534.

19. Chatterjee, D.K., S.T. Kellogg, S. Hamada, and A.M. Chakrabarty (1981) Plasmid specifying total degradation of 3-chlorobenzoate by a modified ortho pathway. J. Bact. 146:639–646.

20. Colby, J., D.I. Stirling, and H. Dalton (1977) The soluble methane mono-oxygenase of Methylococcus capsulatus (Bath). Its ability to oxygenate n-alkanes, n-alkenes, ethers and alicyclic, aromatic and heterocyclic compounds. Biochem. J. 165:395–402.

21. Dagley, S. (1979) Pathways for the utilization of organic growth substrates. In The Bacteria. A Treatise on Structure and Function, I.C. Gunsalus, chief ed., L.N. Ornston and J.R. Sokatch, vol. eds. Academic Press, New York, Vol. 7, pp. 305–388.

22. Dénarié, J., C. Rosenberg, B. Bergeron, C. Boucher, M. Michel, and M. Barate de Bertalinio (1977) Potential of RP4::Mu plasmids for in vivo genetic engineering of gram-negative bacteria. In DNA Insertion Elements, Plasmids and Episomes, A.I. Bukharia, J.A. Shapiro, and S. Adhya, eds. Cold Spring Harbor Press, Cold Spring Harbor, New York, pp. 507–520.

23. Ditta, G., S. Stanfield, D. Cerbin, and D.R. Helinski (1981) Cloning DNA from Rhizobium meliloti using a new broad host range, binary vehicle system. In Genetic Engineering of Symbiotic Nitrogen Fixation and Conservation of Fixed Nitrogen, Basic Life Sciences, A. Hollaender, ed. Plenum Press, New York, vol. 17, pp. 31–40.

24. Don, R.H., (1983) Isolation and Genetic and Physical Analysis of Six Bacterial Plasmids Encoding Degradation of the Herbicide 2,4-Dichlorophenoxyacetic Acid. Ph.D. Thesis, University of Queensland, Australia.

25. Don, R.H., and J.M. Pemberton (1981) Properties of six pesticide degrading plasmids isolated from Alcaligenes paradoxus and Alcaligenes eutrophus. J. Bact. 145:681–686.

26. Dorn, E., and H-J. Knackmuss (1978) Chemical structure and biodegradability of halogenated aromatic compounds. Substituent effects on 1,2-dioxygenation of catechol. Biochem. J. 174:85–94.

27. Dunn, N.W., and I.C. Gunsalus (1973) Transmissible plasmid coding early enzymes of naphthalene oxidation in Pseudomonas putida. J. Bact. 114:974–979.

28. Duxbury, J.M., J.M. Tiedje, M. Alexander, and J.E. Dawson (1970). 2,4-D metabolism: enzymatic conversion of chloromaleyacetic acid to succinic acid. J. of Agri & Food Chem. 18:199–201.

29. Eaton, R.W., and K.N. Timmis (1983) Genetics of xenobiotic degradation. In Current Perspectives in Microbial Ecology, American Society for Microbiology, Washington, USA (in press).

30. Ely, B. (1979) Transfer of drug resistance factors to the di-morphic bacterium Caulobacter crescentus. Genetics 91:371-380.
31. Ely, B., and R.H. Croft (1982) Transposon mutagenesis in Caulo-bacter crescentus. J. Bact. 149:620-625.
32. Engesser, K-H., E. Schmidt, and H-J. Knackmuss (1980) Adaption of Alcaligenes eutrophus B9 and Pseudomonas sp. B13 to 2-fluorobenzoate as growth substrate. Appl. Envir. Microbiol. 39:68-73.
33. Evans, W.C., B.S.W. Smith, H.N. Fernley, and J.I. Davies (1971) Bacterial metabolism of 2,4-dichlorophenoxyacetate. Biochem. J. 122:543-551.
34. Fennewald, M., and J.A. Shapiro (1979) Transposition of Tn7 in Pseudomonas aeruginosa and isolation of alk::Tn7 mutations. J. of Bacter. 139:264-269.
35. Fisher, P.R., J. Appleton, and J.M. Pemberton (1978) Isolation and characterization of the pesticide-degrading plasmid pJP1 from Alcaligenes paradoxus. J. Bact. 135:798-804.
36. Foster, T.J. (1983) Transposon mapping and the use of plasmids in genetics. Analysis of plasmid functions with transposons. Methods in Microbiology, G. Grinstead and P.M. Bennett, eds. Academic Press, London (in press).
37. Franklin, F.C.H., M. Bagdasarian, M.M. Bagdasarian, and K.N. Timmis (1981) Molecular and functional analysis of the TOL plasmid pWWO from Pseudomonas putida and cloning of the genes for the entire regulated aromatic ring meta-cleavage pathway. Proc. Nat. Acad. Sci., USA 78:7458-7462.
38. Franklin, F.C.H., P.R. Lehrbach, R. Lurz, B. Rueckert, M. Bagdasarian, and K.N. Timmis (1983) Localization and functional analysis of transposon mutations in regulatory genes of the TOL catabolic pathway. J. Bact. 154:676-685.
39. Frey, J., M. Bagdasarian, D. Feiss, F.C.H. Franklin, and J. Deshusses (1983) Stable cosmid vectors that enable the intro-duction of cloned fragments into a wide range of Gram-negative bacteria. Gene (in press).
40. Furakawa, K., and A.M. Chakrabarty (1982) Involvement of plas-mids in the total degradation of chlorinated biphenyls. Appl. Envir. Microbiol. 44:619-626.
41. Gamar, Y., and J.K. Gaunt (1971) Bacterial metabolism of 4-chlorophenoxyacetate. Formation of glyoxylate by side chain cleavage. Biochem. J. 122:527-531.
42. Gaunt, J.K., and W.C. Evans (1971) Metabolism of 4-chloro-2-methylphenoxyacetate by a soil pseudomonad. Ring fission, lac-tonizing and delactonizing enzymes. Biochem. J. 122:533-542.
43. Goldman, P. (1972) Enzymology of the carbon-halogen bond. In Degradation of Synthetic Organic Molecules in the Biosphere, National Academy of Sciences, Washington, pp. 147-165.
44. Guroff, G., J.W. Daly, D.M. Jernia, J. Renson, B. Witkop, and S. Undenfriend (1967) Hydroxylation-induced migration: the NIH shift. Science 157:1524-1530.
45. Harayama S., M. Tsuda, and T. Iino (1980) High frequency mobil-

ization of the chromosome of Escherichia coli by a mutant of
plasmid RP4 temperature-sensitive for maintenance. Mol. Gen.
Genet. 180:47–56.

46. Harayama, S., M. Tsuda, and T. Iino (1981) Tnl insertion mutagenesis in Escherichia coli K-12 using a temperature-sensitive
mutant of plasmid RP4. Mol. Gen. Genet. 184:52–55.

47. Holmes, D.S., and M. Quigly (1981) A rapid boiling method for
the preparation of bacterial plasmids. Analyt. Biochem. 114:
193–197.

48. Husain, M., B. Entsch, D.P. Ballou, V. Massey, and P.J. Chapman
(1980) Fluoride elimination from substrates in hydroxylation
reactions catalyzed by p-hydroxybenzoate hydroxylase. J. Biol.
Chem. 255:4189–4197.

49. Huzinger, O., and W. Veerkamp (1981) Xenobiotic chemicals with
pollution potential. In Microbial Degradation of Xenobiotics
and Recalcitrant Compounds, T. Leisinger, A.M. Cook, R. Hütter,
and J. Nüesch, eds. Academic Press, London, pp. 3–45.

50. Jeenes, D.J., W. Reineke, H-J. Knackmuss, and P.A. Williams
(1982) TOL plasmid pWWO in constructed halobenzoate-degrading
Pseudomonas strains: enzyme regulation and DNA structure. J.
Bact. 150:180–187.

51. Jeenes, D.J., and P.A. Williams (1982) Excision and integration
of degradative pathway genes from TOL plasmid pWWO. J. Bact.
150:188–194.

52. Kaufman, D.D., and P.C. Kearney (1976) Microbial transformations in the soil. In Herbicides, Physiology, Biochemistry,
Ecology, L.J. Audus, ed. Academic Press, London, Vol. 2, pp.
29–64.

53. Keil, H., U. Klages, and F. Lingens (1981) Degradation of 4-
chlorobenzoic acid by Pseudomonas sp. CBS3: induction of catabolic enzymes. FEMS Microbiol. Lett. 10:213–215.

54. Keith, L.H., and W.A. Teilliard (1979) Priority pollutants I –
A perspective view. Env. Sci. and Tech. 13:416–423.

55. Kellogg, S.T., D.K. Chatterjee, and A.M. Chakrabarty (1981)
Plasmid-assisted molecular breeding: new technique for enhanced
biodegradation of persistent toxic chemicals. Science 214:
1133–1135.

56. Kilbane, J.J., D.K. Chatterjee, and A.M. Chakrabarty (1983) Detoxification of 2,4,5-trichlorophenoxyacetic acid from contaminated soil by Pseudomonas cepacia. Appl. Envir. Microbiol.
45: 1697–1700.

57. Kilbane, J.J., D.K. Chatterjee, J.S. Karns, S.T. Kellogg, and
A.M. Chakrabarty (1982) Biodegradation of 2,4,5-trichlorophen-
oxyacetic acid by a pure culture of Pseudomonas cepacia. Appl.
Envir. Microbiol. 44:72–78.

58. Klages, U., and F. Lingens (1979) Degradation of 4-chloroben-
zoic acid by a Nocardia species. FEMS Microbiol. Lett. 6:201–
203.

59. Klages, U., and F. Lingens (1980) Degradation of 4-chloroben-
zoic acid by a Pseudomonas sp. Zentrablatt für Bakteriologie

Mikrobiologie und Hygiene 1. Abteilung Originale C1: 215-223.

60. Klages, U., A. Markus, and F. Lingens (1981) Degradation of 4-
    chloro-phenylacetic acid by a Pseudomonas species. J. Bact.
    146:64-68.

61. Kleckner, N., R.K. Chan, B-K. Tye, and D. Botstein (1975) Muta-
    genesis by insertion of a drug-resistance element carrying an
    inverted repetition. J. Mol. Biol. 94:561-575.

62. Knackmuss, H-J. (1981) Degradation of halogenated and sulfonat-
    ed hydrocarbons. In Microbial Degradation of Xenobiotic and
    Recalcitrant Compounds, T. Leisinger, A.M. Cook. R. Hütter and
    J. Nüesch, eds. Academic Press, London, pp. 189-212.

63. Knackmuss, H.J., M. Hellwig, H. Lackner, and W. Otting (1976)
    Cometabolism of 3-methylbenzoate and methylcatechols by a 3-
    chlorobenzoate utilizing Pseudomonas: accumulation of (+)-2,5-
    dihydro-4-methyl - and (+)-2,5-dihydro-2-methyl-5-oxo-furan-2-
    acetic acid.

64. Kuner, J.M., and D. Kaiser (1981) Introduction of transposon
    Tn5 into Myxococcus for analysis of developmental and other
    nonselectable mutants. Proc. Nat. Acad. Sci., USA 78:425-429.

65. Kunz, D.A., and P.J. Chapman (1981) Catabolism of pseudocumene
    and 3-ethyltoluene by Pseudomonas putida (arvilla) mt-2:
    Evidence for new functions of the TOL (pWWO) plasmid. J. Bact.
    146:179-191.

66. Leemans, J., J. Langenakeus, H. De Greve, R. Deblaere, M. Van
    Montagu, and J. Schell (1982) Broad-host range vectors derived
    from the W-plasmid Sa. Gene 19:361-364.

67. Little, M., and P.A. Williams (1971) A bacterial halidohydrol-
    ase. Its purification, some properties and its modification by
    specific amino-acid reagents. Eur. J. Biochem. 21:99-109.

68. Meynell, E., and M. Cooke (1969) Repressor minus and operator
    constitutive derepressed mutants of F-like R-factors, Their
    effect on chromosomal transfer by HfrC. Genetical Research
    (Camb.) 14:309-320.

69. Ornston, L.N. (1970) Conversion of catechol and protocatechuate
    to β-ketoadipate (Pseudomonas putida). Meth. in Enzym.
    17A:529-549.

70. Pemberton, J.M., B. Corney, and R.H. Don (1979) Evolution and
    spread of pesticide degrading ability among soil microorgan-
    isms. In Plasmids of Medical, Environmental and Commercial
    Importance, K.N. Timmis and A. Pühler eds. Elsevier, N.
    Holland, Biomedical Press, pp. 287-299.

71. Pemberton, J.M., and P.R. Fisher (1977) 2,4-D plasmids and per-
    sistence. Nature (London) 268:732-733.

72. Reineke, W., D.J. Jeenes, P.A. Williams, and H.J. Knackmuss
    (1982) TOL plasmid pWWO in constructed halobenzoate-degrading
    Pseudomonas strains: prevention of meta pathway. J. Bact.
    150:195-201.

73. Reineke, W., and H-J. Knackmuss (1978) Chemical structure and
    biodegradability of halogenated aromatic compounds. Substitu-
    ent effects on 1,2-dioxygenation of benzoic acid. Biochim.

Biophys. Acta 542:412–423.

74. Reineke, W., and H–J. Knackmuss (1978) Chemical structure and biodegradability of halogenated aromatic compounds. Substituent effects on dehydrogenation of 3,5-cyclohexadiene-1,2-diol-1-carboxylic acid. Biochim. Biophys. Acta 542:424–429.

75. Reineke, W., and H–J. Knackmuss (1979) Construction of haloaromatic utilizing bacteria. Nature (London) 277:385–386.

76. Reineke, W., and H–J. Knackmuss (1980) Hybrid pathway for chlorobenzoate metabolism in Pseudomonas sp. B13 derivatives. J. Bact. 142:467–473.

77. Reineke, W., S.W. Wessels, M.A. Rubio, J. Latorre, U. Schwien, E. Schmidt, M. Schlömann, and H–J. Knackmuss (1982) Degradation of monochlorinated aromatics following transfer of genes encoding chlorocatechol catabolism. FEMS Microbiol. Lett. 14:291–294.

78. Robinson, M.K., P.M. Bennett, S. Falkow, and H.M. Dodd (1980) Isolation of a temperature-sensitive derivative of RP1. Plasmid 3:343–347.

79. Rothstein, S.J., and W.S. Reznikoff (1981) The functional differences in the inverted repeats of the Tn5 are caused by a single basepair nonhomology. Cell 23:191–200.

80. Ruisinger, S., U. Klages, and F. Lingens (1976) Abbau der 4-chlorobenzoesäure durche eine Arthrobacter-species (Degradation of 4-chlorobenzoic acid by an Arthrobacter species). Arch. Microb. 110:253–256.

81. Sato, M., B.J. Staskawicz, N.J. Panopoulos, S. Peters, and M. Honma (1981). A host-dependent hybrid plasmid suitable as a suicidal carrier for transposable elements. Plasmid 6:325–331.

82. Schell, M.A. (1983) Cloning and expression in Escherichia coli of the naphthalene degradation genes from plasmid NAH7. J. Bact. 153:822–829.

83. Schmidt, E., and H–J. Knackmuss (1980) Chemical structure and biodegradability of halogenated aromatic compounds. Conversion of chlorinated muconic acids into maleoylacetic acid. Biochem. J. 192:339–347.

84. Schreiber, A., M. Hellwig, E. Dorn, W. Reineke, and H–J. Knackmuss (1980) Critical reactions in fluorbenzoic acid degradation by Pseudomonas sp. B13. Appl. Envir. Microbiol. 39:58–67.

85. Schröder, J., A. Hillebrand, W. Klipp, and A. Pühler (1981) Expression of plant tumor-specific proteins in minicells of Escherichia coli: a fusion protein of lysopine dehydrogenase with chloroamphenicol acetyltransferase. Nuc. Acid Res. 9:5187–5202.

86. Schwien, U., and E. Schmidt (1982) Improved degradation of monochlorophenols by a constructed strain. Appl. Envir. Microbiol. 44:33–39.

87. Sharpee, K.W., J.M. Duxbury, and M. Alexander (1973) 2,4-Dichlorophenoxyacetate metabolism by Arthrobacter sp.: accumulation of a chlorobutenolide. Appl. Microb. 26:445–447.

88. Simon, R., U. Priefer, and A. Pühler (1983) Vector plasmids for in vivo and in vitro manipulations of Gram-negative bacteria. In Molecular Genetics of the Bacteria-Plant Interaction: Rhizobium, Agrobacterium and Plant Pathogenic Bacteria, A. Pühler, ed. Springer-Verlag, New York (in press).

89. Slater, J.H., D. Lovatt, A.J. Weightman, E. Senior, and A.T. Bull (1979) The growth of Pseudomonas putida on chlorinated aliphatic acids and its dehalogenase activity. J. Gen. Microb. 114:125-136.

90. Stanier, R.Y., and L.N. Ornston (1973) The β-ketoadipate pathway. Adv. Microb. Phys. 9:89-151.

91. Stanlake, G.J., and R.K. Finn (1982) Isolation and characterization of a pentachlorophenol degrading bacterium. Appl. Envir. Microbiol. 44:1421-1427.

92. Stirling, D.I., and H. Dalton (1979) The fortuitous oxidation and cometabolism of various carbon compounds by whole-cell suspensions of Methylococcus capsulatus (Bath). FEMS Microb. Lett. 5:315-318.

93. Stirling, D.I., and H. Dalton (1980) Oxidation of dimethyl ether, methyl formate and bromomethane by Methylococcus capsulatus (Bath). J. Gen. Microb. 116:277-283.

94. Stucki, G., W. Brunner, D. Staub, and T. Leisinger (1981) Microbial degradation of chlorinated C1 and C2 hydrocarbons. In Microbial Degradation of Xenobiotics and Recalcitrant Compounds, T. Leisinger, A.M. Cook, R. Hütter, and J. Nüesch, eds. Academic Press, London, pp. 131-137.

95. Suida, J.F., and J.F. DeBernardis (1973) Naturally occurring halogenated organic compounds. Lloydia 36:107-143.

96. Thomson, J.A., M. Hendson, and R.M. Magnes (1981) Mutagenesis by insertion of drug-resistance transposon Tn7 into a Vibrio species. J. Bact. 148:374-378.

97. Tiedje, J.M., J.M. Duxbury, M. Alexander, and J.E. Dawson (1969) 2,4-D metabolism: pathway of degradation of chlorocatechols by Arthrobacter sp. J. Agri. Food Chem. 17:1021-1026.

98. Van Vliet, F., B. Silva, M. Van Montagu, and J. Schell (1978) Transfer of RP4::Mu plasmids to Agrobacterium tumefaciens. Plasmid 1:446-455.

99. Vandenbergh, P.A., R.H. Olsen, and J.F. Colarnotolo (1981) Isolation and genetic characterization of bacteria that degrade chloroaromatic compounds. Appl. Envir. Microbiol. 42:737-739.

100. Weightman, A.J., A.L. Weightman, and J.H. Slater (1982) Stereospecificity of 2-monochloropropionate dehalogenation by the two dehalogenases of Pseudomonas putida PP3: evidence for two different dehalogenation mechanisms. J. Gen. Microb. 124:433-437.

101. Williams, P.A., and K. Murray (1974) Metabolism of benzoate and the methyl-benzoates by Pseudomonas putida (arvilla) mt-2: Evidence for the existence of a TOL plasmid. J. Bact. 120:416-423.

102. Worsey, M.J., and P.A. Williams (1975) Metabolism of toluene and xylenes by Pseudomonas putida (arvilla) mt-2: Evidence for

a new function of the TOL plasmid. J. Bact. 124:7-13.

103. Yen, K-M. and I.C. Gunsalus (1982) Plasmid gene organization: naphthalene/salicylate oxidation. Proc. Nat. Acad., USA 79: 874-878.

104. Yen, K-M., M. Sullivan, and I.C. Gunsalus (1983) Electron microscope heteroduplex mapping of naphthalene oxidation genes on the NAH7 and SAL1 plasmids. Plasmid 9:105-111.

GENERAL DISCUSSION: ENVIRONMENTAL TOXICANTS

Participants: A.M. Chakrabarty, University of Illinois
Gilbert S. Omenn (Moderator), University of Washington
Simon Silver, Washington University
Andrew Weightman, Université de Genève

G.S. OMENN: Dr. Silver, besides developing these organisms for degradation of persistent chemicals in particular environments, it may be very useful to have particular organisms as tools for monitoring the presence, in this case, of heavy metals, and heavy metals of particular chemical species. Such monitoring could be useful to follow environmental pathways, to determine the extent of a problem, and to assess the success, if any, in a clean-up program. Would you comment, especially with regard to the kinds of strains you have developed and which you study?

S. SILVER: First, the strains are basically not developed. They are just around. In fact, that is the amazing and very useful point. You can go and seek them when you want them. In highly sophisticated laboratories, such as you would have here in Seattle, and as government agencies would have in the United States, there is little advantage in using these bacteria as biological monitors of pollution, compared with direct chemical analysis by atomic absorption spectrometry and other methods.

There are two situations in which they might be of use as biological monitors: 1) in less affluent laboratories where it is easier to follow petri dishes than it is to use $20,000 analytical machines; and 2) persuading oneself that bacterial resistance does go along with environmental pollution. For example, Rita Colwell and her collaborators have shown more than 90% frequency of mercury resistance among pseudomonads in the Chesapeake Bay area in Baltimore Harbor, which is heavily polluted. By contrast, down at the mouth of the Bay, where the water is rather clean, the frequency might be 1 or 2%. It is important to show that these resistances do go along with environmental pollution, to demonstrate both that the heavy metal levels that are found in polluted waters and soils are

81

high enough to disturb the normal bacterial flora and select for resistant organisms, and to show biologically that these resistance
determinants disappear when you clean up the environment. Let me
give another example.

About ten years ago, the use of mercurials in hospitals in the
United States and Japan was essentially forbidden, and phenylmercuric acetate was removed abruptly from all the hospital soaps. The
frequency of mercury resistant Staphylococcus aureus, E. coli, and
Pseudomonas strains among hospital collections has gone down about
5-fold in the last 10 years. Once you remove the selective pressure, these determinants are decreased; such results from environmental monitoring can enhance efforts to get rid of major sources of
toxic heavy metals.

M. ALEXANDER: With some notable exceptions, most of our chemical pollution problems show chemicals either at very low concentrations or in complex mixtures, as in disposal sites. There may be
20, 30, or 50 organic compounds present, many of which are toxic to
the organisms. What do you do about these situations?

A.M. CHAKRABARTY: First, when it comes down to a toxic chemical in the range of less than 5 ppm of 2,4,5-T, as an example, it
looks as though either the pollutant is bound to the soil or is not
available to the microorganisms for some reason. However, microorganisms are extremely adaptive. One oligotrophic underground Pseudomonas isolate could utilize its substrates only when presented in
very low concentrations. The concentration of organics at that
depth of the soil is very low. I think that as we learn more about
bacteria that can thrive with low substrate concentrations, particularly if they happen to be Pseudomonas, it may be possible to transfer the biodegradative capabilities cloned in plasmids to these bacteria. Then it would be necessary to check whether they express the
genes and whether they would actually attack the compounds at very
low substrate concentration. As we learn more about the distribution of genes for degradation of toxic chemical compounds, I think
it will be possible to develop microorganisms that assist the clean-
up of toxic substrates in very low concentration. These organisms
might be of special value in treating drinking water.

To answer your second question, I admit that if there are 20 or
30 highly toxic chemicals in a toxic dumpsite, it would be very difficult to use genetically engineered or adapted microorganisms. In
some cases, however, toxic chemical dumpsites have only a few chemicals that are present in high concentrations. Let's say we are interested in getting rid of dioxins and pentachlorophenols in the
presence of other toxic chemicals. It may not be very difficult to
make bugs resistant to various toxic chemicals. So my approach
would be to take the bug that can eat the dioxin or phentachloro-
phenol, make it resistant to all the other toxic chemicals known to
be present in high concentrations, and then use it.

A.J. WEIGHTMAN: I might add a specific point which concerns microbial degradation of substrate mixtures. A big problem associated with the degradation of haloaromatic substrates is interference by methyl-substituted compounds. In continuous-flow systems one observes poisoning of mixed cultures as a result of accumulation of catechols during the utilization of substrate mixtures containing methyl- and chloro-substituted aromatics. The problem seems to result from the induction of <u>meta</u>-ring cleavage enzymes by methylaromatic substrates in cultures which are also producing chlorocatechols. In collaboration with Hans Knackmuss' group (Göttingen, W. Germany) we are attempting to construct strains which can channel methyl-substituted catechols down on <u>ortho</u>-cleavage pathway and which do not induce the interfering <u>meta</u>-cleavage activities. The catabolic pathway on which we are basing our study is one about which I talked earlier: the plasmid encoded <u>ortho</u>-pathway in <u>Alcaligenes</u> <u>eutrophus</u> JMP134, which can degrade methylchloro-substituted catechols. It looks as though this approach will be successful. That's just one specific example. Obviously, as mixtures become more complex the problems may increase, depending on the nature of the mixture.

G.S. OMENN: Also, we should note, as targets of opportunity, sites with very high concentrations of very few toxic compounds. Good examples are the Air Force sites Dr. Chakrabarty described which have up to 33,000 ppm of 2,4,5-T.

J.C. LOPER: Your approach is clearly very practical and pragmatic. It's fun to see how much real science becomes more available as you dig further into this problem. As you have manipulated and selected a lot of plasmids and examined enzymatic degradation of a specific compound, what do you think is happening? Are you primarily recruiting different genes from a variety of different undescribed organisms in assembling pathways? Or are you seeing a lot of information from point mutations for subtle changes in substrate specificity? What would you predict as being a good strategy for tackling an unknown problem?

A.M. CHAKRABARTY: We really know very little. For example, we would very much like to know how the 2,4,5-T genes evolved. At present, we have no direct evidence that the plasmid has anything to do with 2,4,5-T degradation. We are trying to clone the 2,4,5-T genes; once we have cloned them, we will hybridize them with the plasmid to see if the genes came from the plasmid. If we find that the genes actually came from the plasmid, then we would cut the plasmid into pieces and hybridize each fragment with all the other plasmids we put into the chemostat to find out if any particular plasmid provided the fragment for an alternate enzyme. What you really need is a molecular anatomy of the 2,4,5-T plasmids.

In terms of the biochemistry of the process, you can demonstrate that 2,4,5-T goes through trichlorophenol to dichloro-cate-

chol. You can also detect by GC/mass spec hydroxylated 2,4,5-T,
dihydroxylated 2,4,5-T, and then dichloro-catechol. So it is clear
that there is dechlorination before the aromaticity has been broken.
What we are really trying to do is to clone the gene that would allow dechlorination from an aromatic nucleus, with substitution of a
hydrogen or hydroxyl group. If we can clone such a gene in a broad
host-range plasmid, then one can put the cloned gene in the chemostat and introduce selective pressures by supplying TCDD, for example. This kind of a gene might undergo mutations to produce enzymes
that recognize TCDD, and dechlorinate it partially without even
breaking the ring.

We don't have to depend upon total degradation of the toxic
chlorinated compound. Once it is dechlorinated, even partially, it
is much less toxic than the highly chlorinated compound. There may
be natural evolution of genes for the degradation of lower chlorinated compounds, so we are working with the hypothesis that it would
be possible to clone genes that code for dechlorination directly
from the aromatic nucleus.

A. DEMAIN: We have been mainly discussing clean-up of problems
that already exist. It is very exciting to hear about these approaches and of the new organisms being developed. But, I wonder
whether the panel can address questions of the present and the
future of chemical wastes. I assume that these chlorinated compounds are still being used. I'd like to know what is going on to
prevent accumulation of these materials. Personally, as one versed
in secondary metabolism, I'm amazed at the lack of interest that I
perceive in the development of biodegradable replacements for present day herbicides, fungicides, and insecticides. For example, I
believe mercuric pesticides were banned in Japan a number of years
ago. They have been replaced by agricultural antibiotics made by
streptomycetes.

A.M. CHAKRABARTY: Why don't the chemical industries use natural products or do something about making sure that these products do
not accumulate in nature? There is no incentive for the chemical
industry to do so. EPA has to force them not to pollute the environment. Persistence of the chemicals in the agricultural environment is desired both in terms of decreased frequency of application
and decreased costs for pest control. The chemical industry has
been forced to do toxicological studies for new synthetic compounds.
In addition to toxicological studies, we should require some microbial genetics to come up with a bug to degrade any new chemical.
That way the chemical industry would have two products: the chemical and the antidote.

S. SILVER: I think you knew the answer to your question when
you asked it, Arnie. Environmental pollutants are not going to go
away, they're simply going to change. None of us expects to live to
see a time when there aren't serious social problems from environmental pollutants. They are just going to change from year to year.

Mercury from agricultural mercurials has apparently disappeared as a problem in many countries because of strong governmental pressure. At any stage we see a balance among economic costs, social benefits, and governmental regulatory restraints on social or health costs of using different products. So some things will go away; other things will stay. Organomercurials are gone, but arsenicals are still used extensively in agriculture. You are never going to get rid of the use of arsenicals in the chemical industry, where the economic and social benefits are high. We will have to have a balance between local health risks in Tacoma, or elsewhere, and overall economic benefits. The social, political, and economic problems are complex.

However, the scientific and technical challenges in studying bacteria and fungi which can degrade many of these compounds are complex, as well. It behooves us to understand these phenomena in detail, point by point by point. The three speakers in this session are all reductionists who, when faced with a complex problem, feel that the best way to approach it is to understand it bit by bit. That is the only way we'll understand it and make progress on various aspects of the problem of environmental pollutants.

G.S. OMENN: Does anyone want to add some information about the development and use of biodegradable products for agricultural applications?

B. ZIMMERMAN: There is a rather high level of interest among some of the independent biotechnological companies and some of their larger agricultural chemical investors in developing species-specific biological pesticides, particularly herbicides and insecticides. The problems, especially of developing species specificity, are not simple. There is a lot of interest among companies such as Dow and Monsanto, and a number of partnerships are being explored. The technology being considered is quite revolutionary, having certain things in common with some of the technology being developed as diagnostic agents for medicine or cancer therapeutics. With a little twist, some of these compounds might be useful as pesticides.

M. ALEXANDER: As an agronomist, I think it's naive to assume that the agricultural chemical industry is living with pesticides which were important 15-20 years ago. In fact, we have very few persistent chemicals left in agriculture. The pressure has been real. The chemicals are going to be very different. It's an economic incentive. If Company A has a biodegradable, effective chemical which is reasonably cheap in contrast with Company B, which doesn't have that, Company A usually wins.

There is another important source of chlorinated compounds. We still chlorinate waters. Many of the pollutants are not synthetics that are added to water, but reaction products of chlorine plus na-

tural organic compounds. For the present, I think most of the concern is with the priority water pollutants and the industrial chemicals, some of whose total production exceeds 10^9 pounds per year in
the United States.

D. VOLK: I'm in the Southwest regional office of the Department of Environmental Resources in Pennsylvania. It seems that
every week we have to deal with a problem of disposal. A farmer may
report finding two or three drums of an herbicide or a pesticide in
his barn. He may not know where they came from or what exactly they
contain. Our corner of the state had approximately 100-150 preliminary applications for hazardous waste management facilities because
of the types of chemical industries we have. Since the preliminary
applications were brought in late last year about half have been
withdrawn because of loopholes. For example, if they no longer
store those chemicals for more than 90 days, they can avoid the
whole gambit of technical review of their engineering and safety
programs. Nevertheless, wherever disposal is carried out, many
years down the road we may face release of the contents. The problem does not go away. We are going to have the same chemicals come
back to haunt us again whenever various types of waste management
facilities break down, because nothing engineered like that can last
forever.

A. HOLLANDER: Dr. Chakrabarty, in your discussion about the
2,4,5-T experiments, you showed that after you've applied 2,4,5-T to
soil and also added the microorganisms, the plants never can grow
quite as well as they could in uncontaminated soil. You postulated
that the reason was that the 2,4,5-T was never completely degraded.
I wonder whether other explanations have been investigated, including the possibility that the microorganisms, while degrading the
2,4,5-T, could be causing other environmental problems, or contamin-
ating the soil in some other way.

A.M. CHAKRABARTY: We have looked for accumulation of any toxic
intermediates by HPLC or by GC-mass spectrometry, and we have never
been able to find anything. Dechlorination through mineralization
is complete to the extent of 99% or more. We believe that the
residual effect that we see in the soil is due to the traces of
2,4,5-T that is being bound to the soil, not adequately available
for bacterial degradation. We cannot see any accumulation of
anything else in the soil.

S. SILVER: But the 2,4,5-T is available for plants?

A.M. CHAKRABARTY: Yes, it seems to be available for plants in
terms of partially inhibiting the growth.

F. TAUB: Dr. Chakrabarty, when you find 2,4,5-T in a dump, it
is indeed a pollutant. However, people who are manufacturing it and

using it as a plant control agent are going to resist the development and the marketing of an organism that will make their product
much shorter lived and much less effective. Most of the concern
that I've heard about the insecticides has been based on the dioxin
contaminant, not so much on the 2,4,5-T itself, although that can
become a problem when it migrates someplace where it wasn't intended
to be. Given your figures, it would look as though there would be
the potential for small numbers of these organisms to find their
way, perhaps on wind-blown soil, into areas where these compounds
are used--rights of way, fields, and so forth. The 2,4,5-T would
break down much more quickly. I wonder if you are not going to find
resistance then from pesticides users.

A.M. CHAKRABARTY: Again, I view the problem from a different
angle. Instead of finding resistance, I think I would find wide acceptance from the chemical industry, as well as the consumers. You
are right, if you use bugs for the degradation of 2,4,5-T, then obviously the next time you apply the 2,4,5-T, some of the pesticide
would be degraded by the bug, and each time you'll have to keep on
applying more. But that means that the chemical industry would be
able to sell more. Just as we pay more to buy automobiles with catalytic converters, I would rather buy some more 2,4,5-T, hoping that
as the chemical industry would sell more, the price would go down
and perhaps there would be a better balance in the environment.

G.S. OMENN: In fact, scientists at the U.S. Department of Agriculture laboratory in Beltsville, Maryland, and elsewhere have begun systematic investigations of the capabilities of microorganisms
in certain soils to degrade pesticides. Reduced pesticide efficacy
has been recognized in the Corn Belt, in managed forests, and with
certain vegetable crops. Carbofuran insecticides and thiocarbonate
herbicides seem to be most susceptible to biodegradation. Soils
vary tremendously. Apparently, no general mechanism has been discovered, but it is widely speculated that genes for pesticide degradation may be carried on plasmids, analogous to antibiotic resistance genes, as Dr. Chakrabarty and Dr. Silver have discussed. The
agricultural scientists and we environmental scientists need to
bridge our efforts and our findings.

S. STRAND: Getting back to the question of the degradation of
these compounds at very low concentrations and in terms of the kinetics in suspended cultures without soil present, have you any idea
of the K_m's of these overall reactions; the half-saturation coeffi-
cients of 2,4,5-T degradation, for instance?

M. ALEXANDER: I think the half-saturation constants in soil
probably have little meaning, because you have sorption and the concentration of chemical on the soil particle is far, far greater than
that in soil solution. In water, the concentrations of chemicals
are far lower that the K_m's.

R. COLWELL: We might want to consider the gene pool from an area of the world that we have not considered before, namely, the deep ocean. We've isolated metal resistant organisms from sediments from the African and Bissel plain. We have found plasmids present in samples that were collected that were geologically quite ancient; so plasmids have been around for a long time. With regard to the utilization of substrates at very low concentrations, there are microorganisms in the ocean that function very well at very low concentrations, where the concentrations of nutrients are in milligram quantities per liter. In fact, in some of our work at the ocean dumping site off Puerto Rico, we have found that there are organisms that will degrade the compounds that are in the pharmaceutical wastes, like toluenes and benzenes, at very, very low concentrations.

We have found that many of the organisms that are metal resistant will be cross resistant to a variety of heavy metals; rarely is an organism in the environment resistant only to a single metal. Dr. Silver, would you agree that really we need not be specific in engineering organisms but that, in the environment, we could very well pick up useful mixed plasmids?

S. SILVER: I think, Rita, that there is a good analogy with the history of antibiotic resistance organisms. The chemical industry will have the same sort of experience that the antibiotic industry has had. Bugs that evolved in natural settings, in that case, the clinic, had resistances to all of the antibiotics that were being used. The pharmaceutical industry invented better antibiotics to get around the bugs. Then better bugs were encountered. There really will not be an end point. For the chlorinated hydrocarbons, as for the antibiotics, we must continue to address this year's problems, then deal with next year's problems, and later the problems ten years from now.

In recent isolates studied by Nakahara, more than 90% of the mercury resistance plasmids also had arsenic resistance; depending on whether they were clinical or river isolates, 90% or 10% also had resistances to tetracycline and streptomycin. In each case, however, the resistance determinant genes are separate. Although these resistances are carried together on plasmids, we have another analogy with the antibiotic resistance plasmids, which now carry 5 or 7 different antibiotic resistance determinants on a single plasmid. The mechanisms are different, the genes are different, and the enzymes or whatever other proteins determine the resistances are different. There are no examples that I am aware of, in your collections or the ones that you've frequently made available to me, where there is a common mechanism for multiple resistances. When you see arsenic, mercury, and cadmium resistance on the same plasmid, and you do very often, it is because all three of these are in the environment; there has been selection for all three, and plasmids are convenient for packaging. Therefore, the resistance genes go together in the same package, even though they are really different.

R. COLWELL: I agree that there is no single mechanism, but you yourself find that the metal resistance genes are linked. In fact, even though perhaps the heaviest concentrated metal might be zinc or mercury or another, you'll still have the other metal resistance genes in the plasmid of the organisms.

S. SILVER: Very much so.

M. ROGUL: Dr. Chakrabarty, most of the research you have done has been designed to manufacture organisms that are to be used in a deliberate release into the environment for the decontamination of these pollutants. We know two organisms that you are involved with, one to decontaminate 2,4,5-T and the other one for the cleanup of oil spills. As far as I know, neither one of these organisms has ever been put to field test or utilized commercially. Can you tell us why, especially, your patented organism hasn't been utilized yet? What does that portend for the future?

A.M. CHAKRABARTY: I think I'll direct your question to my former boss at General Electric, Dr. Ron Brooks. In response to an article in the New York Times, last week I received the first letter I ever got from any GE people to tell me what is happening. GE is now trying to license the microorganism to appropriate licensees. However, considering it is not the main business for GE and also that there are potential problems in terms of application of microorganisms in an open environment, this GE official doesn't expect a quick licensing. You have to realize that I have absolutely no control over the application of the bug. It is GE's business.

In terms of 2,4,5-T, I am eager to identify an appropriate field application for the bug. I should mention a discouraging experience. I was contacted by a company on the West Coast. They had lots of hexachlorophene, trichlorophenol, and pentachlorophenol in a dumpsite in Missouri. They said, "Would you come and see if at least you could get rid of the trichlorophenol or pentachlorophenol, because, after all, they are toxic and they are potential sources of dioxins?" We made all kinds of arrangements. The lawyers from the University worked with the lawyers of this company to make sure that the patent rights were protected for the University, and so forth. I was willing to provide the bug and show them how to grow it. For the next six or eight months we were in communication. They were doing all the preparative work. They had a good microbiological lab, so they could grow the bugs. Suddenly, in 1982, they stopped talking. I was told, "Well, you know, I think we found another way." Six or eight months later I saw a paper describing the "solution." The solution is that they installed two plastic liners to

contain the chlorophenols and the dioxins, plus some kind of sand to
reduce permeation. So you can understand why I say we need better
incentives and better regulatory policies to develop a new technology or to use the best available technology (BAT), as required by
law.

R. BROOKS: Dr. Chakrabarty has pretty well covered the situation. In addition, however, I might indicate that there is another
level of complexity to the question of toxic wastes in the environment, microorganisms, concentrations, and effects thereof. We've
simplified the fact that commercial aspects of the approaches are
also multiple and they have different economic consequences. In the
case of the oil-eating organisms, I think even a modest calculation
will allow you to come to the conclusion that the frequency of those
spills does not entail a major new business opportunity. That's
General Electric's primary reason for not being interested. However, other people may be interested. Even then, the question comes
up about the desirability, timing, and procedure for admitting such
organisms into the environment. EPA has some responsibility for
making policy in that area. So far as I know, that responsibility
hasn't been advanced to a point where I'm clear whether or not that
release is even permissible today. I think that industry as well as
government scientists need to have some forum other than pure economics for deciding at what pace the developments in biotechnology
that are in the open environment can proceed. I would hope that the
government would have the initial insight in declaring the guidelines, rather than leaving the matter to industry.

G.S. OMENN: I think this discussion has been a fine preamble
to subsequent panel discussions.

ENGINEERING ORGANISMS TO SURVIVE

INTRODUCTION

Morris Levin and Mark Segal

Office of Research and Development
U.S. Environmental Protection Agency
Washington, DC   20460

In this conference on Genetic Control of Environmental Pollutants, we have already heard about needs and strategies related to
specific types of environmental toxicants. This session will address the challenge of engineering organisms to survive in marine,
anaerobic, and highly unusual environments, both in terms of the organism itself and in terms of what the organism will encounter. We
will discuss important aspects of the application of genetic engineering and biotechnology to environmental problems. The objectives
of this conference are to consider mechanisms and to assess strategies for more effectively and safely managing wastes and toxic substances in the environment. This automatically involves both degradation and monitoring, since the process of degradation presents the
problem of end products and changes in the organisms involved.
Clearly, safe management of wastes imposes the need to ascertain
that no adverse environmental or health impacts will result from the
tools (microorganisms) or the products (metabolites).

Agricultural products, in addition to the well known chemical
pesticides, include the Erwinia and Pseudomonas organisms now being
tested for use on citrus and tobacco crops, and involve the deliber
ate release of exotic organisms into the environment. These genet
ically engineered organisms can be considered to be pesticides if
you think of them as controlling the natural flora which induce ice
formation, and, thus, are "pests." There are also chemical pesticides which are not used because of toxicological or other adverse
effects. These compounds could be used if an organism could be
developed to degrade them by application of the microbe after the
need for pest control has passed, and before the harvest. In this
situation the ecological implications of the pesticide as well as
the organism and the end product must be considered.

91

In the study of waste treatment, there is much ongoing research focused on the use of plasmids (natural or engineered) to enable organisms to more rapidly degrade a wider and wider variety of compounds. Many articles have appeared over the past 3 to 4 years which describe the degradative ability associated with specific organisms or plasmids. The technique of plasmid-assisted molecular breeding has been successfully applied in producing microorganisms with very specific abilities. In general, the approach to utilization of microbes has been to select a desired characteristic; obtain the specific genome; and, using a plasmid, insert the information into the organism to be used for expression of the function. Relatively little consideration has been given to the possibility of designing an enzyme and then preparing the nucleic acid required to produce it. Although the number of characteristics available for isolation via selection from naturally occurring heritable characteristics is great, it could be expanded manyfold.

On the surface, the general area of public health appears to be far afield of the topic of this conference; however, we could consider aflatoxins as being environmental pollutants, and devise biological techniques for their degradation or the inhibition of their production. The use of microorganisms to concentrate metals has been well documented. These same organisms could be used to remove pollutants from potable water, either in the treatment plant or at the site, and could also be used as assay material to determine the level of a particular metal in the water by measuring the increased concentration attached to the cell. Organisms can be engineered to be sensitive to a particular compound and hence provide an inexpensive, highly specific determination of the presence and concentration of a particular pollutant. Samples of water, air, soil, leachate, etc. could be either extracted or washed, and a battery of organisms could be exposed to the unknown material. Presence of the compound in question would be indicated either by death of the bacterium or by observing a particular reaction (color or pH shift). These organisms would be cultivated under laboratory conditions with stock cultures carefully maintained.

To stretch a little further, consider the use of engineered microorganisms to prevent pollution problems. Reduction of the sulfur content of fuels and flue gas is now being studied, aiming at application to specific industrial sites. The fuel for these plants (oil and coal) is transported long distances via trains, ships, or pipelines. There are approximately 275 miles of a coal slurry pipeline in operation, compared to the 800-mile long Alaskan Oil Pipeline. Temperature, sulfur content, and residence time for coal and oil in the pipeline are given in Tab. 1. Note the lower temperatures for coal and the possibility of sulfur reduction while en route. Lower sulfur content would benefit in terms of cost of fuel utilization, processing of oil to produce gasoline, and ecological impacts of acid deposition. It might be possible to select for

Table 1. Some characteristics of coal and oil pipelines.

	Temperature (°F)	Sulfur (%)	Residence time (hr)
OIL	140–180	0.3 – 3.0	40 – 80
COAL	Winter 40 Summer 50	0.3 – 4.5	48 – 72

resistance to such negative features of this environment as toxic effects on the microorganisms, lack of oxygen, and build-up of metabolites.

Organisms designed for release into semi-contained environments, as for sewage treatment, or more widely, as for oil degradation, must have certain characteristics which can be considered "qualifiers for success" (Tab. 2). The list is deliberately short and general, since this topic will receive attention in subsequent chapters. The need for an ability to resist extremes and antagonists is self-evident. Examples of enhanced competitive ability are rapid growth rate and metabolic efficiency. The ability to be highly flexible or to utilize a material which is not sought after by other organisms will result in energy for multiplication. The point which must be stressed is that these characteristics are identical to those which would appear if a list were being made of characteristics of microorganisms with adverse ecological effects.

Table 3 lists characteristics to assess for effectiveness of a deliberately released organism. The product must be released at a

Table 2. Qualities for successful colonization.

A. SURVIVE		Ability to resist environmental extremes Ability to resist antagonists Strong competitive ability
B. MULTIPLY		Competitive advantage
	Cell	Nutritional flexibility Nutritional specialization
	Genome	Stability Transformability Transmissibility

reasonably high concentration, must withstand chemical and temperature changes, must not be rapidly degraded or inactivated, and must
be specific. Adverse end products of the degradation process or
metabolites from the organism must be avoided. The specificity factor is central in the selection of a characteristic to manipulate
and to assure that the procedure will not result in adverse effects.
Specificity is, of course, related to the accuracy with which the
nucleotide sequence has been characterized. Again, most of these
features describe microorganisms which could have adverse effects.

Thus, while there is a great potential for enhanced control of
environmental pollutants, there is also a potential for adverse
effects which is unknown, but is probably small. It is appropriate
to ask how we can estimate and reduce this probability. There are
three basic approaches to consider in risk reduction: 1) elimination of the organism from the environment; 2) use of a product of
the organism; and 3) containment, either biological or physical.
Elimination, as we know from many actual cases, is almost impossible
and is exceedingly expensive. On a macro-scale, we have the Medfly
as an example, and the effort involved in eradication of smallpox
provides an example of elimination of a microorganism. However,
inclusion of a repressed lethal gene would provide a safety factor.
For example, a situation in which the production of lysozyme is
repressed by detergent would permit the use of the organism in a
sewage treatment plant with some assurance that in other environments it would not survive. Another example of conditional lethali-
ty is the "runaway plasmid" wherein the organism produces many copies of the plasmid and hence much product only when the cultural
conditions are manipulated, resulting in a situation which is toxic
to the cells.

Use of the product instead of the whole organism depends on the
ability to cultivate the organism (either in batch culture or immobilized culture) and recover the product. This is perhaps safest
and is being successfully applied in many cases, e.g., production of
detergents. The problem then involves the potential for some type
of equipment failure and accidental release to the environment.

Table 3. Characteristics of product of released organism.

Production
Release
Persistence
Resistance
Specificity
Efficiency
End Product

Containment problems associated with industrial scale fermenters are
being studied. Data from a study nearing completion at the University of Rhode Island indicate that the probability of transmission
of genetic information in a model sewage treatment plant is very
small [2.5 x 10^{-9}, using Escherichia coli, K12 (REC+, pBR322 or
pBR328), and < 10^{-11} if the E. coli is REC-]. Transfer was only observed between E. coli organisms, although a large number of other
genera were monitored.

Although biological containment appears to afford a certain
degree of security, the concept of physical containment for organisms to be used in situ should not be ignored. A device could be
envisioned which permits the use of immobilized microorganisms in
environmental situations wherein contaminated water can be passed
through, while the organisms are retained and only the end products
are released. Given this approach, an ion exchange or charcoal filter could be used to remove the end products as well. This could be
very similar to the immobilized enzyme or organism devices currently
in use in industrial settings. The optimal characteristics of the
organism to be used would differ significantly from those designed
for deliberate release.

In summary, the point of this commentary is not to stress the
potential dangers of using genetically engineered microbes to enhance our environment, but rather to suggest that, with some fore-
thought, these efforts can result in procedures which are least
likely to have adverse effects.

BIODEGRADATION IN THE ESTUARINE-MARINE ENVIRONMENTS

AND THE GENETICALLY ALTERED MICROBE

Al W. Bourquin

U.S. Environmental Protection Agency
Environmental Research Laboratory
Gulf Breeze, Florida   32561

Many chemicals enter the marine and estuarine environment through a variety of routes. These routes include dumping, direct application, outfalls, accidental spills, and land runoff or rainfall. Some of these compounds are toxic to the biota or may be converted to toxic products in nature. The fate and ecological effects of these chemicals in estuarine environments is part of the concern of the U.S. Environmental Protection Agency (EPA) Laboratory at Gulf Breeze, Florida. Toxicity results when an organism is exposed to a sufficient concentration of a compound. Therefore, fate greatly influences the cumulative effect of a chemical on the biota.

Toxicity effects can be attenuated by dilution of the pollutant below its toxic threshold or by physically removing it into a phase (sediments) where the chemical may not be available to indigenous organisms. Neither process alters the chemical structure of the toxicant. Chemical, photochemical, and some biological processes bring about changes in chemical structure which may or may not alter the toxicity of the chemical or product. Whereas microbial degradation can produce major changes in the chemical structure of the introduced chemical, mineralization is often the end result of bacterial and fungal activities.

The purposes of this paper are to: 1) provide selected examples in the marine and estuarine environments of known introductions of toxic chemicals; 2) describe how habitat differences affect biodegradation potentials in freshwater, estuarine, and marine environments; and 3) express some applications and concerns for the release of genetically altered organisms into the environment.

97

CHEMICAL POLLUTANTS IN ESTUARINE AND MARINE ENVIRONMENTS

Historically, some organic and inorganic compounds have been considered serious environmental pollutants based on quantity produced, bioaccumulation, toxicity, or adverse environmental effects. Although many of the problem chemicals, e.g., chlorinated pesticides, are no longer produced or have been greatly reduced in use, some pose contemporary problems in our estuaries. Examples of pesticide residues accumulated by various marine organisms are shown in Tab. 1. Thus, while chlorinated hydrocarbon pesticides have been banned or restricted in use for years, they are still detected in marine biota. In some cases (California coast), the concentration appears to be higher than that found in other areas (Gulf of Mexico) years earlier (1). Kepone, a very persistent compound which accumulated in marine biota and sediments to significant levels, has caused a serious problem in the James River-Chesapeake Bay areas. Interestingly, results from field studies sometimes contradict laboratory studies; some monitoring studies have detected in marine biota compounds known to be degradable in the laboratory, e.g., pentachlorophenol (PCP) and parathion. These are examples of some of the kinds of problems that we are attempting to understand in our studies on microbial degradation of pollutants in the aquatic environments.

Other compounds which pose an environmental health hazard have accumulated in various estuarine-marine ecosystems (Tab. 2). Most sorb and accumulate in sediments. Recent evidence shows that polychlorinated biphenyls (PCBs) contained in the sediment are still bioavailable through the food chain and accumulate in estuarine organisms (4). Chemicals, such as those in Tab. 2, pose a number of problems for biodegradation or detoxification technology. They are almost always located in anaerobic sediments, and large variations in chemical structures require different biodegradation pathways (5). For example, chlorinated substitutions on aromatic hydro carbons can prevent bond cleavage which normally occurs on the

Table 1. Pesticide residues in various marine biota (1,2,3).

Compound	Species	Location	Residues
DDT	Striped Bass	Gulf of Mexico	0.63 µg/g
	Fish (various)	Gulf of Mexico	0.1 - 6.0 µg/kg
	Spanish Mackerel	Gulf of Mexico	0.008 - 0.319 µg/ℓ
	Common Dolphin	California Coast	13 - 36 mg/ℓ
Kepone	Blue Crab	James River	0.01 - 0.55 µg/g
	Blue Crab	Chesapeake Bay	0.634 - 1.36 µg/g
PCP	Oyster	Galveston Bay	3.40 - 8.30 ng/g
Parathion	Clam	Massachusetts	0.02 - 0.03 mg/g

Table 2. Pollutants found in estuarine/marine environments (1,2,3,4).

Compound	Location	Concentration*
Polychlorinated Biphenyls	Hudson River	0.15 - 1.59 µg/g
Brominated Organics	Sewage Treatment Plant Effluents	0.1 - 50 µg/ℓ
Hydrocarbons		
Naphthalenes	--	0.2 - 496 µg/kg
Polycyclic		
Benzo-pyrene	Charles River	8000 µg/kg
Anthracene Gp.	Mobile Bay	2 - 50 µg/kg
Acenaphthene Gp.	--	320 - 100 µg/ℓ
Crude Oil		
Heavy Metals		
Mercury	New England	305 - 568 µg/g
Cadmium	New York	1.9 - 119.7 µg/g
Lead	Mass.	0 - 8.56 µg/g

* kg or g = sediments; ℓ = water

unsubstituted hydrocarbon. Usually another biochemical pathway or different enzyme is required to achieve degradation. Additionally, they are almost always sequestered in sediments with compounds, such as heavy metals or pesticides, that may be toxic to the microbial population or at least inhibitory to the degradation of the other toxicants (6,7). Some compounds (Tab. 2) found in the environment are known to be biodegradable, at least in laboratory studies; therefore, the enzymatic sequences exist in certain species, but are apparently not active within these environments. This may be due to a lack of capability, i.e., lack of enzymes or to a physical-chemical factor of the environment which prevents expression of the genetic capability. The evolution of plasmids or the addition of plasmids that confer the ability to withstand toxic concentrations of a variety of inorganic metal ions, Hg, Cd, and others (8,9), or to express a greater degree of versatility in degradative pathways (10), could help to develop organisms that are tolerant of these toxicant combinations.

BIODEGRADATION IN AQUATIC ENVIRONMENTS

Laboratory studies have determined the biodegradability of chemical pollutants, such as hydrocarbons, chlorinated hydrocarbons, and various pesticides, including microbial biocides. Genetic

studies have shown that the application of biotechnology can increase the detoxification capability of many organisms (11). Recent
studies have demonstrated that the transfer of genetic information
in nature is much more prevalent than previously perceived (12,13).
This versatility within the microbial community would suggest eventual biodegradation of any susceptible compound that enters the environment. However, we continue to find that biodegradation in the
field differs from that predicted in laboratory studies.

A number of reasons for our inability to rely on laboratory-
generated data to predict field results can be noted, and usually is
related to laboratory design (high nutrients, optimized oxygen concentration, etc.) or to the nature of the microorganisms found in
the field. A number of these conditions are listed in Tab. 3.

The environment in which an organism exists affects how it can
function. Generally, organic compounds degrade more rapidly under
aerobic conditions; therefore, oxygen level can affect the rate at
which a compound degrades. Other environmental conditions include
pH, temperature, and salinity. I will present information on the
effect of salinity on biodegradation of xenobiotics. Low nutrient
levels, both organic and inorganic, can retard biodegradation. An
area requiring extensive study is the effect of sorption on biodegradation of organic compounds. Sediment, for example, sometimes
stimulates degradation and other times may retard degradation (P. H.
Pritchard, personal communication).

The chemical structure and concentration of the substrate are
important considerations in biodegradation. Some chemical structures have never been demonstrated to be degradable by microorganisms even under the most optimal growth conditions, i.e., they are

Table 3. Conditions affecting the environmental biodegradation of
          organic toxicants.

1. Environmental Conditions

   - Anaerobiosis (Eh)
   - pH, Temperature, (Salinity)
   - Nutrient Levels (Organic and Inorganic)
   - Sorption to Particulates

2. Chemical Parameters

   - Structure
   - Concentration
   - Toxic Chemicals (Mixtures)
       Metals, Organics

3. Microbial Parameters

   - Genetic Capabilities (Including Transport)
   - Size of Polulation
   - Microbial Products
   - Predation/Parasitism

recalcitrant. Polyaromatic hydrocarbons above three rings undergo some transformation, but no significant degradation has been demonstrated. Microbial degradation at low concentrations of toxic organic chemicals may utilize different degradative pathways than occur with the same compounds at high concentrations (M. Alexander, personal communication). Combinations of organic chemicals or chemicals and metals can affect the degradation of certain pollutants; evidence will be presented later to demonstrate such an effect. This may be an area of application of genetic engineering to develop organisms that are resistant to heavy metal contamination but retain the ability to degrade organic contaminants in the environment. The third major consideration of factors controlling biodegradation in the environment is the microbial population. The organisms must possess the genetic capability to degrade the pollutant, including transport of the substrate across the membrane. The number of bacteria in a system has a direct relationship with the rate of degradation of the pollutant, especially the number of the specific degraders in a given environment. Products of catabolism can inhibit the degradation process resulting in intermediate accumulation (5). Predation of the microbial population, although considered important in biodegradation of organic compounds, has not been fully investigated. These conditions all affect how a compound will or will not be degraded in an aquatic environment. Our goal is to determine how such conditions, individually or collectively, affect the degradation process.

Kaplan (14) pointed out that in order to extrapolate laboratory data to the field, we must reorient our approach to understanding quantitatively those environmental factors that control biodegradation in the environment. This approach considers the microorganism as the driving mechanism, but identifies the environment and substrate as the controlling and limiting factors. For example, Di-2-ethylhexyl phthalate (DEHP), when it occurs as a plasticizer in polyvinyl chloride (PVC) films, is resistant to microbial degradation, but DEHP alone is susceptible to microbial attack in the laboratory, and can even be mineralized (15). Giam (16) has shown that DEHP is present in the open-ocean to the extent that he considers phthalate esters to be a class of marine pollutants. Generally, higher concentrations of DEHP are found in water, sediment, and air in coastal regions than in the open Gulf of Mexico. If these compounds can be metabolized, why do they accumulate in the marine environment, not only in anaerobic areas, but also in habitats where one can assume dissolved oxygen to be present?

These and other cases have led my laboratory to probe the differences in biodegradation potential between estuarine and freshwater habitats, with the overall goal of characterizing the environment and understanding the role of the microbial community in the biodegradation process. Several case studies on selected synthetic organic chemicals suggest that degradative processes in estuarine and marine environments differ fundamentally from those in terrestrial and freshwater environments.

Early studies in our laboratory on nitrilotriacetic acid (NTA), a proposed phosphate substitute for detergent mixtures, showed that NTA is not degraded by estuarine microorganisms found in the water column (17). Other studies, however, showed that NTA is biodegradable in river water (18), sewage treatment plants (19), and soils (20). We found no evidence of NTA degradation in the saline environments. Whether the NTA-degrading bacteria (entering from the freshwater river) failed to survive in the estuarine areas, or if the enzymes of surviving microbes were not functional, was not determined. For certain freshwater microbes, the latter phenomenon has been observed (J. M. Tiedje, Michigan State University, personal communication). Interestingly, NTA-degrading bacteria have been observed in ocean environments (3.5% salinity) (Wm. Gledhill, Monsanto Co., personal communication). These later studies confirmed the lack of NTA-degradation in estuarine environments, but showed the capability in higher, constant salinity environments. No explanations have been given for these differences within saline environments.

Other investigators (21) have demonstrated that organic compounds (glucose and acetate), which usually degrade rapidly in freshwater environments, become almost refractory in saline wastewaters. These studies showed a 50% decrease in utilization of organic carbon, as measured by biochemical oxygen demand (BOD), when salt concentration was increased from 0% to 3%. No evidence was presented for the cause of the reduced degradation, but it appears that the salinity affected the enzymatic activity of the microbial populations. Ward and Brock (22) extended this evidence to hypersaline environments (< 3%) in a study that strongly suggests occurrence of a general reduction of metabolic rate at extreme salinities and raises doubt about biodegradation of simple hydrocarbons in hypersaline environments. Investigations into the activity and population densities in various coastal environments by Wright (23) have shown decreased specific activities and population densities as water depth and salinity increase. However, he postulates an adaptive strategy for the natural heterotrophic bacteria that involves reversible changes from functional dormancy to a high degree of activity. Therefore, it is possible that populations in estuaries can adjust to faster metabolic activity if the proper conditions are present when pollutant enrichment occurs.

Experimental Studies with Eco-core

To determine how estuarine microbial communities respond after introduction of a xenobiotic, we devised experiments in a laboratory test system called "eco-core" (24). Early in our studies using this system, we examined the effect that one toxic chemical may have on the degradation of another known, biodegradable toxicant. Eco-cores from Kepone-contaminated sediments of the James River (Virginia) were used to determine the effect of Kepone on the biodegradation of methyl parathion. Additional cores were taken from an uncontaminated area in a Florida saltmarsh (Range Point) and treated with Kepone

prior to testing for methyl parathion degradation. These studies
showed that Kepone is inhibitory to biodegradation processes that
normally occur (Fig. 1). Results indicate that inhibition is proportional to Kepone sediment concentration. These results indicate
serious impairment of a degradation process by another pollutant and
emphasize the effects of environmental conditions and other contaminants on the degradation potential of indigenous microorganisms.

   Other eco-core studies examined the degradation rates of the
"natural" microbial community when allowed to "adapt" after exposure
to a xenobiotic. Studies were performed with water-sediment systems
(eco-cores) taken from a salt marsh and riverine sources. Systems
were tested for biodegradation of the model compounds methyl parathion (MP) and p-nitrophenol (PNP) (25). $^{14}CO_2$ released from radioactive parent compounds was used as a measure of mineralization.
River bacterial communities preexposed to PNP at concentrations
as low as 45 µM degraded the nitrophenol much faster than did control communities (Fig. 2). Similar results were obtained with
MP; river bacterial communities adapted to faster degradation, although higher substrate concentrations were required. Saltmarsh
bacterial communities did <u>not</u> adapt to degrade PNP or MP (Fig. 3).

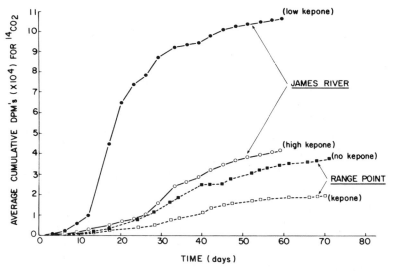

Fig. 1.   Effects of Kepone on Methyl Parathion (MP) mineralization
           in saltwater eco-cores. Range Point (Florida saltmarsh)
           eco-cores sediments were supplemented immediately with 500
           ppm Kepone and the water treated with 200 ppb ^{14}C-MP.
           James River cores were constructed with Kepone-contaminat-
           ed sediments (high = 600 ppm Kepone, low = 140 ppm Kepone)
           from sites in the James River Estuary and Range Point
           water which was treated with 200 ppb ^{14}C-MP. $^{14}CO_2$ was
           trapped and measured as radioactivity. Source: <u>Proceed.</u>
           <u>12th Ann. Conf. on Environ. Toxicol.</u> 1981, p. 354.

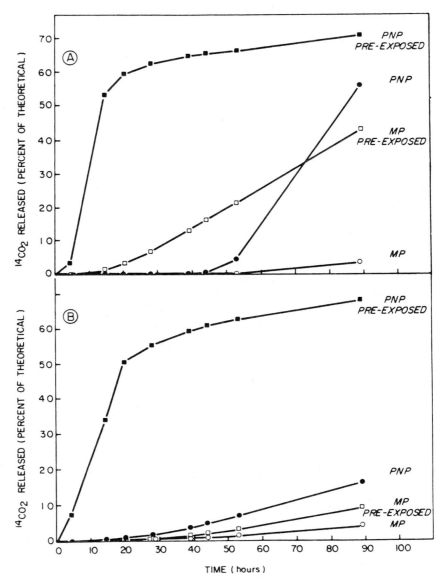

Fig. 2.   Mineralization in preexposed Escambia River cores. Eco-
          cores were taken at the Escambia River site and spiked im-
          mediately with unlabeled MP or PNP at concentrations of
          0.45 and 180 μM.   Control cores received no supplement.
          Cores were incubated 100 hr, water was removed and re-
          placed with filter-sterilized river water, and cores were
          respiked with (^{14}C)MP or (^{14}C)PNP at a concentration of
          180 μM (A) or 0.45 μM (B). $^{14}CO_2$ release was followed
          during subsequent incubation. Source: Appl. Environ.
          Microbiol. 40:726-734.

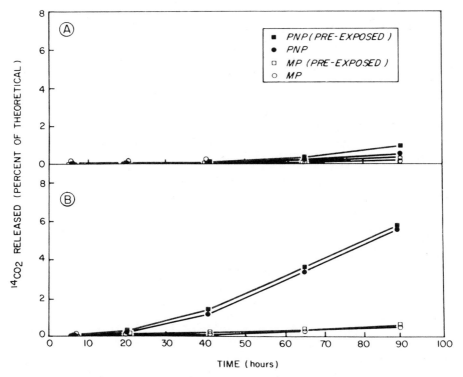

Fig. 3.   Mineralization in preexposed Range Point eco-cores. Cores
          were prepared at the Range Point sampling site and spiked
          immediately with unlabeled MP or PNP at concentrations of
          180 μM (A) or 0.45 μM (B). Control cores received no sup-
          plement. Cores were incubated 250 hr, water was removed
          and replaced with filtered Range Point water, preexposed
          and control cores were then respiked with (^{14}C) MP or
          (^{14}C)PNP at concentrations of 180 μM (A) or 0.45 μM (B),
          and $^{14}CO_2$ release was followed during subsequent incuba-
          tion. Note the x-axis scale relative to that in Fig. 3.
          Source: Appl. Environ. Microbiol. 40:726-734.

Para-nitrophenol-degrading bacteria were isolated from freshwater
river samples, but could not be detected in saltmarsh samples.
These studies suggest that specific biodegradation capabilities may
be present in one aquatic environment, but not in another aquatic
environment. The exact cause of these differences in biodegradation
rates was not determined; however, there appeared to be an absence
of microorganisms in the saltwater system capable of degrading PNP,
although PNP-degrading organisms were carried by freshwater into the
estuary (25).

   Additional estuarine and marine sites (6 sites) and freshwater

sites (5 sites) were sampled to determine if the previous results
were truly representative of the subject environments. All freshwater sampling sites adapted to a faster rate of degradation after
exposure to PNP. When the experiment was repeated with estuarine
and marine samples there was no adaption to faster biodegradation.

    To determine if the microbial response phenomenon was compound-
dependent, trifluralin, PNP, p-cresol, and 2,4,–dichlorophenyoxy-
acetic acid (2,4-D) were tested in eco-cores with water and sediment
samples from the river. Figure 4 shows the disappearance of parent

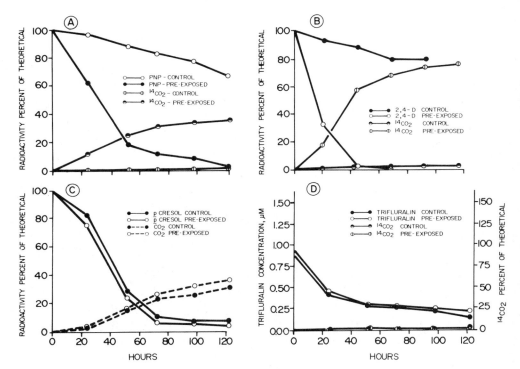

Fig. 4.   Mineralization of radiolabeled test compounds by preex-
           posed and control populations from the Escambia River.
           (A) PNP, (B) 2,4-D, (C) p-Cresol, (D) Trifluralin. Eco-
           cores from the Escambia River test site were exposed to
           the test compounds at concentrations of 1.08 μM; control
           cores received no supplement. After 8 days of incubation
           at 20°C, all cores were tested with 1.08 μM radiolabeled
           compound. During subsequent incubation $^{14}CO_2$ release was
           measured, and water samples were analyzed for parent com-
           pounds by high-pressure liquid chromatography or gas chro-
           matography. The values shown are averages of data from
           duplicate cores; sample-to-sample variation never exceeded
           10% of the mean. Source: Appl. Environ. Microbiol.
           45:428–435.

compound and the evolution of $^{14}CO_2$ from control and pre-exposed cores. The systems adapted to a faster degradation rate for PNP and 2,4-D, but not for p-cresol or trifluralin (26).

Such studies clearly indicate the differences in microbial communities of two nearby aquatic systems. However, no explanation was established as to the nature or cause of the differences. Although no PNP-degrading microorganisms were isolated from the estuarine system, this does not mean the genetic information or the potential was not present. It may not have been expressed or it may have been inhibited by some environmental parameter. Although it is assumed that organisms carrying the genetic information entered the estuarine environment because they were isolated in the freshwater flowing into the estuary, the genetic information was not expressed or was lost. No specific genus was indicated in these studies although G(-) rods were the morphological-type cells isolated as PNP-degraders.

Investigations using four test chemicals, para-chlorophenol (4-CP), para-nitrophenol (PNP), methyl parathion (MP), and pentachlorophenol (PCP) in 3 different saline environments and a river were conducted to empirically determine differences in degradation rates and mineralization rates in these distinctly different but adjacent aquatic environments. Radiolabeled compounds were added to eco-cores filled with samples from the four sites. Degradation rates were measured by collecting $^{14}CO_2$ evolved, then extracting and quantitating parent compound, metabolites, and unextractable C-14.

PNP degradation was fastest in the river system, followed by the saltmarsh, bay, and Gulf systems (Fig. 5). 4-CP was degraded quite rapidly in all systems, but more slowly in the saltmarsh system. Interestingly, 4-CP was mineralized more extensively as the salinity increased and biomass decreased (Fig. 6) with 100% of the theoretical ^{14}C being evolved as $^{14}CO_2$ in the Gulf systems. PCP was not mineralized to any significant extent in any system, although some $^{14}CO_2$ was evolved in the river and Gulf systems. The parent compound was degraded extensively in the river and saltmarsh systems (Fig. 7), but only limited degradation occurred in the higher salinity environments. Methyl parathion hydrolyzes in aquatic environments to PNP, which is subsequently degraded (24). The parent compound, MP, hydrolyzed at essentially the same rate in all systems and the evolution of $^{14}CO_2$ was the same as for PNP (Fig. 5).

Correlations of heterotrophic activity with biomass data do not fully explain the results of these studies. Biomass decreased with increasing salinities, but in some cases, i.e., mineralization of 4-CP in the Gulf system, activity was much greater. In the case of MP and PNP, the decrease in biodegradation rate correlates with the decrease in biomass. However, even here mineralization is not proportional to the biomass or activities of the environment. These results indicate that varied degradative responses to organic substrates by microbial communities from different environments

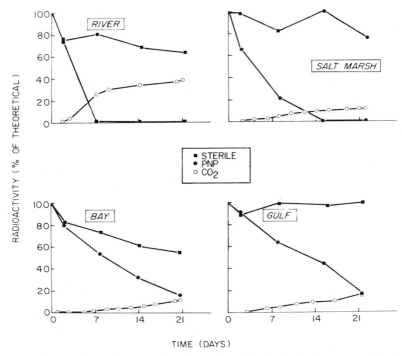

TIME (DAYS)

Fig. 5.   Mineralization and loss of radiolabeled p-nitrophenol
(PNP) from Ecocores taken from Escambia River (10°/oo salinity), Range Point saltmarsh (15°/oo), Escambia Bay
(20°/oo) and near off-shore Gulf of Mexico (35°/oo).
Cores were taken in various environments, treated with 200
ppm $^{14}C_7$-PNP and incubated 21 days at 25°C. During incubation, $^{14}CO_2$ release was measured daily and a core was sacrificed every 7 days and parent compound analyzed by gas-
chromatography. Sterile cores were treated with 2% formalin and analyzed as above.

probably result from differences in growth limiting conditions at
each environmental site.

The examples cited demonstrate the variable response of microbial populations in adjacent environments. It would seem highly
probable that microbes existing in one environment (river) would be
transported into the other (bay or saltmarsh). Their existence and
proliferation would be dependent upon nutrient content, pH, temperatures, oxygen level, and environmental and other factors within the
receiving environment (27).

In addition, it seems highly probable that certain enzyme functions expressed in one environment could be inhibited in another because of salt-induced conformational changes in the enzyme. Before

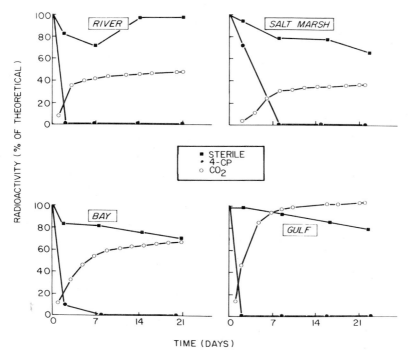

Fig. 6. Mineralization and loss of radiolabeled 4-chlorophenol
(4-CP) from Ecocores taken from Escambia River (10°/oo salinity), Range Point saltmarsh (15°/oo), Escambia Bay
(20°/oo) and near off-shore Gulf of Mexico (35°/oo).
Cores were taken in various environments, treated with
200 ppm ^{14}C-4-CP and incubated 21 days at 25°C. During
incubation, ^{14}CO$_2$ release was measured daily and a core
was sacrificed every 7 days and parent compound analyzed
by gas-chromatography. Sterile cores were treated with 2%
formalin and analyzed as above.

we can predict if a particular organism can survive and function in
a new environment, we need to understand more about how environmental factors affect the functions of a microbial population.

CONCERNS FOR RELEASE OF GENETICALLY ALTERED ORGANISMS

Any discussion of the application of genetically altered organisms should include the conditions and circumstances which may
affect the survival and perpetuation of a genetically altered species in the environment and the potential hazards involved with its
release. For purposes of this discussion, survival differs from
perpetuation in that an organism or trait could survive in an environment for a duration of time but not perpetuate itself through

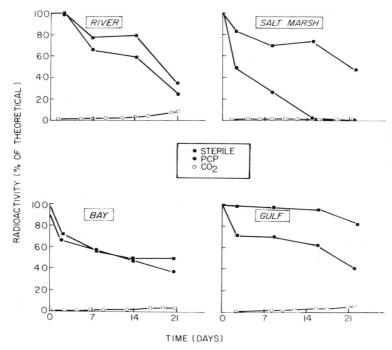

Fig. 7.   Mineralization and loss of radiolabeled pentachlorophenol
           (PCP) from Eco-cores taken from Escambia River (10°/oo sa-
           linity), Range Point saltmarsh (15°/oo), Escambia Bay
           (20°/oo) and near off-shore Gulf of Mexico (35°/oo).
           Cores were taken in various environments, treated with 200
           ppm ^{14}C-PCP and incubated 21 days at 25°C. During incuba-
           tion, $^{14}CO_2$ release was measured daily and a core was sac-
           rificed every 7 days and parent compound analyzed by gas-
           chromatography. Sterile cores were treated with 2% for-
           malin and analyzed as above.

multiplication and thus would eventually be "diluted" out of the
ecosystem. Table 4 condenses and summarizes concerns for the survival and potential hazards of genetically altered microorganisms as
discussed by Curtiss (28).

Survival and Perpetuation

    In order to achieve, functionally, the purpose for which an
organism was developed for release into the environment, it almost
always must be able to survive and perpetuate within a given environment. As noted earlier, the characteristics of the receiving
environment will affect whether and how the organism can exist and
function. Even in natural systems, certain traits or capabilities
can be lost when environmental conditions change. The lack of the

Table 4.   Survival and perpetuation of genetically altered organisms or traits.

A. Nature of microbial host and cloning vectors

   1. Host survival depends on suitable environment for multiplication
   2. Trait survival by transfer of foreign DNA to environmental recipient

B. Ecological niche of altered organism and original

   1. Natural ecological niche of host organism
   2. Contribution of foreign DNA to alter ecological niche
   3. Distance between occupiable niche and laboratory or containment facility

C. Transmissibility

   1. Foreign DNA fragments frequently transferred in nature or in laboratory
      - Transduction via phage
      - Plasmid transfer via conjugation
   2. Recipient of foreign DNA in nature would have higher probability of survival

D. Contributation of foreign DNA

   1. Offers selective advantage (or no disadvantage) to survival of host of vector
   2. Most cases, cloned DNA will be detrimental to competitive survival of cells or vectors

NTA-degrading potential of bacteria within a freshwater river flow-ing into an estuary is an example. The nature of the organism it-self must be considered. A totally laboratory-attenuated host may not survive under conditions in a natural environment. On the other hand, the additional DNA could alter the environment to allow sur-vival of the host. The ability of genetically engineered organisms or the trait to reproduce is a critical factor for the perpetuation of the population or characteristic. If the organism is unable to reproduce, the population will die out. The survival and perpetua-tion of the host necessitates that the foreign DNA confer some se-lective advantage or at least no disadvantage to the genetically engineered organism.

Survival of the genetically altered trait can be affected by survival of the host cell or the vector involved in the genetic transfer. If the host does not survive, the trait will more than likely die with it. However, the trait's survival could be in-creased if the foreign DNA or altered DNA fragment is passed to another organism in the environment. The potential for trait sur-vival seems highly probable with certain genetically altered species carrying promiscuous plasmids capable of infecting a broad spectrum of microorganisms (i.e., gram-negative bacteria). The survival and perpetuation of the DNA and new trait could be facilitated by transfer to another vector or host in the environment which would be better adapted to growth within a particular ecological niche.

Some information on survival and trait transfer can be developed from methods using simulated environments (microcosms), such as eco-core. It will not be practicable to simulate all of the environmental conditions or the combinations of environmental conditions that might allow reproduction, growth, and survival of genetically altered organisms. But these methods have been used to simulate environmental conditions in the laboratory on a site-specific basis.

Transmissibility

The exchange of genetic material between species and genera of bacteria is so common that it is highly likely that transfer of altered DNA will occur if the host survives, and that transfer will more than likely occur via transduction or conjugational plasmid transfer (28). However, with sufficient information on the nature of the host cell, transmissibility in the laboratory, and the nature of the receiving environment, we may be able to evaluate this potential. Laboratory studies can evaluate the potential for transfer of genetic material from one microbe to another. However, those studies will provide data on only the potential for genetic exchange among the species tested and under the conditions employed in the laboratory. The likelihood for exchange with other species in the environment remains unknown and requires investigation. It is not practical to test all possible situations with some altered organism; it may be possible to anticipate probable transfer through laboratory testing.

CONCLUSIONS

Many factors control and regulate biodegradation in aquatic environments. Some of these factors have been discussed in this paper. In addition to the more obvious constituents of an environment necessary for the organism's growth, certain physical/chemical factors may inhibit or alter the function within a particular ecosystem. One of the more obvious discussed here was the loss of certain biodegradation functions in the transfer from freshwater to a saline environment. Another factor was the inhibitory effect of one pollutant on the biodegradation of another. Biodegradation potentials in different saline environments for xenobiotics of varied chemical structures were dramatic when comparisons among freshwater, saltmarsh, estuarine, and marine environments were more. Some of the reasons for how each factor affects the biodegradation functions were discussed briefly. Certainly a lot of work remains to be done to understand the biodegradation function in a particular environment.

The release of genetically altered microorganisms in the environment creates a whole new set of questions which relate to the investigations just presented. It is necessary, of course, to know how and why a particular function exists in one environment and not in another in order to achieve the results desired from releasing genetically altered organisms. If it is known that a particular trait can function in a particular environment, then it is possible to genetically manipulate an organism that contains the desired traits. Release of that organism creates another set of questions related to interference and destruction of natural ecosystem functions. The questions of survival of the host (or altered organism), transmissibility of the trait, or ecosystem disruption can be answered somewhat through studies similar to those presented here. These studies using laboratory microcosms and the problems of control of biodegradation in the environment as well as the limitations and applications of genetic engineering and interrelated advancements in any area will contribute to advancement in the other areas.

REFERENCES

1. Reish, D.R., S. Steven, A.J. Mearns, P.S. Oshida, and F.G. Wilkes (1979) Marine and estuarine pollution. J. Water Pollut. Control Fed. 51(6):1477-1517.
2. Reish, D.J., G.G. Geesey, T.J. Kauwling, F.G. Wilkes, A.J. Mearns, P.S. Oshida, and S.S. Rossi (1980) Marine and estuarine pollution. J. Water Pollut. Control Fed. 52(6):1533-1575.
3. Reish, D.J., G.G. Geesey, F.G. Wilkes, P.S. Oshida, A.J. Mearns, S.S. Rossi, and T.C. Ginn (1982) Marine and estuarine pollution. J. Water Pollut. Control Fed. 54(6):786-812.
4. Rubinstein, N.I., E. Lores, and N.R. Gregory (1983) Accumulation of PCB's, mercury and cadmium by Nereis virens, Mercenaria mercenaria and Palaemonetes pugio from contaminated harbor sediments. Aquatic Toxicol. 3:249-260.
5. Hedgement, G.D. (1972) The evolution of metabolic pathways in bacteria. In Degradation of Synthetic Organic Molecules in the Biosphere, I.C. Gunsalus, ed. National Academy of Sciences, Washington, D.C., pp. 56-72.
6. Bourquin, A.W., P.H. Pritchard, and W.R. Mahaffey (1978) Effects of kepone on estuarine microorganisms. Dev. Ind. Microbiol. 19:489-497.
7. Bourquin, A.W., J.C. Spain, and P.H. Pritchard (1981) Microbial degradation of xenobiotic compounds. In Proceedings of the 12th Annual Conference on Environmental Toxicology, AFMRL-TR-81-149, Wright Patterson AFB, Ohio, pp. 354-369.
8. Novick, R.P. and C. Roth (1968) Plasmid linked resistance to inorganic salts in Staphylococcus aurenus. J. Bacteriol. 95:1335-42.
9. Smith, D.H. (1967) R-Factors mediate resistance to mercury, nickel and cobalt. Science 156:1114-16.
10. Chakrabarty, A.M. (1976) Plasmids in Pseudomonas. In Annual

Rev. Genet., L. Roman, A. Campbell, and L.M. Sadler, eds.
10:7-30.

11. Johnston, J.B., and S.G. Robinson (1982) The development of new
     pollution control technologies using genetic engineering
     methods-assessment of problems and opportunities. In Confer-
     ence on Genetic Engineering, Raven Press, New York, p. 24.

12. Weinberg, S.R., and G. Strotzky (1972) Conjugation and genetic
     recombination of Escherichia coli in soil. Soil Biol. Biochem.
     4:171-180.

13. Graham, J.B., and C.A. Istock (1978) Genetic exchange in
     Bacillus subtilis in soil. Mol. Gen. 166:287-290.

14. Kaplan, A.M. (1979) Prediction from laboratory studies of bio-
     degradation of pollutants in "natural" environments. In Pro-
     ceedings of the Workshop Microbial Degradation of Pollutants in
     Marine Environments, A.W. Bourquin and P.H. Pritchard, eds.
     EPA-600/979-012, pp. 497-484.

15. Kaplan, A.M. (1977) Microbial degradation of materials in lab-
     oratory and natural environments. Dev. Ind. Microbiol.
     18:203-211.

16. Giam, C.S. (1978) Pthalate ester plasticizers, DDT, DDE, and
     polychlorinated biphenyls in biota from the Gulf of Mexico.
     Marine Pollut. Bull. (G.B.) 9:249.

17. Bourquin, A.W. and V.A. Przybyszewski (1977) Distribution of
     bacteria with nitrilotriacetate-degrading potential in an
     estuarine environment. Appl. Environ. Microbiol.
     34(4):411-418.

18. Thompson, J.E., and J.R. Dunthrie (1968) The biodegradability
     and treatability of NTA. J. Water Pollut. Control Fed.
     40:306-319.

19. Swisher, R.D., M.M. Crutchfield, and D.W. Caldwell (1967) De-
     gradation of nitrilotriacetic acid in activated sludge.
     Environ. Sci. Technol. 1:820-827.

20. Tiedge, J.M., and B.B. Mason (1974) Biodegradation of nitrilo-
     triacetate (NTA) in soils. Soil Sci. 38:278-283.

21. Davis, E.M., J. Bishop, and R.K. Guthrie (1979) Resistance of
     pollutants to degradation in saline environments. In Proceed-
     ings of Workshop: Microbial Degradation of Pollutants in Marine
     Environments, A.W. Bourquin and P.H. Pritchard, eds. EPA-600/
     9-79-012, pp. 337-347.

22. Ward, D.M., and T.D. Brock (1978) Hydrocarbon biodegradaton
     in hypersaline Environments. Appl. Environ. Microbiol.
     35:353-359.

23. Wright, R.T. (1979) Natural heterotrophic activity in estuarine
     and coastal waters. In Proceedings of the Workshop: Microbial
     Degradation of Pollutants in Marine Environments, A.W. Bourquin
     and P.H. Pritchard, eds. EPA-600/9-79-012, pp. 119-134.

24. Pritchard, P.H., A.W. Bourquin, H.L. Frederickson, and T.
     Maziarz (1979) System design factors affecting environmental
     fate studies in microcosms. In Proceedings of the Workshop:
     Microbial Degradation of Pollutants in Marine Environments,

A.W. Bourquin and P.H. Pritchard, eds. EPA-600/9-79-012, pp. 251-272.

25. Spain, J.C., P.H. Pritchard, and A.W. Bourquin (1980) Effects of adaption on biodegradation rates in sediment/water cores from estuarine and freshwater environments. Appl. Environ. Microbiol. 40:726-734.

26. Spain, J.C., and P.A. VanVeld (1983) Adaption of natural microbiol communities to degradation of xenobiotic compounds: effects of concentration, exposure time, inoculum, and chemical structure. Appl. Environ. Microbiol. 45(2):428-435.

27. Stotzky, G., and V.N. Krasovsky (1981) Ecological factors that affect the survival, establishment, growth and genetic recombination of microbes in natural habitats. In Molecular Biology, Pathogenicity, and Ecology of Bacterial Plasmids, S.B. Levy, R.C. Clowes, and E.L. Koenig, eds. Plenum Press, New York, pp. 31-42.

28. Curtiss III, R. (1976) Genetic Manipulation of Microorganisms: Potential Benefits and Biohazards. Ann. Rev. Microbiol. 30:307-533.

PLASMID-MEDIATED BIODEGRADATIVE FATE OF MONOHALOGENATED

BIPHENYLS IN FACULTATIVELY ANAEROBIC SEDIMENTS

Gary S. Sayler, Hay-Long Kong, and Malcolm S. Shields

Department of Microbiology and
The Graduate Program in Ecology
The University of Tennessee
Knoxville, Tennessee 37996

INTRODUCTION

Interactions between bacterial populations and environmental
pollutants which result in the partial or complete biodegradation of
the pollutant are of multifaceted importance. Studying these interactions can provide useful information for predicting the persistence of pollutants and needs for discharge and release regulations.
Additional information can be obtained to quantify and assess pollutant exposure levels from both ecological and environmental health
perspectives. Such studies may also be a source of new bacterial
isolates containing genetic information potentially useful for
wastewater treatment and pollution abatement. Finally, qualitative
and quantitative descriptions of these interactions may provide
insights into microbial evolution and natural selection, ranging
from the population level to the molecular level. The objective of
this report is to review some fundamental concepts and problems
related to the microbial ecology of pollutant biodegradation in
anaerobic and facultatively anaerobic sediments, and to describe in
greater detail current research on the biodegradation of monohalogenated biphenyls (as models for polychlorinated biphenyls) by sediment bacterial populations.

Anaerobic Environments and Environmental Pollutants

Aquatic sediments and wastewater treatment facilities represent
two anaerobic environments of obvious interest with respect to the
fate of potential environmental contaminants. However, additional
concerns can include other anaerobic environments such as water-
logged soils, ground waters, coal storage and refuse piles, as well

as coal slurry transport lines. All represent either sources or
sinks for environmental pollutants. By definition, anaerobic
environments are devoid of oxygen. Lack of oxygen is the result of
either chemical oxygen demand (COD) or biological utilization of
oxygen as a terminal electron acceptor during respiration on organic
or inorganic substrates. An example of an anaerobic system driven
by COD is coal slurry transport lines which become anaerobic in a
matter of minutes as a result of reduced sulfur and iron compounds
reacting with a limited supply of molecular dissolved oxygen.
Anaerobic conditions in digesters are maintained by an organic carbon load and biochemical oxygen demand.

The anaerobic nature of some systems is variable at both the
macro- and microenvironmental level. Reservoir sediments, the
object of the bulk of this report, may be highly anaerobic (methanogenic) on a seasonal basis. However, seasonal stratification and
turnover of water masses can result in the reaeration and oxidation
of the sediment surface. Summer pool drawdown can result in exposing anaerobic sediment to the atmosphere. In addition, even methanogenic sediments can be oxygenated at the microenvironmental level
in the rhizomatous zone of rooted aquatic macrophytes. Consequently, the reduction potential of aquatic sediments may range from moderately oxidized (100 mV) to highly reduced (-400 mV), depending
upon oxygen reaeration, carbon loads, and sediment composition.
General characteristics of reservoir sediments demonstrating PCB
degradative bacterial populations are given in Tab. 1.

Microbial communities in most natural and artificial environments represent a complex array of interacting eukaryotic and

Table 1.   Characteristics of East Tennessee Reservoir sediments
           examined in PCB biodegradation studies.

Sediment Characteristic	Winter	Summer
Water Column Depth	2-4 m	0-2 m
Interfacial Dissolved O_2	3-6 mgl^{-1}	0-2 mgl^{-1}
Eh (-0.5 mm)	-100 to -200 mV	-150 to -330 mV
pH	7.0-8.0	6.5-7.0
Temperature	4-6°C	15-25°C
Organic Matter	2-7.5%	2-8%
Total Bacterial Density	$10^8-10^9 \, g^{-1}$	$10^8-10^9 \, g^{-1}$
Culturable Anaerobes	$10^6-10^8 \, g^{-1}$	$10^6-10^8 \, g^{-1}$
Diversity (H̄)	3-4	3-4
PCB Burden (Aroclor 1242-1254)	0-5 $mg \, kg^{-1}$	0-5 $mg \, kg^{-1}$

prokaryotic organisms. These biological interactions are further modified by selective pressures imposed by specific physical and chemical characteristics of the surrounding microenvironment. These environmental and biological interactions result in dynamic community structure and function. However, during sampling, recovery, isolation, and characterization of community members and their environment, the community is treated as being in a pseudo-equilibrium condition. It is necessary to be aware of the competition among populations and individuals for a finite and generally limited supply of carbon and energy sources, electron acceptors, micronutrients, and growth factors that maintain the underlying dynamic structure of the communities sampled (14). Such competition may in part explain the existence and maintenance of bacterial populations capable of biodegradation or biotransformation of environmental pollutants.

In aquatic environments, sediments are generally richer in total numbers of bacteria, but not necessarily total diversity, when compared to the overlying water column. The enrichment of total population density is the combined result of accumulation of both autochthonous and allochthonous organic matter as well as the existence of colonizable physical substrates for microbial attachment. These same factors affecting microbial densities also contribute to the enrichment of sediments with environmental pollutants. For example, sediment contamination by inorganic pollutants such as heavy metals is well documented. In addition, nonpolar, low solubility organic pollutants such as PCBs partition to sediment and suspended sediment (7,11), bringing them in close proximity to the highest density of potentially degradative bacteria in aquatic environments. Under these conditions it is hypothesized that the greatest potential selection for degradative bacteria can occur among competing bacterial species.

PCB BIODEGRADATION

Over the past several years our investigations have dealt with aromatic and chlorinated aromatic pollutants in aquatic sediments, their biodegradative fate, and selective pressure imposed upon microbial populations. The biochemical pathways for biodegradation of aromatic pollutants under aerobic conditions have been described by other investigators. Initial biochemical events in catabolism of aromatic compounds are mono- or dioxygenase catalyzed molecular oxygen insertion onto and cleavage of the aromatic ring (5). It may be presumed that in oxygen limited environments this process would be slow or nonexistent. Anaerobic reductive pathways for metabolism of aromatic rings proceed via saturation of the aromatic ring, followed by hydrolytic cleavage of the molecule (6). Tiedje and co-workers have recently provided evidence that enzymatic dehalogenation of chlorinated benzoates, prior to aromatic ring reduction, can occur under obligately anaerobic (methanogenic) conditions (28). This

particular pathway may be an alternative reductive dehalogenation
pathway for anaerobic biodegradation of chlorinated aromatic compounds.

Using existing knowledge about the biochemistry of catabolism
of aromatic compounds, we have attempted to investigate the factors
affecting the fate of environmentally persistent polychlorinated
biphenyls (PCBs). PCBs represent a significant environmental burden
of chlorinated aromatic hydrocarbons as indicated by Fig. 1 and cor-
respond to ten pounds per capita. The pollutants are of low solubility and vapor pressure and tend to partition to sediments as
well as to bioaccumulate (11). As indicated in Fig. 2, their environmental fate and rate of removal from the environment are governed
by a complex interaction of physical, chemical, and biochemical processes resulting in three primary fates, namely, sediment deposition
and burial, photochemical destruction, or biodegradation.

It has been reported that many of the 209 congeners of PCBs are
subject to biodegradation (2,3,7,8,9,10,15,21,29). Yet this apparent microbial catabolism is limited to the lesser chlorinated congeners and is usually incomplete, with the accumulation of chlorobenzoates as a primary biodegradation product. Similar results have
been reported for the environmental fate of PCB congeners (4,20,25,
26). We have demonstrated that PCBs do not represent a toxic threat
to a variety of heterotrophic bacterial processes under aerobic or
anaerobic conditions (18,19,22,23). However, PCBs do significantly
inhibit autotrophic nitrification at concentrations as low as 1 μg/L
(24). Conclusive results have been obtained that at least one mono-
chlorobiphenyl congener is subject to incomplete biodegradation in
uncontaminated reservoir water, resulting in the accumulation of
environmentally stable chlorophenyl glyoxylic acid and chlorobenzoic
acids (26).

Bacterial Isolation and Cultivation

Studies were undertaken to determine factors affecting biodegradative fate of model PCBs in PCB contaminated reservoir sediments.
Sediment grab samples were obtained from the Little River Embayment
of Fort Loudon Reservoir in the vicinity of Knoxville, Tennessee.
Historically, this reservoir is contaminated by both industrial and
domestic pollutants, including multiple sources of PCB. Reservoir
sediment samples were returned to the laboratory and were immediately subsampled and subjected to enrichment cultivation by inoculating
1-10 g sediment samples into 10 ml autoclaved reservoir water supplemented with 60 μg/ml (60 ppm) 4-chlorobiphenyl. Following incubation at room temperature for up to 60 days, subsamples were withdrawn and subjected to streak plate isolation on PCB agar (23) (minimal medium containing 1 g/L Aroclor 1254, Monsanto Chemical Company, St. Louis, Missouri) or Yeast Extract Peptone Glucose agar
(YEPG) (23). Apparent pure cultures were removed from these media.
However, staining and light microscopy revealed multiple monomorpho-
logical types suggesting up to four individual species per colony.

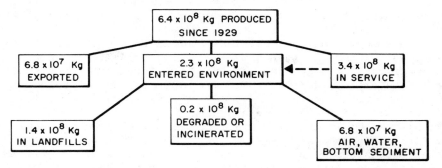

Fig. 1.   A history of PCB production and fate in the United States
           [reproduced from Hutzinger and Roof (11)].

[More detailed procedures have been recently reported (13)].   The
mixed cultures were separated and isolated as pure cultures by purification on YEPG agar.   These pure and mixed cultures, as well as
the natural sediments, were examined to determine their capacity
for, and mechanisms of, biodegradation of model PCBs.

Biodegradation of PCB Substrates by Sediment Bacteria

        Chemicals.   Reagent grade 2-chlorobiphenyl (2CBP), 3-chlorobi-
phenyl (3CBP), 4-chlorobiphenyl (4CBP), 2-bromobiphenyl (2BB), and
3-bromobiphenyl (3BB) were obtained from Analabs Inc. (North Haven,
Connecticut).   4-bromobiphenyl (4BBP) was obtained from Fluka

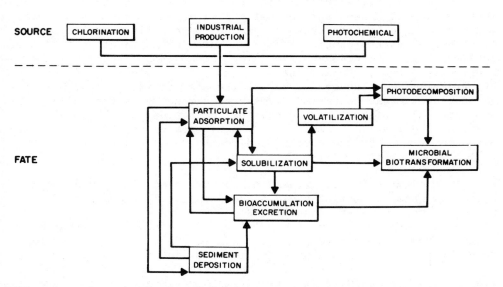

Fig. 2.   A conceptual model of integrated sources and fate of PCB
           in the environment.

Chemical Corporation (Hauppauge, New York). Monochlorinated benzoates were obtained from Pfaltz and Bauer Inc. (Stamford, Connecticut). 4-bromobenzoate was obtained from Aldrich Chemical Company
(Milwaukee, Wisconsin). Fluorisil and organic solvents (HPLC grade)
used in extraction and chromatography were obtained from Fisher
Scientific Company (Fairlawn, New Jersey). Carbon-14, uniformly
chlorophenyl ring labeled, 4CBP, and 2CBP (specific activities:
11.09 Ci/mole and 18.05 Ci/mole, respectively), and (U-^{14}C), 2,4,5,
2',4',5'-hexachlorobiphenyl (HCB), (14.09 Ci/mole) were purchased
from Pathfinder Laboratories Inc. (St. Louis, Missouri). All ^{14}C-
labeled substrates were of ~98% radiochemical purity. Liquid scintillation grade dioxane and toluene (Burdick and Jackson Laboratories, Muskegon, Michigan) were used in preparing Omnifluor (New England Nuclear, New Haven, Connecticut) liquid scintillation cock-
tails.

     PCB biodegradation assessment. PCB biodegradation was measured
in batch cultures or sediment supplemented with the desired model
substrate. Specific details have been previously reported (13).
Biodegradation was measured using high performance liquid chromatographic (HPLC) separation and isolation of biodegradation products
and/or liquid scintillation spectrometry of radioactive degradation
products (13). Where needed, mass spectrometry and infrared spectrometry were used in identification of degradation products (13,
25).

RESULTS

     Initial experiments indicated that 4CBP was removed from a lake
water medium by a sediment population. This biodegradative removal
was accompanied by the transient production and removal of a series
of biodegradation products (Fig. 3). These biodegradation products,
detected by HPLC, included a yellow colored metabolite, most likely
2-hydroxy-6-oxo-6-(4-chlorophenyl)-hexa-2,4-dienoic acid, described
by Furukawa (9). The second metabolite was not identified, but
chlorobenzoate was confirmed by mass spectrometry as the third product (Fig. 3). After 15 to 30 days of incubation, virtually all
(99%) of the initial 60 mg/L 4CBP was removed by the 4CBP-acclimated
mixed culture or by the natural sediment after a 4-day lag period
(13).

     As indicated by Tab. 2, all monochlorinated and brominated
biphenyls were subject to rapid biodegradation by the non-PCB-accli-
mated sediment populations examined. First order biodegradation
rate constants (K_t, where t=days) for the degradable substrates
ranged from 3.6 x 10^{-2} for 2CB to 1.4 x 10^{-1} for 3BB. Respective
turnover times (in this case, the time for biotransformation of the
parent substrate to any product) ranged from 27 to 7 days. The
results also demonstrate differences in biodegradation-structure

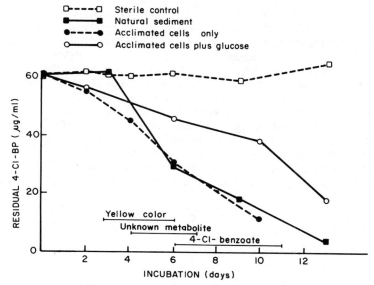

Fig. 3.   Biodegradation of 4CBP in sediments and mixed culture.
Each of the 2 ml cultures were inoculated with 0.2 ml
natural river sediment. 4CBP-acclimated cells inoculated
at 2,000/ml. Glucose at 60 ppm was dosed with the acclimated cells. Brackets indicate the transient appearance
of biotransformation products.

Table 2.   Average degradation rates of monochlorinated and monobro-
minated biphenyls.

Substrate	Degradation rate (μ g/ml-day) ($\pm$ Standard Deviation)	Rate Constant (day^{-1})	Turnover Time (days)
2CB	1.1 ($\pm$ 0.6)	3.6×10^{-2}	27
3CB	1.6 ($\pm$ 0.1)	5.3×10^{-2}	19
4CB	2.0 ($\pm$ 0.3)	6.7×10^{-2}	5
2BB	2.3 ($\pm$ 0.3)	7.7×10^{-2}	13
3BB	4.2 ($\pm$ 0.2)	1.4×10^{-1}	7
4BB	1.4 ($\pm$ 0.2)	4.7×10^{-2}	21

0.1 mg fresh river sediment was inoculated into 2 ml culture dosed with 30 ppm of substrate.
Incubation time was 6 or 9 days.

activity relationships for chlorine and bromine substituted biphenyls, in that rates of oxidation for the same isomer of the different halogenated substrates were not correlated (13).

    Monohalogenated biphenyl (MHB) substrates and metabolite remov-
al patterns in these initial studies suggested that the biodegradation of the halogenated substrates was not merely a co-metabolic
event, or the result of nonspecific enzymatic attack. Consequently,
studies were undertaken to evaluate the terminal fate of a model
substrate, 4CBP. Using ^{14}C-chlorophenyl ring labeled 4CBP, it was
observed that significant mineralization of the chlorinated ring
was promoted by the acclimated mixed populations recovered from
sediments (Fig. 4). A series of experiments was then conducted to

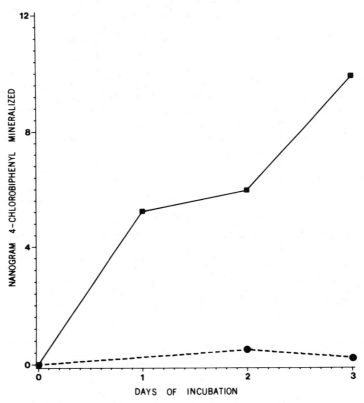

Fig. 4.   Mineralization of 4CBP by acclimated cells. Each 0.6 ml
           culture contained 0.1 ml heat-sterilized river sediment,
           420 ng (0.7 ppm) carbon-14 chlorophenyl-ring labeled 4CBP,
           0.4 ml filter-sterilized river water, and 0.1 ml suspen-
           sion of 4CBP-acclimated cells (approximately 10[5] cells).
           Broken line represents sterile control. Data are means of
           triplicate measurements.

determine environmental factors potentially limiting the rate and
extent of $^{14}CO_2$ production from ^{14}C-4CBP in sediment. When the density of the 4CBP-degrading mixed population recovered from sediment
was varied, it was observed that the rate of 4CBP mineralization was
not a function of the density of total degradative bacteria (within
the range employed), but was directly related to the concentration
of 4CBP in the reaction mixture (Fig. 5). Assuming a first order
reaction relative to 4CBP concentration, a mineralization rate
constant (k) of 6 x 10^2 (day 1) was calculated, indicating a turnover time of approximately 17 days for the total destruction of
4CBP. This mineralization rate constant was essentially identical
to that calculated for conversion of 4CBP to a degradation product,
as determined by HPLC techniques (Tab. 2). These results indicate
that once oxidation of the the substrate is initiated by the population, there are no biochemical rate limiting reactions that retard
the complete destruction of 4CBP. As indicated by the radioactive
materials balance for acclimated, mixed culture biodegradation of
4CBP, nearly 25% of the added 4CBP is converted to CO_2 during a
3-day incubation (Tab. 3).

The addition of <u>Escherichia coli</u> cells (1 x 10^5 ml^{-1}) to sediment resulted in a 25% decrease in cumulative 4CBP mineralization.

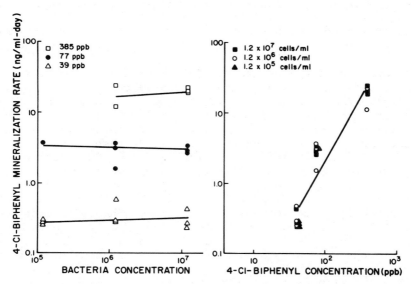

Fig. 5.   Effect of 4CBP and bacterial concentration on mineraliza-
           tion rate. Left panel: mineralization rate vs. bacterial
           concentration; right panel: mineralization rate vs. 4CBP
           concentration. Solid line indicates trend of changes.
           Volume of culture was 1.3 ml; incubation time was 2 days.

Table 3. Distribution of radioactivity in ^{14}C-labeled 4CBP culture[a].

SOURCE	RADIOACTIVITY	
	cpm	% OF INPUT
4CBP in solution	22317	24.2
Metabolites	8055	8.7
[14]CO_2	23095	25.1
Adsorbed to reactor[b]	6597	7.2
TOTAL RECOVERED	60064	65.2
UNACCOUNTED FOR[c]	32096	34.8

[a] 4CBP acclimated culture was dosed with ^{14}C-labeled 4CBP (370 ng equivalent to 92160 cpm was added) and incubated for 3 days.

[b] Associated with Teflon-rubber reactor seal.

[c] Most likely due to volatilization loss.

These results may suggest competitive partitioning of availiable PCB residues by nondegradative bacterial populations. However, exposures of the sediment culture to artificial sunlight resulted in a 400% increase in cumulative 4CBP mineralization and may represent synergistic interaction with microbial metabolism (data not shown; Ref. 13).

In comparing the kinetics of 4CBP mineralization by the mixed culture in sediment and lake water at equivalent cell concentrations ($\sim 10^5$ ml^{-1}), it was noted that mineralization kinetics in sediment were an order of magnitude slower than in lake water. This result and the failure to demonstrate a bacterial concentration vs. mineralization rate dependency suggest competitive adsorptive partitioning of the 4CBP to the sediment matrix and/or nondegradative cells in the mixed culture. Such PCB partitioning dynamics have been reported (16,17,27). The rate of 4CBP accumulation by bacterial cells in filtered lake water was found to be instantaneous and reached an equilibrium between 2 and 20 min. The cells maintained approximately a 5-fold higher concentration of 4CPB than either the water phase or a heat-killed bacterial suspension (data not shown). However, in the case of HCB adsorbed to clay, accumulation by bacterial cells was dependent on the length of contact time with the clay-HCB suspension (Fig. 6). Bacterial cells accumulated HCB at a rate of approximately 10 μg mg^{-1} min^{-1} during the first 15 min of contact time, then reaching a pseudo-equilibrium with an accumulation rate of 0.5 μg mg^{-1} min^{-1} up to 1,440 hr. These results

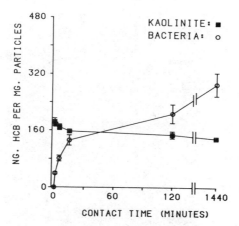

Fig. 6.   Kinetics of bacterial accumulation of clay-adsorbed hexa-
chlorobiphenyl.

indicate that PCB residues in sediment are bioavailable, but that
partitioning kinetics may influence observed rates of biodegradation.

Plasmid-Mediated Catabolism of 4CBP

Several bacterial isolates, tentatively identified as Alcaligenes spp., were isolated from the mixed culture and were found
capable of 4CBP mineralization. On original isolation, these
strains contain plasmid DNA of approximately 50 mdal in size
(Fig. 7). Strains designated A8 and A2 were originally chosen to
determine if the observed plasmids were involved in 4CBP catabolism.
Strain A8 was subject to heat curing at 42°C which resulted in the
isolation of cured strains designated ACS8. The A2 strain (4CBP$^+$)
was then filtered and mated with ACS8 (4CBP$^-$), and an exconjugant
strain, AX2 (4CBP$^+$), was recovered after nalidixic acid resistance
selection. The phenotypes of the four strains studied are given in
Tab. 4.

During laboratory maintenance, the original 50 mdal plasmid had
undergone a spontaneous deletion giving rise to a 35 mdal plasmid in
the A8, A2 strains and the resulting AX2 strain, as well as other
strains maintained under laboratory conditions. Electrophoretic
plasmid profiles, after the mating experiment, are given in Fig. 8.
However, the strains harboring the deletion derivative plasmids and
the exconjugent strain promoted both the production of ^{14}C-chloro-
benzoate and ^{14}CO$_2$ from 4CBP, while the cured strain ACS8 was unable
to metabolize the substrate (Figs. 9 and 10). On prolonged laboratory maintenance and transfer, several isolates harboring the

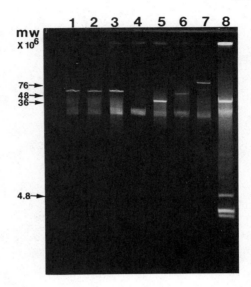

Fig. 7.   Detection of plasmids in bacterial strains isolated from a
           mixed culture capable of 4CBP mineralization [detected by
           horizontal agarose gel electrophoresis using methods
           described by Kado and Liu (12)].   (Vertical numbers indi-
           cate approximate plasmid molecular weight in daltons).
           Lanes 1-6, environmental isolates A1, A2, A3, A4, A5, and
           A8, respectively; Lane 7, Pseudomonas putida Tol plasmid
           DNA; Lane 8, Escherichia coli V517 containing size refer-
           ence control plasmids).

Table 4.   Phenotypes of bacterial strains used in demonstrating
            plasmid involvement in PCB biodegradation.

Strain	Phenotype						
A8[a]	4-CBP$^+$	Starch$^+$	Str^s	Cm^s	Ap^s	Pen^s	Na^r
ACS8[b]	4-CBP$^-$	Starch$^+$	Str^s	Cm^s	Ap^s	Pen^s	Na^r
A2[c]	4-CBP$^+$	Starch$^-$	Str^r	Cm^r	Ap^r	Pen^r	Na^s
AX2[d]	4-CBP$^+$	Starch$^+$	Str^s	Cm^s	Ap^s	Pen^s	Na^r

[a] Strain harboring 35 mdal plasmid.
[b] Heat cured derivative of A8, recipient strain.
[c] Donor strain harboring 35 mdal plasmid.
[d] Exconjugant derived from filter mating of A2 and ACS8.

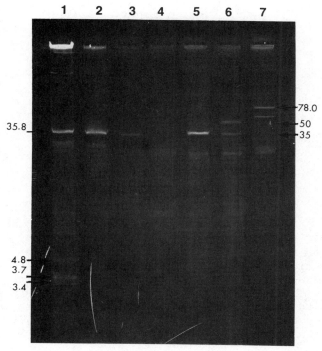

Fig. 8.   Detection of Plasmid DNA in 4-chlorobiphenyl mineralizing
bacteria, cured derivative, and exconjugant. [Kado and
Liu (12) procedure using 0.5% ME agarose electrophoresis
for 4 hr at 100V.] (Vertical numbers indicate molecular
weight of Plasmid DNA in megadaltons). [Lane 1, Escherichia coli V517 containing size reference control plasmids;
Lanes 2 and 3, strain A2 and A8, respectively, capable of
4-chlorobiphenyl mineralization demonstrating 36.5 mdal
Plasmid DNA; Lane 4, strain ACS8 cured derivative of A8
showing no Plasmid DNA; Lane 5, strain AX2 exconjugant
derived from a mating of A2 and ACS8 demonstrating
transfer of Plasmid DNA of 36.5 mdal; Lane 6, strain ALP
original isolate demonstrating size conversion of
degradative Plasmid DNA; Lane 7, Pseudomonas putida
toluene plasmid reference.]

35 mdal plasmid demonstrated a loss in 4CBP mineralization ability.
A 4CBP material balance, calculated after re-examining the biodegradative ability of several strains, indicated that the A8 strain containing the 35 mdal plasmid converted virtually all available 4CBP
to 4-chlorobenzoate (Tab. 5). A frozen stock culture, designated
ALP-1-8, harbored both plasmid varieties and promoted significant
mineralization of 4CBP. As expected, the cured derivative of A8

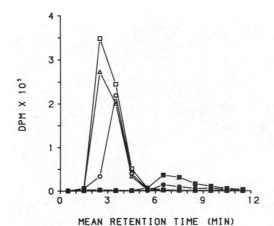

MEAN RETENTION TIME (MIN)

Fig. 9.   HPLC comparison of 4-chlorobenzoate produced during the
           plasmid-mediated biodegradation of ^{14}C-4-chlorobiphenyl
           (radioactive peak at approximately 3.0 min retention time
           is 4-chlorobenzoate). (Symbols: open squares, triangles,
           and circles are A2, A8, and AX2 strain, respectively;
           solid squares, ACS8 cured strain; solid circles, Escheri-
           chia coli negative control).

(ACS8) did not metabolize the substrate.

    Mixed culture and pure culture mineralization experiments con-
ducted in lake water or chemically defined media were performed
under aerobic conditions. However, mineralization of 4CBP in natural sediments or sedements supplemented with biodegradative bacteria
demonstrated a redox potential of $\sim$-150 mV. The results suggest
anaerobic conditions are variable in the sediment or that
mineralization may proceed through an anaerobic pathway. Consequently, an experiment was conducted in a lake water medium maintained under anaerobic conditions using methods described by Adler
and Crow (1). This procedure utilized E. coli membrane vesicles to
catalytically reduce oxygen by a functionally intact cytochrome system. Preliminary results indicate that, under these conditions at
an initial redox potential of -90 mV, some plasmid bearing sediment
isolates could biotransform 4CBP to both metabolites as well as CO_2
(Tab. 6). Plasmid bearing strain ALP-1-8, ALP, and A8 harbor the
35 mdal plasmid, yet only the ALP-1-8 strain was capable of 4CBP
mineralization. Strain A8 demonstrated no anaerobic metabolism of
4CBP, and as previously described, was examined under aerobic conditions and was found to produce chlorobenzoate from 4CBP, but had
lost the ability to mineralize the substrate. This partial loss in
catabolic activity was not associated with plasmid loss or detectable size conversion.

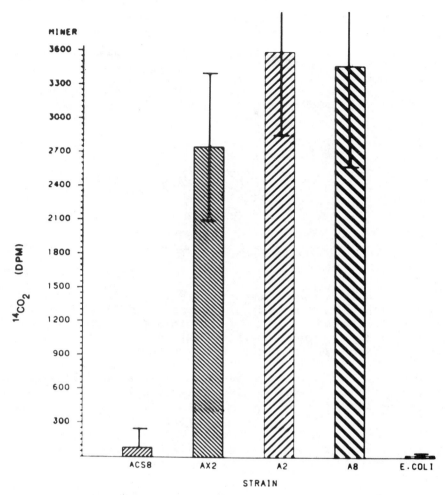

Fig. 10.   Comparative mineralization of 4-chlorobiphenyl by plasmid
           carrying and plasmid cured bacterial strains. (A8 and A2,
           original plasmid bearing environmental isolates; ACS8,
           cured derivative of A8; AX2, exconjugant from filter mat-
           ing of A2 with ACS8; Escherichia coli, negative control;
           Brackets indicate standard deviation).

Summary and Limitations

The results of these studies have demonstrated that model PCB
substrates can be mineralized by indigenous microbial population in
contaminated sediments. This catabolic function can be rate limited

Table 5.   Material balance for plasmid-mediated aerobic catabolism of 4-chlorobiphenyl.[a]

Strain	Phenotype	% Conversion of 4-CBP		% Recovery
		^{14}C Metabolite	$^{14}CO_2$	
A8[b]	4CBP[+]	92	0	95
ACS8[b]	4CBP[-]	0	0	84
ALP-1-8[d]	4CBP[+]	5	34	87

[a] Cultures incubated 10 days in the presence of 2.8 µg ml^{-1} (U-^{14}C) chlorophyll ring labeled 4CBP.

[b] A8 strain haboring 35 mdal plasmid after loss of 4-CBP mineralization ability.

[c] Original cured derivative of A8.

[d] Frozen stock culture harboring the 50 mdal plasmid and 35 mdal deletion derivative plasmid.

at the microenvironmental level by physical-chemical processes such as physical partitioning and accumulation.   At the biochemical level, this catabolic function is determined by the existence of plasmid borne genes that, under laboratory conditions, can be maintained and expressed in pure or mixed culture.

Numerous limitations are encountered in establishing the significance of these biodegradative bacteria and the catabolic plasmids at the environmental level.   Relatively little information is

Table 6.   Plasmid-mediated catabolism of 4-chlorobiphenyl by sediment bacteria under anaerobic conditions.[a]

Strain	% Conversion of 4-CBP	
	^{14}C-Metabolites	$^{14}CO_2$
ALP-1-8[b]	40.9 ± 10.80	7.80 ± 2.00
ALP[b]	62.7 ± 4.80	0.20 ± 0.05
ACS8[c]	0.7 ± 0.40	0.13 ± 0.08
A8[d]	0.5 ± 0.02	0.20 ± 0.20
Sterile Control	0.5 ± 0.05	0.05 ± 0.002

[a] 8 day incubation with 2.8 µg ml^{-1} (U-^{14}C) chlorophenyl ring labeled 4-CBP.

[b] 50 mdal plasmid bearing strains.

[c] Cured derivative of A8.

[d] 35 mdal plasmid bearing strain, after loss of mineralization ability on laboratory maintenance.

available concerning frequencies and stability of the bacteria or
the plasmid encoded genes within the community. There is no information on the incompatibility grouping of the isolated plasmid relative to other plasmids maintained within the populations. Such factors will influence the development of gene screening techniques to
monitor gene frequency distributions in the sediment community.
Although mineralization of 4CBP was observed under moderately reducing conditions, it remains suspect that transient or trace levels of
dissoved oxygen may have permitted conventional aerobic metabolism
of the substrate. If this is true, demonstrating anaerobic metabolism of environmental contaminants will require strict and tedious
cultivation under highly reduced conditions ($\sim$-300 mV). Large
deletions of cryptic DNA observed under laboratory conditions may
affect bacterial survival and gene maintenance and transfer under
environmental conditions. Little information exists on regulation
of catabolic activity of selective pressures required to maintain
the degradative genes under environmental conditions. Such limitation encountered in these studies are shared by virtually all
attempts to utilize genetically manipulated bacteria or newly
isolated strains and plamids. Perhaps the fundamental question is
whether the catabolic genes are maintained and expressed within the
community rather than whether the host bacterium can survive in the
environment.

ACKNOWLEDGEMENTS

These studies were supported by a grant, R-808457-01, from the
U. S. Environmental Protection Agency, Office of Exploratory
Research. G. S. Sayler is also supported by a Research Career
Development Award from the National Institute for Environmental
Health Sciences, Department of Health and Human Services.

REFERENCES

1. Adler, H.I., and W.D. Crow (1981) A novel approach to the
    growth of anaerobic microorganisms. Biotech. Bioeng. Symp.
    11:533-540.
2. Ahmed, M., and D.D. Focht (1973) Degradation of polychlorinated
    biphenyls by two species of Achromobacter. Can. J. Microbiol.
    19:45-52.
3. Ballschmiter, K., Ch. Unglert, and H.J. Neu (1977) Abbau von
    chlorienten aromaten: Mikrobiologischer abbau der polychlor-
    ierten biphenyls (PCB) III: Chlorierte benzoesauren als metabo-
    lite der PCB. Chemosphere 7:51-56.
4. Carey, A.E., and G.R. Harvey (1978) Metabolism of polychlorin-
    ated biphenyls by marine bacteria. Bull. Environ. Contam.
    Toxicol. 20:527-534.
5. Dagley, S. (1971) Catabolism of aromatic compounds by micro-
    organisms. Adv. Microbial Physiol. 6:1-46.

6. Evans, W.C. (1977) Biochemistry of the bacterial catabolism of aromatic compounds in anaerobic environments. Nature 270: 17–22.
7. Furukawa, K., K. Tonomura, and A. Kamibayashi (1978) Effect of chlorine substitution on biodegradability of polychlorinated biphenyls. Appl. Environ. Microbiol. 35:223–227.
8. Furukawa, K., F. Matsumura, and K. Tonomura (1978) Alcaligenes and Acinetobacter strains capable of degrading polychlorinated biphenyls. Agric. Biol. Chem. 42:543–548.
9. Furukawa, K., and F. Matsumura (1976) Microbial metabolism of polychlorinated biphenyl components by Alcaligenes sp. Agr. Food Chem. 24:251–256.
10. Furukawa, K., and A.M. Chakrabarty (1982) Involvement of plasmids in total degradation of chlorinated biphenyls. Appl. Environ. Microbiol. 44:619–626.
11. Hutzinger, O., and A.A.M. Roof (1980) Polychlorinated biphenyls and related halogenated compounds. In Analytical Techniques in Environmental Chemistry, J. Albaiges, ed. Pergamon Press, Oxford, pp. 167–184.
12. Kado, C.I., and S.T. Liu (1981) Rapid procedure for detection and isolation of large and small plamids. J. Bacteriol. 145: 1365–1373.
13. Kong, H.L., and G.S. Sayler (1983) Degradation and total mineralization of monohalogeneated biphenyls in natural sediment and mixed bacterial culture. Appl. Environ. Microbiol. 46(3) (in press).
14. Mallory, L.M., and G.S. Sayler (1983) Heterotrophic bacterial guild structure: Relationship to biodegradative populations. Microbial Ecol. 9 (in review).
15. Neu, H.J., and K. Ballschmiter (1977) Abbau von chlorierten aromaten: Mikrobiologischer abbau der polychlorierten biphenyls (PCB). II: Biphenylole als metabolite der (PCB). Chemosphere 7:419–423.
16. Paris, D.F., W.C. Steen, and G.L. Baughman (1978) Role of physico-chemical properties of Aroclors 1016 and 1242 determining their fate and transport in aquatic environments. Chemosphere 7:319–325.
17. Pavlou, S.P., and R.N. Dexter (1979) Distribution of polychlorinated biphenyls (PCB) in estuarine ecosystems. Testing the concept of equilibrium partitioning in marine environments. Environ. Sci. Technol. 13:65–71.
18. Pedersen, D.P., and G.S. Sayler (1980) Methanogenesis in freshwater sediments: Inherent variability and effect of environmental contaminants. Can. J. Microbiol. 27:198–205.
19. Perkins, R.E., and G.S. Sayler (1983) Comparative effects of synthetic oil and environmental pollutants on organic matter mineralization rates in aquatic sediments. Can. J. Microbiol. (in review).
20. Reichardt, P.B., B.L. Chadwick, M.A. Cole, B.R. Roberson, and D.K. Button (1981) Kinetic study of the biodegradation of

biphenyl and its monochlorinated analogues by a mixed marine microbial community. Environ. Sci. Technol. 15:75–79.

21. Sayler, G.S., M. Shon, and R.R. Colwell (1977) Growth of an estuarine Pseudomonas sp. on polychlorinated biphenyls. Microbial. Ecol. 3:241–255.

22. Sayler, G.S., M. Puziss, and M. Silver (1979) Alkaline phosphatase assay for aquatic sediments: Application to perturbed sediment systems. Appl. Environ. Microbiol. 38:922–927.

23. Sayler, G.S., L.C. Lund, M.P. Shiaris, T.W. Sherrill, and R.E. Perkins (1979) Comparative effects of Aroclor 1254 (PCB) and phenanthrene on glucose uptake velocities by freshwater microbial populations. Appl. Environ. Microbiol. 37:878–885.

24. Sayler, G.S., M.P. Shiaris, W. Beck, and S. Held (1982) Effects of polychlorinated biphenyls and environmental biotransformation products on aquatic nitrification. Appl. Environ. Microbiol. 43:949–952.

25. Sayler, G.S., M.C. Reid, B.K. Perkins, R.M. Pagni, R.L. Smith, T.K. Rao, J.L. Epler, W.D. Morrison, and R. DuFrain (1982) Evaluation of the mutagenic potential of bacterial polychlorinated biphenyl biodegradation products. Arch. Environ. Contam. Toxicol. 11:577–581.

26. Shiaris, M.P., and G.S. Sayler (1982) Biotransformation of PCB by natural assemblages of freshwater microorganisms. Environ. Sci. Technol. 16:367–369.

27. Steen, W.C., D.F. Paris, and G.L. Baughman (1978) Partitioning of selected polychlorinated biphenyls to natural sediments. Water Res. 12:655–657.

28. Suflita, J.M., A. Horowitz, D.R. Shelton, and J.M. Tiedje (1982) Dehalogenation: A novel pathway for the anaerobic biodegradation of haloaromatic compounds. Science 218:115–116.

29. Yagi, O., and R. Sudo (1980) Degradation of polychlorinated biphenyls by microorganisms. J. Water. Poll. Cont. Fed. 52:1035–1043.

LAND DISPOSAL AND SPILL SITE ENVIRONMENTS

A. C. Middleton

Koppers Company, Inc.
Monroeville, Pennsylvania 15146

ABSTRACT

Land is a receptor of many chemicals through both intentional and unintentional depositions. Mitigation methods for control of the chemicals resulting from unintentional depositions such as unsuccessful landfills, spills, and leaks include excavation and disposal, entombment in place, and in some situations, in situ bio-degradation. If genetically engineered bacteria could expand the number of situations where in situ degradation is applicable, then more economically efficient control methods resulting in the destruction of chemicals would be available.

This paper outlines the various processes affecting the fate of organic chemicals in the soil environment, summarizes the environmental conditions encountered by organisms, and reviews two case histories of biodegradation of chemicals within the soil environment.

Environmental conditions encountered by organisms are distinctly different in the two major soil zones: the unsaturated zone and the saturated zone. Chemicals may be present within the soil environment including the vapor phase, the adsorbed phase, and the soluble phase. These differences affect the fates of each chemical and result in greatly different rates of biodegradation of chemicals by naturally occurring microorganisms. Case histories discussed are that of a spray irrigation field treating wastewater from a creosote wood treating process, and that of an in situ biodegradation program for clean up of surface soils contaminated with pentachlorophenol. Recommendations for bacterial characteristics that could be

engineered to greatly expand the applicability of in situ biodegradation are made.

INTRODUCTION

The soil environment is the receptor of many chemicals. Intentional deposition of chemicals includes landfilling and land treatment systems. Unintentional deposition includes chemical spills,
leakage, and unsuccessful landfills. Various mitigation techniques
exist for the unintentional depositions, including excavation and
disposal, entombment in place, and, in the case of biodegradable
organic chemicals, in situ biotreatment. Genetic engineering of
bacteria may present opportunities for enhancement of in situ biotreatment and land treatment systems for biodegradable organic chemicals.

The objectives of this paper are 1) to outline processes affecting the fate of organic chemicals in soil environments; 2) to
summarize environmental conditions encountered by organisms in the
soil environment; and 3) to review two specific case histories involving biodegradation of organic chemicals in the soil environment.

FATE OF CHEMICALS IN SOIL ENVIRONMENT

General

The fate of biodegradable organic chemicals in soil environments is a complex process. Figure 1 is a schematic diagram of the
various factors affecting such chemicals in soil environments. The
chemicals have three phases of interest: vapor, aqueous or soluble,
and adsorbed. Each of these phases is subject to different transformations and transport, depending to some extent on its location
in either the unsaturated zone or the saturated zone of the soil
environment. The unsaturated zone is the layer of soil from the
surface to the top of the water table; the saturated zone, the layer
below the water table. Biodegradation and chemical transformation
can take place in both zones. In the unsaturated zone, volatilization can be a factor in the fate of the chemical. Transport of the
chemicals is normally by water movement, which is different in each
zone. These processes are discussed in more detail in subsequent
sections.

Chemical Phases

Vapor phase. If the chemical has a significantly high vapor
pressure, it can volatilize in a gaseous environment. This process
is significant in the unsaturated zone where the void spaces within
the soil are not filled with water. Vapor can diffuse through the

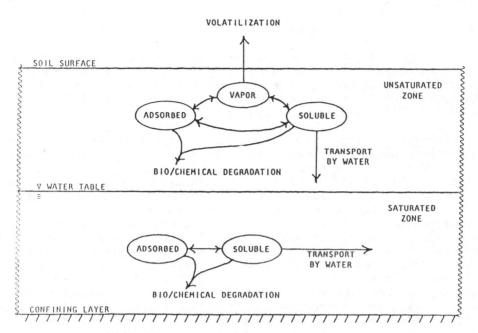

Fig. 1.   Schematic diagram of factors affecting chemicals in soil
           environments.

void spaces and escape to the atmosphere at the soil surface. In
its movement through the void spaces, it can also be adsorbed to the
surface of soil particles, or be dissolved in soil moisture. Factors affecting such processes include soil type, soil organic content, and soil porosity.

     Adsorption phase. Many soil types, e.g., clays, are very sur-
face active and can adsorb a variety of chemicals. Chemicals can be
adsorbed from the vapor phase or from the aqueous phase. Adsorption
can occur in both the unsaturated and saturated zones. In a like
manner the chemical may desorb from the soil particles and reenter
the vapor or aqueous phases. While adsorbed, the chemical is considered to be stationary, in that soil particles do not significantly move within the soil environment.

     Aqueous phase. The aqueous or soluble phase includes chemicals
dissolved in water or the chemical itself if it is a liquid moving
through the soil environment. In the unsaturated zone, the dissolved chemical is contained in the soil moisture, and in the saturated zone, it is a solute in the groundwater. While soluble, the
chemical is available for biodegradation, chemical transformation,

or adsorption. It moves with groundwater, and in the unsaturated
zone it can also volatilize.

Environmental Conditions

General. As stated earlier, the major zones of interest in a
soil environment are the unsaturated and saturated zones. Physical
conditions are different in each of these zones resulting in different processes affecting the fate of chemicals. These differences
are discussed in subsequent sections.

Unsaturated zone. The unsaturated zone exists above the water
table where the void spaces between the soil particles are not completely filled with water. The gaseous content of these void spaces
can be similar to air or can be significantly different as a result
of biological and physical processes. The oxygen content results
from the net effect of two competing processes: oxygen demand of
biodegradable chemical, and atmospheric reaeration. Atmospheric
reaeration is the diffusion of oxygen through the pore spaces down
into the unsaturated zone. It depends upon soil-type and soil porosity. Oxygen demand depends upon the concentration of biodegradable chemicals and the rate at which they are being degraded. The
rate depends upon the type of chemical and, usually, temperature.
If reaeration can resupply oxygen at a rate greater than the oxygen
demanding substances are consuming it, then the unsaturated zone
remains aerobic. If not, it is anaerobic.

A good example of an anaerobic unsaturated zone is that of a
municipal landfill above the water table. Here, the biodegradation
of the organics is so rapid that not only is oxygen depleted, but
the redox potential is reduced to the point where significant
amounts of methane can be generated. Decomposition gases, such as
carbon dioxide and hydrogen sulfide, will make up part of the gaseous content of the unsaturated zone, depending upon the net effect
of the rate of production and the rate of diffusion to escape the
unsaturated zone.

The temperature in the unsaturated zone will follow the air
temperature throughout the year near the surface and approach the
average annual air temperature at depth. Hence, temperature dependent reactions within this zone vary in rate over an annual period.

Movement of chemicals through the unsaturated zone is by transport in water percolating through it. Chemicals spilled in the unsaturated zone may be totally captured by it depending on the soil
type and the soil liquid holding capacity. If this has been the
case, movement of chemicals out of it will depend upon their transport by water percolating through it. Water percolation is normally
vertically downward through the unsaturated zone with minor horizontal movement, except in cases where impermeable lenses exist.

New landfills are designed to be constructed entirely within
the unsaturated zone. Such landfills, when completed, can be capped
at the surface to limit flow of water through them, thereby greatly
reducing the transport of chemicals from them. Land treatment systems, such as spray irrigation fields for wastewaters, are also
designed to be aerobic and to be within the unsaturated zone. This
design takes advantage of the more rapid aerobic degradation of
waste.

Saturated zone. The saturated zone is below the water table,
and is characterized by the void spaces within the soil being completely filled with liquid.. Water will move through the saturated
zone in the direction of the groundwater gradient. The groundwater
gradient can be viewed as the slope of the water table and has a
horizontal and vertical component. The vertical component can be
upward or downward, depending on local hydrogeologic conditions.
The flow is laminar or nonturbulent, and can range from a few feet
per year to tens of feet per day, depending on the soil type and
localized hydrogeologic conditions.

Reaeration with oxygen can be considered negligible in the saturated zone. Oxygen addition is only by diffusion of oxygen at the
surface of the water table. For oxygen to reach to the water table,
the unsaturated zone above must be sufficiently low in organics to
permit oxygen to penetrate to that depth. Then, the organic content
of the water table must also be sufficiently low, such that the oxygen is consumed at a rate much slower than the diffusion rate. Such
a situation contrasts greatly with the oxygen reaeration processes
of surface waters, where high turbulence provides a significant
reaeration rate. It is rare to find aerobic conditions in the saturated zone where biodegradable organic chemicals are present in any
concentration.

Normally, the temperature in the saturated zone will be approximately constant throughout the year, near the average annual air
temperature. Average annual temperatures may be in the range of 10°
to 15°C in many locations. Hence, temperature-dependent reactions
may be relatively constant throughout the year at rates corresponding to this temperature range.

In the case of biodegradation reactions, the combination of
lower constant temperature and anaerobic conditions result in relatively slow biological transformations in the saturated zone.
Hence, it is not surprising to find that many chemicals which are
rapidly biodegraded in warmer, aerobic conditions persist for long
periods of time in the saturated zone.

Chemicals are transported in the saturated zone by groundwater
movement being spread out by dispersion and diffusion processes.
As the chemicals move in the saturated zone, they are subject to

biodegradation, chemical transformation, and adsorption/desorption
processes. These processes can act like a chromatographic medium in
that soil may retard movement of some chemicals and give a separation of a mixture of chemicals with distance from the source.

SITE ENVIRONMENTS

Spray Irrigation

     General. Spray irrigation of wastewaters containing biodegrad-
able chemicals has been a long established process in many industries. It is widely used in the wood preserving industry to treat
wastewaters containing organic components from the wood mixed with
wood preserving chemicals, e.g., creosote or pentachlorophenol.
Figure 2 is a schematic diagram of a spray irrigation field. Wastewater is intermittently applied to the soil surface. It percolates
down through an aerobic degradation zone within the unsaturated
zone. It is within the unsaturated zone that biological degradation
takes place. Treated water can reach the water table and move with
the groundwater in the saturated zone. The amount reaching the

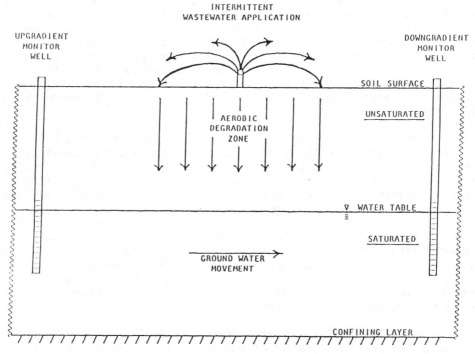

Fig. 2.   Schematic diagram of spray irrigation field.

water table is normally less than that applied, due to water losses
by evapo-transpiration near the surface. The performance of such a
system is normally monitored by wells upgradient and downgradient of
the application point.

   The application of wastewater must be intermittent so that the
unsaturated zone does not become saturated, thereby restricting
reaeration. A variety of organisms in the unsaturated zone participate in the degradation process including bacteria, actinomycetes,
and fungi. Adsorption/desorption of chemicals and volatilization
can play a role in the transformation processes. Biological films
on the soil particles are the primary site of degradation. The use
of such systems is limited to the part of the season where the
ground is nonfrozen and the air temperature is sufficiently warm to
permit biological activity to occur. In addition, it cannot be used
when the ground has been saturated by precipitation. Thus a major
component of such a system is a relatively large waste storage system that permits storage of the waste up to several months of the
year.

   Case history. One spray irrigation field treating wastewater
from a wood preserving plant utilizing creosote was investigated in
detail. The soils consist of silty clays at the surface with sandy
clays and clayey sands beneath. Bedrock is at a depth of approximately 20 feet. The water table varies from 4 feet below the surface to 15 feet below the surface over the spray field. The mean
annual air temperature is 11.6°C.

   Wastewater is pretreated by oil separation and stored in a
lagoon system prior to application to the spray field. The area
sprayed is approximately 4.4 acres. Wastewater is sprayed seven
days a week from April through November, except during periods of
soil saturation due to precipitation. Normally, wastewater is supplied once per day for a period of three hours at a loading of
approximately 4,300 gpd/acre. The operator ensures that this application rate does not flood the field, especially in times of precipitation. No nutrients are added to the field and no tilling of the
soil is performed. The field maintains a complete grass cover during operational months, and normally requires cutting at least four
times a year. Performance is monitored with wells upgradient and
downgradient of the field to measure appropriate water quality constituents.

   The wastewater contains a total organic content (TOC) of
approximately 33 mg/L and phenols of approximately 6 mg/L. Poly-
nuclear aromatic hydrocarbons (PAH), e.g., acenaphthene, phenanthrene, chrysene, etc., normally range from 0.05 µg/L to 100 µg/L.
Naphthalene may range up to 5 mg/L. These ranges will vary from
plant to plant, depending upon the exact nature of the preserving
process.

    Downgradient wells showed nondetectable phenol (<0.005 mg/L),
TOC ranging from 13 mg/L - 16 mg/L, and nondetectable PAH concentrations [<5-100 nanograms per liter or parts per trillion (ng/L)]
for samples taken in July. For samples taken in November, one out
of four wells showed detectable phenol at 0.01 mg/L, TOC
concentrations ranged from 6 mg/L - 8 mg/L. One out of four wells
showed naphthalene detect-
able at 64 ng/L, phenanthrene detectable in the range of 13 ng/L -
61 ng/L, and fluoranthene detectable in the range of 10 ng/L -
25 ng/L, pyrene detectable in the range of 15 ng/L - 48 ng/L, chrysene detectable in the range of 10 ng/L - 60 ng/L. Other PAH concentrations were nondetectable.

    The average annual July air temperature is 23.6°C; October,
12.7°C; and November, 6.4°C. Hence, some decrease in biological
degradation as the colder months approached was apparent. As it was
mentioned, November is the last month of the year in which wastewater is applied to the field.

Spill Site

    General. Two general situations can be defined for spills of
chemicals onto the ground. The first is that in which the chemical
contamination is contained entirely within the unsaturated zone
(Case A). The second is the case in which the chemical contamination in the unsaturated zone passes through it and begins to contaminate the saturated zone due to the liquid percolation of the spill
itself. Figure 3 is a schematic diagram of spill sites illustrating
these two cases.

    Case A can occur when the chemical spill is completely adsorbed
or held by the soil. This is possible when there is a relatively
small spill or a highly adsorptive soil. Another case in which this
can occur is when the chemical itself is relatively viscous and
seals the voids of the soil, thereby greatly reducing permeability
of the soil and preventing further spread of the chemical. This
situation has been observed in the case of coal tar.

    Movement of chemicals out of the unsaturated zone to the water
table is by water percolating downward through the spill site. Relatively little horizontal movement would be expected. The water
mobilizes the chemicals in the spill by dissolving them. The rate
of movement is governed by the amount of water moving through the
spill site, which depends upon permeability of the soil with the
chemical present, and the amount of precipitation incident on the
surface of the spill site.

    Case B occurs when the adsorptive and holding capacity of the
soil is overwhelmed. This would be the situation for a large spill
on a nonadsorptive soil. The chemical moves downward through the

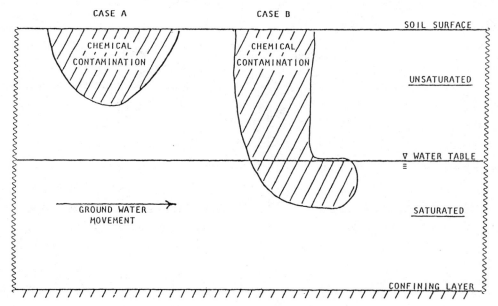

.Fig. 3.   Schematic diagram of spill site.

unsaturated zone to the water table and then moves with the groundwater.

   Mitigation methods.   There are several mitigation methods currently popular for spill site control.   These include excavation and
disposal of contaminated material, entombment of the spill site, and
in some cases in situ biodegradation.

   Excavation and disposal is applicable for spill sites that are
relatively small and near the surface.   It becomes less practical
with larger sites and deeper ones.   If chemicals penetrate the water
table, its applicability greatly decreases because excavation of
materials in the water table becomes very difficult due to the instability of the excavation pit.   Disposal is almost universally on
land either in a secure landfill or a land farming operation.

   Figure 4 is a schematic diagram of entombment systems for spill
sites.   For a case where the chemical contamination is limited to
the unsaturated zone, capping the surface of the site with a low
permeability material provides for suitable control.   Since percolation of incident precipitation through the zone of chemical contamination is responsible for mobility of the chemical contaminants, a
low permeability cap greatly reduces such percolation, thereby
greatly reducing the migration of chemicals away from the spill
site.

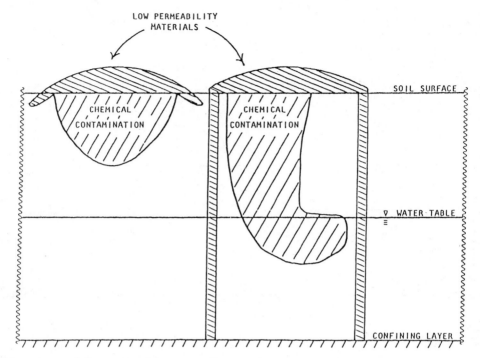

Fig. 4.   Schematic diagram of entombment systems for spill sites.

For the case where the chemicals have reached the water table surrounding the spill, enclosing the part in the water table with a low permeability material as well as on the surface, provides a suitable entombment system. Such a system greatly reduces the movement of groundwater through the chemical contamination, again reducing the movement of chemical contaminants from the spill site.

In certain instances, in situ biodegradation is a very suitable means of clean up of a spill site. Normally, applicability of this method has been limited to spills in the unsaturated zone near the surface of the soil. For such a case, a site can be fertilized to obtain an appropriate carbon:nitrogen:phosphorus ratio; periodically tilled to mix and dilute the concentrated chemicals and aid aeration; and, watered to provide moisture content control which aids degradation in that degradation decreases very rapidly in dry soils. If the spill site is such that this can be done practically then such a method is appropriate.

Case history. One wood treating site became contaminated at the surface with pentachlorophenol, such that the soil content was approximately 700 ppm pentachlorophenol. This site was prepared for in situ biodegradation by fertilizer application, tilling, and

moisture content control. Figure 5 shows the soil pentachlorophenol
concentration as a function of time. The concentration decreased
from approximately 700 ppm to 150 ppm in about 140 days. The cli-
mate was moderate at this site over this period. The contamination
was near the surface and over a relatively widespread area, making
it a very suitable site for in situ biodegradation clean up. The
biodegradation process is still under way. The scatter of the data
points in Fig. 5 is due in part to the difficulty in obtaining and
analyzing representative soil samples especially where there is a
large gradation of soil particles. Such analytical difficulties are
inherent to the nature of evaluating such activities.

DISCUSSION

     Biological degradation has a definite role for mitigation of
chemicals in the soil environment. Applicability can be for cases
of either intentional or unintentional deposition of chemicals in
the soil. The fate of chemicals in the soil is determined by a number of complex biological, chemical, and physical processes as well
as the environmental conditions that are specific to the soils.
Consideration must be given to the two major soil zones of interest:

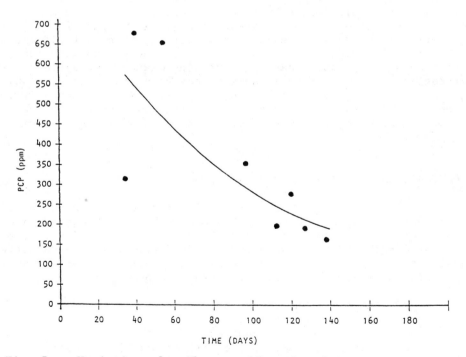

Fig. 5.   Variation of soil pentachlorophenol concentration with
          time.

the saturated and unsaturated zones, because each affects chemicals
differently. The unsaturated zone can be aerobic and will have
temperatures tracking the daily air temperature at the site. It is
specifically used for the intentional deposition of chemicals on
land in spray irrigation fields for wastewater treatment, land farms
for sludge decomposition, and landfills. Movement of chemicals
through the saturated zone is due to the percolation of liquids
downward through it transporting the chemicals.

The unsaturated zone at depth is normally characterized by an
approximate constant temperature near the average annual air temperature of the site and anaerobic conditions, if any significant biodegradable organic concentrations are present. These conditions
limit biodegradation to that which is obtainable by anaerobic decomposition at temperatures in the range of 10° to 15°C. This contrasts to the normal optimal anaerobic biodegradation temperature
range of 30° to 35°C. Adsorption/desorption processes involving the
chemicals and soil particles result in attenuation of the chemicals
with distance traveled in the soil, and can give chromatographic-
like separation of mixtures of chemicals. Chemical transport in the
saturated zone is by movement with the groundwater.

Presently utilized biodegradation systems for soil environments
have taken advantage of the natural microorganism community that
exists in such environments. The characteristics of these microorganisms have limited, to some extent, the applicability of the biodegradation techniques. The limitation for significant rapid biodegradation of organic chemicals has been to the unsaturated zone,
where concentrated wastes can be diluted by mixing, and aerobic
degradation can have a role in warmer seasons of the year. Aerobic
degradation has been used in wastewater applications to spray irrigation fields. Anaerobic degradation in the unsaturated zone has
been a long standing consequence of sanitary landfilling of municipal refuse.

RECOMMENDATIONS

To expand the applications of in situ biodegradation, it will
be necessary to expand the conditions under which such degradation
could occur. Given the environmental conditions that exist in the
unsaturated and saturated zones and the fact that relatively little
degradation presently occurs in the saturated zone, bacterial characteristics to improve the situation can be suggested:

- Active at low temperatures (0° to 15°C).
- Active in anaerobic environments.
- Active in high concentrations of chemicals.
- Production costs sufficiently low to be competitive
  with other mitigation methods.
- Active against chemicals in adsorbed phase.

Development of organisms with such characteristics would greatly expand the capabilities of in situ biodegradation for control of
chemical contaminants in the soil environment. Desirable characteristics existing in certain bacteria might be transferred to other
bacteria with a good match to the environmental conditions of the
particular soils.

REFERENCES

1.   Alexander, M. (1981) Biodegradation of chemicals of environmen-
     tal concern. Science 211:132–138.
2.   Elrlich, G.G., D.F. Goerlitz, et al. (1982) Degradation of
     phenolic contaminants in ground water by anaerobic bacteria:
     St. Louis Park, Minnesota. Groundwater Vol. 20.
3.   McCarty, P.L., M. Reinhard, B.E. Rittmann (1981) Trace organics
     in groundwater. Env. Sci. and Tech., 15:40–51.
4.   Freeze, R.A., J.A. Cherry (1979) Groundwater. Prentice-Hall,
     Inc., New Jersey.
5.   Loehr, R.C., W.J. Jewell, et al. (1979) Land Application of
     Wastes, Vols. I & II. Van Nostrand Reinhold Environmental En-
     gineering Series, New York.

ECOLOGICAL CONSTRAINTS ON GENETIC ENGINEERING

Martin Alexander

Laboratory of Soil Microbiology
Department of Agronomy
Cornell University
Ithaca, New York 14853

INTRODUCTION

The aim of this paper is to present, briefly to be sure, the views of a microbial ecologist with a strong practical bent. These views, I believe, have relevance to genetic engineering to control environmental pollutants. I shall point out several ways by which the chances of success can be increased and some of the problems that may be encountered.

Ecology has much to offer to the research and technology designed to develop genetic means to control environmental pollutants. Although much of ecology is not directed at issues of current environmental concern, a large literature is directed to practical problems that relate to the behavior of organisms and the interrelationships between organisms and environmental stresses. Some of the basic aspects of ecology are highly relevant and should be brought to bear in considerations being given to genetic approaches to minimize environmental pollution. Nevertheless, molecular geneticists, microbiologists, and biochemists have not applied ecological insights or turned to ecologists to assess whether that field has information and approaches that might be useful. It is also unfortunate that ecologists have not been significantly involved in devising technologies to minimize environmental problems arising from organic chemicals.

It is my purpose to address two issues. The first is the application of information from microbial ecology that should be useful in devising genetic approaches and microbial technologies to destroy chemical pollutants. In this area of my discussion, I shall deal with possible failure modes, that is, environmental or ecological problems that may result in failures in the currently used

151

genetic approaches. By focusing on failure modes, I do not want to
leave the impression that I am pessimistic about the use of modern
genetics for answering some major environmental problems; quite the
contrary. I believe that an approach involving genetics, microbiology, environmental engineering, and ecology will allow us to minimize the number of failures and maximize the number of successes.

My second issue is the possible ecological consequences of genetic engineering. The nay-sayers on the one side frequently have
been prophets of doom, whereas many of the proponents of the new
technologies have paid little attention to unpredictable effects of
novel technologies.

EFFECT OF CONCENTRATION

Pollutants are commonly distinguished on the basis of whether
they are derived from single, discrete sites (point sources) or from
multiple sites (nonpoint sources). Point sources include effluents
from factories that manufacture chemicals, for example, and nonpoint
sources include pesticides applied to agricultural land. The concentrations in the former instance are often high; those in the latter instance are almost invariably low. However, if a chemical derived from a point source is not readily destroyed, it may exist in
many areas at low levels as it is diluted in adjacent waterways or
moves through soil to enter groundwaters.

Microbiologists, molecular geneticists, and biochemists rarely
are concerned with concentrations in the ranges at which organic
pollutants occur in natural water or soils. They use substrates in
the range of several percent or, if they are adventuresome, high
parts-per-million range. Alas, such are not the levels commonly encountered in rivers, lakes, groundwaters, estuaries, soils, or sediments, and never in the open ocean. It was taken as incontrovert-
ible fact that reactions which occurred at the concentration convenient for the laboratory-oriented scientist would also take place in
nature. The rate might be slower, presumably in direct relationship
to the concentration, but all else would be the same.

Let us consider a few cases in point. First, no microorganism
has yet been shown to grow on a defined substrate at concentrations
at which pollutants are frequently of practical concern, such as
10 ppb (10 ng/ml). The data in Fig. 1, for example, show the microbial mineralization of a test chemical at low concentrations but not
at still lower concentration. If a microorganism will not grow at
low pollutant concentrations, genetically engineered strains may not
function in nature because it is probably not feasible to introduce
sufficient numbers to saturate the environment with the cataboli-
cally active cells. I do not mean to suggest that genetic engineering is useless in these circumstances; possibly genetics should be

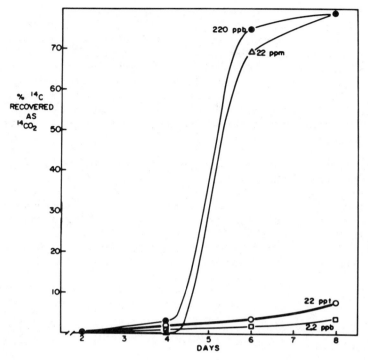

Fig. 1.   Mineralization of 2,4-D in stream water. Reproduced with
           permission of American Society of Microbiology from R. S.
           Boethling and M. Alexander (1979) Effect of concentration
           of organic chemicals on their biodegradation by natural
           microbial communities. <u>Appl. Environ. Microbiol.</u>
           37:1211-1216.

applied to oligotrophs, to species that grow on dissolved organic
carbon of waters, and to species that utilize humus of soil. Such
organisms are not in the present lists of pet species of microbiologists, molecular geneticists, and biochemists. If theirs is the
game, these microorganisms must be the players.

     Second, some chemicals in natural waters at ppb or ppt (ng or
pg/ml) levels are mineralized (that is, transformed to CO_2 and other
inorganic products), but carbon from the substrate is not converted
to microbial cells (2,12). If carbon is not assimilated, the species responsible for the biodegradation are not replicating at the
expense of their substrate. If they do not multiply using the test
substance as a carbon source, there will be no favoring in nature of
genetically modified isolates whose selective advantage is linked
with their growth on the substrate for which the genetic modification is being performed.

Third, although some chemicals are mineralized and destroyed in certain environments at the levels of concern in pollution control, no such reactions occur at the higher levels used in most laboratory investigations (8,12). The data in Fig. 2 indicate that the herbicide 2,4-D is mineralized in certain natural waters at levels below 0.2 μg/ml but not above. This suggests that success in the real world might be achieved if the laboratory scientists would begin their inquiries with knowledge of environmentally relevant levels rather than attempting to address the problem of concentration late in their studies.

Fourth, models of the rates of biodegradation and attempts to predict the persistence of pollutants, whether the process is brought about by natural or genetically engineered species, require information on kinetics. The kinetics of chemical transformations brought about by pure cultures of bacteria growing on high substrate concentrations are exponential. Few microbiologists question the sanctity of the classical bacterial growth curve. However, in natural environments, biodegradation of individual chemicals is sometimes linear (12) (Fig. 3), or it follows first-order kinetics (3), possibly second-order kinetics (6), or none of these patterns of breakdown. These differences are not trivial because conversions

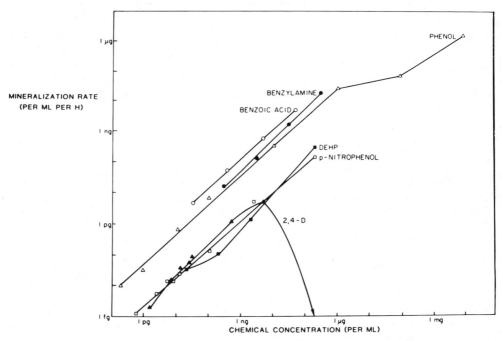

Fig. 2.   Mineralization in lake water of a range of concentrations of several organic compounds (8).

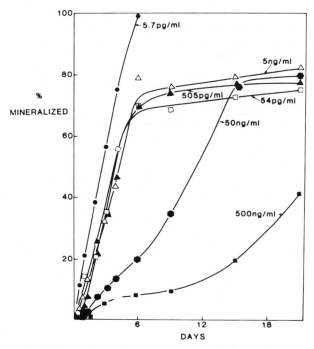

Fig. 3.   Aniline mineralization in White Lake water (12).

that follow these kinetics increase rapidly if they are exponential, remain constant if the process is linear, or decrease rapidly with time if the conversion is first-order.

STARVATION STRESS

The culture medium that is the elixir of life for our pet organisms is rich in nutrients. When the nutrient supply falls, the organisms are rushed to the refrigerator or into fresh media lest they fail to survive. Those species that fail to survive an occasional period of starvation stress are either elevated to the status of being perpetually pampered or are relegated to oblivion.

Rivers, lakes, soils, and sediments are poor in readily available nutrients. The organic matter levels are either very low or, if high, as in the case of soils, very little of that carbon is readily available to bacteria. These are the environments in which it is hoped to introduce many genetically engineered isolates. One can easily predict what will happen when a starvation-susceptible organism successfully completes its biodegradative work in such habitats: both the chemical and its destroyer will be gone. Loss of

the pollutant will surely be good for some environments and loss of
the active organisms undoubtedly is desired by companies seeking to
make profit by selling inoculants. However, for environments receiving pollutants intermittently and for municipalities and industries seeking to reduce the costs of pollution control; a more sen-
sible approach is to rely on starvation-resistant organisms.

    Assessing the tolerance of microorganisms to starvation is not
part of the research programs of specialists in genetic engineering.
Such evaluations are easy to perform, and starvation susceptibility
in culture appears to be correlated with susceptibility in nature.
Moreover, some of the species that have been the subject of considerable genetic inquiry are resistant to nutrient deprivation. The
results in Fig. 4 and 5 show the rapid decline in samples of natural

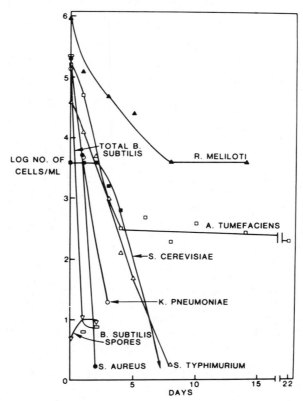

Fig. 4.   Survival of several bacteria in lake water. Reproduced
           with permission of American Society of Microbiology from
           L. N. Liang, J. L. Sinclair, L. M. Mallory, and M.
           Alexander (1982) Fate in model ecosystems of microbial
           species of potential use in genetic engineering. Appl.
           Environ. Microbiol. 44:708-714.

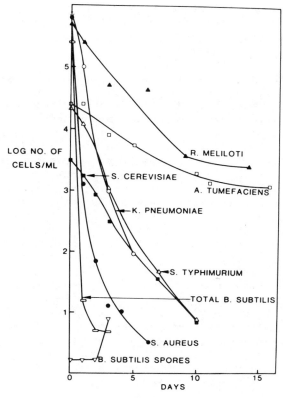

Fig. 5.   Survival of several bacteria in sewage. Reproduced with
           permission of American Society of Microbiology from L. N.
           Liang, J. L. Sinclair, L. M. Mallory, and M. Alexander
           (1982) Fate in model ecosystems of microbial species of
           potential use in genetic engineering. Appl. Environ.
           Microbiol. 44:708-714.

ecosystems of starvation-susceptible but not -resistant organisms.
This resistance was shown in recent studies. Nevertheless, caution
must be exercised because starvation-resistance appears to be necessary but not sufficient for persistence in nutrient-poor environments (9), so that, even if an organism can endure in the absence of
its nutrients, it may still be eliminated in nature.

PREDATION AS A STRESS

     Many natural ecosystems are populated by a variety of predators
able to feed on microorganisms. These predators include protozoa,
various metazoa, myxobacteria, and cellular slime molds. Although
the grazing habits of these predators are well documented, their

roles in modifying the activity of microorganisms that destroy pollutants has scarcely been explored. Let us examine their potential role in environments with high chemical concentrations and with low levels.

In an environment rich in readily utilizable organic nutrients, such as in sewage, bacterial populations are large. It is because of the very abundance of bacteria that the organic matter load in the waste water is quickly reduced. This abundance also is linked with active feeding by predators--in this instance, protozoa. Do these predators enhance or diminish the rates of microbial processes? The question has been addressed to some degree (10), but not with reference to the types and concentrations of chemicals that are important as pollutants. Suppose, however, an organism is introduced to carry out a specific, desired function. If protozoan grazing enhances its activity, all is for the best. However, these predators might reduce the activity or eliminate the introduced organisms. Such considerations appear to be entirely absent from discussions of genetic engineering for environmental improvement. However, even in the event that predators have a catastrophic effect on some introduced organisms, the impact of predators may be minimized or avoided by use of introduced species that withstand grazing. For example, although most species of free-living bacteria seem to be excellent prey for one or another member of the protozoan community; the same may not be true of bacteria that grow in flocs or that are retained on solid surfaces in waste-treatment units. Such problems of predation may be real and substantial, yet the means of overcoming the problems may be easily found.

Protozoa do not seem to be particularly active in nutrient-poor environments. The reason is probably that they need a high density of prey cells in order to feed and multiply. This density often is in the vicinity of 10^6 bacterial cells per ml (1). In environments poor in organic matter but which contain trace levels of synthetic chemicals, as in most natural waters, the density of bacterial prey is probably low; hence, protozoa are unlikely to affect the biodegradation.

On the other hand, an effect may occur if a polluting chemical is present at low levels in an environment rich in organic matter. Such an effect might not be expected because to support enough bacteria to reach the threshold prey density of about 10^6/ml, the pollutant must exist at an initial level of approximately 1 ppm ($1 \mu g/ml$). However, for the protozoan, the theshold is not ca. 10^6/ml for one bacterium but rather for all prey bacteria. The predator feeds with a low degree of discrimination both on the organisms of interest and on cells that serve as an alternate prey, and it continues to feed until the prey density falls to the threshold value. Under these conditions, an introduced bacterium may thus be eliminated (Figs. 6 and 7). In view of the likelihood of

predation being a major ecological constraint on microorganisms inoculated into municipal and industrial waste-treatment systems as
well as other environments, means should be found to overcome or
minimize predation as a stress to genetically engineered organisms.

Microbiologists have a vast literature on bacteriophages. However, parasitism by these viruses is also dependent on the density
of the bacteria that sustain them. This density appears to be reasonably high (Fig. 8) (1,13). Moreover, differing from protozoa,
which feed on a range of bacteria, bacteriophages are highly host
specific and attack only individual strains or species. Therefore,
it is unlikely that bacteriophages have a significant impact on the
organisms responsible for the biodegradation of most synthetic organic pollutants at low concentrations.

PHYSICAL BARRIERS

Microorganisms, by definition, are small. Hence, to the microbiologist whose professional efforts are not directed to ecological
issues, they can be transported readily and for long distances. The
history of water-borne epidemics attests to the ease of bacterial
dissemination. However, soils are a striking contrast to waters.
The pores in soils are minute, and clay and colloidal organic matter coupled with the small pores impede the movement of nearly all

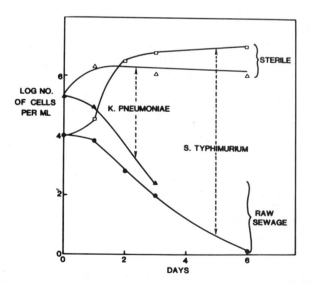

Fig. 6.   Changes in populations of two bacteria in raw and filter-
          sterilized sewage. From L. M. Mallory, R. M. Goldstein,
          and M. Alexander (unpublished data).

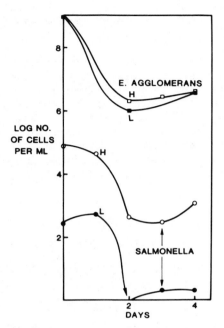

Fig. 7.   Tetrahymena feeding on enterobacter at high (H) and low
           (L) numbers of salmonella (4).

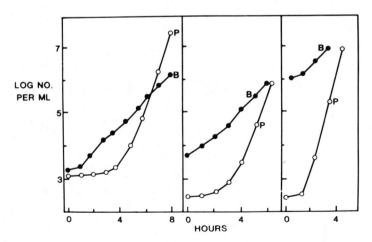

Fig. 8.   Replication of bacteriophage 80α (P) on three initial
           densities of Staphylococcus aureus (B) (13).

cells of an introduced population. A distance as short as a few
centimeters may be too great in habitats with these barriers. Even
a highly sandy soil, which has large pores and little colloidal
material, impedes the movement of nearly all cells added to it at
individual sites; the impedance in this case may be associated with
the tortuous twists and turns that an organism must undergo to accomplish any appreciable transport through these pores. Admittedly,
a few cells will be moved passively for some distance, but these
probably are transported through channels left by burrowing inverte-
brates and plant roots and through cracks that appear in soil as a
result of abiotic factors such as wetting and drying. The data in
Table 1 show the inconsequential extent of movement of Rhizobium
through soil and the few cells that are moved. Cells are restricted
in movement; they may grow where they alight, but they do not dis-
tribute themselves widely or homogeneously through the soil matrix.
The same considerations probably apply to sediments.

    Let us consider the case of a water-soluble synthetic chemical
that moves quickly through soil. Many chemicals behave in this way,
especially if they are not cationic and hence are not retained by
the negatively charged soil colloids. Such chemicals pass downward
through the soil, but few cells of an inoculum strain will be able
to follow the substrate under conditions that prevail in the field;
that is, in soils that have some depth, as they nearly all do, and
which are not mixed, as they are only occasionally. Of the few
cells that are transported, these individuals will multiply in their
newly found haven and destroy the chemical, but the organisms are
locked within a microhabitat, and they will not act on the bulk of
the chemical present in this environment.

Table 1. Movement of R. japonicum to various soil depths after
          inoculation at surface. From E. L. Madsen and M.
          Alexander (1982) Transport of Rhizobium and Pseudomonas
          through soil. Soil Sci. Soc. Am. J. 46:557-560.

| | No./g soil | | | | | |
Depth	Un treated	Soy-bean	Earth-worm	0.5 cm water	Plant & water	Worm & water
2.8-4.2	0	0	5	100	6500	1000
4.3-5.7	0	0	50	0	1300	400
5.8-7.2	0	0	50	0	10	300
7.3-10.0	0	0	8	0	0	0

Count at 0.0-2.7 cm: 3 to X 10^5/g

Hopefully, this pessimistic view of the success of soil inoculation is incorrect. The available data suggest that it is not.

SORBED CHEMICALS

A general rule for microbiologists is to grow cultures in media in which all constituents are fully soluble in water. A few hardy souls introduce water-insoluble substrates such as aliphatic hydrocarbons or cellulose, but these investigators are clearly in the minority. In contrast with these ideal circumstances, an untold number of organic compounds, although quite soluble in water, are not in the liquid phase in natural ecosystems, at least not to a significant extent. These chemicals are retained by the clays and colloidal organic matter of soils or sediments, the sludge and flocs of sewage, or the organic detritus of natural waters. In this form, much or nearly all of certain organic substrates is not readily available, even when the same compound in solution is metabolized quickly and completely. Such compounds often constitute special pollution problems because they are transported for considerable distances with eroding soil particles, river sediments, or dredge materials, or because of difficulties in their final disposal if retained by sewage sludge.

The microbiology of sorbed substrates has been almost totally ignored. A few studies have shown that some sorbed compounds are mineralized or that only a part of the sorbed chemical is mineralized by the existing populations (5,11). Although physical barriers may prevent contact between sorbed chemicals and active microorganisms in soils and sediments in situ, reasonably frequent contact between organism and pollutant is possible in systems that are mixed, as in sewage during aerobic treatment. Achieving success with novel genotypes obviously requires a better knowledge of the microbiology of these sorbed molecules, but ultimate success in this area would contribute greatly to minimize water pollution.

ABIOTIC STRESSES

Microbial ecologists are aware of the major importance of abiotic factors. Individual organisms may be eliminated by the lethal action of sunlight, salts, toxic metals, extremes of temperature, sulfide levels, etc. In one study, for example, a test compound was found to be destroyed only slowly in sewage (Fig. 9) (L. M. Mallory, R. Morrison, and M. Alexander, unpublished data). An organism was then isolated that rapidly mineralized the chemical in culture. Addition of that organism to nonsterile sewage did not result in enhanced decomposition. The reason: abiotic factors present in sewage (i.e., found in sterile sewage) prevented the organism from

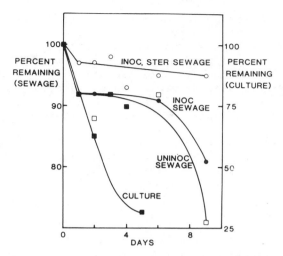

Fig. 9.   Degradation of 10 μg 2,4-dichlorophenol/ml in sewage and
culture. From L. M. Mallory, R. M. Goldstein, and M.
Alexander (unpublished data).

functioning. The composition of the microbial community of any ecosystem is governed by these factors as well as by biological stresses, and a species unable to cope with all of the ambient stresses
will not survive, or if it survives, it will not grow.

Nevertheless, it seems to be commonly held that if a bacterium
grows at 30°C in the dark in rich media in the absence of the inorganic toxicants so common in polluted environments, the same organism will not only endure in nature but it will flourish there. This
approach does not go far in solving practical problems.

ORGANISMS OF CHOICE

It is my contention that for the control of environmental pollution, the organisms to be used must be selected to have not only
the correct catabolic potential but also the full array of ecologically important traits needed for success in nature. One without the
other is worthless. Possibly, it would be more appropriate to do
the genetic manipulation on the ecologically important traits rather
than on those related to catabolic function. Biodegradative activities may be more widespread in the microbial realm than are the
traits needed for ecological success.

For nutrient-poor environments, oligotrophs (7) could be
selected rather than the eutrophic species most of us study. For

habitats in which the pollutant concentration is below the threshold that allows for growth, organisms could be chosen that could use the natural organic nutrients, and possibly some, as they grow at the expense of the natural products, also would metabolize synthetic molecules. In environments where predation is a major stress, floc-forming bacteria or species protected by sorption to surfaces could be used. Where salinity, sunlight, or other abiotic factors are significant, strains resistant to such stresses could be utilized.

The answer, thus, will not come solely from genetic engineer-ing. It will come from a mixture of that discipline together with a strong infusion of good, new-fashioned ecology.

ECOLOGICAL HAZARDS

My comments so far have been those of a believer in the poten-tial usefulness of genetic engineering for minimizing environmental pollution. My views are obviously those of a microbial ecologist who has little knowledge of modern genetics, its methodologies, and its problems. Let me now approach, again from the point of view of an ecologist, a different facet of the use of genetic engineering--its possible hazards. (Some of these remarks were presented recent-ly to the House of Representatives Subcommittees on Science, Re-search and Technology and on Investigations and Oversight.)

Some interesting generalizations appear if one reviews the his-tory of new technologies. In most instances, the risks of these technologies were not initially evident, but they became quite clear as the technology became widespread. Often, the risk occurred at a very low frequency, but the impact was quite large. Antibiotics revolutionized our approach to chemotherapy, but a significant num-ber of people suffered severe and often irreversible consequences from the use of these drugs. DDT prevented an enormous amount of human misery and widespread mortality resulting from insect vectors of human, animal, and crop diseases, but the harmful effect of this insecticide became evident with time. The Industrial Revolution im-proved our standard of living and provided materials which would never have been available otherwise, but it was the prelude to air pollution. Atomic energy offers enormous promise where fuels for energy production are in short supply, but many people feel that the dangers are quite substantial. The proponents of these technolo-gies, any many others that could be cited, minimized or ignored the risks in the past or still do so. The lure of major benefits from these new technologies has been so great that their proponents have been unwilling to consider the possible undesirable consequences. Few, if any, major technologies have been introduced without some untoward effect.

I, for one, do not know whether there will or will not be unde-sirable ecological consequences arising from the deliberate release of new genotypes into waters and soils, but I am bothered by the historical precedents. The likelihood of untoward ecological damage is probably small, but can we say it is zero? How small a probability of risk should be entertained without any guidelines, restrictions, or regulations? If a new genotype is deliberately released to perform some useful environmental function, and it grows to do what is expected of it, what is the probability that it will make contact with a species that it can harm and that the new genotype will bring about some deleterious change?

It is frequently stated that the slight changes arising from genetic engineering will not alter the harmfulness of organisms. To a non-geneticist, it seems that slight genetic changes, admittedly induced in the era before genetic engineering, can bring about major modifications in the potential harmfulness of some microorganisms. The changes that modify the antigenicity of the influenza virus become evident in the low immunity in humans exposed to the virus. Slight modifications in the metabolism of pathogens make them resistant to the drugs used for their control, so that antibiotics and other chemotherapeutic agents are no longer effective. The slight genetic changes that result in a capsule to be formed around certain bacteria make them resistant to the defense mechanisms of humans and animals.

We have no history of the effects of genotypes created by man. However, much is known about deleterious effects of new genotypes that have arisen spontaneously. Such new organisms become prominent because they possess some selective advantage. Thus, the use of antibiotics allowed for the widespread occurrence of new genotypes of the organisms causing gonorrhea and staphyloccocal infections. The use of fungicides in agriculture has allowed new genotypes of plant pathogens to proliferate and have harmful effects on major crops. Similarly, the influenza virus presumably undergoes regular genetic changes in nature, and these genetic changes lead to the widespread dissemination of the virus, periodically with large numbers of human deaths; here, the selective advantage of the new genotype is not obvious. It is difficult for me to see why a man-made genetic change would necessarily behave any differently from those occurring spontaneously in nature: it too could proliferate, spread, and do harm to susceptible humans, animals, or plants, or to microorganisms important to natural environmental functions. Obviously, no responsible scientist would knowingly bring about such changes, but what is our degree of assuredness that they will not occur? A risk of absolute zero can probably never be assumed, but regulatory agencies and the public at large need some assessment of how small is a small risk.

Disasters arising from introduced microorganisms are well known. Ceratocystis ulmi, the fungus causing Dutch elm disease, in a few years nearly wiped out the population of susceptible trees. The fungus Endothia parasitica is estimated to have eliminated most

chestnuts from 50,000,000 acres of the United States in only a few
years. In the 1970s, <u>Helminthosporium</u> spread rapidly through the
corn crop of the United States, and the disease induced is estimated
to have reduced the corn yield in this country by 10 percent, clearly a major impact. The myxoma virus deliberately introduced into
Australia nearly wiped out the rabbit population of that country.
Influenza affects many humans each year, but when a new genetic variant of the influenza virus appeared in 1918, millions of people
were killed. In most but not all such instances, the microorganisms
did not represent new genotypes, but rather they were existing organisms that moved to a new environment. The reason I cite these
well known epidemiological facts is to illustrate that a microorganism having the capacity to grow in nature (as is our aim in environmental use of new genotypes) may, if it makes contact with an appropriate host, spread rapidly through the host population and cause
disastrous changes.

Probably thousands of species of plants and animals have been
introduced deliberately into a region or a specific country, and
these introduced populations did not become established. The exotic
organisms usually died out. During the colonization of the Western
Hemisphere and of Africa, many attempts were made to establish species in environments in which they were initially absent. I feel
confident that if asked, the person in these earlier days who would
be introducing a new plant or animal would cite these many failures.
A perfectly reasonable statement might be that, "I know of no evidence that species introduced to do one thing would escape, do something I did not intend of them, and cause damage." Based upon the
bulk of the available evidence, most of us would agree. I can ima-
gine just a statement from a person introducing an exotic plant to
control erosion, or insects to produce a silk substitute in a limited area. On the other hand, if that introduced plant is kudzu, or
the introduced insect is the gypsy moth, both of which have done
enormous harm to natural ecosystems, one might see why some ecologists would be concerned about the introductions.

Fortunately, there are no illustrations of genetically engineered species causing harm. Hopefully, we never will have an illus-
tration. Nevertheless, meaningful tests of the probabilities of
these changes have not yet been performed. The prudent course of
action is to establish the risks and develop procedures to assess
deleterious effects. Procedures do not now exist to measure deleterious effects of microorganisms on natural populations at low
cost, but there has not been a significant amount of research to develop such procedures.

CONCLUSION

It is my firm belief that genetic approaches have much to offer
to help minimize or overcome problems of environmental pollution.
The potential approaches and the range of genetic material available

are truly large. Research and subsequent technology will surely find many areas where environmental problems can be solved by these new methods. However, it is critical that the chances of success be increased by applying information from microbial ecology and, indeed, by employing ecological approaches that will aid in accomplishing the successful introduction of genotypes able to destroy unwanted chemicals.

One must also consider the likelihood, however small, that there may be unexpected and undesired consequences from the release of novel genotypes into natural ecosystems. At this time, there are few convincing reasons to propose that some new genotype will, or will not, cause a detrimental effect in addition to bringing about the desired changes. Our topic at this meeting reflects in part the fact that chemists and the chemical manufacturing industry were not sufficiently aware of some of the difficulties associated with large-scale chemical production and use to foresee the consequences of inadvertent or deliberate releases of organic compounds into natural ecosystems.

With a meaningful blending of ecology with other scientific as well as engineering disciplines, I am convinced that much progress will be made in reducing environmental pollution by the application of appropriate microbial technologies. I grant you that ecology in the era of molecular biology occasionally appears as a scientific anomaly. Moreover, to the laboratory-oriented scientist, a natural ecosystem is, at best, an enigma. However, if you plan to modify the anomaly that is our science and cope with the enigma that is our working place, it might also be prudent to learn some of the confusing rules that govern our game.

REFERENCES

1. Alexander, M. (1981) Why microbial predators and parasites do not eliminate their prey and hosts. Annu. Rev. Microbiol. 35:113–133.
2. Larson, R.J. (1980) Role of biodegradation kinetics in predicting environmental fate. In Biotransformation and Fate of Chemicals in the Aquatic Environment, A.W. Maki, K.L. Dickson, and J. Cairns, Jr., eds. American Society for Microbiology, Washington, pp. 67–86.
3. Larson, R.J., and L.M. Games (1981) Biodegradation of linear alcohol ethoxylates in natural waters. Environ. Sci. Technol. 15:1488–1493.
4. Mallory, L.M., C.-S. Yuk, L.-N. Liang, and M. Alexander Appl. Environ. Microbiol. (in press).
5. Moyer, J.R., R.J. Hance, and C.E. McKone (1972) The effect of adsorbents on the rate of degradation of herbicides incubated with soil. Soil Biol. Biochem. 4:307–311.
6. Paris, D.F., W.C. Steen, G.L. Baughman, and J.T. Barnett, Jr. (1981) Second-order model to predict microbial degradation of

organic compounds in natural waters. Appl. Environ. Microbiol. 41:603-609.

7. Poindexter, J.S. (1981) Oligotrophy: Fast and famine exist-
    ence. Adv. Microb. Ecol. 5:63-89.

8. Rubin, H.E., R.V. Subba-Rao, and M. Alexander (1982) Rates of
    mineralization of trace concentrations of aromatic compounds in
    lake water and sewage samples. Appl. Environ. Microbiol.
    43:1133-1138.

9. Sinclair, J.L., and M. Alexander (manuscript in preparation).

10. Stout, J.D. (1980) The role of protozoa in nutrient cycling and
    energy flow. Adv. Microb. Ecol. 4:1-50.

11. Subba-Rao, R.V., and M. Alexander (1982) Effect of sorption on
    mineralization of low concentrations of aromatic compounds in
    lake water. Appl. Environ. Microbiol. 44:659-668.

12. Subba-Rao, R.V., H.E. Rubin, and M. Alexander (1982) Kinetics
    and extent of mineralization of organic compounds at trace
    levels in freshwater and sewage. Appl. Environ. Microbiol.
    43:1139-1150.

13. Wiggins, B.A., and M. Alexander (manuscript in preparation).

PANEL DISCUSSION: VULNERABILITY OF ECOSYSTEMS

A. M. Chakrabarty, University of Illinois
Rita Colwell, University of Maryland
Gordon H. Orians (Moderator), University of Washington
James A. Shapiro, University of Illinois
James Staley, University of Washington
Andrew Weightman, Université de Genève

G. ORIANS: The panelists doubtless include people who are
stimulated, outraged, and infuriated by the comments of our keynote
speaker!

J. SHAPIRO: I have to confess to a certain feeling of confu-
sion. I study bacteria in the laboratory, and even there I think
that our understanding of how the bacteria do what they do is minimal compared to the magnitude of the problems. When we address
questions like we're addressing here, we have to realize that we are
really groping in the dark.

I am confused at four levels. First, at a scientific level, a
lot of organisms can metabolize compounds that are man-made and
which we presume have not existed before in nature. I am confused
as to where the information that allows the bacteria to do this
comes from. That is an exciting question because we might learn
something about evolution through studying these organisms.

Second, I am confused when I hear presentations such as Dr.
Alexander's about the complexities of understanding what organisms
do in natural ecosystems. To me, that is just an incredibly complicated "black box." I have trouble understanding what happens in my
petri dishes in the laboratory where I think I can control many
things. What is happening in estuaries and in soils is an enormous
enigma; it is very, very complicated.

Third, I am a little confused on the issue of release of the
organisms that we engineer to degrade some of these compounds. I
think that the concern expressed about these organisms is probably a

169

"red herring." There are real reasons for concern about certain kinds of experiments that can be done, especially where we take infectious agents and link them up, creating new means of propagating them through genetic engineering research. However, when we take the metabolic capabilities of soil organisms and, keeping them in the soil organisms, rearrange them in ways that we know can happen in nature, I have great difficulty in seeing why that is going to be a problem. Nevertheless, I admit we are ignorant about these systems.

Finally, based on what was said by the EPA Regional Administrator at the opening session of this conference, I am not sure what people see as the scientist's role in public discussion about these questions. I am confused as to whether officials think that scientists should be purely technicians and make technical recommendations and let other people make the decisions, or whether we are permitted to be equal citizens and full participants in public discussions.

A. WEIGHTMAN: I appear to be stuck between poles in the views expressed by other speakers. Dr. Middleton wanted organisms to withstand high concentrations of toxic pollutants in order to degrade them, while Dr. Alexander is dealing with problems of organisms surviving in very low concentrations of substrates. Dr. Alexander advances the problem of what it may take for an organism to be successful at all in the environment and the possibility that, if that organism is successful, would it overtake all other organisms or otherwise present ecological hazards within the environment.

As a geneticist, I look at the genes of microorganisms in an attempt to piece together catabolic pathways within a laboratory microorganism. I do not think that it is fair to equate a laboratory microorganism with a "pet species" that goes out into real life off the petri plate. In our laboratory we are dealing with organisms that have been isolated recently from the soil, and which are pretty well uncharacterized. Hopefully, these organisms will be engineered and reintroduced into the soil. The fact that they were isolated from the soil presumably means that they survived in that environment somehow despite the starvational stresses, low concentrations, predation, and physical barriers. With regard to adsorption of chemicals, I see no problem dealing with substrates that are not soluble in aqueous solution. We are dealing with naphthalenes and with several solvents. I think that the gene pool within these sorts of microorganisms can be used effectively to extend the metabolic capabilities of the microorganisms. It has to be a stepwise process. The studies that we are undertaking and, as far as I am aware, those that other laboratories are undertaking, are only on the first rung of the ladder. I would like to address myself more to questions of the survival of these organisms in the environment, but I feel more compelled to deal with the first questions first, and to look at the potential for genetic manipulation of soil microorganisms. I do not foresee any insurmountable problems in re-introducing microorganisms that have just been isolated from the soil back into their environment.

J. STALEY: First, I believe much good can come from the use of genetically engineered microorganisms in the area of environmental pollution. I am not too concerned about undesirable effects caused by some newly engineered strain wreaking havoc in the environment, though there is certainly a possibility, as Dr. Alexander has point-ed out. I would be much more concerned in this respect with the use of genetic engineering in the manipulation of the human genome or in the transfer of characteristics from one kingdom to another kingdom. Thus, as I see it, with regard to pollution control, the major ques-tions are not primarily ethical questions, but technical questions. And the foremost of these questions is, can the engineered organism with the appropriate traits survive in the environment and perform its desired activity? It is one thing to engineer $E.$ $coli$ to pro-duce insulin in the laboratory, but quite another to introduce a genetically engineered bacterium into a natural environment.

This is much less of a problem if we are talking about some sort of manmade treatment system, a semicontained environment, like a wastewater treatment system. Here, one can control the process to a large extent, as well as the organisms that are introduced. Gen-erally, concentrations of nutrients are relatively high, and a lot of the problems Dr. Alexander addressed are not real problems. I think it is in these semicontained systems that genetic engineering can play a very promising role.

For the more difficult situations of the natural soil and aqua-tic habitats, I would like to suggest a general approach for devel-oping strains suitable for genetic engineering. First, it is logi-cal to get the organism of choice from the habitat. It is likely that more genomic features are necessary to enable an organism from a habitat to survive there than can be readily genetically engi-neered, at least initially. So I would start with an organism from the habitat. Before it is genetically engineered, it would be im-portant to determine its physiological features in the laboratory, as these may preclude its selection. For example, one would hope to obtain an isolate that could grow well in the environment and simi-lar environments under the widest possible range of conditions of pH, temperature, water availability, and so forth. Such a strain would be useful, therefore, in a variety of similar habitats.

Furthermore, we want a strain that is not only a seasonally im-portant organism, but an organism that is going to be able to grow and be important in the habitat in the year-round situation. By consideration of such features, strain selection can be made, and the strain can then be engineered to acquire the appropriate traits

with which you wish to endow it. I hasten to add that genetic engineering may not be as important in these cases of environmental
pollution as old-fashioned strain selection and mutagenesis, which
could play a very important role.

The next step would be to test the strain of choice by using
microcosms and similar laboratory testing devices to see whether or
not the strain really works before you go to the field situation.
On the matter of oligotrophy, I certainly share Dr. Alexander's concerns about the problems of low concentrations at which the toxic
compounds would be expected to be found in many environments. The
oligotroph is a possible solution; however, it may be somewhat pre-
mature. Obligate oligotrophs are organisms that cannot grow to a
visible turbidity in the laboratory. I am not aware that any of
these strains have been well characterized. There are some facultative oligotrophs that can be grown and manipulated in the laboratory. But, at the present time, only the best physiologist would be
able to cultivate and study the obligate oligotrophs.

R. COLWELL: We have discovered over the past year a phenomenon
which may change our views about oligotrophy, viability, and recoverability of bacteria in natural waters. For example, if one monitors the number of Escherichia coli cells in sea water over a 3-week
period, the typical "die off" of E. coli is observed by the plate
counting method. Eventually, no recoverable cells will be detectable. But, in fact, if the technique of epifluorescent microscopy
is used for direct counting, there isn't any change in cell number
at all. We have done such studies with Vibrio cholerae and E. coli
[Xu, Huai-Shu, N. Roberts, F.L. Singleton, R.W. Attwell, D.J.
Grimes, and R.R. Colwell (1982) Survival and viability of nonicultur-
able Escherichia coli and Vibrio cholerae in the estuarine and marine environment. Microb. Ecol. 8:257-262]

Furthermore, if an immune serum linked to a fluorescent stain
(in place of the acridine orange stain) is substituted, intact, viable cells are observed even though they do not grow on agar or in
broth. Indeed, the direct counts do not change, even though a "die-
off" by plate count is observed. One might conclude that these
cells, seen under a microscope as intact cells, are not necessarily
viable cells. However, using the method of Kogure et al., [Kogure,
K., U. Simidu, and N. Taga (1979) A tentative direct microscopic
method for counting living bacteria. Can. J. Microbiol. 25:415-
420], it can be shown that these bacteria remain viable, even if
unable to grow on the usual laboratory media. If these cells are
collected on a filter of 0.2 μ pore size, the filter can be placed
in a salts solution for 6 or more hours. The salts solution should
contain a small amount of yeast extract and nalidixic acid. The
latter prevents cells from dividing, but allows them to enlarge as
they take up substrate. Under the microscope, the cells, even

though nonculturable by routine plating methods, will enlarge and
grow. If the suspension of cells is mixed, in a separate experiment, with radiolabeled acetate or glutamate, utilization of the
substrate can be shown by release of $^{14}CO_2$. Thus, these bacteria
undergo a "nonrecoverable stage," but maintain viability. We have
observed this phenomenon for Salmonella spp. suspended in Potomac
River water, E. coli in sea water, and Vibrio cholerae in distilled
water and in Chesapeake Bay water. Thus, we have cases of not being
able to recover cells that are actually alive, even metabolizing
substrates, but not growing on routine laboratory media. The evidence given by Dr. Alexander and his conclusion that some substrates
simply are not being utilized because the cells don't proliferate,
may in some cases, really be rapidly metabolizing and proliferating
cells, but not recoverable cells, using presently available methods.
Thus, recoverability must be separated from viability because cells
may remain viable, but not be recoverable.

With regard to some of the other points raised by Dr.
Alexander, it would seem that those cells showing long generation
times, reported to be about several hundred hours or days long, may
be organisms that are in the mini-cell, "round body" state. In the
marine environment, these cells are essentially endogenously respir-
ing, and present very long generation times. Again, we must differentiate those microorganisms that are culturable and those that are
not. Those microorganisms growing in situ, i.e., in the natural
environment, are not the same as microorganisms growing in a petri
dish.

It may not always be wrong to use high concentrations of substrate to test for biodegradative capacity of a mixed culture or
pure culture system. Heterotrophic potential has long been measured
using elevated concentrations of a given substrate, i.e., concentrations not found in sea water or fresh water in nature, mainly to
determine whether the microorganisms can respond sufficiently to
degrade the allochthonous compound. Obviously, there are concentrations above which one would not choose to use in a test medium. For
example, it has been demonstrated that there are some concentrations
of materials in the environment, that are present at such high concentrations that cells cannot degrade the material when, if they
were presented in the material at lower concentrations, the bacteria
would utilize it.

We have done some mixed culture studies, including bacteria,
fungi, and ciliated protozoa, which show interesting successions
occurring in the environment. For example, in the initial stages of
oil degradation, bacterial populations increase significantly in
size; usually the bacteria are readily able to utilize simple alkanes in oil. After 2 or 3 weeks of exposure of the natural water
sample to which oil was added in a microcosm system, the autochthonous yeasts become dominant, being able to utilize the long chain-

alkanes and more complex hydrocarbon components of the oil. After 1
or 2 months, the autochthonous fungi in the natural water sample
gain ascendency, being able to utilize the more recalcitrant molecules. Thus, succession is important, in terms of biodegradation in
natural systems, a phenomenon we should consider.

With regard to protozoans, we must also remember that they do,
in fact, carry out some substrate conversions and can carry the
original and/or converted substrates into the higher levels of the
food chain and/or web. One can readily show metals and other potentially toxic substances being accumulated by bacteria which, in
turn, are grazed upon by ciliates; the ciliates, in turn, being
grazed upon by copepods; and the latter eventually consumed by fish
larvae. Thus, metals or toxic compounds can be carried through the
food chain and into the food web [Berk, S.G., and R.R. Colwell
(1981) Transfer of mercury through a marine microbial food web. J.
Exp. Marine Biol. and Ecol. 52:157-172]. Thus, we need to know at
what stage these conversions occur and/or whether or not transport
into the higher levels of the food chain occurs. What has been em-
phasized in this conference are abiotic stresses. Dr. Alexander has
pointed out several abiotic stresses to be considered, including
temperature and salinity. In the ocean, one must consider hydrostatic pressure, as well. If toxic chemicals are dumped into the
deeper parts of the ocean, the hydrostatic pressure can be such that
terrestrial microorganisms cannot function. For example, E. coli,
at 180 atm. pressure--that occurring at 1,800 meters depth--may not
be able to metabolize substrates. Thus, if we wish to use the ocean
as a dumping site, genetically engineered marine bacteria are better
agents of biodegradation since they are more likely to be barotoler-
ant, functioning also very well at low temperatures and elevated
salinities relative to microorganisms in fresh water systems.

This is a serious problem which deserves attention from genetic
engineers. Marine bacteria should be relied upon to degrade toxic
wastes in the ocean, not the terrestrial forms in the waste itself.
I would point out, as others have, that the microorganisms should be
from the natural environment. Thus, the genes involved in growth of
marine bacteria in the natural environment should be cloned into -
terrestrial bacteria or we should clone those genes that are involved in degradation into marine bacteria. With these genes transferred to marine bacteria, the engineered marine bacteria can then
serve as inoculum for the waste. The result is, we will have bacteria found to occur naturally in the environment able to degrade
the wastes. We should be looking at organisms like Vibrio spp. that
are found in the ocean, and naturally occurring therein, rather than
bacteria from soil, if degradation is to be carried out in the
ocean. Thus, microorganisms such as Beggiatoa, Cytophaga, and Myxobacteria, not familiar to E. coli workers and for which there is not
yet much information about their genetic systems, are of real interest. This is where the rich "mother lode" of genetic material will

derive for the kinds of activities we need to engineer for the natural environment.

We may want to question whether we should bother with whole cells, if we have all these problems of dealing with living cells in the natural environment. Why not just clone the genes, produce the enzymes, and throw away the "bag" that the genes came in. Immobilize the enzymes that are produced for waste treatment. Thus, we would use the genetic material, i.e., the genes, to produce the enzymes for degradation.

I find it a bit amusing to observe the concern raised about the release of genetically engineered organisms in the environment. We have been engineering such organisms over the past several decades. In any harbor, like Baltimore Harbor, which I know very well, we are unknowingly engineering organisms every day. By discharging sewage waste, heavy metals, hydrocarbons, etc., into a single receiving water body, we thereby place selective pressures on microorganisms entering with those wastes and on microorganisms which naturally occur in that body of water. It has been shown that transfer of drug resistance genes from E. coli to Vibrio parahaemolyticus can occur, the latter being a naturally occurring organism in Chesapeake Bay and a potential human pathogen. There are probably many other genes being transferred that we don't know about. So we are already engineering organisms simply because the organisms are picking up "survival genes," allowing them to survive in an environment where certain substances, like heavy metals, have to be dealt with. Thus, we are changing the genetic constitution of these bacteria by introducing genetic material via plasmids. It is very likely that there are new pathogens emerging from such waste disposal practices, i.e., bacteria, picking up "invasive genes," i.e., genes coding for proteases, elastases, depolymerases, and perhaps even toxin-producing genes. Thus, microorganisms that survive in wastes containing increased concentrations of heavy metals, and other toxic chemicals, may pick up plasmids carrying genes involved in detoxifying the wastes but the plasmids may also be carrying genes coding for toxin production or other traits that are potentially harmful for humans. So we may be enhancing the invasiveness of bacteria in these situations, of which we are not aware. The "new pathogens" may be nothing more than old pathogens with new information! These are aspects of microbial ecology we should pay attention to and try to understand better.

I would also suggest that it is appropriate to study what I would term "survival genes" in bacteria, i.e., those genes enabling microorganisms to survive in given environments whereby they outcompete other microorganisms. What it comes down to, and of course this is the fundamental basis of microbial ecology, is that a strategy of survival exists for microorganisms which they develop in given environments. Basic information about the microbial ecology

of such situations is needed, especially community structure, species diversity, and the taxonomy of microorganisms found in the
natural environment. If we don't know the species composition of
natural systems, we will not be able to learn much about interactions of microorganisms in the natural environment. Knowledge of
cell-cell interactions is lacking, not interactions of one E. coli
cell with another, but the interactions of E. coli with Beggiatoa
spp. or interactions of Myxobacteria with E. coli and Vibrio spp.,
and other organisms found in the environment. It is irreverent, I
suppose, to say that we know very little about the "real" bacteria
in nature, i.e., the odd and unusual generic types such as Beggiatoa, Vitreoscilla, Acinetobacter, Moraxella, and Cyanobacteria spp.
We need to understand the activities of these organisms under in
situ conditions. Chemostats are helpful, but we need to know the
processes that occur in situ, at low nutrient concentrations, and
under conditions of low temperature, high salinity, and high pressure. A lot of basic microbial ecology is necessary, especially by
creative application of microbial ecology, deduced from natural ecosystems.

Finally, we need to develop a construct analogous to a "synthetic cow," whereby controlled mixtures of substrate and paired or
multiple combinations of microorganisms from the natural environment
are monitored for substrate conversions, both synthesis and degradation, in serriation using microcosms.

New ideas for recovery of materials via waste treatment are
needed, especially for considering waste treatment as resource recycling. Many heavy metals, such as vanadium, titanium, cobalt,
chromium, and others of strategic importance, could be recovered
from domestic and industrial wastes. Methane is presently lost in
uncontrolled digestions but could be a source of energy. It is also
possible that steroids and other products could be recovered from
wastes so that we can then use the waste as a resource, rather than
to create a societal problem, by discharge into the environment.

Finally, we should develop a strategy for dealing with accidental spills or deliberate discharge of wastes in the environment.
Site-specific microorganisms should be employed, that is, microorganisms from those sites where the spills and/or discharges occur
and capable of surviving and returning to their natural proportion
in the community structure after degradation of the waste. At the
present time, discharge of waste occurs and the allochthonous microorganisms in the waste itself or the naturally occurring bacteria
are relied upon to degrade the wastes. It would be better to engineer microorganisms to degrade wastes that are to be discharged at
sea or at land sites, using microorganisms from the given site as
the agents of degradation. The microorganisms should return to
their proportional representation in the natural system after the
spill or discharge is cleared. Introduction of foreign microorgan-

isms is not necessary, only the introduction of specific genes or
gene complexes into the bacteria, permitting the bacteria to carry
out the degradative processes desired, and resuming their natural
"place" in the ecosystem when the toxic chemical "pressure" sub-
sides, upon degradation and/or mineralization.

In the future, I predict activities of microorganisms in paired
or multiple combinations of cultures will be able to be controlled
and applied for a variety of tasks. As microbial ecology develops,
combinations of microbial species will yield new products and new
processes. However, the ecology of mixed cultures remains to be
understood.

In summary, microbial ecology is in a rapid growth phase, with
regard to gaining an understanding of processes occurring in the
natural environment. Control of such populations represents a challenge. Naturally occurring organisms for which genetic systems are
not yet known, as well as the interactions of these organisms with
protozoa and algae need to be studied. Treatment of discharges,
whether accidental or deliberate, will require use of microorganisms
with the capacity to function in a given site, whether it be the
Sargasso Sea, the Sahara Desert, or Tierra del Fuego, and with a
"self-destructing" capability. That is, the microorganisms at the
given sites are engineered to carry the genes needed for degradation. Once the wastes are degraded, the microorganisms resume their
proportional representation in the microbial community.

The future for microbial ecology is particularly exciting at
this time, when the tools of biotechnology are available, and readily applied. Wise use of these tools and clever application in microbial ecology should provide an entirely new and exciting dimension to the problems of managing the environment.

A. M. CHAKRABARTY: Whatever the mode of regulation is--guide-
lines, legislation, or other--there should be panels where ecologists are represented along with lawyers, biochemists, geneticists,
and everyone else. I think it is very important to recognize that
people have been manipulating the genes of bacteria for years any-
how, not only in the Chesapeake Bay, but also through the lab sink
into the environment. As far as I know, there has been no environmental ecological havoc. I don't really think there is anything
hazardous in terms of manipulating the genes of bacteria and putting
the bacteria back into their environments. I think there should be
concern when the genes you are putting in are from eukaryotic organisms, as Dr. Staley mentioned in terms of moving genes from kingdom
to kingdom. Such steps might overcome some natural barriers.

Some of you may underestimate the potential of genetic engineering. If you do genetic engineering and you find that you have
made a bug that does not perform well in sewage, you can do a few

more manipulations to make sure that it does what is desired,
including avoiding toxins or predators. There are all kinds of conditions where the amount of pollution is really due to high concentrations of the toxic chemicals, rather than low concentrations; at
the least, we could take care of those pollution problems. Nevertheless, I do want the ecologists and others on that panel to tell
me what might be the causes of concern. Your word of caution is
well taken. I think we should not rush into it. But then we must
also realize that environmental pollutants themselves cause all
kinds of environmental and health damage.

G. ORIANS: As moderator, I would like to make a few comments
from the point of view of a vertebrate ecologist. I am struck with
the parallels that exist between the insights that Dr. Alexander of-
fered and those that derive from the studies of macro-ecology. For
example, he spoke about the problem of the structural complexity of
the system in which the interaction is taking place--surfaces, barriers, etc. It is a basic principle of macro-ecology that stability
of interactions in the systems is greatly enhanced by imposing
structural complexity. That is the basis of inter-cropping in agriculture: mixing things up a bit to reduce the ability of insects to
find plants. I am not suggesting that the sewage bed is a mixed
agricultural system, but I think the role of structural complexity
in affecting the dynamics of the system is very similar.

Another issue that Dr. Alexander raised was the ability of certain organisms to take prey, which in this case would be a toxic
chemical, essentially down to zero. Their ability to do so depends
on their having an alternative energy source in the system, so that
they can prey upon the toxic target as the second prey. This is, in
a sense, why the whales are in trouble. When we go whaling we are
depending on rice and wheat carbon energy sources. Whales can be
hunted to extinction because we are not dependent on the energy we
are getting from whales to make a living, but from the subsidy provided by alternative sources. In macroecology, a lot of the cases
of extinction are due to organisms that have alternative energy
sources; they are not dependent on the prey for which they would
have a threshold problem. The parallel I see is very striking.
There may be others that are drawn from our insights from working
with higher organisms that may enlighten the manipulations that we
might try with microorganisms.

At the same time, I am impressed with the difficulty of predicting how organisms are going to work. The organisms I study are
perhaps the best known ecologically, namely birds, and we just do
not understand what is going to work with them. If you walk around
Seattle or any other city in North America, one of the most abundant
birds you will see is the house sparrow, which was introduced in the
mid-1800s into New York City from some location in the English Mid-
lands, because the English who had come to the New World missed

house sparrows. Most people do not realize that a very close relative in the same genus as the house sparrow, the European tree
sparrow, was also introduced into North America, into St. Louis,
Missouri. The European tree sparrow is extremely widespread in its
native habitat; in fact, it goes all across Europe and Asia. It
functions as a yard bird, and is, indeed, the "house sparrow" of
Japan. If you go to Japan, those little sparrows that are chirping
all over town by the thousands are the European tree sparrows; it
looks like a house sparrow with a little black patch in the middle
of the cheek.

    In contrast, if you wish to see the European tree sparrow in
North America, you must go to St. Louis or East St. Louis, Illinois.
There is no one who can explain why it is that one of these species
spread out to take over all of North America, and the other has
spread at most about forty miles from the point of introduction in
roughly the same period of time.

    These organisms are well known ecologically, compared to the
microorganisms that we are discussing in this program, yet we cannot
predict what these birds are going to do. We face a lot of troubles
in attempting to predict what organisms will do when they are introduced into different environments. This situation makes me a bit
more cautious than are some other people.

    J. ROGERS: So far almost all of you except Rita Colwell have
talked about the survival of the "bug." Isn't it more appropriate
to talk about the survival of the DNA that is inside the bug?

    G. ORIANS: Who wishes to speak on behalf of DNA?

    J. SHAPIRO: The organisms are not really created in the labo-
ratory; they are selected, especially in the chemostat approach.
Dr. Chakrabarty really does not know how they came about. The organisms are extremely good genetic engineers and certainly much better chemists than any human being. They have done whatever reorganization they have to do to their DNA and the rest of the cellular
structure, and they have developed some novel metabolic capabilities. If we take those organisms and put them back in the environment, we may find, after a period of time, that certain reactions
take place and that pollutants disappear. Even then we do not know
for sure that it is the organisms that were put back in there which
have done that. For example, they may have transferred information
to other organisms, as has been reported by Knackmuss and his colleagues in Germany from studies of mixed cultures with certain industrial effluents.

    I would like to elaborate on what both Dr. Alexander and Dr.
Colwell said about picking better organisms. It may be that there
is one category of microorganisms with which one can do genetics;

that surely includes <u>Pseudomonas</u>, which was notably absent from some
of Dr. Alexander's slides. One can use them, because they do grow
well in the laboratory and because we do know something about their
plasmids, their phages, their chromosome genetics, and how to engineer them. There may be another set of organisms which are extremely important in nature, but which do not form good-sized colonies or
any colonies at all on petri dishes, or which cannot be isolated in
pure form. It is illusory to think that you could do genetics, at
least as we understand it, with these organisms. Nonetheless, I
think we can anticipate that the organisms that can be constructed
in the laboratory and then be put back into natural systems eventually will contribute to the production of surviving organisms which
carry out some of these novel biochemical pathways. The new activities are recovered from enrichment cultures, signifying that those
capabilities are somehow present in the wild flora. Sometimes those
enrichment cultures take quite a long time to come up in a form
which can be utilized in a laboratory, indicating that we may be
pulling out organisms which do not express those capabilities in
nature but do have them in the chemostat or on the petri dish.
Eventually one gets something that you can work with in the laboratory. From the point of view of genetics, we may not be using our
time profitably to find those organisms which can metabolize chemicals at very low concentrations, because they may not be suitable
for what we can do in terms of genetics.

     R. COLWELL: I think the question really was directed toward
harvesting the genes, rather than the cells. We have many problems
in understanding the ecology of the whole cell. If we can clone the
gene to get the appropriate enzyme, it may well be that with immobilized enzyme systems we may be able to do the kinds of things we
need to do. It turns out then to be more of a bulk processing kind
of a problem, an old-fashioned engineering problem. We focused the
entire day on putting whole cells into the environment. I think it
might be more productive to take advantage of the appropriate DNA
sequences in the tremendous gene pool in the environment by harvesting the appropriate DNA sequences to do the things we want done.

     G.S. OMENN: Strategies for identifying and cloning specific
genes are advancing remarkably rapidly. Later in this volume, Hood
describes the synergy of microchemical instrumentation, recombinant
DNA technology, and monoclonal antibody techniques to produce DNA
probes and synthesize genes and peptides. These techniques will
permit development of "synthetic enzymes" with physical, binding,
and catalytic properties designed for specific applications. In
fact, Bendix and Genex have formed a joint venture, called
"Proteus," to pursue such protein engineering objectives. In some
situations the cloned genes and their protein products may be useful
directly and could avoid problems of survival, safety, and uptake of
substrates into the cells. However, if an enzyme depends on cellular production and regeneration of such cofactors as NADH or NADPH,

the isolated enzyme may be less useful than intact cells.

F. TAUB: The fact that we have toxic waste dumps certainly suggests that these organisms are evolving in "polluted" or "enriched" local environments, where toxic chemicals have been in contact with soil, marine waters, fresh waters, or sediments. There seems to be some selection for organisms that can break down these chemicals. Many of you have started by taking samples from these sites and then doing further enrichment and further isolation. What is it that you are doing in the lab? What is it that is happening in your continuous cultures that is not happening naturally? If all of the processes that you are carrying out are essentially the same kind of genetic transfer as you would expect to happen in natural environments anyway, why is this not happening fast enough in natural environments? Why is it that you are feeling the need to supplement it with laboratory efforts?

R. COLWELL: I think that the situation is akin to the problem in the production of penicillin. What we are trying to do is amplify, enhance, make more efficient. In the case of penicillin, a discovery we all know was made in the late 1920s, progress depended upon the work in the 1940s that was really to develop a hyper-producer. I think what we try to do when we work with strains in the laboratory is to develop an organism that does more of that which we want done, under conditions we can control.

M. ALEXANDER: Dr. Taub has a very important point, because these simple chemicals, which can be degraded readily in the laboratory, are very persistent in nature. Catabolic activity is not the entire game. The world was not made for the destruction of organic compounds. There are a lot of other stresses; there are a lot of other factors. There must be good reasons why orthochloronitrobenzene moves down the Mississippi River without any significant destruction. There are reasons why phthalate esters are persistent in natural waters. There are reasons why there is organic carbon in the oceans. It is biodegradable, but it is there.

A. CHAKRABARTY: There are not enough microorganisms present to carry out all those conversions, therefore, if I can come up with a microorganism that can do the conversion, why can I not use it in an open environment? Remember that the burden of proof is on the genetic engineers who do come up with bugs that can perform certain things to demonstrate their place. If the genetic engineer can come up with bugs that, for instance, can eat dioxin, the question is, "What do we do, what sort of guidelines do we set up so that we can go ahead and use the microorganisms and help to solve the dioxin problem?" Whether the problem will be solved or not, of course, will depend upon how effective and safe this microorganism would be. I think once we try these microorganisms in an open environment, we will very soon know the answers, so I think that we need not have to

rely on speculation. We should figure out what sort of guidelines
there should be to regulate the application of appropriate microorganisms once they are made.

W. LANDIS: We would know a lot better what guidelines to give
you if we knew a lot more microbial ecology. We are working in an
environment that is stochastic; 24 hr is 4 generations to a parame-
cium, about 6 or 7 for a tetrahymena. Not only do they feed on bacteria, but most protozoa also can crop large numbers of organic molecules from the detritus. Thus, protozoa may survive at far less
than 10^6 bacteria per ml, the usual minimal estimate. These mobile
organisms also find sites with higher densities of bacteria when the
mean density is too low. We need to study the ecosystems and the
interactions a lot more before we can be of much help on guidelines.

M. ALEXANDER: Just a point of clarification. The number 10^6
is not the number of cells consumed by a protozoan, which tends to
be in the vicinity of 10^3 to 10^4 per division, but the threshold
population below which protozoa feeding on cultures of bacteria will
not reduce the bacterial population any further. We worked very
hard to get the number.

A. COLWELL: Ciliates can be highly selective in their feeding,
accepting some bacteria as a food source and rejecting others. We
have carried out experiments with ciliates, giving the ciliates a
choice of Vibrio, Pseudomonas, and Bacillus spp. They will feed
selectively on one species and not on the others, selecting cells
out very nicely [Berk, S.G., and R.R. Colwell (1981) Transfer of
mercury through a marine microbial food web. J. Exp. Marine Biol.
and Ecol. 52:157-172].

B. ZIMMERMAN: I would like to return to the point that Dr.
Chakrabarty had opened up concerning what mode of regulation, if
any, is appropriate for the introduction of soil organisms. During
the debates over accidental laboratory hazards, people were constructing some hypothetical scenarios, however improbable those
might have been, which the regulations were designed to prevent.
Even though there has been talk about ecological disasters resulting
from misuse of genetically engineered soil organisms, nobody has
said what these hypothetical scenarios might be. I can think of a
few things, but I would really like to hear the comments of the
microbial ecologists. What is it that people are worried about?

J. STALEY: I am not too concerned about the use of genetically
engineered organisms to control environmental pollutants problems,
but I think you have to realize that bacteria play very important
roles in the environment. I will cite just one. Nitrifying bacteria, which oxidize nitrite to nitrate, keep the level of nitrite
very low. Nitrite is highly toxic to plants, bacteria, and animals.
If something should happen to the rather select group of nitrifying

organisms, many plants and animals could not survive. I do not expect such an effect to occur, but I suppose it is possible.

A. ALEXANDER: If you are looking at natural ecosystems, it is very simple to propose horrible scenarios. Hopefully, no one will do these experiments! There are a lot of critical reactions that microorganisms and higher plants bring about, and a stress on one of these reactions could have a very serious impact. An example was discussed at EPA. Suppose you had an organism which would nitrify a little bit faster, converting ammonium to nitrates, an exergonic reaction. The organisms they would be competing with are very slow growers. Therefore, anything that grows with a generation time less than 30 hr is going to take over. It is going to get into the ocean, and there is a lot of ammonia in the ocean, so it converts the ammonia to nitrate. But suppose that the yield of nitrous oxide, which is now very low, goes up some hypothetical value, let us say 1% to 2%. What is that going to do with the ozone layer that protects against ultraviolet radiation? This is a real problem; we would like to have enhanced nitrification, because it is a slow reaction. Take another reaction which you would like to bring about but where there is a potential danger, and dream up your own bad dreams!

I do agree with the panelists; I think the probability is very low, but when I hear over and over again, "I am confused," "I am not sure," then I think somebody needs to look at the public welfare.

J. SHAPIRO: In terms of the kinds of organisms we are talking about, this issue is a red herring. How much PCB is there for every man, woman, and child in this country? Ten pounds per capita. We know about that. We know about a number of other pollutants. Those are real dangers and hazards. Even though we do not understand microbial ecology well, we know that ecosystems are pretty resilient and highly buffered. I think, if we come up with a microbial solution to PCBs, we have to apply it. Someone would have to come up with a concrete and specific objection to say that this is something that we should not do. I think there is a very important difference between the analogies to Agent Orange and the nuclear power industry. In both of those cases there was a lot of very disturbing information which was not made available to the general public.

M. ALEXANDER: I think we need a stronger degree of assurance than a group of scientists saying "I think," "I believe," "we have no precedents for it." We want to have the technologies. We want to have pesticides. We want nuclear energy, but we have to have more assurance than my statement or your statement that "I do not think there is a problem; we have no precedent for a problem." We need some solid system of assessing the potential dangers, not to reduce the risk to zero, which we cannot do, but at least to reduce the risks substantially.

(UNIDENTIFIED SPEAKER): When the decisions were being made to begin generation of electricity by fission in the fifties we had lots of evidence that radioactive substances were dangerous, but that evidence was not as fully debated and as widely known as it is now. I think that is a very salient difference from what we are discussing now. Likewise, the toxicity of some of the contaminants in herbicides was very closely held information. I think that when you get to the point of having bugs that you think might be useful, you will have had some experience with them. It is incumbent on anybody who may develop one to use every means of characterization possible, but I find it very difficult to see a serious objection to these kinds of organisms. On the other hand, organisms which may produce pharmacologically active agents or which may contain infectious sequences require a great deal of caution and perhaps guidelines or regulation for their use.

R. COLWELL: When changes are observed and recorded, we may not really now how to cope with those changes. For example, over the past 10 years, my research group and I have been studying the microbial ecology of an ocean dumpsite located in the Atlantic Ocean, north of Puerto Rico. We have completed at least 11 cruises to the dumpsite, where pharmaceutical wastes are released from barges deliverying composited waste to the dumping area from Aricebo, Puerto Rico.

We have documented changes in the community structure and species composition of the microbial populations of the surface waters at the dumpsite. Despite the evidence, some colleagues absolutely will not accept the fact that, in an area of the ocean this large, one can induce changes in the microbial community composition. They say that because it is such a big area of the ocean the dilution factor is tremendously large. Well, the changes have occurred and they have been documented.

Now the question is: What difference does it make? I am not sure what the correct answer to that question is, at the present time. It may be that, in a decade from now, an irreversible, traumatic change will occur as a result of the long-term environmental insult, if the dumpsite is resumed and continued. For now it is a "change," resulting from the decade of dumping millions of gallons of pharmaceutical waste in one place in the Atlantic Ocean, a site badly chosen, incidentally, because the circulation of the water at that site is such that it is not flushed out. The wastes are retained a longer time than predicted, before moving off in an eastward direction. We know so relatively little about the microbial ecology of the ocean that we cannot predict consequences of these kinds of changes at higher levels of the food chain and food web in the world oceans.

R. BROOKS: I am a little concerned. Professor Taub asked what

a geneticist is doing in the laboratory that is not going on in the
outside. Most of the discussion here today has been about catabolic
pathways. I doubt that the geneticists are able to threaten ecological systems by merely taking organisms, retaining them in the laboratory and processing them through transfer. I think they cannot
do anything but accelerate natural processes. As far as we know,
all of those pathways or at least their components exist in nature.
So, if we confine the discussion to catabolic pathways, I do not see
what is going to suddenly appear on a catabolic pathway to endanger
anybody's ecosystem that nature has not experimented with several
times over.

L. RIGGS: For the past two and a half years I have worked with
an experimental program in California (GENREC), where we have tried
to integrate ecological considerations, genetic considerations, and
work with a variety of interest groups that are using genetic resources. I hear two kinds of concerns. The geneticists are concerned that someone will say, "Don't do that, you are going to create an organism that is too dangerous to let loose on the earth."
The ecologists fear unpredictable effects on ecosystems. As an
example, let us consider macroorganisms: salmon. In fall, 1981, a
sea ranching operation released several million smolts of artifici-
ally reared salmon at a coastal facility where they were supposed to
convert to the salt water mode and move out into the ocean. This
had been done before, on a smaller scale, and had worked. No one
saw any particular reason not to do it on the scale that was attempted. However, physiological processes are complex, and these
several million fish decided that it was not yet time to go to sea.
They turned around and jammed up into a very small watershed, one
selected because, theoretically, it would be less impacted by any
such problems. All of the native fish in that watershed were then
subjected to tremendous levels of competition for the duration of
the winter. The kinds of problems that I think our ecologist speakers are highlighting are not problems that have to do with violation
of the genetic integrity of organisms in other taxa, but small performance differences. Small differences in the organization of the
gene might tell the organism to do something a little bit different
from what we expect. Those kinds of things can make a big difference in the way our applications work. Once you get the organisms
and they have the kind of catabolic and other capabilities that you
are interested in, guidelines for testing these organisms may help
avoid such impacts.

F. TAUB: I cannot resist rising to the bait, especially on the
salmon, being from the School of Fisheries! Many years ago, there
was a conflict between the wild salmon people and the hatchery people, in which the wild salmon people said it is ridiculous to think
that Dr. So and So can outwit Mother Nature. They predicted that
all the salmon and trout would drop dead as soon as they leave the
hatchery because they are too fat, they have grown too fast, and

they cannot possibly compete against wild stock. Now the concern is
that the hatchery fish are going to drive the wild stock to extinction, because you can harvest 90% of the hatchery stock and still
have enough to have eggs and sperm for your hatchery, but if you try
harvesting 90% of your wild stock they are going to become extinct,
so we have gone from one worry to an opposite worry.

I think we are ignoring a lot of the ways that we test for hazard assessment in new chemicals. There are analogies. We do not
test every pair of things that might have been on the earth. We do
not test them one-by-one or two-by-two, each of them reproducing.
It is fairly easy to pick a few typical organisms, hoping that they
somehow represent larger numbers of organisms. In the poster session we have described laboratory microcosms and their application.
I have given some thought to the differences between trying to assess environmental safety of new chemicals and the environmental
safety of new organisms. One important difference is that new organisms can reproduce. In microcosms we can test safety and survival under conditions where, if the organism turns out to be a bad
actor, you can sterilize the whole experiment. We are not totally
lacking in ways to study some of these concerns. Perhaps once we
have studied them a bit, we will either be much more concerned or
much less concerned. While we cannot totally eliminate the unique
circumstance where something that looks harmless in every test could
yet prove hazardous under some special circumstances, we certainly
can do enough testing that we do not have to say, "we do not know
where to start."

G. ORIANS: I am pleased to report there is enough wild stock
salmon still left that it is possible for all of you visiting
Seattle to enjoy the salmon dinner. While the questioning is still
very active, I prefer to terminate the discussion while it is still
vigorous rather than to let entropy prevail. As H. L. Mencken said,
"It is very difficult to make predictions, especially about the
future."

PERSPECTIVE ON OPPORTUNITIES FOR GENETIC ENGINEERING

APPLICATIONS IN INDUSTRIAL POLLUTION CONTROL

James W. Patterson

Pritzker Department of Environmental Engineering
Industrial Waste Elimination Research Center
Illinois Institute of Technology
Chicago, Illinois 60616

OVERVIEW

Biological systems have been employed successfully for many years in both industrial and domestic pollution control. Such systems, while "engineered" to the extent of the operational conditions imposed (hydraulic residence time, population growth rate, etc.), are essentially chemostatic in nature, with populations consisting of those species which can either survive or thrive under the conditions of wastewater characteristics and process operational parameters. Table 1 presents characteristics of existing biological processes utilized in pollution control.

The systems contain mixed populations, capable in the aggregate of a wide range of biochemical functions. The systems are either aerobic (normally containing both aerobic and facultative species), or anaerobic (containing anaerobes and perhaps facultative species). Most systems operate as heterotrophic processes, although some are designed to encourage autotrophic performance either simultaneous with or separate from heterotrophic functions. However, the primary goal of almost every application of biological systems is mineralization of organic constituents. As I shall discuss later, this goal may not be the most appropriate for genetic engineering applications.

Both cell residence time and time of population contact with the waste may range (independently) from a few hours to several days or even weeks. The existing systems are characterized by low population densities and/or biochemical reaction rates, at least in comparison with other biochemical systems, such as pharmaceutical fermentation processes. This is also an aspect where genetically

Table 1. Characteristics of existing biological processes utilized
          in pollution control.

MIXED POPULATIONS
- AEROBIC
- ANAEROBIC
- FACULTATIVE

GOAL IS MINERALIZATION

SHORT (HOURS) TO LONG (WEEKS)
CONTACT TIMES

LOW POPULATION DENSITIES AND/OR
BIOCHEMICAL REACTION RATES

DILUTE AND TIME-VARIANT WASTE
STREAMS

BIOLOGICAL SYSTEMS OFTEN PRECEDED
BY PROTECTIVE PHYSICAL-CHEMICAL
PRETREATMENT PROCESSES

---

engineered systems will likely deviate from conventional biological
systems.

A key characteristic of existing biological systems is that
they normally must accept and efficiently mineralize relatively dilute and time-variant waste streams varying in flow rate, chemical
constituents, individual chemical concentrations, and relative chemical compound concentrations. Existing systems are designed and operated to achieve a high degree of performance despite varying influent conditions. This constraint may not be necessary for many
cost-effective genetically engineered systems, however.

A final important characteristic, at least for existing systems
utilized in many industrial wastewater applications, is that such
systems must often be preceded by protective physical-chemical pretreatment processes such as cooling, pH adjustment, toxic constituents segregation, and nutrient balance. I anticipate that this
characteristic will be equally important in genetically engineered
processes.

Although there are physical-chemical systems available to handle most industrial pollutants, biological systems have many actual
or potential advantages including: 1) low capital investment; 2)
low energy consumption; 3) self-sustaining operation; and 4) possible product recovery. However, if biological systems, genetically
engineered or otherwise, are to be utilized in industrial pollution
control, they must meet several fundamental requirements. For example, they should have the following characteristics: 1) self-sustaining operation; 2) biochemical specificity; 3) rapid kinetics;

and 4) stable performance. Systems which do not meet such requirements may be functionally successful, but not competitive with alternative techniques of pollution control.

OPPORTUNITIES FOR GENETIC ENGINEERING

     It is apparent that, within the field of industrial pollution
control, there are numerous opportunities for the application of
genetic engineering. However, I do not believe that viable opportunities exist in head-to-head competition with existing biological
systems, insofar as end-of-pipe utilization for relatively dilute,
composite, and time variant wastes, where the primary objective is
simply mineralization. Existing processes are relatively economical, well-established, and risk-free. Genetically engineered processes, at least initially, will not be comparable and must therefore be well-targeted in their applications. They must present
unique advantages and opportunities. Table 2 presents some general
areas of opportunity for genetically engineered processes. The
first two areas listed, biomass production and mineralization, are
well recognized. I believe that the latter three areas of Tab. 2
represent targets of even greater opportunity.

     Fermentation technology is certainly well established in pol-
lution control, although its primary by-product, methane, is far
less significant than is the ability of the process to stabilize
concentrated soluble and particulate organic waste streams.

Table 2.   General areas of opportunity for genetically engineered
           processes.

           BIOMASS PRODUCTION

           MINERALIZATION
           - GENERAL
           - COMPOUND SPECIFIC

           FERMENTATION
           - METHANE
           - ORGANIC ACIDS
           - OTHER INTERMEDIATES

           PRODUCT/BY-PRODUCT RECOVERY
           - DEHALOGENATION
           - DEAMINATION
           - DENITRATION
           - RING CLEAVAGE

           OTHER AREAS
           - RATE ENHANCEMENT
           - INCREASED SPECIFICITY
           - RESISTANCE TO INHIBITION

Fermentation as applied today proceeds fully through acidogenesis to methanogenesis to reach the lowest free energy level, as represented by the end products methane and carbon dioxide. Far greater value may be achievable with genetically engineered systems which produce selected organic acids or other intermediates. This is an unlikely scenario where fermentation is applied at the end-of-pipe to a complex and time-variant wastestream.

The potential is far greater if we move from the end-of-pipe to a particular manufacturing unit process which produces a more simple, consistent, and concentrated waste stream. This may be the key to the successful application of genetic engineering in industrial pollution control. That is, it is likely to be simpler, more economical, and advantageous to genetically engineer a biological system to handle a waste stream at its point of generation, where it is in its most consistent and concentrated form, prior to blending that stream with others for end-of-pipe treatment. In its simplest form, we might consider such an approach to represent a manufacturing process modification, rather than pollution control in the conventional sense. Yet the end result is equivalent, with the added potential to recover valuable by-products.

Direct raw material or product, as well as by-product, recovery is also possible when we evaluate the opportunities of point-of-generation application of genetically engineered systems. Among the most powerful biochemical techniques which might be exploited are dehalogenation, deamination, denitration, and ring-cleavage. The opportunities derive from the chemical classes of industrial pollutants regulated, as we shall discuss later.

Finally, there are several other areas of opportunity which should not be neglected. These include rate enhancement, increased biochemical specificity, and increased resistance to inhibitory or toxic response. The latter area is obvious, and requires no further explanation. With regard to rate enhancement, enzymes are the catalysts of biochemical processes. Increased enzyme density or turnover rate will enhance process kinetics, and thereby process economics. Biochemical specificity is highly desirable, if it allows the biological population to ignore extraneous chemicals and strip out the single chemical for which the population is targeted. Specificity extends even further, to the performance of a single chemical modification (such as ring-cleavage) on the target compound.

Let us now return to those four biochemical functions which, I believe, represent the pot of gold at the rainbow's end: dehalogenation, deamination, denitration, and ring-cleavage. In the United States and other industrialized nations, millions of gallons of concentrated wastes are disposed of each year by methods such as landfill, incineration, or chemical oxidation. These wastes are disposed of because there is either no viable recovery alternative, or because disposal is the most economical alternative available. By

employing disposal, industry not only loses the value of the disposed raw material, product, or by-product, but must pay the cost of
disposal. This cost is not insignificant, and for some wastes can
reach $2-$3 per gallon of waste. The lists of chemicals regulated
as pollutants identify hundreds of compounds requiring special control measures. Certain categories of compounds, however, dominate
the lists. These are halogenated, benzo-, amino-, and nitro-com-
pounds. These classes of chemicals, and many others, are strictly
regulated under 1) the Resource Conservation and Recovery Act (RCRA)
as hazardous wastes, and/or 2) the Clean Water Act (CWA) as priority
water pollutants. Table 3 presents examples of chemicals regulated
under such laws. The lists of regulated chemicals controlled under
RCRA and CWA may be considered as directories of opportunity for genetic engineering.

SIGNPOSTS FOR SUCCESS

    We can be encouraged in the potential opportunities for genet-
ic engineering applications such as I have described. For example,
it is well established that acclimated conventional biological systems are able to mineralize phenol, and that this accomplishment
is achieved by Pseudomonas sp. The organism proceeds sequentially
though ring disruption, generation of organic acids of decreasing
molecular weight, and finally, carbon oxidation to CO_2. Mutant

Table 3. Examples of regulated chemicals.

TYPE	CHEMICAL	LAW[1]
HALOGENATED	CHLOROBENZENE	RCRA/CWA
	CHLOROPHENOL	RCRA/CWA
	DICHLORODIFLUOROMETHANE	RCRA
	PENTACHLOROETHANE	RCRA/CWA
	DIBROMOMETHANE	CWA
BENZO-	BENZENE	RCRA/CWA
	BENZOPYRENE	RCRA/CWA
	PHENOL	RCRA/CWA
	TOLUENE	RCRA/CWA
AMINO-	DIAMINOTOLUENE	RCRA
	PROPYLENIMINE	RCRA
	PYRIDINAMINE	RCRA
NITRO-	NITROBENZENE	RCRA/CWA
	NITROPHENOL	RCRA/CWA
	NITROPROPANE	RCRA

[1] RCRA is the Resource Conservation and Recovery Act. CWA
is the Clean Water Act.

Table 4.   Rates of ring disruption* (Pseudomonas).

COMPOUND	INITIAL CONDITIONS	TIME, HOURS PARENT	MUTANT
PHENOL	500 mg/l, 30°C	25	8
TRICHLOROPHENOL	200 mg/l, 30°C	120	50

* TIME TO ACHIEVE 100 PERCENT RING DISRUPTION

Pseudomonas species are much faster at ring disruption than is the parent population (Tab. 4), and even highly halogenated phenols are disrupted, although at much lower rates.

There are many other biochemical phenomena which reinforce our confidence in the potential of genetic engineering, and a few are listed in Tab. 5. A biohydrometallurgical process for extraction of copper plus elemental sulfur from crude ore has recently been patented. The process relies upon Thiobacillus ferrooxidans for the initial extraction step. We have already discussed methane production--a thoroughly researched and well understood biochemical process.

International concern for polychlorinated biphenyl (PCB) pollution has generated extensive research on biochemical mineralization of PCBs. Over 20 different bacterial species have demonstrated

Table 5.   Example biochemical processes.

BIOHYDROMETALLURGICAL EXTRACTION OF COPPER PLUS
ELEMENTAL SULFUR - THIOBACILLUS FERROOXIDANS

METHANE PRODUCTION - ACIDOGENIC + ACETOGENIC
+ METHANOGENIC BACTERIA

PCB MINERALIZATION - 20 DIFFERENT BACTERIA

TRACE METALS CONCENTRATION - THIOBACILLUS SP.

CONCENTRATION OF CHROMIUM, SILVER, OR URANIUM -
PSEUDOMONAS FLUORESCENS OR P. AERUGINOSA

HALOGENATED AROMATICS MINERALIZATION - ANEROBIC SP.

ELEMENTAL SULFUR RECOVERY FROM POWER PLANT
SCRUBBER SLUDGES - DESULFOVIBRIO SP. PLUS
CHLOROBRIUM OR CHROMATIUM SP.

PCB mineralization capability. Mineralization rates are extremely slow, however. Trace metals are present in many diverse industrial waste streams. Many of these metals are strategic materials, and certain <u>Thiobacillus</u> species display an intriguing capability to strongly concentrate these trace metals. <u>Pseudomonas</u> organisms also display this talent, although they appear to be more selective (specific) in the metals that they will accumulate. Anaerobic organisms isolated from lake sediments have been observed to mineralize a wide array of halogenated aromatic compounds. Perhaps some have biochemical talents which could be utilized for intermediate by-product production.

Finally, I would like to note an extremely interesting process now being explored through support from the National Science Foundation. The process is concerned with the recovery of H_2S and SO_2 air pollutants to yield elemental sulfur. Sulfur dioxide has been implicated as the principal culprit of acid rain, and the control technologies for SO_2 produce voluminous quantities of sludge requiring disposal. Both <u>Chlorobium</u> and <u>Chromatium</u> species have the ability to convert sulfate to elemental sulfur. For control of hydrogen sulfide, <u>Desulfovibrio</u> will convert sulfide to sulfate, and in a second step the sulfate would be converted to elemental sulfur.

CONCLUSION

There is tremendous potential for the application of genetic engineering in industrial pollution control. However, the greatest opportunities exist where we can exploit a very specific biochemical talent, and target that talent at specific locations in manufacturing processes where the waste stream is in it most consistent and concentrated form.

APPLICATION OF GENETIC ENGINEERING TO

INDUSTRIAL WASTE/WASTEWATER TREATMENT

Hester A. Kobayashi

Standard Oil of Ohio Research Center
Cleveland, Ohio 44128

INTRODUCTION

Despite the many recent advances in various aspects of genetic engineering, application of the technology to waste/wastewater treatment is still in its infancy. The genetics of microorganisms important in biological treatment is almost unknown except for that of the most common organisms, and the state of the art is to a large extent still in the laboratory (1-12). In addition, the ways in which genetic engineering can be most effectively applied to waste/wastewater are as yet poorly defined.

Current attempts at using genetic engineering appear to be rather narrow, being directed toward merely creating organisms that can degrade specific compounds. There has been no attempt to consider the physical and complex chemical characteristics of the waste/wastewaters to be treated. Directly engineered genetic manipulation in waste/wastewater treatment is still limited to plasmid assisted transfers in the few species of organisms understood well enough for such manipulations (2-6).

The only application of any type of genetic engineering of waste/wastewater treatment systems appears to be that practiced by a number of biotechnology firms. The methods used involve preparation of desirable inocula by the classical techniques of either selecting natural mutants from populations exposed to waste of a certain type, or by inducing mutations by use of physical or chemical agents. Inocula prepared by these methods show some success in treatment of specialized wastes, and in general appear to be effective for system start-up (13-17).

There has been much discussion of the need for studies on microbe/microbe interactions at the cellular as well as at the

biochemical level, and for studies of interactions between microorganisms and the environment (2,4,8,9,18,19). Detailed genetic
characterization and studies of genetic control mechanisms of various organisms of potential value in treatment, especially those
organisms which exist in extreme environments, are needed (1,2,4).
Populations could be stabilized by creating stable mutants and by
counteracting the pressures of competition between the introduced
mutants and the local organisms (4,7,8). In addition, improved
reactor technology is yet another major requirement before genetic
engineering applications can be fully effective (8,20).

There is still a large gap between directly engineered genetic
manipulation as a laboratory science and as an applied technology.
In order for a new technology to be well accepted, it must be proved
to be significantly more effective and economical in accomplishing
the task than existing, conventional techniques can be. None of the
current applications or suggested applications yet appear to be associated with a means to significantly influence waste/wastewater
treatment technology.

The purpose of this paper is to suggest a potentially valuable
application of genetic engineering to treatment of industrial
wastes/wastewaters, which may be viewed as extreme environments.
This application is one of using genetic engineering to minimize
pretreatment adjustments often necessary before conventional biological treatment. The approach involves using organisms from extreme
environments in nature, similar to the waste/wastewaters, and developing mutants or communities of mutants capable of degrading the material to be treated. The mutants would be used in appropriate reactor systems which would be capable of helping maintain population
stability.

In order to acquaint you with the nature of industrial wastes/
wastewaters and the problems they present in conventional treatment
systems, examples of a few selected types will be described. A discussion of some extreme environments will illustrate the proposed
application. Finally, biofilm reactors will be discussed as an appropriate reactor type for growing mutant organisms.

Interdisciplinary activity among microbiologists in physiology,
ecology, biochemistry, and molecular biology, as well as with engineers well acquainted with biotechnology will be stressed as an important ingredient in this approach.

EXAMPLES OF INDUSTRIAL WASTE/WASTEWATERS WHICH ARE EXTREME
ENVIRONMENTS AND THEIR TREATMENT BY CONVENTIONAL TECHNIQUES

Industrial wastes/wastewaters are often extreme environments
with physical and chemical characteristics beyond the normal physiological range of organisms found commonly in the aquatic environment
and in domestic treatment systems. Conventional treatment, however,

often is based upon domestic waste/wastewater treatment techniques and are often started with inocula taken from such systems. Because of the extreme nature of many industrial wastes/wastewaters, various adjustments are often necessary before they can be treated by conventional techniques.

"Conventional treatment" in this paper refers to the following biological treatment methods: aerated lagoons, aerated activated sludge treatment, landfarming, landfilling, and activated anaerobic sludge treatment. Detailed discussion of these techniques can be found in general textbooks on environmental engineering.

Table 1 is a list of the characteristics which are often found singularly or in combination in industrial waste/wastewater. Examples of industrial wastewaters with extreme characteristics are listed in Tab. 2. The following is a discussion of the different extremes and the problems they present in conventional wastewater treatment methods.

Complexity of Wastes

Industrial wastes/wastewaters are rarely simple solutions of well defined compounds. They are generally complex mixtures which vary quantitatively and qualitatively with changes in process conditions. Some of the constituents may be refractory to immediate biological degradation, and hence, they require long retention times in treatment systems for adequate removal.

The complexity issue is further complicated in certain cases by very low concentrations (<1 to a few mg/L) of individual constituents of environmental concern. Though the total organic composition

Table 1. Characteristics of industrial waste/wastewater which make them extreme environments.

1. Temperature extremes

2. Low dissolved oxygen and Eh

3. pH extremes

4. Inadequacy of nutrient concentrations

5. Inadequate moisture content

6. Extremes in salinity and ionic composition

7. Complexity and variability (qualitative and quantitative) of organic matter

8. Presence of recalcitrant anthropogenic compounds

9. Presence of high concentrations of potentially toxic substances

10. Exotic composition of gases

Table 2. Examples of industrial wastewaters which are extreme environments.

Industry (Refs. 24, 46–50)	pH (high)	pH (low)	Temperature (high)	Eh (low)	Sulfur Compounds S²⁻	SO₃²⁻	Thiosulfate	Nitrogen NO₃⁻	NH₃ (high)	Organic Concentration (low)	Oxygen (low)	CN (high)	Salinity (high)	Oil
Textile	+		+			+					+			+
Leather		Variable		+	+						+		+	
Explosives	+			+				+						+
Pesticides	+					+								
Pulp & Paper	+					+								
Petroleum, Petrochemical		Variable	+	+	+	+			+	+	+	+	+	+
Glue Manufacture	+		+											
Synfuels Coal gasification	+		+						+				+	
Shale Oil	+		+	+	+		+		+				+	+
Steel Mill Waste		Variable	+						+			+		
Cellulose Factory	+		+		+	+								

Table 3.   Example of complex mixture of organic compounds in re-
            finery wastewater (21).

	Mean (mg/L)	Range
Benzene	10.833	ND* - 80.000
Chloroform	.175	ND - .440
Ethylbenzene	.543	ND - 12.000
Toluene	5.491	ND - 14.000
Phenol	.562	ND - .800
Naphthalene	.440	ND - .830
Anthracene/phenanthrene	.031	ND - .066
BOD (Biochemical oxygen demand)	249	127 - 625
COD (Chemical oxygen demand)	654	353 - 2500

* ND - Not detected

may be considerable, the individual compounds may be below the substrate concentration which can sustain a rapid decomposition rate.
Low concentrations result in poor opportunity for mass transfer from
the liquid phase to the specific microorganisms capable of degrading
specific compounds, resulting in long retention times and low treatment efficiency. The cost of long retention times is high, because
of high capital costs for construction of larger reactors and longer
periods of aeration. A good example of this problem is seen in refinery waste/wastewater treatment (Tab. 3). Although the total organic concentration in refinery wastewater is about that of domestic
wastewater, the retention time of biological treatment at oil refin-
eries must be extended to days, while domestic wastewater can be
treated in hours.

Complexity may reflect the presence of various compounds which
may be toxic and interfere or compete with microbial activity.
Compounds found in industrial wastes include ammonia, cyanide, various forms of sulfur, and metals. Pretreatment, and/or adjustment is
often necessary to overcome the toxic effects.

Complexity also may result from biochemical interactions between organisms and constituents of the waste/wastewater. Such interactions may favor metabolic pathways other than those necessary
to meet treatment requirements (8,12,22).

Extremes in pH

The pH of industrial waste/wastewater is often acidic, basic,
or variable. Adjustments to pH by acid or base addition is common

practice in current industrial biological treatment techniques because systems are operated at about pH 7 following the convention of
domestic wastewater treatment. In domestic wastewater, a pH of
about 7 is optimal, and organisms used are selectively those which
grow optimally at that pH.

In order to treat industrial waste/wastewater, however, much
adjustment is often necessary to meet the required pH conditions in
order to assure treatment efficiency. This adjustment represents
considerable expense in chemicals and worker time, as well as the
risk of being unable to meet effluent requirements when adjustment
is inadequate.

Exotic Atmospheric Composition

Industrial processes often result in production of gases such
as NH_3, CO_2, H_2S, and various volatile organic compounds. These
gases exist in equilibrium with the liquid phase, creating an environment with an exotic atmosphere. Concentrations of these substances, consequently, are higher than commonly found in domestic
waste. Concentrations of several thousand ppm are common. Some of
these substances cause wastes to have low Eh (oxidation-reduction
potential), to have unusually high or low pH values, or high toxicity. Thus, such industrial pollutants in high concentrations may
cause interference with conventional wastewater and may have to be
removed before biological treatment.

The common practice is to remove these substances by physical
treatment followed by further treatment or release to the atmosphere. Pretreatment, however, is expensive. Furthermore, disposal
of the substances may not be the best alternative when there may be
a recovery value for the substance in solution.

Temperature Extremes

Many industrial wastes/wastewaters come from high temperature
processes and are often above 40°C. However, the optimal temperature for microorganisms in conventional wastewater systems is about
35°C or lower. Therefore, the current practice is to allow the
waste/wastewater to cool to an acceptable temperature before treatment. This practice does not take advantage of the higher kinetic
rates possible at elevated temperatures. Treatment processes are
not as efficient as they might be if elevated temperatures could be
used and reactor detention times reduced.

Wastes generated at low temperatures or in locations where
ambient temperatures are low (less than about 15°C) present another
problem. Low kinetic rates at low temperatures make treatment very
costly because long detention times are necessary: this may mean
high construction costs due to need for large reactors, or operation
of costly heating systems.

Low Organic Nutrient Concentration

Another frequent extreme situation in industrial waste/waste-
waters is deficiency of inorganic nutrients, especially phosphorus
and nitrogen. The deficiency of various micronutrients also can be
a problem. These substances are commonly added as a preadjustment
prior to biological treatment.

Oxygen Concentration and Eh

Availability of oxygen in wastewater is an important issue in
treatment. Wastewater from high-temperature processes and those
which contain reducing compounds such as H_2S have little to no dissolved oxygen and a low Eh (Tab. 2). Conventional aerobic treatment
processes cannot operate until reducing compounds are removed and
oxygen is reintroduced. This often involves use of energy-intensive
techniques such as aeration and/or stream stripping of pollutants
(23,24,25).

Moisture Content

In certain wastes very little moisture is available. This
makes the waste an extreme environment, because few microorganisms
can survive and proliferate without an aqueous medium (33,34,35).
Without adequate moisture the cells would be isolated from the substrate source, or limited to a very small substrate surface area to
attack. Examples of low moisture waste are sludge in general and
oily waste. Both are normally treated by landfarming and landfilling; unless moisture content is kept up, degradation does not occur
significantly.

Salinity and Ionic Composition

A wide range of salt concentrations occur in industrial waste/
wastewaters. Depending upon the process, there may be almost no
salt, while from other processes wastewaters may be a brine solution. The ionic composition of the salt may also vary. It may consist of abnormal proportions of the different inorganic ions as compared to common aquatic environments. High salinity approaching
that of seawater (about 3% w/v) and of variable ionic composition
may lead to inhibition of growth in conventional systems. A common
practice is to dilute wastes before treatment; however, with immi-
nent water shortages in different parts of the country, treatment at
high salinities may become an economic necessity.

EXTREME ENVIRONMENTS IN NATURE AND THEIR SIMILARITY TO CERTAIN
INDUSTRIAL WASTEWATERS

The wastes/wastewaters described earlier were described as
extreme environments. These environments are not unique; in fact,
they are similar to a number of natural environments, many of which

support microbial life. Much research has been done on extreme environments in nature, and results of such research can be used as
the basis for genetic engineering (26,27,28). Table 4 lists examples of extreme environments in nature which support microbial life.
Extremes in physical and chemical characteristics of interest in
waste/wastewater and at which microorganisms proliferate are listed
in Tab. 5, while types of organisms which exist are listed in
Tab. 4. The following is a brief description of a few selected
extreme environments of interest in waste/wastewater treatment.

Hot Spring Environments

    Areas within the hot spring environment (29,30,31,32) are good
examples of the situation commonly found in industrial wastes/waste-
waters. There are extremes in pH, high temperatures, and dispropor-
tionately large concentrations of gases found normally only in small
quantities in the atmosphere. Frequently, the composition of inorganic ionic species is significantly different from that in the more
common aquatic environment. Because of the presence of H_2S, the Eh
is low, similar to many industrial waste/wastewaters. However, an
important difference between the hot spring and industrial waste/
wastewaters is that the organic concentration is generally low in
the hot springs and anthropogenic compounds are not normally found.

    Although diverse organisms ranging from algae to methanogens
inhabit hot springs, the number of species which can exist is limited. This is significant because it shows that the principle of ubiquity so often assumed in conventional waste/wastewater treatment
apparently does not apply. Chemolithotrophy appears to be common,
but organisms with potential for heterotrophy are present. The importance of genetic potential to develop adaptations is evident from
this observation. Among interesting organisms are the cyanobacteria
which occur in hot springs. The proliferation of cyanobacteria is
interesting because, from the standpoint of treatment processes,
they are tolerant of low oxygen concentrations, and are often capable of being heterotrophic.

    Thermophilic organisms predominate in areas where the tempera-
tures extend from 45°C to 100°C. Studies show that they are dras-
tically different from the dominant organisms at lower temperatures,
possibly due to large scale genetic differences from their mesophilic counterparts (30,31,32). A number of mechanisms have been proposed regarding the ability of these organisms to proliferate at extreme temperatures. They include: thermostability of most proteins
due to amino acid alteration and increased interaction within the
protein molecules; thiolation of tRNA molecules, and stabilization
by extrinsic molecules, such as divalent cations or organic bases.
In addition to these thermophilic microorganisms, mesophiles capable
of proliferating under moderately thermophilic and lower temperatures can be expected. These organisms and their complex adaptations are interesting because of their tolerance to temperature

Table 4. Characteristics of selected natural extreme environments.

Site	pH	Temperature (°C)	Organic Concentration	Gases	Type of Microorganisms	Alkalinity (mg/L) (CaCO$_3$)	Salinity (%w/v)	Ref.
Acid hot springs	<4	>45 to 100	low	—	limited species of aerobic and anaerobic bacteria, cyanobacteria	—	0.1-0.3	30,32,54,55
Alkaline	5 to 11	>45 to 100	low	$+H_2$, $+CH_4$, $+NH_3$, $+H_2S$, $+CO_2$		—	0.1-0.3	30,29
Hypersaline water Dead Sea, Salt Lake	11	ambient	—	—			3.5-39.2	
Big Soda Lake	9.7	ambient	low	H_2S	anaerobic, aerobic	24,000	8.7	41
Distilled water	—	ambient	trace	—	oligotrophic	—	0	43,44
Submarine hydro-thermal vents	4.24-7.53	3 to 306	high	CH_4,CO_2,H_2	anaerobic, aerobic bacteria	—	3	39,40
*Domestic wastewater	6.5 to 7.5	ambient	100-500 mg/L	air	wide variety	50-200	0.1-0.3	25
Soil (low moisture)	—	ambient	variable	air	fungi predominate	—	—	33,52

*Domestic wastewater is given for comparison purposes.

Table 5. Environmental extremes at which microorganisms have been
found reported to live.

Factor	Range	Ref.
Eh/pH	-450 to 850 mV	28
pH	<1 to 11 s.u.·	28, 51
Temperature	-18 to 104°C	28
Salinity	0 to 30%	28
Substrate concentration	from <75 g/L	37
Sulfide	0 to 500 mg/L	41
Ammonia	500 mg/L	52
*Water activity (a_w)	1.0 to 0.61	34, 35
Toxic Substances		
CN	0 to 280 mg/L	53
Phenol	0 to 1000 mg/L	28
Metals	Variable tolerance depending upon previous exposure	52

$$*a_w = \frac{Po}{P} \quad \text{when } Po = \text{vapor of water} \quad P = \text{vapor pressure}$$

variations; such changes occasionally occur under actual industrial
process conditions.

Submarine Hydrothermal Vents

Hydrothermal vents (39,40) offer very extreme thermophilic conditions and high pressures. As marine environments they are considerably more saline than hot springs. A wide variety of bacteria
which have been collected from these vents range from aerobes to
anaerobes, and include methylotrophs, methanotrophs, methanogens,
and sulfur bacteria.

Alkaline, Hypersaline Lakes

Alkaline, hypersaline lakes such as the Big Soda Lake in Nevada
present a good similarity with waste/wastewaters with high alkalin-
ity, high sulfide concentrations, and extreme salinity (41). The
organisms found appear to be predominantly obligate heterotrophs.
Methanogens also appear to be present, but the mechanism of their
methanogenic activity is not yet known. Such organisms found in hypersaline conditions are uniquely adapted to their environments by
what appear to be multigenic adaptations which have made their protein structures dependent upon high salt concentrations. They have

also developed mechanisms which prevent dehydration, including production of glycerol of other polyols, accumulation of KCl, or use of
sodium pump mechanisms (6).

Low Moisture Environments

Soil and other environments with considerable organic content
but low in moisture (33,34,35,52) are interesting extreme environments from the standpoint of waste treatment. These environments
support organisms which can proliferate even when moisture conditions become low enough to limit the aquatic medium. Generally,
bacterial activity is limited to areas where enough moisture is
available for accessibility to nutrients. However, certain organisms, especially filamentous fungi appear to predominate in other
areas. Fungi are successful because they are able to extend their
hyphae from one moist area to another, passing through the drier
areas between. They appear to predominate because of lack of competition by bacteria, which tend to be moisture-limited.

Fungi are very flexible in their metabolic activity. They
appear to contain enzymes which are able to function with multiple
substrates, while bacteria tend to be relatively specialized (36,
37). Fungi from low moisture environments adapted to specific types
of wastes can be the source of a valuable gene pool for enhancement
of land application-type waste treatment processes. They can offer
a possible alternative for treatment processes which depend upon
bacterial activity.

APPLICATION OF GENETIC ENGINEERING

Wastes/wastewaters which have extreme physical and chemical
characteristics provide a unique opportunity to apply genetic engineering and significantly improve treatment processes. As discussed
above, various wastes/wastewaters require costly and complicated adjustments before they can be treated biologically. Uses of genetic
engineering and appropriate reactor technology may minimize the need
for these adjustments.

Proposed Scheme

The proposed approach is shown schematically in Fig. 1 and is
contrasted with conventional treatment. Instead of the numerous adjustments used in conventional treatment systems (pH, temperature,
salinity, O_2, moisture, etc.), treatment is done directly in the
waste/wastewater with little or no adjustment. Organisms from extreme environments similar to the waste/wastewater are used. Because organisms which evolve in remote, unusual environments will
not necessarily be able to degrade anthropogenic compounds in industrial waste/wastewater, mutants may be very valuable. These mutants would be prepared from organisms from the extreme environments

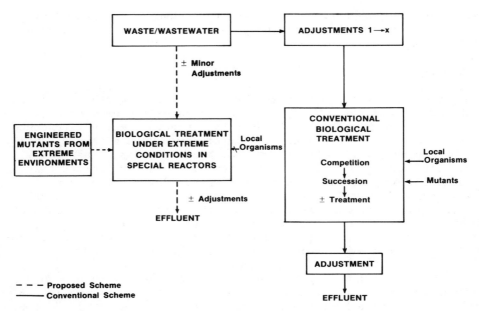

Fig. 1.   Proposed scheme for application of genetic engineering to
           waste/wastewater treatment contrasted with scheme for con-
           ventional wastewater treatment.

similar to the waste/wastewater to take maximal advantage of the
multigenic changes which have occurred in nature over time, adapting
the organism to the environment.

     Because these organisms will be well adapted to the environ-
ment, the major problem of competition which would be expected in a
conventional system could be negligible. In addition, the problem
of accidentally releasing mutant organisms would be at least partially minimized because organisms proliferating under extreme conditions would find it difficult to survive outside of the reactor.

     Post-treatment adjustments before discharge may be necessary in
certain cases in order to meet discharge requirements. This, however, would be relatively simple in the final clarifier, containing
a well mixed and equilibrated batch.

Generally Useful Traits

     In dealing with industrial waste/wastewaters, there are traits
which would be of universal value if they could be introduced into
the bacteria involved. Among these traits are: flexible substrate
uptake, enhancement of enzyme production, and capability to use multiple substrates.

Flexibility in uptake is an important consideration, for without this characteristic, organisms genetically altered to metabolize particular compounds would not be able to function as intended (42). This would be a very valuable trait in application of genetic engineering to complex waste/wastewaters.

Development of organisms capable of handling multiple substances simultaneously would be a valuable accomplishment because of the complexity and variability of many wastes/wastewaters. This can be accomplished if organisms could have nonspecific enzymes and/or multiple inducible enzymes, with little or no catabolite repression. Flexible enzymes appear to be common among fungi (36) and certain bacteria. Multiple enzyme induction is found among oligotrophs, bacteria which occur under low carbon flux conditions (42,43). Transfer of genetic material from such organisms to selected organisms to be used, or manipulation of existing genes which may control a possible inherent ability to handle multiple substrates, can be a valuable contribution.

Enhancement of production of enzymes necessary for degradation of compounds in waste/wastewater would mean increased kinetic rates and improved process efficiency. Those processes which occur slowly because of low temperature and/or under anaerobic conditions would be significantly improved.

Specific Applications

Examples of possible specific applications for genetic engineering in treatment of industrial waste/wastewaters are listed in Tab. 6 and are discussed in this section. These applications will depend upon the advances in the basic biology and biochemistry of organisms involved, and upon demonstrations that the necessary transfer of genetic material can be achieved, stabilized, and expressed.

Anaerobic conditions. Anaerobic wastes/wastewaters would be matched with similar environments such as areas within hot springs, submarine hydrothermal vents, regions in alkaline lakes, and well established industrial waste storage sites. Organisms endemic to the selected environment would then be genetically manipulated. Under anaerobic conditions there would be much to be gained by using methanogenic consortia of microorganisms because of the savings to be realized by eliminating aeration intreatment, reduction of sludge production, and, depending upon the concentration of the waste/wastewater, the potential of offset treatment costs by methane production. The following characteristics would be valuable: that the methanogens must be able to use acetate and other simple organic substrates, and the associated consortia must be capable of attacking a wide range of compounds and break them down to forms that can be used by the methanogens. Flexibility in substrate uptake and flexible enzyme systems in key organisms would be essential.

Table 6. Examples of application of organisms from extreme environments.

Waste/Wastewater Type	Natural Environment Type	Traits Desired	Advantage
complex, little or no dissolved oxygen, low Eh, high temperature, H_2S, NH_3, relatively reduced compounds	anaerobic, high mesophilic to thermophilic, e.g., hot springs, hydrothermal vent, hypersaline lakes	flexible substrates flexible uptake	no aeration, shorter retention time, greater treatment efficiency
low temperature, complex waste	low temperature	flexible substrates flexible uptake enhanced enzyme levels	shorter retention time, little to no heating
low moisture, complex, variable temperature	well drained soil in areas used for treatment of similar material	flexible substrates flexible uptake enhanced enzyme levels aerobic/anoxic metabolism	minimal attention needed
low pH, complex waste, high temperature	low pH, temperatures in high mesophilic to thermophilic range, e.g., acid hot spring	flexible substrates flexible uptake	minimize pH adjustment

A function which would be particularly valuable if transferred to methanogens is the ability to withstand exposure to air or dissolved oxygen without loss of viability. This is an important problem in commercial efforts in start-up of anaerobic treatment systems when inocula must be transferred over long distances to reactor sites.

Cyanobacteria (blue-green algae) are also interesting organisms for use in anoxic to anaerobic conditions. Their value in wastewater treatment systems was described earlier. Because they appear to be relatively simple to manipulate, they are good candidates for this work (38). Because they are capable of both heterotrophic and photosynthetics growth, they may be especially useful where concentrations of the organic substrate may be low. However, because genetic material is readily exchanged in these organisms, considerable effort must be put into stabilizing any planned genetic transfer.

Low moisture environments. Treatment in low moisture situations as in land application treatment, can benefit greatly from genetic engineering. Fungi, as described earlier, are well equipped to survive and thrive under low moisture conditions. If land application sites can be populated predominantly by fungi, then the cost of adjusting the site for moisture can be minimized. Fungi manipulated for enhanced enzyme production and ability to metabolize efficiently under anoxic conditions may be useful for the purpose. This potential would allow efficient performance even under low temperature conditions which commonly occur in land applications, and provide the fungi with the ability to function efficiently even below the soil surface.

Low pH condition. Acid hot springs appear to be good locations to find organisms which might be able to proliferate in low pH wastes. However, because organisms in the hot spring environment are not normally exposed to high concentrations of organic compounds, especially anthropogenic compounds, their ability to degrade such compounds may be limited. Enhancement of this ability may be necessary, and genetic engineering may be an important tool for the purpose.

Population Stability and Improvement of Reactor Technology

Population stability is a major issue in the attempt to put genetic engineering to use in waste/wastewater treatment. Conventional, continuously stirred reactors can readily lose organisms to the environment because the microorganisms are in free floating suspension. When very special organisms are involved, their retention is critical for a number of reasons:

1. to perpetuate the population in the reactor because contin-
    uous inoculation can be very costly

2. to be able to maintain a varied population of organisms if
    necessary so that the treatment process can continue effi-
    ciently even when the composition of the waste varies

3. to provide good opportunity for mass transfer of compounds
    in the waste/wastewater to the organisms.

4. to prevent release of genetic recombinants to the environ-
    ment, because of the many questions which remain regarding
    possible problems the organisms may cause if they are re-
    leased.

A method for achieving this need, often mentioned in the biotechnology literature today, is the use of biofilms. Biofilm techniques available today are fixed packed bed reactors, fluidized bed
reactors, upflow sludge reactors, rotating biological contactors,
and the age old trickling filters. These methods are under active
investigation as a possible means to conserve energy in waste/waste-
water treatment in general. Modifications to these techniques may
be necessary to accommodate use of mutant organisms. In cases where
the extreme conditions are not markedly different from the local
environment, other means of assuring that the desired organisms will
predominate may be necessary. Reactors with special features to
assure environmental control may be a solution. These would be
reactors which allow for selection of particular types of organisms
by using a characteristic different from that possessed by competing
organisms.

An example of possible reactor modification is the use of light
to selectively culture phototrophs on fixed films from a wastewater
effluent stream. In previous work the author has selectively developed populations of photosynthetic sulfur bacteria for sulfide removal, by providing a low intensity light source to a fixed film
reactor (45). The light in the reactor favored the growth of the
phototrophs and allowed them to predominate over other organisms
coming from an anaerobic reactor/system.

In addition to recognized techniques, there is a number of innovative methods appearing in the literature today based upon small-
scale laboratory studies. However, as a word of caution, it is always important to consider the methodology from the standpoint of
feasibility for eventual scale-up. The feasibility of construction
on a large scale (e.g. 5×10^5 gallons/day) and the associated economics must be considered. This requires a background in structural
engineering; hence, the attempt to consider means to apply genetic
engineering to waste/wastewater control requires interdisciplinary

activity among microbiologists, molecular biologists, and engineers with a good understanding of biotechnology.

CONCLUSION

Genetic engineering has the potential to play an important role in making industrial waste/wastewater treatment more efficient and economical by minimizing the need for pretreatment adjustments. Before genetic engineering can be applied, however, much basic research will be necessary on the physiology, biochemistry, and genetics of organisms to be used. The ecology of the extreme environments to be used as inoculum sources and the interactions of the organisms in those environments also must be elucidated. Methods to accomplish gene transfer, stabilize mutants, and assure gene expression appropriate for this application must also be developed.

This application can only become a reality through the interdisciplinary activity of the genetic engineer with microbiologists of appropriate specialties and with environmental engineers well versed in biotechnology.

REFERENCES

1. American Society of Microbiologists (1983) Opportunities in Microbiological Research. ASM Committee on Genetic & Molecular Microbiology of the Public & Scientific Affairs Board and the NSF, Washington, D.C.
2. Chakrabarty, A.M. (1982) Genetic mechanisms in the dissimilation of chlorinated compounds. In Biodegradation and Detoxification of Environmental Pollutants. CRC Press, Boca Raton, pp. 127-139.
3. Chakrabarty, A.M. (1981) Microbial Genetic Engineering and Environmental Pollution. Proc. Batelle Conf. Genetic Engineering 5:211-219.
4. Chatterjee, D.K., S.T. Kellogg, K. Furukawa, J.J. Kilbane, and A.M. Chakrabarty (1981) Genetic Approaches to the Problems of Toxic Chemical Pollution. Proc. Third Cleveland Symposium on Macromolecules, Cleveland, Ohio, 22-26 June, A.G. Walton, ed., Elsevier Scientific Publishing Co., Amsterdam, pp. 199-212.
5. Kellogg, S.T., D.K. Chatterjee, and A.M. Chakrabarty (1981) Plasmid-assisted molecular breeding: New technique for enhanced biodegradation of persistent toxic chemicals. Science 214:1133-1135.
6. Knackmuss, H.J., and W. Reineke (1979) Construction of haloaromatics utilizing bacteria. Nature 277:385-386.
7. Pierce, G. (1982) Development of genetically engineered micro-

organisms to degrade hazardous organic compounds. In Hazardous
Waste Management for the 80's, T.C. Sweeny, R.M. Sykes, and
O.J. Sproul, eds. Ann Arbor Sciences, Ann Arbor, pp. 431-439.

8. Pierce, G. (1982) Potential role of genetically engineered
microorganisms to degrade toxic chemical hydrocarbons.
Presented at the Cleveland Meeting of the AICHE.

9. Pierce, G.E., J.B. Robinson, T.J. Facklam, and J.M. Rice (1982)
Physiological and genetic comparisons of environmental strains
of Pseudomonas capable of degrading the herbicide 2,4-D. In
Developments in Industrial Microbiology 23:407-417.

10. Pierce, G.E., J.J. Facklum, and J.M. Rice (1981) Isolation and
characterization of plasmids from environmental strains of bacteria capable of degrading the herbicide 2,4-D. In
Developments in Industrial Microbiology 22:401-407.

11. Devereux, R., and R.K. Sizemore (1982) Plasmid incidence in
marine bacteria isolated from petroleum polluted sites on
different petroleum hydrocarbons. Marine Pollution Bull.
13(6):198-202.

12. Cane, P.A., and P.A. Williams (1982) The Plasmid-coded metabolism of Naphthalene and V2-methyl naphthalene in Pseudomonas
strains: Phenotypic changes corrected with structural modification of the plasmid pWW60-1. J. Gen. Microb. 128:2281-2290.

13. Ackerman, R.A., J.F. Tobey, S.G. Frasier, and S.K. Birdsall
(1982) Ammonia removal from mixed industrial wastewaters. Presented at the summer meeting AICHE, Cleveland.

14. Nyer, E.K., and H.J. Bourgeois, Jr. (1979) Operational Trouble
Shooting in Industrial Biological Treatment Systems. Proc.
35th Industrial Waste Water Conf., Purdue University, pp. 849-
854.

15. Zikopoulos, J.N., and T.G. Zitrides (1982) Pollution technology
state-of-the-art. Presented at 1982 Summer Meeting, AICHE,
Cleveland.

16. Himebaugh, R.R., and R.L. Heintrich, Jr. (1982) Waste sludge
reduction and biological wastewater treatment optimization
through addition of adapted mutant bacteria of biochemicals.
Presented at the WPCF 55th Annual Conference.

17. Tracy, K.D., and T.G. Zitrides (1979) Mutant bacteria and Exxon
waste system. Hydrocarbon Processing, Oct. 1979, pp. 1-46.

18. Johnston, J. (1981) Genetic Engineering Planning Study.
Advanced Environmental Control Tech. Center, Univ. of Illinois,
Urbana.

19. Liang, L.N., J.L. Sinclair, L.M. Malloy, and M. Alexander
(1982) Fate in model ecosystems of microbial species of potential genetic engineering. Appl. Environ. Micro. 44(3):703-714.

20. Cooney, C.L. (1983) Bioreactors: Design & operation. Science
219(4585):728-733.

21. American Petroleum Institute (1981) Refinery wastewater priority pollutant study - sample analysis and evaluation of data.
API Publication 4346. API, Washington, D.C.

22. Pierce, G.E., J.B. Robinson, and J.R. Colaruotolo (1983) Sub-

strate diversity of Pseudomonas spp. containing chloro-toluene degradative plasmids. (In press.)

23. Jones, H.R. (1973) Pollution Control in the Petroleum Industry. Noyes Data Corporation, Park Ridge, New Jersey.

24. Beychok, M.R. (1979) Characterization of Petroleum Refining Industry and Petroleum Refinery Wastewater. Univ. of Tulsa and USEPA: R.S. Kerr Environmental Research Laboratory.

25. Metcalfe & Eddy, Inc. (1972) Wastewater Engineering. McGraw Hill, Inc., New York.

26. Shilo, Moshe, ed. (1979) Strategies of Microbial Life in Extreme Environments. Proceedings of the Dahlem Konferenzen, Berlin. Verlag Chemie, New York.

27. Alexander, M. (1976) Natural selection and the ecology of microbial adaption in a biosphere. In Extreme Environments, M.R. Heinrich, ed. Academic Press, Inc. New York, pp. 3-25.

28. Vallentyne, J.R. (1963) Environmental biophysics and microbial ubiquity. Annals N.Y. Acad. Sci., 180:342-352.

29. Brock, T.D. (1979) Ecology of saline Lakes. In Strategies of Microbial Life in Extreme Environments, M. Shilo, ed. Verlag Chemie, New York, pp. 29-47.

30. Castenholz, R.W. (1979) Evolution and ecology of thermophilic microorganisms. In Strategies of Microbial Life in Extreme Environments, M. Shilo, ed. Verlag Chemie, New York, pp. 373-392.

31. Langworthy, T.A., et al. (1979) Life at high temperatures, Group Report. In Strategies of Microbial Life in Extreme Environments, M. Shilo, ed. Verlag Chemie, New York, pp. 417-432.

32. Zuber, H. (1979) Structure and function of enzymes from thermophilic microorganisms. In Strategies of Microbial Life in Extreme Environments, M. Shilo, ed. Verlag Chemie, New York, pp. 393-415.

33. Griffin, D.M., and E.J. Luard (1979) Water Stress and Microbial Ecology. In Strategies of Microbial Life in Extreme Environments, M. Shilo, ed. Verlag Chemie, New York, pp. 49-63.

34. Horowitz, N.H. (1979) Biological water requirements. In Strategies of Microbial Life in Extreme Environments. M. Shilo, ed. Verlag Chemie, New York, pp. 125-135.

35. Lanyi, J.K. (1979) Life at low water activity group report II. In Strategies of Microbial Life in Extreme Environments, M. Shilo, ed. Verlag Chemie, New York, pp. 125-135.

36. Gibson, D.T. (1978) Microbial transformation of aromatic pollutants. In Aquatic Pollutants, O. Hutzinger et al., eds. Pergamon Press, New York, pp.

37. Kobayashi, H., and B.E. Rittmann (1982) Microbial removal of hazardous organic compounds. Environ. Sci.& Technol. 16:170A-183A.

38. Sherman, L., (1981) Photosynthesis and cloning in cyanobacteria. Presented at the Genetic Engineering Conference, University of Illinois, Urbana.

39. Baross, J.A., M.D. Lilley, and L.I. Gordon (1982) Is the CH_4 and CO venting from submarine hydrothermal systems produced by thermophilic bacteria? Nature 298:366–368.

40. Jannasch, H.W., and C.O. Wirsen (1981) Morphological survey of microbial mats near deep sea thermal vents. Appl. Environ. Micro. 41:528–538.

41. Oremland, R.S., L. Marsh, and D.J. Des Marais (1982) Methanogenesis in Big Soda Lake, Nevada: an alkaline, moderately hypersaline desert lake. Appl. Environ. Micro. 43(2):462–468.

42. Zeikus, J.G. (Personal communication.)

43. Poindexter, J. (1981) Workshop on Trace Organic Contaminant Removal. Advanced Environmental Control Technology Research Center, University of Illinois, Urbana. July 27–28, 1981.

44. Hirsch, P. et al. (1979) Life under conditions of low nutrient concentrations, Group Report. In Strategies of Microbial Life in Extreme Environments, M. Shilo, ed. Verlag Chemie, New York, pp. 357–372.

45. Kobayashi, H. (1983) Use of Photosynthetic Bacteria for Hydrogen Sulfide Removal from anaerobic waste treatment effluent. Water Research 17(5):579–587.

46. Jackson, L.P., and C.C. Wright, eds. (1981) Analysis of Waters Associated with Alternative Fuel Production. ASTM, Philadelphia.

47. Jones, H.R. (1973) Pollution Control in the Petroleum Industry. Noyes Data Comparison, New Jersey.

48. Nemerow, N.L. (1978) Industrial Water Pollution. Addison-Wesley Publishing Co., Massachusetts.

49. Patterson, J.W. (1977) Wastewater Treatment Technology. Ann Arbor Science Publication, Inc., Ann Arbor.

50. Wilderman, T.R., and S.L. Hoeffner (1981) Paraho waters synfuel – characteristics and analysis of major constituents. In Analysis of Waters Associated with Alternation Fuel Production, L.P. Jackson, and C.C. Wright, eds. ASTM Publication 720, pp. 129–141.

51. Souza, K.A., P.H. Deal, H.M. Mack, and C.E. Turnbill (1975) Growth and reproduction of microorganisms under extremely alkaline conditions. Applied Micro. 28(6):1066–1068.

52. Kobayashi, H. (Unpublished data.)

53. Howe, R. (1972) Toxic wastes degradation and disposal. Process Biochem. (London) 7(317):474–1430.

54. Hickey, C.W., and R.M. Daniel (1979) The electron transport system of extremely thermophilic bacteria. J. Gen. Microbiol. 114:195–200.

55. Jansen, G., R.M. Daniel, B. Nicholson, and H.W. Morgan (1982) Membrane phase transition and succinate oxidase activity in an extremely thermophilic bacteria. Biochem. Biophys. Acta 685:191–195.

NEEDS AND STRATEGIES FOR GENETIC CONTROL: MUNICIPAL WASTES

Bruce E. Rittmann

Department of Civil Engineering
University of Illinois at Urbana-Champaign
Urbana, Illinois 61801

INTRODUCTION

Municipal wastes mainly consist of sewage, sludges generated from treatment of sewage, and refuse. All three types of waste are generated whenever sizable numbers of people live together; treatment and disposal are usually considered a municipal problem, even though private firms sometimes carry out the operations. Table 1 lists approximate values for the total masses of sewage, sludge, and refuse generated annually by all Americans. Although the waste materials have small economic value, their very large mass generation rates make them of major economic significance to the local economy. For urban areas and towns, treatment and disposal often are functions performed by local or regional governmental agencies.

The purposes of this paper are to identify problems encountered in the treatment and disposal of municipal wastes and to indicate how genetic control can be applied fruitfully to ameliorate some of the problems. First, three general classes of problems are identified. Second, strategies, especially those including genetic control, are presented. Third, problems of treatment and disposal are enumerated and placed into the classes for problem type and solution approach. Finally, possible stumbling blocks are addressed.

PROBLEM CLASSES

The problems encountered in the treatment and disposal of municipal wastes can be classified into three types:

1. problems for which no feasible solution is currently iden-
    tified

2. problems for which the existing solutions are expensive

3. problems for which the existing solutions have poor effic-
    iency and/or reliability.

Identification of the problem type is valuable because it
allows us to point toward an appropriate goal. For example, if an
existing method is feasible, economical, but unreliable, the emphasis should be on determining the cause of and mitigating the unreliability. Looking for entirely new approaches is probably unnecessary and unfruitful, as is making changes unrelated to the cause of
the unreliability. On the other hand, classes or problems for which
no feasible solution exists need a wide-ranging, exploratory (and
high risk) approach. Most municipal waste problems fall into the
classes characterized by poor economics and poor reliability/effic-
iency.

SOLUTION APPROACHES

Potential solutions come about through four different strategies, only two of which rely on genetic control. Fruitful use of
genetic control techniques requires that they be applied to problems
whose solutions require them. Attempting genetic control when it is
unnecessary or inappropriate wastes valuable resources and is likely
to be unsucessful.

The first strategy involves enhancing a currently used method
by making a process-related improvement. Genetic control is not
part of the strategy. Since the current process is feasible, the
process improvement strategy addresses problems in economics and
efficiency/reliability. An example of a process improvement that
can enhance economics is the use of denitrification as the first
step in wastewater treatment for biochemical oxygen demand (BOD) and

Table 1. Approximate annual generation rates of sewage, sewage
          sludge, and refuse by all Americans in the 1980s.

Waste	Generation rate, tons/year
Sewage	2×10^{10}
Sewage Sludge	1×10^{7}
Refuse	2×10^{8}

nitrogen removal (1). Performing denitrification first reduces the
oxygen-transfer requirement and the amount of sludge produced, both
of which lower operating costs. Rittmann (2) and Rittmann and
Kobayashi (3) pointed out an example of how a process improvement
can enhance efficiency, even though the same reactions are carried
out by the same organisms. They demonstrated that the use of fluidized-bed biofilm reactors can achieve higher removal efficiencies
than fixed-bed biofilm reactors when a very low effluent concentration is the treatment goal. The process improvement is achieved by
optimizing the distribution of microorganisms within the reactors.

    The second general strategy is to apply an existing process or
reaction to a new problem for which the currently used process is
inadequate or nonexistent. The second strategy requires recognition
that a process used for other purposes is applicable to the problem
and mitigates the shortcomings of current practice. Appropriate use
of this second strategy is primarily technology transfer and does
not necessarily involve genetic control. A good example of the
second strategy would be the use of a methanogenic process for the
treatment of sewage. The economic benefits derived from eliminating
aeration, reducing sludge production, and generating methane gas
would be substantial if the anaerobic technology used for sludges
and industrial wastes could be transferred to municipal sewage.
Likewise, successful anaerobic digestion of municipal refuse could
provide major economic benefits and would reduce the deleterious
environmental impacts of refuse disposal, such as disruptive land
use; pollution of air, groundwater, and surface water; odors; and
propagation of disease vectors.

    The third strategy is to employ the genetic control technique
of selection of novel microorganisms not presently utilized in
treatment. Kobayashi and Rittmann (4) reviewed the wide variety of
microorganisms available, but seldom employed. Successful use of
new microorganisms requires three steps. The first step is the
identification of an organism that can carry out a desired function.
The second step is providing an environment that selects for and allows growth of the organism. Finally, the microorganism must be
utilized in a reactor system that allows it to perform efficiently
the desired reaction and sustain itself. The very large mass and
volume throughputs of municipal wastes requires that the microorganisms reproduce to sustain suitably large numbers in the treatment
reactor.

    Four infrequently used microorganisms might have applications
to municipal wastes (4): fungi, algae, photosynthetic bacteria, and
oligotrophs. The fungi are most valuable because of their ability
to attack and partially degrade complex organic materials. This
makes them particularly useful for degradation of solids, and fungi
are common constituents of the flora of composting sludge and refuse. Fungi are selected in systems that contain complex organics
and relatively high solids contents.

The main advantage of algae is that they grow from the utilization of light as the energy source and water as the electron donor.
Therefore, development of a large algal biomass can be independent
of the usual limiting factors in biological processes -- organic
carbon and energy sources. Algae can be useful for adsorbing refractory organic compounds, providing organic product material for
the growth of heterotrophic microorganisms, and catalyzing photochemical reactions. Although algae are a critical aspect of stabilization lagoons, little has been done to optimize their use for the
above-named functions. Better ways to grow, accumulate, and control
algae are needed.

Photosynthetic bacteria also possess the advantage of growth
with light as the energy source. Again, phototrophy allows growth
of the biomass independently of the organic content of the water.
Photosynthetic bacteria are able to oxidize the H_2S produced in
anaerobic systems (5) and to participate in reductive dechlorination
(4). Light, reduced sulfur, and anaerobic conditions favor
photosynthetic bacteria.

Oligotrophic microorganisms are those that are particularly
adapted to low nutrient concentrations. Although oligotrophs could
come from any microbial group, bacteria are the best studied. Oligotrophs are most advantageously applied when very low concentrations are required. Basic work on the selection and accumulation of
oligotrophs is now under way. Attachment seems to be a critical
factor for the successful use of oligotrophs.

The fourth strategy, also one that employs genetic control, is
genetic alteration of some appropriate microorganism to improve or
add a desirable attribute. This fourth strategy involves application of the genetic engineering tools that have come into prominence
in recent years. Five items are necessary for the successful use of
genetic engineering methods (6):

1.   a desired DNA molecule (passenger) to be replicated

2.   a DNA vehicle which can replicate in living cells after
     the desired DNA molecule is inserted into it

3.   a method of joining the passenger DNA to the vehicle DNA

4.   a means of introducing the joined DNA molecule into an
     appropriate host organism in which it can replicate and
     the desired DNA be expressed

5.   a means of selecting for those cells that have replicated
     and expressed the desired recombinant molecule.

The experimental methods to perform the genetic engineering
manipulations have been reported in other references (e.g., Ref. 7)

and are well beyond the scope and purpose of this paper. Nonetheless, discussion of a few generic types of manipulations that might
be of value illustrates the potential for genetic engineering.
Johnston and Robinson (8) suggested four types of manipulations,
which are discussed below.

The first manipulation is the rearrangement of genes from one
species to another. The proper goal of such a transfer is to introduce a totally new function or an improved version of an existing
function into a microorganism that is otherwise well suited to the
treatment scheme. Achieving the proper goal first requires that the
DNA coding for the new or improved function exists in some other
organism and can be isolated. Then, a suitable receptor organism
that can receive and express the new DNA and that can thrive under
treatment conditions, i.e., temperature, pH, moisture content,
electron donor and acceptor, and other nutrients must be found.
Most of the emphasis in genetic engineering has focused on matters
relating to the first step, while experience using as receptors
environmentally relevant microorganisms, such as bacteria found in
treatment systems or the novel organisms described previously, is
very sparse. Successful application of genetic control to municipal
waste problems absolutely requires the use of organisms suited to
the treatment environment. The large mass and low economic value of
the municipal wastes preclude attempts to modify the waste to the
special requirements of a poorly suited microbe.

Achieving practical results from gene transfer clearly is
limited by the lack of knowledge about how DNA can be transferred
to, replicated in, and expressed in relevant microorganisms. The
relative facility with which we can now manipulate E. coli is not
directly transferrable to other, more relevant species; we can
expect to expend considerable time and effort before we can use
environmentally relevant organisms. On the other hand, employing
convenient, but poorly suited microorganisms is doomed to failure in
practice.

The first step, finding existing DNA that codes for the desired
function, is advanced, but still can limit practical applications,
especially for municipal wastes. The main deficiency is identification of the desired function to be improved or added. Some functions, such as dehalogenation or initial breakdown of complex organic molecules, reside in one gene which is relatively easy to
identify. On the other hand, other functions are complex, poorly
defined, and reside in several genes. Examples of complex functions
are better flocculation of heterotrophic bacteria in activated
sludge, stronger attachment of bacteria to surfaces, increased
growth rates of nitrifying bacteria, improved resistance to low
moisture content by composting organisms, and decreased sensitivity
to inhibitors. Each function is defined according to a physiological factor affecting process performance. Success using genetic

engineering depends critically upon properly recognizing and describing the process-related physiological factors. Translation of
the complex physiological factors into a gene or set of genes is a
major new initiative for genetic engineering.

The second genetic manipulation mentioned by Johnston and
Robinson (8) is amplification of the number of gene copies in an
organism. Presumably, more gene copies would give rise to higher
protein levels, which would increase reaction rates. Gene amplification, to be successful, requires an appropriate organism, recognition of the physiological factor to be enhanced, identification of
the genes controlling that factor, and specific amplification of
those genes. Any step could be limiting, and more gene copies do
not necessarily guarantee faster reactions.

The third type of manipulation is alteration of genetic control
on the expression of genes. For example, making certain biodegradative enzymes permanently constitutive instead of inducible by the
substrate could overcome lag period or threshold affects seen for
low concentrations of some organic compounds (9,10,11). Derepression seems to be the most likely application for alteration of expression. In other words, the goal is to prevent cells from stop-
ping a desired function because of a lack of sufficient inducing
substrate, the presence of a competing substrate, or other unfavorable conditions.

The fourth possible manipulation is site-specific mutagenesis
to alter the gene product. Goals could include making a degradative
enzyme accept more substrates and increasing enzyme affinity for a
substrate. The ability to construct or alter genes to improve gene
products presently is not a reality.

IMPROVEMENTS IN MUNICIPAL WASTE TREATMENT

Tables 2-4 compile desirable improvements in biological treatment of municipal wastewater, sludge, and refuse. The tables indicate the type of problem (no feasible process, poor economics, and
poor reliability/efficiency) and whether the most likely solutions
will come from a process enhancement, utilization of a new process,
the use of a novel microorganism, and/or the application of genetic
manipulation.

Tables 2-4 make it clear that the biggest problems for municipal waste treatment are poor reliability/efficiency and poor economics. Many of the reliability problems can be solved through the
improvement in the current process or a switch to a different, but
known, process. Hence, genetic control is not needed for many problems. Instead, better application of biological and process fundamentals is most effective.

Table 2.   Improvements in biological treatment of municipal waste-
            waters.

Improvement	Problem Type	Likely Solution Type
Eliminate activated sludge bulking	2	a, d
Improve biofilm attachment	2	a, d
Stable nitrification	2	a
	3	d
Prevent sloughing in trickling filters	2	a
Reduce O_2 limitations in aerobic processes	3	d
Reduce energy consumption	2	a, b
Reduce sludge quantities produced	2	a, b
Enhance P removal	2, 3	a, b, c, d
Biodegrade xenobiotic organics	2	a, b, c, d
Resist toxic upsets	2	a, d
Prevent odor generation	2, 3	a, b, c
Make simple efficient processes for small communities	2	a, b

Problem types: 1.   Not feasible
                 2.   Not reliable or efficient
                 3.   Not economic
Solution types: a.   Improve existing process
                 b.   Use of new process
                 c.   Use a novel microorganism
                 d.   Apply genetic manipulation

     The tables point out that several improvements could result
from genetic control approaches. The remainder of this section
briefly describes the physiological requirements or objectives
associated with the most promising improvements.

     Elimination of activated sludge bulking, the phenomenon of poor
sludge settling and solids loss, requires identification of the factors that control the growth of desired flocculant bacteria and undesired filamentous microorganisms. The desired result is a nonfil-
amentous bacterium that flocculates strongly and can function well
with the very low dissolved oxygen concentrations found in the
interior of flocs.

Table 3.   Improvements in biological wastewater sludge treatment.

Improvement	Problem Type	Likely Solution Type
Eliminate anaerobic digester instability	2	a, d
Eliminate odors	2	a, c
Enhance sludge dewaterability	1	d
Make sludge composting occur more quickly	3	a, d
Eliminate heavy metals from sludge	1	d

Problem types: 1. Not feasible
                  2. Not reliable or efficient
                  3. Not economic
Solution types: a. Improve existing process
                  b. Use a new process
                  c. Use a novel microorganism
                  d. Apply genetic manipulation

Table 4.   Improvements in biological refuse treatment.

Improvement	Problem Type	Likely Solution Type
Make refuse composting occur more quickly	3	a, d
Perfect anaerobic digestion of refuse	2, 3	a, d
Biodegrade contaminants in leachate from refuse landfills	2, 3	a, b, c, d
Eliminate heavy metals from refuse	1	d
Eliminate odors	2	a, c

Problem types: 1. Not feasible
                  2. Not reliable or efficient
                  3. Not economic
Solution types: a. Improve existing process
                  b. Use a new process
                  c. Use a novel microorganism
                  d. Apply genetic manipulation

Improved attachment of film-forming bacteria, or biofilms, involves factors that allow strong adhesion and close packing of cells.

Stable nitrification (aerobic oxidation of ammonium) would be more likely if nitrifying bacteria had faster growth rates, more comparable to heterotrophs. Relaxation of dissolved oxygen limitation and the need to fix CO_2 would increase growth rates. Reduction of oxygen limitation seems to require substitution of or modification to make electron transport enzymes with a higher affinity for O_2.

Enhanced biological phosphorus removal would be possible if microorganisms could be selected for or manipulated to have increased P contents in their dry cell material.

Biodegradation of xenobiotic organic compounds requires that the microorganisms which thrive in treatment systems also possess enzymes to degrade the xenobiotics. Such functions could be transferred to the indigenous organisms likely to survive in a practical treatment process.

Odors from the generation of H_2S in anaerobic processes could be prevented by the use of photosynthetic, sulfur-oxidizing bacteria.

Anaerobic digestion or compositing would be improved by increasing the rate at which complex organic solids are hydrolized. In addition, methanogenic processes would be made more reliable if methanogens that had fewer nutrient requirements and are less subject to inhibition were found or constructed.

TWO SPECIFIC EXAMPLES

From all the possible applications of genetic control to municipal wastes, two examples stand out because of their potential impact. The two examples are elimination of activated sludge bulking and reduced sensitivity methanogenic microorganisms. Both examples would have great impact on waste treatment because of the already widespread use of these processes.

Eliminating Sludge Bulking

Figure 1 shows the main parts of activated sludge treatment, which is the main process used today in treatment of sewage, as well as many industrial wastewaters. In the reactor, or aeration basin, a concentrated slurry of aerobic microorganisms comes into contact with dissolved oxygen and organic material that enters in

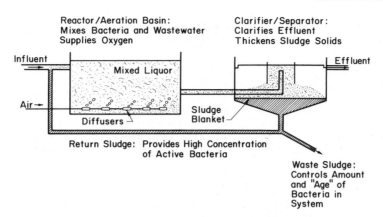

Fig. 1.   Parts of the activated sludge process and their functions.

the influent.   The relatively high concentration of microorganisms
and constant supply of dissolved oxygen allow rapid metabolism of
the organic material, or Biochemical Oxygen Demand (BOD), within the
reactor.   The end products of the metabolic reactions are CO_2, H_2O,
inorganic ions, and more cell mass.

The slurry of microorganisms, called the mixed liquor, passes
from the reactor to the clarifier, or separator.   The clarifier
serves two critical functions.   First, the microorganisms are
removed from the liquid stream that leaves the process.   Thus, the
effluent is clear liquid having only traces of solid material.   The
second function of the clarifier is to concentrate the biological
solids into a relatively thick sludge, which can be returned to the
reactor to provide the necessary high concentration of microorganisms.   The thickened sludge is also removed, or wasted from the process to control the total mass of cells and their "age", which is
the reciprocal of their specific growth rate.

For the activated sludge process to perform properly, the
reactor and the clarifier must achieve their respective objectives.
One relatively common problem with activated sludge treatment is
sludge bulking, which prevents the clarifier from achieving one or
both of its objectives.   Activated sludge that settles and thickens
well is comprised of relatively large and dense aggregates, called
flocs.   When sludge bulks, the flocs are dominated by filamentous
bacteria that extend well out from the floc (12,13).   These fila-
ments slow sludge settling and prevent good compaction.   If severe
enough, bulking prevents the clarifier from attaining a dense return
sludge and a clear effluent.

Recent studies (12,13) indicate two physiological traits of
floc-forming bacteria that prevent them from out-competing filamentous bacteria under certain operating conditions.   When the organic
loading is high, especially when the organic material is composed of

easily degraded, soluble compounds, the dissolved oxygen concentration is depressed. Evidence (12,13) indicates that floc-forming bacteria have poorer affinity for oxygen than do certain filamentous bacteria, which then have a competitive advantage. The most advantageous way in which genetic control can be used to prevent high-load bulking is to enhance the oxygen affinity of floc-forming bacteria.

A second bulking problem occurs when loadings are very low. Low loading favors bacteria that have slow decay/respiration rates. Certain filamentous bacteria are characterized by a slow decay/respiration rate, in comparison to floc formers. An important advantage to floc formers would be a reduced rate of decay/respiration.

Reducing Methanogenic Inhibition

Methanogenic processes are used widely for sludge digestion. The treatment of industrial waste by anaerobic processes is also gaining applications. Treatments of solid waste and sewage have been tried, but are not yet proven and accepted. Despite application to numerous wastes and sludges, methanogenic processes are utilized for only a small fraction of the wastes for which they appear amenable and advantageous. Methanogenic processes are advantageous because of their low energy requirement, small excess sludge production, generation of methane gas, and possible capabilities in detoxification (4).

One of the main reasons that methanogenic processes are not used as often as possible is that they are perceived to be unstable and easily upset. Part of the instability is attributable to poor operations. However, another aspect of instability is the sensitivity of the methanogenic microorganisms to inhibitory materials, particularly the heavy metals and alkaline earth metals (14,15). A related aspect is the methanogens' needs for small concentrations of numerous stimulating metals, such as cobalt, nickel, and iron. The proper balance of stimulating and inhibitory metals is not always present in a waste; the task of diagnosing and correcting a metals imbalance is difficult, time-consuming, and not always successful.

Making methanogens less sensitive to metals concentrations is a worthy goal for genetic control. Such an achievement would improve operations of existing applications and would encourage further applications, especially for solid-waste digestion and treatment of industrial wastes.

STUMBLING BLOCKS

Practical application of genetic control, particularly genetic engineering, to biological treatment of municipal wastes (as well as all other environmental problems) faces many major stumbling blocks.

The first is that we have only a vague idea of the physiological
effects we desire, and virtually no knowledge of the genes that control the effects. Second, we know little genetically about the receptor microorganisms that could thrive in a treatment environment.
Third, we cannot be sure that genetic transfer efficiency would be
sufficiently high or that the transferred DNA would not spontaneously leave the target organisms after some time. Fourth, we are
largely ignorant of how to ensure expression of transferred DNA in a
relevant microbe. Fifth, we must deal with prohibition on the
release of genetically altered organisms. Finally, we must realize
that economic risks are high and may dissuade investors and talented
professionals from entering the area. Risks are related to the following questions: can we achieve the five steps? can we do genetic
manipulation better than do natural processes? and can we market
the products?

SUMMARY AND CONCLUSIONS

     Municipal wastewater, sludge, and refuse constitute major
material flows and area of public concern. Substantial lists of
desired improvements in the biological treatment of each waste can
be formulated. Many improvements can be brought about by better
application of biological and process fundamentals; widespread application of good process control and existing microorganisms is
still not a reality. Nevertheless, several improvements seem amenable to genetic control techniques.

     Whether the genetic control technique involves selection of a
novel microorganism or genetic manipulation of conventional or novel
microorganisms, two key requirements stand out. First, we must
recognize the physiological factor that provides the desired function. Second, we must recombine the genes for the desired function
into a microorganism that can thrive in a treatment process. For
environmental applications, identifying the physiological effect and
an appropriate microorganism are the most critical steps. However,
they are probably the least well developed, as biochemists and genetic engineers have concentrated mainly on isolating, recombining,
and expressing relatively well known genes into convenient laboratory strains. Because of the many different steps associated with
applications of genetic control to municipal-waste treatment, the
successful application requires coordination of biochemistry, microbiology, and process engineering. No one discipline has all the
requisite tools and insight to do the whole job.

                              ACKNOWLEDGEMENT

     Although the information described in this chapter has been
funded wholly by the United States Environmental Protection Agency
under assistance agreement EPA Cooperative Agreement CR 806819 to

the Advanced Environmental Control Technology Research Center, it has not been subjected to the Agency's required peer and administrative review and therefore does not necessarily reflect the views of the Agency and no official endorsement should be inferred.

REFERENCES

1. Burdick, C.R., et al. (1982) Advanced biological treatment to achieve nutrient removal. J. Water Poll. Control. Fed. 54:1078-1086.
2. Rittmann, B.E. (1982) Comparative performance of biofilm reactor types. Biotech. Bioengr. 24:1341-1370.
3. Rittmann, B.E., and H. Kobayashi (1982) Microbiological separations for trace organics removal. In Detoxification of Hazardous Wastes, J.H. Exner, ed. Ann Arbor Science, Ann Arbor, Michigan, pp. 323-347.
4. Kobayashi, H., and B.E. Rittmann (1982) Microbial removal of hazardous organic compounds. Environ. Sci. & Technol. 16:170A-181A.
5. Kobayashi, H., et al. (1983) Use of photosynthetic bacteria for hydrogen sulfide removal from anaerobic waste treatment effluent. Water Res. 17:579-588.
6. Morrow, J.F. (1979) Recombinant DNA techniques. In Methods in Enzymology, Vol. 68, Recombinant DNA, R. Wu, ed. Academic Press, New York, pp. 3-24.
7. Wu, R. (1979) Methods in Enzymology, Vol. 68, Recombinant DNA. Academic Press, New York.
8. Johnston, J.B., and S.G. Robinson (1982) Opportunities for development of new detoxification processes through genetic engineering. In Detoxification of Hazardous Waste, J.H. Exner, ed. Ann Arbor Science, Ann Arbor, Michigan, pp. 301-314.
9. Boethling, R.S., and M. Alexander (1979) Effect of concentration of organic chemicals on their biodegradation by natural microbial communities. Appl. Environ. Microb. 37:1211- 1216.
10. Boethling. R.S., and M. Alexander (1979) Microbial degradation of organic compounds at trace levels. Environ. Sci. & Technol. 13:989-991.
11. Rittmann, B.E., et al. (1980) Biodegradation of trace organic compounds in ground water system. Technical Report No. 255, Department of Civil Engineering, Stanford University, Stanford, California.
12. Sezgin, M., D. Jenkins, and D. Parker (1978) A Unified theory of filamentous activated sludge bulking. Journal of the Water Pollution Control Federation 50:362.
13. Chiesa, S.C., and R.L. Irvine (1982) Growth and control of filamentous microbes in activated sludge - an integrated hypothesis. Presented at the 55th Annual Conference of the Water Pollution Control Federation, St. Louis, Missouri.
14. McCarty, P.L. (1964) Anaerobic waste treatment fundamentals -- Part III. Public Works 95:91.

15. Speece, R.E. (1983) Review -- Environmental requirements for
     anaerobic digestion of biomass. In Advances in Solar Energy --
     An Annual Review of Research and Development. Environmental
     Studies Institute, Drexel University, Philadelphia, Pennsyl-
     vania.

PSEUDOMONAS HYDROCARBON OXIDATION

J. A. Shapiro, D. J. Owen, M. Kok,[1] and G. Eggink[1]

Department of Microbiology
The University of Chicago
Chicago, Illinois 60637

In this paper we will withdraw from the complex world of mixed cultures and multiple substrates that characterize polluted ecosystems and treatment facilities to discuss a simple model system involving petri dishes, vapor phase pure substrates, and genetically defined bacterial strains. The laboratory situation is no less "real" than any other and has many important lessons to teach us if we are ever to be in a position to design pollutant-degrading organisms with the same level of sophistication now employed to produce medically important polypeptides. One of the major points to be made is that even a hydrocarbon oxidation system chosen for maximum simplicity reveals a genetic complexity that is beyond our current understanding.

Many hydrocarbon oxidation pathways begin with the stepwise oxidation of a methyl group to a carboxylic acid moiety. Figure 1 shows examples of gaseous, aliphatic, and aromatic hydrocarbon degradations that start in this manner. Because it is biochemically and technically the easiest to study, we chose the n-alkane oxidation pathway in Pseudomonas putida for genetic analysis. All the substrates and intermediates were readily available, and Coon's group had established conditions for biochemical characterization of the oxidizing activities (1,10,11,12). The pathway consists of the following reactions: 1) an initial hydroxylation catalyzed by a multicomponent mixed-function oxygenase that requires molecular oxygen and NADH cofactor; 2) an alcohol dehydrogenation; 3) an aldehyde dehydrogenation; and 4) β-oxidation of the resulting fatty acid to produce the substrates of intermediary metabolism.

---

[1]Permanent address: Biochemical Laboratory, Groningen State University, The Netherlands.

229

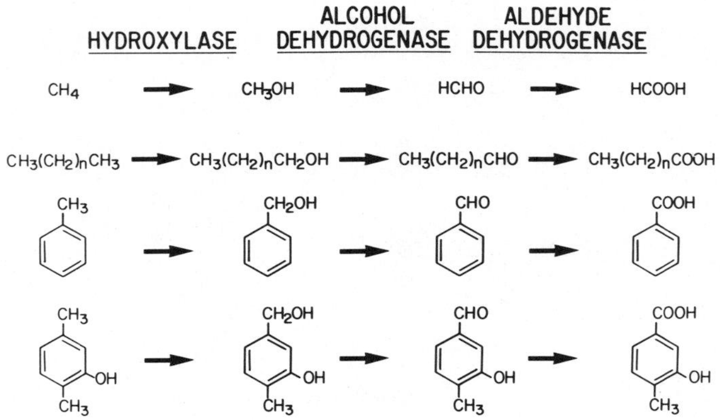

Fig. 1.   Methyl group oxidation to carboxylic acid. The substrates are (top to bottom): methane, n-alkane, toluene, and 2,5-xylenol. Reproduced from J. A. Shapiro et al. (1981) Perspectives for genetic engineering in hydrocarbon-oxidizing bacteria. In Trends in the Biology of Fermentations for Fuels and Chemicals, A. Hollaender et al., eds. Plenum Press, New York, pp. 243-272.

One of the important characteristics which n-alkanes share with many environmental pollutants is their hydrophobicity. This consideration led us to assume that the hydrophobic region of the bacterial cell, namely the membrane, would play a very important role in the physiology of alkane oxidation, and we have managed to obtain evidence in favor of this assumption. Figure 2 is a schematic cartoon that was published some years ago (3) of how we envision the first three steps in n-alkane oxidation. It shows the entry of substrate into the cytoplasmic membrane of P. putida by an unknown process which we believe depends largely on the tendency of alkane molecules to partition from an aqueous phase into a lipid phase. Once in the cytoplasmic membrane bi-layer, the substrate is hydroxylated to the primary alcohol by an elaborate enzyme complex, alkane hydroxylase, with three components. These are the membrane protein oxidase and two soluble proteins, rubredoxin and rubredoxin reductase, which must be somehow associated with the oxidase for the reaction to occur. Then the primary aliphatic alcohol product of hydroxylation is dehydrogenated by a membrane activity to an aliphatic aldehyde. We know little about the subsequent aldehyde dehydrogenation step in P. putida, but there is evidence in P. aeruginosa for inducible membrane aldehyde dehydrogenases that produce the fatty acids (G. Brandon, personal communication). We hypothesize that these products are then taken into the cytoplasm and subjected to β-oxidation to yield acetyl-CoA (and propionyl-CoA if there is an odd number of carbons in the alkane chain).

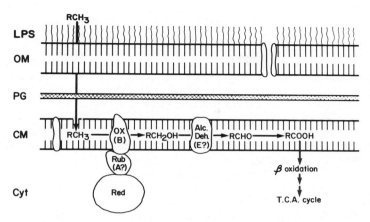

Fig. 2.   A model for the role of the bacterial envelope in n-alkane
           oxidation, reproduced from Reference 3. LPS = lipopoly-
           saccharide; OM = outer membrane; PG = peptidoglycan; CM =
           cytoplasmic membrane; and Cyt = cytoplasm. RCH_3, RCH_2OH,
           RCHO, and RCOOH are, respectively, n-alkane, aliphatic
           alcohol, aldehyde, and fatty acid substrates. OX =
           oxidase component of alkane hydroxylase encoded by alkB;
           Rub = rubredoxin, possibly encoded by alkA; Red =
           rubredoxin reductase; and Alc. Deh. = aliphatic alcohol
           dehydrogenase, possibly encoded by alkE. Reproduced from
           Reference 3.

     Part of the evidence for this scheme comes from the examination
of the polypeptides that are induced when alkane-positive bacteria
carrying the appropriate plasmid alk DNA sequences are exposed to
substrate or gratuitous inducers (3). We find that a number of different membrane polypeptides appear of approximate molecular weights
59,000 daltons, 47,000 daltons, and 40,000 daltons. The two larger
peptides are possibly components of the alcohol dehydrogenase activity. The 40,000 dalton peptide is known to be the oxidase component
of alkane hydroxylase because there is a mutation, alkB1029, which
leads both to an alteration in the electrophoretic mobility of this
peptide and to increased thermolability of oxidase activity. If the
envelopes of alkane-induced bacteria are fractionated, then the
inducible polypeptides, oxidase activity, and alcohol dehydrogenase
activity are all found in the cytoplasmic membrane fraction. It
should be pointed out that hydroxylation activity must reside in
the cytoplasmic membrane, not in the outer membrane, because it requires NADH cofactor. Indeed, such cofactor requirements are characteristic of many of the reactions involved in oxidation of natural
and synthetic hydrocarbons. Thus, the need to regenerate cofactors is one of the reasons why it seems to us that most practical

applications of hydrocarbon-oxidizing organisms will utilize whole
cells (free or immobilized) rather than extracts or other cell-free
systems.

The geneticist's approach to understanding a phenomenon such as
hydrocarbon oxidation is to isolate mutants altered in the relevant
processes and study their properties. In the case of P. putida
alkane oxidation, we were fortunate that Chakrabarty et al. (6) had
already shown that OCT plasmid sequences were involved. We could
therefore analyze both chromosomal and plasmid sequences controlling
the oxidation pathway. Figure 3 summarizes published and unpublished results. By using a chemical mutagen (nitrosoguanidine) we
could isolate strains with chromosomal mutations that prevent utilization of aliphatic primary alcohols. These mutations have not yet
been mapped, but they define loci encoding the conversion of alcohols to aldehydes (alc), the conversion of aldehydes to fatty acids
(ald), and the assimilation of fatty acids (oic). The oic loci
certainly must include several sequences encoding the enzymes of
β-oxidation.

If we introduce the OCT or derivative CAM-OCT plasmid (5,14)
into a P. putida strain, its growth substrate range is extended to
include n-alkanes of six to ten carbon atoms, and the plasmid strain
can synthesize inducible alkane hydroxylase and aliphatic alcohol
dehydrogenase activities. A priori, these results imply the existence of a set of plasmid alk loci which encode proteins for alkane
oxidation. Chemical mutagenesis produces a series of mutant plasmids which lack various components of the alkane oxidation system:
alkA - no soluble alkane hydroxylase component; alkB - no membrane
alkane hydroxylase component; alkC - no inducible aliphatic alcohol
dehydrogenase; alkR - no induction of alkane hydroxylase and aliphatic alcohol dehydrogenase.

The alkR mutations define a locus encoding proteins involved in
transcriptional control of an alkBAC operon. In addition to Alk⁻
phenotypes resulting from alkR mutations, there are also alkR
strains which have altered alk regulation (8): some are constitutive and synthesize alkane hydroxylase and aliphatic alcohol dehydrogenase in the absence of inducer, and others have a more restricted range of inducers (so, for example, they will only grow on
heptane, octane, and nonane but not on hexane or decane). These
latter kinds of alkR mutants are important because they show that
the apparent substrate range of a hydrocarbon-oxidizing organism
deduced from growth tests often reflects regulatory specificity more
than the substrate specificity of the oxidizing activities themselves. We now know that the alkR locus is complex and contains
more than one cistron (D.J.Owen et al., unpublished data).

In addition to chemical mutagens, one can induce mutations with
transposable elements, segments of DNA that can insert themselves
into various loci in the cellular genome. Many such elements,
called transposons, carry sequences encoding specific phenotypes

such as antibiotic resistance. When a transposon inserts into a
particular cistron, it interrupts the continuity of that particular
sequence and also perturbs the pattern of transcription beyond the
site of insertion. Thus, transposon insertion mutations often have
pleiotropic effects. We have used the element called Tn7 which confers resistance to trimethoprim, streptomycin, and spectinomycin
(9). We isolated insertions in alkB which blocked expression of all
three activities (i.e., alkB::Tn7 is BAC$^-$), insertions in alkA which
blocked expression of only the soluble alkane hydroxylase component
and of aliphatic alcohol dehydrogenase (i.e., alkA::Tn7 is B$^+$A$^-$C$^-$),
and insertions in alkC which did not affect alkane hydroxylase expression (i.e., alkC::Tn7 is B$^+$A$^+$C$^-$). These results showed that
there must be coordinated alkBAC transcription starting from a promoter in the position indicated in Fig. 3. There were also insertions into alkR which resulted in a noninducible phenotype which
thus indicated that the products of the alkR cistrons are required
for alkBAC expression.

The presence of Tn7 insertions within and adjacent to alk sequences provided antibiotic resistance markers for genetic mapping.
This was particularly important for the CAM-OCT plasmid which is
very large, perhaps as large as 500,000 base pairs in length, and so
not amenable to simple physical analysis with restriction enzymes or
by heteroduplex methods. Transduction with the P. aeruginosa tem-
perate phage F116 showed the alkR and alkBAC regions to be separated
by about 40,000 base pairs (7). (The previous report that alkC::Tn7
mutations were unlinked to both alkBA and alkR was an error.) The
Tn7 insertions also facilitated recombinant DNA cloning work because

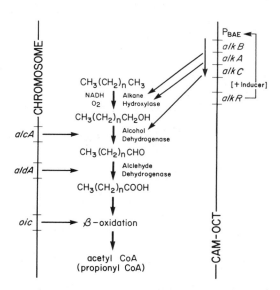

Fig. 3.   The genetic determination of the n-alkane oxidation pathway in P. putida (see text for roles of alk genes).

we could select for expression of the trimethoprim resistance marker
on alk::Tn7 DNA fragments in many different bacteria, such as Escherichia coli, where the Alk phenotype might not express itself.
(It was also unlikely that we could clone both alkR and alkBAC on a
single fragment, and we did not know if these were the only plasmid
sequences needed for the Alk⁺ phenotype.) Figure 4 illustrates the
use in this way of Tn7 and also a further use of transposable elements in our cloning system. We employed a limited host-range vector in E. coli, RSF1596, which carries the mutant transposon
Tn3Δ596. Although Tn3Δ596 is defective, it can be complemented and
transposed in the presence of active Tn3 or Tn1 sequences. Thus,
any DNA fragment inserted within Tn3Δ596 becomes transposable and
can be moved to a broad host-range replicon that can be transferred
to a Pseudomonas host. Although other methods are available for
mobilizing cloned DNA into Pseudomonas strains, we used this one
because it enabled us to place the same fragment into plasmids of
different incompatibility groups.

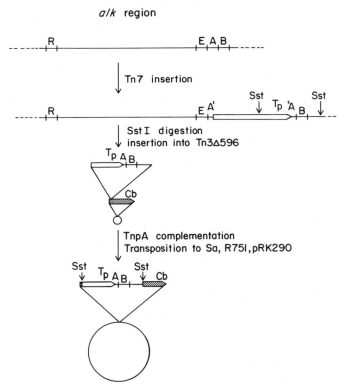

Fig. 4.   The use of transposons in cloning alk DNA sequences.
Reproduced from J. A. Shapiro (1982) Mobile genetic
elements and reorganization of procaryotic genomes. In
Genetics of Industrial Microorganisms 1982, Y. Ikeda and
T. Beppu, eds. Kodansha, Tokyo, pp. 9-32.

Once <u>alk</u> sequences were isolated from <u>alk</u>::Tn7 mutants, they could be used for a variety of genetic experiments. Two such experiments deserve mention here. One is to use Southern hybridization techniques to map the DNA of various <u>alk</u>::Tn7 mutants, and it was this technique which showed that <u>alkC</u>::Tn7 insertions are close to and downstream of <u>alkB</u> and <u>alkA</u>. The second kind of experiment is to connect the sequence encoding β-galactosidase, <u>lacZ</u>, to the cloned fragment. If <u>lacZ</u> has no promoter of its own, β-galactosidase expression serves as a probe for promoter activity (2,4). This is handy because there are several rapid assays for β-galactosidase activity. To confirm that we had indeed isolated an <u>alkBA</u> fragment, we fused <u>lacZ</u> to a restriction site in the <u>alkB</u> sequence, transposed the fusion to a broad host-range plasmid, and then transferred the resulting <u>alk-lacZ</u> plasmid to various <u>Pseudomonas</u> strains. Those with no CAM-OCT plasmid or with a defective <u>alkR</u>⁻ plasmid show low noninducible β-galactosidase levels. If the strain has the normal <u>alkR</u>⁺ plasmid, then β-galactosidase activity is induced by exposure to alkane or an alkane analogue, and if the strain has a constitutive <u>alkR</u>^{c} plasmid, then there is a high β-galactosidase level which can be increased further by alkane or alkane analogue induction. These results confirm that we have isolated an intact <u>alkBAC</u> regulatory sequence because the <u>lacZ</u> fusion shows the correct regulatory responses. They also show that <u>alkR</u> controls transcription of <u>alkBAC</u>. It is interesting to note that the <u>alkBAC</u> promoter shows higher activity by the <u>lacZ</u> fusion assay in <u>E. coli</u> than it does in <u>P. putida</u> <u>alkR</u>⁻.

One of the basic assumptions behind detailed genetic analysis of hydrocarbon-oxidizing bacteria is that the information and mutants produced will be useful in rational strain construction schemes for practical applications. While this will surely turn out to be a valid assumption, some experience with alkane-oxidizing <u>Pseudomonas</u> strains indicates that we are still a long way from the goal of specific designs for bacteria to carry out certain tasks. One potential application for these bacteria lies in the stereospecific epoxidation of alkenes, a process first developed by a group at Exxon and recently extended by the Biotechnology Program at the State University of Groningen in Holland (13,15). The Exxon workers used the original <u>P. oleovorans</u> isolate of Coon, and Schwartz (13) selected derivatives that survived storage in the cold much better than the starting strain. Surprisingly, these organisms had several-fold increased expoxidation activity. In order to analyze the genetic basis of these changes, we have begun to transfer plasmids between the improved epoxidation strain (labeled PPO1 in our laboratory) and our standard <u>P. putida</u> strains. We find that the <u>alk</u> plasmid of PPO1, which we have denoted OCX, shows high frequency transfer, unlike the original OCT plasmid in <u>P. oleovorans</u> (6), but there is no discernible difference in alkane utilization between <u>P. putida</u> strains with with CAM-OCT and those with OCX. Similarly, introduction of CAM-OCT into PPO1 (which results in loss of OCX by reason of incompatibility) does not lead to any change in alkane

utilization. These results suggest (but do not establish) that PPO1
underwent chromosomal rather than plasmid changes in acquiring cold-
resistance and enhanced expoxidation activities. (The epoxidation
assays of all or various strains are not yet complete.) Thus, we
reasoned that an even better strain could be constructed by introducing an $\underline{alkR}^c$ plasmid encoding higher alkane hydroxylase levels
into PPO1. We did this to generate strains PPO5 and PPO6. However,
when we tested them for alkane utilization compared to PPO1 and
other derivatives, we found these constitutive strains to be rather
defective (Fig. 5). Needless to say, this result was unexpected and
showed that our understanding of the genetics and physiology of n-
alkane utlization still has a long way to go before we are in a position to predict with confidence how a particular strain construction will behave.

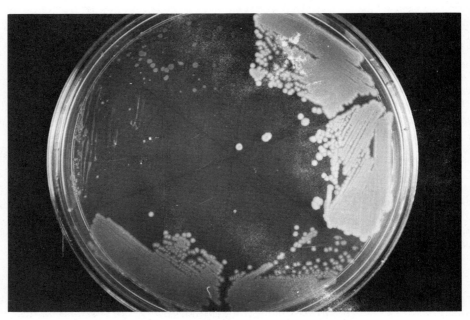

Fig. 5.   Growth on octane of P. putida and P. oleovorans TF4-IL
          (13) derivatives carrying different alkR alleles. Clock-
          wise from top right, the strains on this minimal salts-
          octane plate are PPS2172 = P. putida (CAM-OCT $alkR^c$578),
          PPS2171 = P. putida (CAM-OCT $alkR^c$701), PPO9 = P. oleo-
          vorans TF4-IL (OCX $alkR^c$2184), PPO8 = P. oleovorans TF4-IL
          (OCX $alkR^c$2184), PPO6 = P. oleovorans TF4-IL (CAM-OCT
          $alkR^c$701), and PPO5 = P. oleovorans TF4-IL (CAM-OCT
          $alkR^c$578). PPS2172 and PPS2171 show the heaviest growth,
          PPO8 and PPO9 show weaker growth, and PPO6 and PPO5 show
          poor growth.

There are three conclusions about genetic engineering of bacteria for practical applications that we would like to make from our own work. First, we still have a great deal to learn about the biology of any particular system before we can carry out rational strain construction. The alkane oxidation system was chosen for maximum simplicity and has some of the most detailed genetic analysis of any Pseudomonas pathway, yet it still yields many surprises. It would be amazing if other degradative systems were not to do likewise. This does not mean, however, that we cannot develop very useful genetically manipulated organisms, simply that we should not overestimate our own consciously designed input into the desirable characteristics of any particular strain.

This consideration leads to our second conclusion, namely, that there is still a large role for traditional selection techniques and serendipitous strain improvements, like that of Schwartz (13). Indeed, one of the main challenges in work on biological hydrocarbon oxidation is to understand how the bacteria reorganize their genomes and alter their metabolism to meet the selective challenges placed on them. It may well be that once we have done this for several pathways, we will discover new principles of genetic change and metabolic regulation that will place our genetic engineering efforts on a more solid foundation.

A third conclusion is a corollary of the first two: recombinant DNA analysis is extremely useful for genetic analysis and may have limited application in strain construction, but cloning, in vitro mutagenesis, and other modern techniques will probably not be as important in improving integrated degradative pathways as they have shown themselves to be in the production of specific proteins. While this last point may appear to be negative, it has two positive aspects if correct. These are: 1) freedom from in vitro genetic engineering will remove degradative organisms from irrelevant concerns about synthetic biohazards, and 2) degradative pathways pose puzzling, and therefore scientifically important, problems which well continue to engage the curiosity of microbiologists for some time to come.

ACKNOWLEDGEMENTS

This research has been supported by grants from the National Science Foundation (PCM 8200971), the Petroleum Research Fund administered by the American Chemical Society, and the Biotechnology Center of Groningen State University.

REFERENCES

1. Baptist, J.N., R.K. Gholson, and M.J. Coon (1963) Hydrocarbon oxidation by a bacterial enzyme system. I. Products of octane

    oxidation. Biochim. Biophys. Acta 69:40–47.
2. Bassford, P., J. Beckwith, M. Berman, E. Brickman, M.
    Casadaban, L. Guarente, I. Saint-Girons, A. Sarthy, M.
    Schwartz, H. Shuman, and T. Silhavy (1980) Genetic fusions of
    the lac operon: A new approach to the study of biological
    processes. In The Operon, J.H. Miller and W.S. Reznikoff, eds.
    Cold Spring Harbor Laboratory, Cold Spring Harbor, New York,
    pp. 245–262.
3. Benson, S., M. Oppici, M. Fennewald, and J. Shapiro (1979)
    Regulation of membrane proteins by the Pseudomonas plasmid alk
    (alkane utilization) regulon. J. Bacteriol. 140:754–762.
4. Casadaban, M.J., and S.N. Cohen (1980) Analysis of gene control
    signals by DNA fusion and cloning in Escherichia coli. J. Mol.
    Biol. 138:179–207.
5. Chakrabarty, A.M. (1973) Genetic fusion of incompatible plas-
    mids in Pseudomonas. Proc. Nat. Acad. Sci., U.S.A. 70:1641–
    1644.
6. Chakrabarty, A.M., G. Chou, and I.C. Gunsalus (1973) Genetic
    regulation of octane dissimilation plasmid in Pseudomonas.
    Proc. Nat. Acad. Sci., U.S.A. 70:1137–1140.
7. Fennewald, M., S. Benson, M. Oppici, and J. Shapiro (1979)
    Insertion element analysis and mapping of the Pseudomonas plas-
    mid alk regulon. J. Bacteriol. 139:940–952.
8. Fennewald, M., and J. Shapiro (1977) Regulatory mutations of
    the Pseudomonas plasmid alk regulon. J. Bacteriol. 132:622–
    627.
9. Fennewald, M., and J. Shapiro (1979) Transposition of Tn7 in P.
    aeruginosa and isolation of alk::Tn7 mutations. J. Bacteriol.
    139:264–269.
10. Gholson, R.K., J.N. Baptist, and M.J. Coon (1963) Hydrocarbon
    oxidation by a bacterial enzyme system. II. Cofactor require-
    ments for octanol formation from octane. Biochemistry 2:1155–
    1159.
11. McKenna E.J., and M.J. Coon (1970) Enzymatic ω-oxidation of
    Pseudomonas oleovorans. J. Biol. Chem. 245:3882–3889.
12. Peterson, J.A., D. Basu, and M.J. Coon (1966) Enzymatic co-
    oxidation. I. Electron carriers in fatty acid and hydrocarbon
    oxidation. J. Biol. Chem. 241:5162–5164.
13. Schwartz, R. (1973) Octene epoxidation by a cold-stable alkane-
    oxidizing isolate of Pseudomonas oleovorans. Appl. Microbiol.
    25:574–577.
14. Shapiro, J.A., S. Benson, M. Fennewald, A. Grund, and M. Nieder
    (1976) Genetics of alkane utilization. In Microbiology 1976,
    D. Schlessinger, ed. American Society for Microbiology,
    Washington, D.C., pp. 568–571.
15. de Smet, M.-J., H. Wynberg, and B. Witholt (1981) Synthesis of
    1,2-epoxyoctane by Pseudomonas oleovorans during growth in a
    two-phase system containing high concentrations of 1-octene.
    Appl. Environ. Microbiol. 42:811–816.

MICROBIAL ENZYMES AND LIGNOCELLULOSE UTILIZATION

Ross D. Brown, Jr. [1,2] and Mikelina Gritzali [1]

[1]Department of Food Science and Human Nutrition
Institute of Food and Agricultural Sciences
[2]Department of Biochemistry and Molecular Biology
University of Florida
Gainesville, Florida 32611

INTRODUCTION

Although lignocellulose always has been a principal component of man's food, fuel, and fiber, there has been for the past decade an increased interest in utilization of these materials by new and improved "bioconversion" processes. Since lignocellulose is the most abundant constituent of biomass, attention has been directed to several relatively inexpensive sources, such as agricultural, industrial, and municipal wastes. The biological reactions of the carbon cycle which are responsible for the conversion of lignin and cellulose turn over some 10^{11} tons/year (1). The variety of microorganisms which mediate the reactions, the extracellular conditions under which the reactions take place, and the products to which lignocellulose is converted are of scientific interest as well as being potentially valuable for technological applications. Studies of these processes range from determination of precise chemical mechanisms to analysis of microbial associations responsible for the multiplicity of reactions needed to convert the heterogeneous lignocellulose to metabolic intermediates and end products.

To describe and define an organism's capacity for these reactions, genetic studies have been useful and, with the advent of recombinant DNA technology, may permit development of microbial and/or enzyme systems for specific biotechnological use. Several books and reviews recently have discussed the chemical and biological conversion of lignocellulose (2-19). In this report, emphasis will be placed on the activity and regulation of enzymes catalyzing the initial biochemical steps in the breakdown of lignin and

239

cellulose. [Hemicellulose utilization is referred to here only in
the context of an associated process and has been reviewed elsewhere
(20,21)]. Some examples will be given of recent work on development
of microbial strains, control of enzyme synthesis, and prospects of
genetic engineering for increased enzyme yield or enhanced metabolic
capability.

Most of the enzymes of interest are found to be extracellular
or at the cell surface, since the undegraded macromolecular substrates must be solubilized preliminary to cellular uptake and
metabolism. This implies that the reactions proceed with reactants
such as water or oxygen found in the extracellular milieu and makes
unlikely the use of enzymes which depend on soluble cofactors. As
seen below, the primary attack on lignin is predominantly oxidative,
while cellulose is usually subject to hydrolytic depolymerization.

Lignin

The biochemistry of lignolysis is still incompletely understood, although certain patterns of degradation (5,6,8,13,17,22,23)
and individual enzymatic and nonenzymatic steps have been described
(4-6,8,11,17,24,25). The substrate lignin is a macromolecule of
phenyl propanoid units (Fig. 1) linked through a variety of ether
and carbon-carbon bonds (6,14,15). The phenolic groups are methylated to varying degrees. Lignification or lignin synthesis in plant
cell walls is believed to proceed by a free radical process which
confers a racemic nature to configurations at asymmetric carbon
atoms. Because of the chemical diversity of bonds and functional
groups, as well as lack of stereoregularity, it is thought unlikely
that the initial oxidative cleavage of lignin is enzymatically specified (6,17,23,25). Nevertheless, a number of enzymes have been
identified in the white-rot fungus, Sporotrichum pulverulentum
(=Phanerochaete chrysosporium), which seem to be associated with
lignolysis. Since lignin degradation by this "white-rot" organism
has been studied in great detail (4-6,8,11,13,23,26,27), the
pattern, regulation, and possible mechanisms of the process will be
summarized as the paradigm for lignolysis.

Surfaces of the lignin close to the fungal hyphae apparently
are first attacked. Demethylation reactions (lowering methoxyl

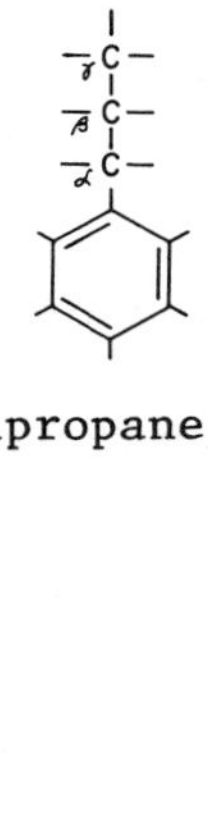

Fig. 1.   Phenylpropane unit of lignin.

content and increasing phenolic hydroxyls) occur early, after which
the aromatic rings are cleaved and carboxylic acids are formed by
extracellular mixed function oxygenases and dioxygenases. An oxidizing enzyme which may activate the phenyl-propanoid side chains
for further reaction also has been reported (11,17).

A number of physico-chemical elements in the microbial environment are prerequisite to active lignin degradation by the white-rot
fungus (6,13,23). Only after mycelial weight has become constant
(i.e., growth has ceased due to nutrient limitation) is there
evidence of conversion of ^{14}C-labelled lignin conversion to $^{14}CO_2$.
Nevertheless, it appears essential that some source of metabolizable
carbohydrate be available during lignolysis (6,26). The increase in
both the titer of the lignolytic system formed (13) and the reaction
rate of lignolysis (17) depends on the partial pressure of oxygen.
It has been suggested that O_2 is involved in the induction of the
lignolytic system as well as serving as a reactant. The presence of
an extracellular nitrogen source (in particular L-glutamate) represses lignolytic activity in P. chrysosporium (13,23). In contrast, the ^{14}C-lignin-solubilizing activity of the basidiomycete
(NRRL 6464) isolated from cattle dung, a nitrogen-rich substrate,
was relatively insensitive to nutrient N levels (28). This has been
interpreted to indicate that the repression by N-sources may be
characteristic of fungi which rot wood where C/N levels are relatively high. Several investigators are examining the metabolic controls imposed by nitrogen limitation (29-31).

Although no extracellular fungal enzyme preparation has been
shown to degrade lignin extensively, a number of enzymes (Fig. 2,
adapted from Eriksson, Ref. 7) have been implicated in lignin

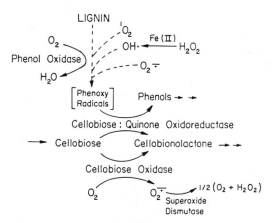

Fig. 2.   Extracellular oxidative reactions hypothetically relevant
           to lignolysis by Sporotrichum (Phanerochaete).

degradation by <u>Sporotrichum pulverulentum</u> (7,17,26). A phenol oxidase-less mutant could not degrade lignin in the presence of cellulose unless exogenous laccase was provided (26), whereas a revertant strain regained its ability to degrade lignin. The precise role of phenol oxidase is unknown but several possibilities include (a) detoxification by removal of low molecular weight phenols which inhibit cellulase or xylanase production (26), (b) demethylation of methoxyl groups (17), or (c) formation of a coupled system with cellobiose:quinone oxidoreductase (cellobiose dehydrogenase, CBDH) to remove cellobiose (arising from cellulose degradation) by oxidation with catalytic levels of phenols.

The significance of the flavoprotein cellobiose dehydrogenase (CBDH) is illustrated by Eriksson's work with the <u>S. pulverulentum</u> cellulase-less mutant Cel 44 which also lacks CBDH (26). This mutant degraded kraft lignin less rapidly than the wild-type. However, in wood, where xylan was available for utilization as cosubstrate, the mutant degraded lignin nearly as rapidly as did the wild-type. Thus, CBDH is likely to play, at best, an ancillary role in preventing accumulation of lignin-derived quinones (or the coupling of phenoxy radicals) or of cellulolytically generated cellobiose. The utility of the Cel 44 mutant lies in its ability to partially degrade lignin with little degradation of cellulose in wood chips preliminary to mechanical pulping. Karl-Erik Eriksson has stated that "biochemical pulping" can produce a savings of some 30% in energy demand (32).

The glycoprotein cellobiose oxidase (CBO) of <u>S. pulverulentum</u> contains both heme and flavin groups and catalyzes the oxidation of cellobiose to cellobionolactone with molecular oxygen (33,34). At least some superoxide ion ($O^{\cdot -}$) but no hydrogen peroxide is produced. As in the case of CBDH, the removal of cellobiose by CBO may relieve end-product inhibition of cellulase enzymes or prevent reformation of glycosidic bonds formed by the glucanases on the surface of cellulose. However, the fate of the superoxide ion is of interest with regard to the degradation of both cellulose and lignin, as discussed below. Eriksson has found that superoxide dismutase (SOD) is produced both intra- and extracellularly by <u>S. pulverulentum</u>. The significance of SOD in regulating superoxide levels or in producing hydrogen peroxide remains to be demonstrated.

One of the most active areas of inquiry is the search for active species of oxygen such as $O^{\cdot -}$, $^1O_2$, or $OH^{\cdot}$ which may be involved directly in lignin degradation. The reported presence of hydrogen peroxide (H_2O_2) in brown-rotted wood (35) led to the suggestion that this compound in the presence of Fe(II) caused the depolymerization of cellulose. More recently this circumstantial evidence has been disputed, but H_2O_2 has been found to be produced by several white-rot fungi (36,37). Moreeover, the production of H_2O_2 was found to coincide with the onset of lignolysis by <u>P</u>.

chrysosporium (37), and the use of $OH^{\bullet}$ trapping agents suggests that this radical arises from the Fe(II)-catalyzed reduction of H_2O_2. By use of other trapping agents it was suggested that singlet oxygen ($^1O_2$) is important for lignin biodegradation by P. chrysosporium (38). These agents demonstrated the formation of $^1O_2$ and by scavenging this active species inhibited oxidation of ^{14}C-lignin, but not ^{14}C-glucose, to $^{14}CO_2$ in cultures. The significance of $^1O_2$ in lignin degradation has been questioned on the basis that its formation by known reactions would be thermodynamically or kinetically unfavorable (37). Since superoxide ion, known to arise from CBO action, can give rise to either $^1O_2$ or $OH^{\bullet}$ by different pathways, it may play a key role in lignin degradation as suggested by Hall (25).

The stimulation of lignin degradation by an atmosphere of 100% oxygen may be due to increased formation of active oxygen species or to the low affinity of phenol oxidase (laccase) for its substrate O_2 (17). Recently it has been proposed that the combined attack of laccase (generating a phenoxy radical) followed by coupling and cleavage with hydroxyl radical may be important for demethoxylation and cleavage of aryl groups from the macromolecule (17). It is remarkable that the lignolytic fungi can grow in high-oxygen environments for long periods. It seems likely that some protective mechanism is necessary such as (a) scavenging of free radicals by lignin or (b) removal of superoxide, SOD which is found both intra- and extracellularly (8).

In summary, genetic studies have been helpful in identifying important elements in lignin degradation by white-rot fungi, such as phenol oxidase and the requirement for a carbohydrate cosubstrate. Understanding the generation and regulation of active oxygen species in the initial oxidative attack may make it possible to enhance biological treatment of lignaceous raw materials and wastes.

Cellulose

Cellulolytic microbes span a wide range of anaerobic and aerobic prokaryotes, as well as fungi which can convert cellulose to cellooligosaccharides and glucose. As for lignin, the principal enzymatic attack on the insoluble substrate is extracellular (or at the cell surface). Hence the synthesis and secretion of cellulase enzymes is expected to be stimulated by products of cellulose hydrolysis. The stereoregularity of the substrate [β (1->4) linked cellobiosyl units] permits a specific type of enzyme, β (1->4) glucan glucanohydrolase (EC 3.2.1.4), to attack any of the exposed glycosidic linkages. Because many of the linkages are buried in the crystalline cellulose fibrils or are shielded by lignin, the degradation of native lignocellulose proceeds very slowly even when catalyzed by enzymes. Therefore, soluble or swollen forms of cellulose are often employed in assays for the depolymerizing cellulase enzymes.

Cellulase Enzymes

     The hydrolytic cellulase enzymes include the β (1->4) glucan
glucanohydrolase (EC 3.2.1.4), β (1->4) glucan exo-cellobiohydrolase
(EC 3.2.1.91) and β-glucosidase (EC 3.2.1.21) (3). [From Penicillium funiculosum there has been reported (39) a β (1->4) glucan glucohydrolase which very slowly cleaves glucose from cellulose]. The
glucanohydrolase (endoglucanase) and β-glucosidase occur nearly universally among cellulolytic microbes. For fungi containing the
"complete" array of cellulolytic enzymes, the endoglucanases and
cellobiohydrolases act synergistically to convert cellulose to cellooligosaccharides. Subsequently, the cellooligosaccharides are converted to glucose, either extra- or intracellularly, by the β-glucosidase. In some bacteria, such as Clostridium thermocellum (40,41)
and Cellvibrio gilvus (42), there are intracellular phosphorylases
which cleave cellobiose or cellooligosaccharides to glucose-1-phos-
phate and either glucose or smaller cellooligosaccharides, respectively. The cellobiose dehydrogenase and cellobiose oxidase of Sporotrichum were discussed above. A list of representative cellulolytic organisms has been published by Mandels and Andreotti (43).

     Among the cellulase producers, several have been of particular
interest due either to the amount of extracellular enzyme produced
or the products arising from the metabolism of cellulose-derived
glucose. Thermophilic species, such as Thermomonospora (44-46),
Thermoascus (47), Talaromyces (48), Clostridium thermocellum (49-
51), and Sporotrichum thermophile (52,53), have been of interest
due to relatively higher growth rates and rates of cellulose degradation. Anaerobes, such as Ruminococcus (54) and Clostridium (51,
55), either alone or in coculture, are potentially valuable for fermentation of cellulose to useful products. Understanding the coordinated attack on cellulose and lignin has required analysis of
the cellulase system of Sporotrichum (7). The most prolific producer of extracellular cellulose enzymes is the imperfect fungus
Trichoderma reesei (18,43). A brief description of some representative cellulase systems will provide a basis for the applications
of these enzymes to bioconversion of cellulose.

     Almost all cellulase systems comprise endoglucanases (EGs) to-
gether with monosaccharide producing enzymes (Table 1) and in some
cases (56-60) exo-cellobiohydrolases (CBHs). The Thermomonospora
cellulase system includes extracellular thermostable endoglucanases
and a cell-bound β-glucosidase (45). From the thermophilic anaerobe
Clostridium thermocellum multicomponent cellulase system, an extracellular endoglucanase (51) and cell-bound β-glucosidase (49) and
phosphorylases (40,41) have been purified. All of these except the
endoglucanase are labile to thiol reagents. Ruminococcus produces a
cellulase which seems to be partially wall-bound in a high molecular
weight form and partially secreted into the medium in the form of an
enzyme with a molecular weight of 30,000 (51). Sporotrichum pulverulentum produces an extracellular cellulase system consisting of

Table 1.   Enzymes producing monosaccharides from β-(1-4) linked glucosyl oligomers or polymers.

β-GLUCOSIDASE

$$(\text{GLUCOSE})_N + H_2O \longrightarrow D\text{-GLUCOSE} + (\text{GLUCOSE})_{N-1}$$

CELLOBIOSE PHOSPHORYLASE (CLOSTRIDIUM, CELLVIBRIO)

$$\text{CELLOBIOSE} + P_I \rightleftharpoons \alpha\text{-}D\text{-GLUCOSE-1-PHOSPHATE} + D\text{-GLUCOSE}$$

CELLODEXTRIN PHOSPHORYLASE (CLOSTRIDIUM)

$$(\text{GLUCOSE})_N + P_I \rightleftharpoons \alpha\text{-}D\text{-GLUCOSE-1-PHOSPHATE} + D\text{-GLUCOSE}$$

$(1\rightarrow 4)$-β-D-GLUCAN GLUCOHYDROLASE (PENICILLIUM)

$$(\text{GLUCOSE})_N + H_2O \longrightarrow D\text{-GLUCOSE} + (\text{GLUCOSE})_{N-1}$$
OR (CELLULOSE)

$(1\rightarrow 4)$-β-D-GLUCAN GLUCANOHYDROLASE (TRICHODERMA)

$$\text{CELLOBIOSE} + H_2O \longrightarrow 2\ D\text{-GLUCOSE}$$

---

five endoglucanases, an exo-1,4-β-glucanase and β-glucosidases
(7,9). The endo- and exoglucanases act synergistically to degrade
cellulose. In addition, the cellobiose-oxidizing enzymes discussed
earlier can convert this end product of cellulose degradation to
cellobionolactone. The ultimate metabolic fate of this lactone has
not been examined in detail.

   Among the truly cellulolytic fungi (61), which include species
of Fusarium, Penicillium, and Trichoderma, there is a substantial
production of enzymes of the exocellobiohydrolase (CBH) type. These
have been demonstrated repeatedly to act synergistically with the
endoglucanases to degrade crystalline cellulose (62). However, a
new type of "exo-exo" synergism has been found (57), for which
additional evidence will be presented. These fungi also produce an
array of intra- and extracellular β-glucosidases which convert
cellobiose or cellooligosaccharides to glucose for metabolism.

   The generally accepted mode of action of the multicomponent
cellulase enzyme system involves a synergistic action at the cellulose surface of both endoglucanase production of glucan chain ends
and CBH solubilization of those polymers as cellobiose. Since the
cellobiohydrolase and endoglucanase are inhibited by the principal
end product cellobiose, its removal by β-glucosidase action stimulates depolymerization. Metabolism of the glucose normally
maintains the activity of the β-glucosidase which is subject to

inhibition by glucose. For many biotechnical applications, exogenous β-glucosidase is added (63) to enhance cellulase activity, and
combining the enzyme system with a fermenting organism in "simultaneous saccharification and fermentation" has been shown to accelerate
cellulose utilization.

Since the Trichoderma reesei enzyme system typifies many features of cellulase biosynthesis, it will be described in some
detail. The enzyme system of T. reesei QM9414 consists of (a) two
CBHs, CBH I and CBH II, (b) one to six electrophoretically distinct
endoglucanases, and (c) one to five β-glucosidase components depending upon culture conditions (56,64–67). Most of these enzymes are
glycoproteins. From crossed immunoelectrophoresis more than twenty
components have been observed (68) in the extracellular medium, although many of these are not cellulase enzymes. Earlier studies
showed that commercial preparations of T. viride cellulase contained
three forms of CBH I which were immunochemically similar, but differed in carbohydrate content (69). Because of the multiplicity of
enzyme forms and the possible loss of enzymes by binding to residual
cellulose, we investigated the rapid synthesis of the cellulase system using a soluble inducer (56). From comparison of the resultant
enzymes to those produced during a brief culture on cellulose, we
concluded that there are initially formed CBH I, CBH II, an endoglucanase, and a β-glucosidase (56) in the approximate proportions of
60:25:15:0.5. That 80-85% of the extracellular protein comprise
CBHs is a distinctive feature of this system and emphasizes the significance of the exoglucanases to its mode of action. For a commercial cellulase preparation from T. reesei, Lützen et al. (68) estimated the protein distribution to be cellobiohydrolases: endoglucanase: cellobiase: "inert protein" 65:20:1:15, in fair agreement with
our estimates for our preparation (56). The multiplicity of proteins we found also is in agreement with Göran Pettersson's analytical determinations (65). The amino acid and carbohydrate composi-
tions as well as the immunochemical characterization and activities
of the cellobiohydrolases reveal that the cellobiohydrolases are
quite distinct (57,70). Fägerstam and Pettersson have determined
partial amino acid sequences for cellobiohydrolase I and cellobiohydrolase II. It was found that for CBH I at least 80% of the neutral
carbohydrate is bound to a small region of the polypeptide. Recently we have determined that this carbohydrate is bound in the form of
O-linked trisaccharides which produce ^{13}C NMR spectra (Fig. 3) in-
dicative of only three types of anomeric carbons (C. du Mée, unpublished results).

Fägerstam and Pettersson also described a new type of "exo-exo"
cellulolytic synergism, since the activity on cellulose of CBH I and
CBH II together is greater than the sum of the activities of the
individual enzymes acting alone (57). We found (Figs. 4 and 5) that
this synergism is important in the intact cellulase system as it
degrades crystalline cellulose. Variation of the fraction of CBH

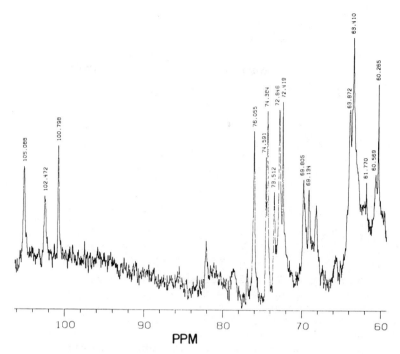

Fig. 3. Natural abundance carbon-13 nuclear magnetic resonance spectrum of cellobiohydrolase I (D) from _Trichoderma reesei_ QM9414. The region from 60 to 106 ppm of the proton-decoupled spectrum (obtained at 75.46 MHz) of 210 mg of the glycoprotein dissolved in 3.8 ml of D_2O after 35,712 scans is shown. Three signals from the anomeric carbon atoms of the mannosyl and glucosyl residues of trisaccharide side chains are evident at about 105.1, 102.5, and 100.8 ppm.

protein represented by CBH I and CBH II (together with fixed levels of endoglucanase and β-glucosidase) revealed an optimum composition for the system when acting on microcrystalline cellulose. However, on amorphous (swollen) cellulose, the utilization of CBH II as the sole CBH enzyme provided the optimum rate, as one might expect from the 5- to 10-fold greater activity for CBH II relative to CBH I. The synergistic activity on crystalline cellulose is a fundamental property of the _Trichoderma_ system.

For species of _Trichoderma_ several mutants have been selected which exhibit improved growth or cellulase enzyme production (Tab. 2). These mutants usually have been selected by cellulose plate-clearing assays (71-73) in the presence or absence of (a) easily metabolized substrates (e.g., glucose or glycerol), (b) transport or

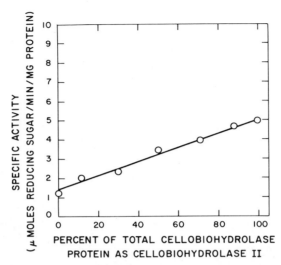

Fig. 4.   Activity of the cellulase system reconstituted from puri-
           fied T. reesei QM9414 glucanases and T. viride β-glucosi-
           dase on phosphoric acid-swollen cellulose as a function of
           cellobiohydrolase II concentration. A 1% suspension of
           swollen cellulose served as the substrate, and activity
           was determined by measuring reducing sugars released after
           a 30 min incubation with enzyme at 40°. In combining the
           pure components, endoglucanase and β-glucosidase concen-
           trations were kept constant at 15% and 0.6%, respectively,
           by weight, of the total enzyme protein, whereas the
           remaining 84.4% of enzyme protein was provided as cello-
           biohydrolase protein and comprised varying proportions of
           cellobiohydrolases I (D) and II. All reported values are
           averages of replicates differing by less than 3%.

metabolic inhibitors (e.g., 2-deoxyglucose), or (c) agents to limit
colony growth or facilitate enzyme diffusion (e.g., Phosfon D,
oxgall) (72). Such screening techniques together with a variety of
mutagens have led to great increases (74) in enzyme production relative to wild-type organisms. Some of the additional features
achieved include increased β-glucosidase production (75-80), rapid
cellulase production (81), and derepressed cellulase production during growth on glucose (71,82-84). Although most of these studies
resulted in mutants which produce more extracellular protein and
enzyme activity, the basic array of enzyme activities remained
similar or identical to the parent strains (85). One striking
feature of the hyperproducing/catabolite resistant mutant (RUT-C30)
is the abundance of endoplasmic reticulum (86). It was suggested
that the regulation of endoplasmic reticulum biogenesis may have

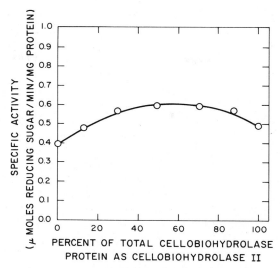

Fig. 5.   Activity of the cellulase system reconstituted from pur-
           ified T. reesei QM9414 glucanases and T. viride β-glucosi-
           dase on microcrystalline cellulose as a function of cello-
           biohydrolase II concentration. A 2% suspension of micro-
           crystalline cellulose (Avicel) served as the substrate.
           Activity determination, assay conditions, and enzyme
           proportions were identical to those described in Fig. 4.
           All reported values are averages of replicates which
           differed by less than 3%.

been affected by the mutation, leading to enhanced potential for
enzyme synthesis and secretion.

Cellulase Induction

        In addition to growth on cellulose, for some organisms growth
or exposure to related compounds such as carboxymethylcellulose or
cellobiose also stimulate cellulase production (51,87). It was
found in 1961 by Mandels and Reese that sophorose [O-β-D-glucopyran-
osyl-(1->2)-α-D-glucopyranose] (Fig. 6) is a potent inducer of cellulase activity in Trichoderma (88). Nisizawa et al. extended the
study of sophorose stimulation to show that (a) sophorose induces de
novo synthesis of cellulase enzymes, (b) glucose represses the synthesis, and (c) RNA synthesis is necessary for the induction (89,
90). Zhu and co-workers (84), using Trichoderma pseudokoningii,
have studied the induction of cellulase by sophorose and found (a)
that all of the activities of the cellulase system were induced and
(b) that total RNA and poly A-RNA increased in the induced mycelia.
This is consistent with our results with T. reesei which had shown
that β-glucosidase is induced by sophorose (Tab. 3) after a slightly

Table 2.   Improved <u>Trichoderma</u> strains.

STRAIN	PROPERTIES	INVESTIGATORS
T. REESEI		
QM9414	HIGH CELLULASE PRODUCTION	MANDEL (111)
RUT-C30	HYPERPRODUCTION OF CELLULASE CATABOLITE REPRESSION RESISTANT	MONTENECOURT AND EVELEIGH (71)
MCG 77	HIGH CELLULASE PRODUCTION	GALLO ET AL. (112)
MCG 80	HIGH CELLULASE PRODUCTIVITY RAPID CELLULASE PRODUCTION	GALLO (81)
C-5	CONSTITUTIVE CELLULASE PRODUCTION	MISHRA ET AL. (82)
QM9414-M5	PRODUCES BETA GLUCOSIDASE ON GLUCOSE	DACOSTA & VAN UDEN (76)
L-27	HIGH CELLULASE PRODUCTIVITY CONSTITUTIVE CELLULASE PRODUCTION	SHOEMAKER ET AL. (83)
VTT-D-80133	HIGH BETA GLUCOSIDASE STABLE STRAIN RESISTANT TO STIRRING	BAILEY AND NEVALAINEN (75)
CL-847	HIGH CELLULASE PRODUCTION HIGH BETA GLUCOSIDASE CATABOLITE REPRESSION RESISTANT	WARZYWODA ET AL. (79)
T. VIRIDE		
E 58	HIGH BETA GLUCOSIDASE	SADDLER (80)
T. PSEUDOKONINGII		
EA$_3$-867, N$_2$-78	HIGH CELLULASE PRODUCTION RESISTANT TO CATABOLITE REPRESSION	ZHU ET AL. (84)
SE1 A8	BETA-1,3 GLUCANASE PRODUCTION HIGH BETA GLUCOSIDASE	KUBICEK (78)

longer lag period than is required for induction of the depolymerizing enzymes (Fig. 7) (56).   Addition of compounds (e.g., nojirimycin
or 1-deoxynojirimycin) which inhibit β-glucosidase (Tab. 4) cleavage
of sophorose increased the levels of induced enzyme; similarly,
addition of 2-deoxyglucose, which interferes with glucose uptake and
metabolism, also increased enzyme levels.   However, tunicamycin, an
antibiotic which interferes with the synthesis of <u>N</u>-linked oligosac-
charide synthesis prior to protein glycosylation, had no effect.
This is consistent with the <u>O</u>-linkage of carbohydrate to protein
which we have observed (91).

By isolation of the poly A-RNA (mRNA) present on polyribo-
somes obtained from induced and noninduced cells, it was possible to

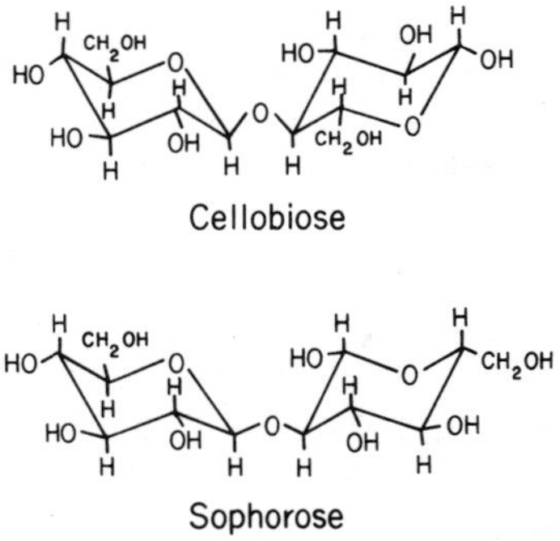

Cellobiose

Sophorose

Fig. 6.   Disaccharide structures.

estimate relative levels of active message for specific proteins. Using in vitro translation with rabbit reticulocyte lysate, we found the proportion of CBH I and CBH II message increased by about 200-fold after induction (Tab. 5). This is about the same fold increase as noted in extracellular Avicelase activity during the same induction period. This suggests closely coordinated control of transcription, translation, and secretion of cellulase enzymes by Trichoderma.

Cellulolytic Fermentations

Most of the work on improved cellulolytic strains has been devoted to an increase in extracellular cellulase activity. However, some selected or improved strains, such as a derepressed

Table 3.   Effect of sophorose concentration on the production of cellulase enzymes by T. reesei.[A]

SOPHOROSE CONCENTRATION (mM)	PROTEIN (MG/ML SUPERNATE)	ENZYME ACTIVITY (MILLIUNITS/ML SUPERNATE)		
		ARYL –β– D– GLUCOSIDASE	ENDO-1,4-β- D-GLUCANASE	AVICELASE
0.0	0.08	0.6	0.0	0.6
0.1	0.23	62	4000	80
0.5	0.25	70	6000	86
1.0	0.28	85	6500	140
5.1	0.20	75	2000	45

[A]ENZYME ACTIVITY OBSERVED AFTER 8 H OF INCUBATION. THE CELL SUSPENSION CONTAINED 1.9 MG/ML OF CELLS. ALL REPORTED VALUES ARE AVERAGES OF REPLICATES WHICH DIFFERED BY LESS THAN 10%. (108)

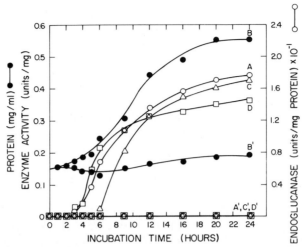

Fig. 7.   Enzyme production by T. reesei QM9414 when incubated in
           the presence of Sophorose. Lines A, C, and D represent
           specific endoglucanase, β-glucosidase, and Avicelase
           activity, respectively. Lines A', C', and D' represent
           the corresponding controls which lack Sophorose. Lines B
           and B' represent extracellular protein in the sophorose-
           containing and control incubation mixtures, respectively.
           The cell suspension contained 3.6 mg dry weight mycel-
           ium/ml (108).

Cellulomonas (92), Aspergillus terreus (93), and Chaetomium (94),
are considered valuable for the production of enzyme and microbial
biomass as a proteinaceous foodstuff. A more complex adaptation is
the use of either the cellulase or the cellulolytic (saccharifying)
organism together with a fermenting organism to convert lignocellulose to useful end products, such as ethanol, methane, or hydrogen
(Tab. 6). These "simultaneoussaccharification-fermentation" (SSF)
systems or cocultures often afford both a directed synthesis of end
product and enhanced cellulolysis due to removal of soluble sugars.
The cellulase enzymes with Saccharomyces cerevisiae yield ethanol
with few byproducts (95); with Zymomonas mobilis there is a potential for higher ethanol yields (96). Trichoderma reesei plus Candida wickerhamii permits utilization of the yeast β-glucosidase instead of supplementing the Trichoderma system with another fungal
β-glucosidase (97,98). Thermomonospora sp. and Thermoanaerobacter
ethanolicus have been proposed as a thermophilic coculture for ethanol production (109). Clostridium thermosaccharolyticum ferments
xylose from hemicellulose together with the Cl. thermocellum saccharification and hexose fermentation. Wang et al. produced superior strains of both organisms capable of increased fermentation
rates and lower proportions of glucose diverted to lactic, acetic,

Table 4. Effect of various compounds on sophorose-stimulated cellulase enzyme production by resting mycelia of T. reesei
QM9414.[A]

ADDITIONS	EXTRACELLULAR PROTEIN	ENZYME ACTIVITY	
		ENDO-1,4 β-D-GLUCANASE[B]	AVICELASE[C]
	MG/ML SUPERNATE	U/ML	
NONE	0.43	7.60	0.15
NOJIRIMYCIN (0.01MM)	0.92	18.00	0.33
1-DEOXYNOJIRIMYCIN (0.01MM)	0.88	17.60	0.32
2-DEOXYGLUCOSE (1MM)	0.65	11.60	0.22
TUNICAMYCIN (20 µG/ML)	0.42	7.60	0.14

[A] INCUBATIONS WERE CARRIED OUT FOR 24 HOURS IN 17MM POTASSIUM PHOSPHATE
BUFFER, PH 6.0. SOPHOROSE CONCENTRATION WAS 1 MM, AND BIOMASS CONCEN-
TRATION WAS 5.2 MG DRY WEIGHT MYCELIUM PER ML OF INCUBATION MIXTURE.
ALL REPORTED VALUES ARE AVERAGES OF REPLICATES WHICH DIFFERED BY LESS
THAN 5%.

[B] DETERMINED BY THE REDUCTION IN VISCOSITY OF A SOLUTION OF CARBOXYMETHYL-
CELLULOSE, AND EXPRESSED AS CHANGE IN SPECIFIC FLUIDITY/MIN/MG OF PROTEIN.

[C] AVICELASE ACTIVITY IS DETERMINED BY MEASURING TOTAL REDUCING SUGAR
RELEASED FROM AVICEL, A MICROCRYSTALLINE CELLULOSE AS A RESULT OF ENZYME
ACTION. THIS TERM DOES NOT SIGNIFY THE ACTIVITY OF A SINGLE ENZYME,
BUT RATHER THAT OF THE ENTIRE CELLULASE SYSTEM.

and butyric acids (55). Among many possible complex cocultures involving methanogens, the Acetivibrio cellulolyticus plus Methanosarcina Barkeri system yielded nearly theoretical amounts of CH_4 and
CO_2 from cellulose (99). The combined fermentation of Bacteroides
succinogenes and Selenomonas ruminantium takes advantage of the saccharification by the former and a conversion of succinate to prop-
ionate by the latter (100). In a coculture of Cellulomonas and
Rhodopseudomonas, the organic acids produced by the former were used
as a source of reducing power for photosynthetic hydrogen production

Table 5. Cellulase polypeptides synthesized in vitro by mRNA isolated from T. reesei QM9414 resting cells.[A]

SERUM	PERCENT IMMUNOPRECIPITABLE RADIOACTIVITY	
	INDUCED	CONTROL
ANTI CBHI(D)	3.92	0.016
ANTI CBH II	2.36	0.013

[A] IMMUNOPRECIPITATIONS WERE CARRIED OUT USING, IN EACH CASE, IN
VITRO TRANSLATES WHICH CONTAINED APPROXIMATELY EQUAL AMOUNTS
OF TCA PRECIPITABLE RADIOACTIVITY.

Table 6.   Examples of microbial/enzyme combined conversion systems.

ORGANISMS	PRODUCTS	INVESTIGATORS
ETHANOL		
T. REESEI CELLULASE PLUS SACCHAROMYCES CEREVISIAE	ETHANOL	TAKAGI ET AL. (95)
T. REESEI CELLULASE PLUS ZYMOMONAS MOBILIS OR SACCHAROMYCES CEREVISIAE	ETHANOL	SADDLER ET AL. (96)
T. REESEI CELLULASE PLUS CANDIDA WICKERHAMII	ETHANOL	FREER AND DETROY (97)
THERMOMONOSPORA THERMOANAEROBACTER ETHANOLICUS	ETHANOL	MITCHELL ET AL. (109)
CELLULOLYTIC ANAEROBE CLOSTRIDIUM THERMOSACCHAROLYTICUM	ETHANOL ACETIC ACID PROPIONIC ACID	KHAN AND MURRAY (110)
CLOSTRIDIUM THERMOCELLUM S-7 CLOSTRIDIUM THERMOSACCHAROLYTICUM HG-4	ETHANOL ACETIC ACID LACTIC ACID	WANG ET AL. (55)
METHANE ACETOVIBRIO CELLULOLYTICUS METHANOSARCINA BARKERI	METHANE	KHAN (99)
PROPIONATE BACTEROIDES SUCCINOGENES SELENOMONAS RUMINANTIUM	PROPIONATE AND ACETATE	WOLIN AND MILLER (100)
HYDROGEN CELLULOMONAS SP. RHODOPSEUDOMONAS CAPSULATA	H_2	ODOM AND WALL (101)

(101). These examples indicate some of the diverse simple gnotobi-
otic cultures which have been shown to convert cellulose to products
of practical value.

Genetic Engineering

As a prelude to a recent symposium, Dr. W. A. Wood (102) proposed some desirable new organisms (Tab. 7). In the description of
each organism the terms "cellulolytic" and "thermophilic" appeared,
perhaps indicating a general wish to rapidly convert cellulose or

Table 7. Desirable new organisms (W.A. Wood).

YEAST	THERMOPHILIC, ETHANOL-TOLERANT, CELLULOLYTIC
METHANOGEN	THERMOPHILIC, HETEROTROPHIC, CELLULOLYTIC
BUTANOL PRODUCER	THERMOPHILIC, HOMOFERMENTATIVE, CELLULOLYTIC

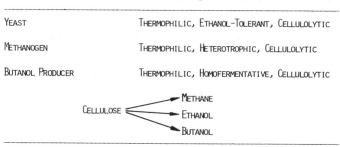

lignocellulose into fuels or chemicals — a process commensurate with
the availability of the substrate and market for the products.
Among the known cellulolytic or cellobiose fermenting organisms,
several have now been examined and the use of recombinant DNA technology employed to transfer the DNA coding for some specific enzymes
to host organisms in prospect of eventual design of simple "desirable microbes." Some of these studies are listed in Table 8, and
the research is summarized briefly below.

Since cellobiose is often the predominant product of cellulose
degradation, a β-glucosidase gene of Escherichia adecarboxylata was
transferred to E. coli as a first step in expanding the range of
microbes which can utilize cellobiose (103). After digestion of E.
adecarboxylata DNA with EcoRI and alkaline phosphatase, it was incubated with EcoRI-treated pBR322 DNA and T_4 ligase. The ligated DNA
was used to transform E. coli HB101, and selection for β-glucosidase
was carried out on minimal broth containing cellobiose and tetracycline. Two hundred colonies per μg ligated DNA were able to grow.
The plasmid DNA (pBA2) from the cellobiose culture of one colony was
isolated and digested with a number of restriction endonucleases.
Cellobiose-utilizing subclones of the pBA2 (25 kb insert) fragments
yielded first a plasmid pBA24 (11 kb insert) and, subsequently,
through subcloning, a plasmid pBA2410 (5.1 kb insert). The β-glucosidase containing E. coli HB101 grew on cellobiose with a doubling
time of 66 min (compared to 50-60 min for growth on glucose). All
of the enzyme was cell-associated and constitutively expressed.
Because of an observed stimulation of activity by P_i, the authors
considered it possible that the enzyme was really cellobiose phosphorylase. It is difficult to assess the significance of this
research without more specific information regarding the structure
and properties of the enzyme both in E. adecarboxylata and the
transformed strains.

The molecular cloning of Cellulomonas fimi gene(s) into E. coli
was also carried out using pBR322 and a Bam HI digest of C. fimi
DNA (104). After ligation, the plasmid was used to transform E.
coli C600 to ampicillin resistance. Screening of clones employed
antisera to the extracellular medium of C. fimi and ^{125}I-labelled

Table 8.   Cloning of genes for cellulose utilization.

Donor	Cloning Vehicle	Acceptor	Activity	Investigator
Escherichia adecarboxylata	pBR322	E. coli HB101	β-Glucosidase	Armentrout and Brown (103)
Cellulomonas fimi	pBR322	E. coli C600	CM-cellulase	Whittle et al. (104)
Clostridium thermocellum	cosmid pHC79	E. coli 4282	CM-cellulase	Cornet et al. (105)
(Preliminary Reports)				
Thermomonospora	pBR322	E. coli HB101	Endocellulase	Wilson (106)
Schizophyllum commune	pBR322	E. coli	'Cellulase'	Seligy (107)
Trichoderma reesei QM9414	λ	E. coli	Cellobiohydrolase I	Stafford (107)

protein A.   Proteins from lysed colonies were transferred to CNBr-activated filter papers (or plain filter papers) which then were exposed sequentially to the antiserum and ^{125}I-protein A.   The specificity of this technique is questionable on the basis of the uncertain number and nature of cellulases secreted by the organism and used as the antigen probe.   One positive clone was obtained in the initial screening of 1,000 clones and the plasmid designated pDW1. Cell-free extracts of the transformed E. coli contained 5 units of cellulase/ml culture, using the dinitrosalicylic acid (DNS) method for reducing sugars liberated from carboxymethylcellulose.   The plasmid pDW1 was estimated to contain a 20.2 kb insert.   At this point further work will be required to determine whether a plasmid/host combination can be found which will produce and export large quantities of cellulase.

The Clostridium thermocellum cellulase system consists of a number of enzymes (51) which together (at 60°C) efficiently degrade cotton (50) and thus are attractive as candidates for cloning into noncellulolytic hosts.   The Cl. thermocellum NCIB10682 total DNA was digested with Sau3Al and ligated to Bam HI digested cosmid pHC79 DNA (105).   After in vitro packaging into lambda phage heads, the phage was plated on E. coli 4282.   The clone bank consisted of 1,200 Amp^r Tet^s clones with randomly selected plasmid DNAs containing inserts of between 25-40 kb.   Of these 1,200 clones, pooled in groups of ten, crude extracts of two pools gave a positive test when assayed viscosimetrically for carboxymethylcellulase activity.   From each pool one clone was identified as the CMCase source.   These two clones carried cosmids designated pCT182 and pCT262. To an antiserum against a purified endoglucanase from Cl. thermocellum, the extract of E. coli 4282 (pCT182) gave a precipitin line which fused completely with that formed to the homologous antigen. There was no reaction with extracts of strains carrying pCT262 or pHC79. The antiserum inhibited the CMCase activity of E. coli 4282 (pCT182) by 85%, but caused no inhibition of the extract of E. coli 4282 (pCT262). About 30% as much CMCase (color release test) was produced per mg of all proteins in E. coli 4282 (pCT182) as in Cl. thermocellum, suggesting that expression is about 30% as great.

There have been several preliminary reports of cloning cellulase genes (106,107), and abstracts of papers dealing with this subject have appeared. The cloning of a cellulase gene from Thermomonospora in E. coli using pBR322 was found by Wilson et al. to result not only in expression, but secretion of the enzyme into the medium. The transforming plasmid D316 showed an insert of an 8.3 kb segment of the Thermomonospora DNA. An antibody to the "endocellulase" inhibited the enzyme. Approximately one third of the enzyme activity was found in the cells, in the periplasmic space, and in the medium, respectively. The enzyme synthesis in E. coli was observed only after growth had stopped, whereas Thermomonospora synthesizes cellulases during growth. The thermophilic actinomycete also makes about 100 times as much cellulase enzyme as does the E. coli. Using mRNA from cellulose-induced Schizophyllum commune, Seligy et al. have constructed cDNA which was ligated into pBR322 and used to transform E. coli. At this point a small amount of enzyme is reported to be synthesized, as judged by reaction with antibody to the pure enzyme. Using cellulose-grown Trichoderma reesei, Stafford and co-workers have made cDNA to mRNA enriched in cellulase enzyme message. E. coli clones resulting from infection by a recombinant lambda phage did not exhibit cellulase activity. Although oligonucleotide probes based on the established amino acid sequence of CBH I (57) were used in an attempt to identify the specific mRNA in the E. coli, no translatable message was detected. However, this probe did permit the identification of an oligonucleotide sequence in T. reesei mRNA which apparently codes for a signal peptide sequence.

The future success of genetic studies for lignocellulose conversion will continue to include profitably a rich variety of approaches. Useful and unique organisms continue to be isolated, strains are improved by mutagenesis and selection, and, as more precise knowledge of enzyme structure and function is revealed and cloning systems are developed, there should be increasingly sophisticated organisms "engineered." The recently reported purification of a H_2O_2-requiring enzyme which degrades lignin should stimulate genetic and enzymological studies in this field (113).

The area is not without its potential problems, as organisms which perform well under laboratory conditions may not compete or react satisfactorily under actual pilot plant or reactor conditions. Since some plant diseases may involve degradation of lignocellulose, it is of some concern that newly constructed organisms be screened for pathogenicity. At present there is no shortage of interesting and important projects which may enhance bioconversion of lignocellulosic wastes.

ACKNOWLEDGEMENT

This work was supported in part by a cooperative program with The Gas Research Institute.

REFERENCES

1. Hall, D.O. (1982) Solar energy through biology: Fuels from biomass. Experientia 38:3-10.
2. Brown, D.E. (1983) Lignocellulose hydrolysis. Phil. Trans. R. Soc. Lond. B300:305-322.
3. Brown, Jr., R.D., and L. Jurasek, eds. (1979) Hydrolysis of Cellulose: Mechanisms of Enzymatic and Acid Catalysis, Adv. Chem. Ser., Vol. 181. American Chemical Society, Washington, D.C., Vol. 181.
4. Chen, C.L., M.G.S. Chua, J.E. Evans, H.M. Chang, and T.K. Kirk (1981) Chemistry of lignin biodegradation by Phanerochaete chrysosporium. The Ekman Days Symp. III:75-87.
5. Crawford, D.L., and R.L. Crawford (1980) Microbial degradation of lignin. Enzyme Microb. Technol. 2:11-22.
6. Crawford, R.L. (1981) Lignin Biodegradation and Transformation. John Wiley & Sons, Inc., New York.
7. Eriksson, K.-E. (1978) Enzyme mechanisms involved in cellulose hydrolysis by the rot fungus Sporotrichum pulverulentum. Biotechnol. Bioeng. 20:317-332.
8. Eriksson, K.-E. (1981) Microbial degradation of cellulose and lignin. The Ekman Days Symp. III:60-65.
9. Eriksson, K.-E. (1982) Degradation of cellulose. Experientia 38:156-159.
10. Flickinger, M. (1980) Current biological research in conversion of cellulosic carbohydrates into liquid fuels: How far have we come? Biotechnol. Bioeng. 21:27-48.
11. Higuchi, T. (1982) Biodegradation of lignin: Biochemistry and potential applications. Experientia 38:159-166.
12. Hollaender, A., ed. (1981) Trends in the Biology of Fermentations for Fuels and Chemicals. Basic Life Sciences, Vol. 18, Plenum Press, New York.
13. Kirk, T.K. (1981) Principles of lignin degradation by white-rot fungi. The Ekman Days Symp. III:66-70.
14. Kirk, T.K., T. Higuchi, and H.M. Chang, eds. (1980) Lignin Biodegradation: Microbiology, Chemistry and Potential Applications. Vol. I, CRC Press, Inc., Boca Raton, Florida.

15. Kirk, T.K., T. Higuchi, and H.M. Chang, eds. (1980) Lignin Bio-degradation: Microbiology, Chemistry and Potential Applica-tions. Vol. II, CRC Press, Inc., Boca Raton, Florida.
16. Ladisch, M.R., K.W. Lin, M. Voloch, and G.T. Tsao (1983) Process considerations in the enzymatic hydrolysis of biomass. Enzyme Microb. Technol. 5:82–102.
17. Palmer, J.M., and C.S. Evans (1983) The enzymic degradation of lignin by white-rot fungi. Phil. Trans. R. Soc. Lond. B300:293–303.
18. Ryu, D.D.Y., and M. Mandels (1980) Cellulases: Biosynthesis and applications. Enzyme Microb. Technol. 2:91–101.
19. Scott, C.D., ed. (1982) Fourth Symposium on Biotechnology in Energy Production and Conservation. Biotech. Bioeng. Symp. No. 12. John Wiley & Sons, New York.
20. Reilly, P.J. (1981) Xylanases: Structure and function. In Trends in the Biology of Fermentations for Fuels and Chemicals, Basic Life Sciences, A. Hollaender, ed. Plenum Press, New York. Vol. 18, pp. 111–129.
21. Gong, C.S. (1983) Recent advances in D-xylose conversion by yeasts. In Annual Reports on Fermentations Processes, G.T. Tsao, ed., Vol. 6, pp. 253–297.
22. Kirk, T.K. (1980) Studies on the physiology of lignin metabo-lism by white-rot fungi. In Lignin Biodegradation: Microbiol-ogy, Chemistry, and Potential Applications, T.K. Kirk, T. Higuchi, and H. Chang, eds. CRC Press, Inc., Boca RAton, Florida, Vol. II:51–63.
23. Kirk, T.K. (1981) Toward elucidating the mechanism of action of the ligninolytic system in Basidiomycetes. In Trends in the Biology of Fermentations for Fuels and Chemicals, Basic Life Sciences, A. Hollaender, ed. Plenum Press, New York. Vol.18, pp. 131–149.
24. Hall, P., W. Glasser, and S. Drew (1980) Enzymatic transforma-tions of lignin. In Lignin Biodegradation: Microbiology, Chem-istry, and Potential Applications, T.K. Kirk, T. Higuchi, and H. Chang, eds. CRC Press, Inc., Boca Raton, Florida, Vol. II:33–49.
25. Hall, P.L. (1980) Enzymatic transformations in lignin II. Enzyme Microb. Technol. 2:170–178.
26. Ander, P., A. Hatakka, and K.-E. Eriksson (1980) Degradation of lignin – related substances by Sporotrichum pulverulentum. In Lignin Biodegradation: Microbiology, Chemistry, and Potential Applications, T.K. Kirk, T. Higuchi, and H. Chang, eds. CRC Press, Inc., Boca Raton, Florida, Vol. II:1–15.
27. Ander, P., K.-E. Eriksson, P. Mansson, and B. Pettersson (1981) Lignin degradation by Sporotrichum pulverulentum: A new culti-vation method to study fungal lignin degradation. The Ekman Days Symp. III:71–74.
28. Freer, S.N., and R.W. Detroy (1982) Biological delignification of ^{14}C-labelled lignocelluloses by Basidiomycetes: Degradation and solubilization of the lignin and cellulose components. Mycologia 74:943–951.

29. Buswell, J.A., P. Ander, and K.-E. Eriksson (1982) Lignolytic
    activity and levels of ammonia assimilating enzymes in Sporo-
    trichum pulverulentum. Arch. Microbiol. 133:165-171.
30. Reid, I.D. (1983) Effects of nitrogen supplements on degrada-
    tion of aspen wood lignin and carbohydrate components by Phan-
    erochaete chrysosporium. Appl. Environ. Microbiol. 45:830-837.
31. Reid, I.D. (1983) Effects of nitrogen sources on cellulose and
    synthetic lignin degradation by Phanerochaete chrysosporium.
    Appl. Environ. Microbiol. 45:838-842.
32. Eriksson, K.-E., A. Grünewald, and L. Vallander (1980) Studies
    of growth conditions in wood for three white-rot fungi and
    their cellulaseless mutants. Biotechnol. Bioeng. 22:363-376.
33. Ayers, A.R., S.B. Ayers, and K.-E. Eriksson (1978) Cellobiose
    oxidase, purification and partial characterization of a hemo-
    protein from Sporotrichum pulverulentum. Eur. J. Biochem.
    90:171-181.
34. Ayers, A.R., and K.-E. Eriksson (1982) Cellobiose oxidase from
    Sporotrichum pulverulentum. In Methods in Enzymology, W.A.
    Wood, ed. Academic Press, Inc., New York, Vol. 89, pp.
    129-135.
35. Koenigs, J. (1974) Production of hydrogen peroxide by wood-
    rotting fungi in wood and its correlation with weight loss,
    depolymerization, and pH changes. Arch. Microbiol. 99:129.
36. Highley, T.L. (1982) Is extracellular hydrogen peroxide
    involved in cellulose degradation by brown-rot fungi?
    Materialen und Organismen 17:205-214.
37. Forney, L.J., C.A. Reddy, M. Tien, and S.D. Aust (1982) The
    involvement of hydroxyl radical derived from hydrogen peroxide
    in lignin degradation by the white rot fungus Phanerochaete
    chrysosporium. J. Biol. Chem. 257:11455-11462.
38. Nakatsubo, F., I.D. Reid, and T.K. Kirk (1981) Involvement of
    singlet oxygen in fungal degradation of lignin. Biochem.
    Biophys. Res. Comm. 102:484-491.
39. Wood, T.M., and S.I. McCrae (1982) Purification and some prop-
    erties of a (1->4)-β-D-glucan glucohydrolase associated with
    the cellulase from the fungus Penicillium funiculosum.
    Carbohyd. Res. 110:291-303.
40. Alexander, J.K. (1972) Cellobiose phosphorylase from Clostrid-
    ium thermocellum. In Methods in Enzymology, V. Ginsburg, ed.
    Academic Press, Inc., New York, Vol. 28, pp. 944-948.
41. Alexander, J.K. (1972) Cellodextrin phosphorylase from Clos-
    tridium thermocellum. In Methods in Enzymology, V. Ginsburg,
    ed. Academic Press, Inc., New York, Vol. 28, pp. 948-953.
42. Sasaki, T., T. Tanaka, S. Nakagawa, and K. Kainuma (1983) Pur-
    ification and properties of Cellvibrio gilvus cellobiose phos-
    phorylase. Biochem. J. 209:803-807.
43. Mandels, M., and R.E. Andreotti (1978) Problems and challenges
    in the cellulose to cellulase fermentation. Process Biochem.
    13:6-13.
44. Fennington, G., D. Lupo, and F. Stutzenberger (1982) Enhanced
    cellulase production in mutants of Thermomonospora curvata.
    Biotechnol. Bioeng. 24:2487-2497.

45. Hagerdal, B., H. Harris, and E.K. Pye (1979) Association of β-glucosidase with intact cells of thermoactinomyces. Biotechnol. Bioeng. 21:345-355.
46. Meyer, H.P., and A.E. Humphrey (1982) Cellulase production by a wild and a new mutant strain of Thermomonospora sp. Biotechnol. Bioeng. 24:1901-1904.
47. Tong, C.C., A.L. Cole, and M.G. Shepherd (1980) Purification and properties of the cellulases from the thermophilic fungus Thermoascus aurantiacus. Biochem. J. 191:83-94.
48. Folan, M.A., and M.P. Coughlan (1979) The saccharifying ability of the cellulase complex of Talaromyces emersonii and comparison with that of other fungal species. Int. J. Biochem. 10:505-510.
49. Ait, N., N. Creuzet, and J. Cannáneo (1982) Properties of β-glucosidase purified from Clostridium thermocellum. J. Gen. Microbiol. 128:569-577.
50. Johnson, E.A., M. Sakajoh, G. Halliwell, A. Madia, and A.L. Demain (1982) Saccharification of complex cellulosic substrates by the cellulase system from Clostridium thermocellum. Appl. Environ. Microbiol. 43:1125-1132.
51. Ng, T.K., and J.G. Zeikus (1981) Comparison of extracellular cellulase activities of Clostridium thermocellum LQRI and Trichoderma reesei QM9414. Appl. Environ. Microbiol. 42:231-240.
52. Canevascini, G., M.R. Coudray, J.P. Rey, R.J.G. Southgate, and H. Meier (1979) Induction and catabolite repression of cellulase synthesis in the thermophilic fungus Sporotrichum thermophile. J. Gen. Microbiol. 110:291-303.
53. Margaritis, A., and M. Merchant (1983) Xylanase, CM-cellulase and Avicelase production by the thermophilic fungus Sporotrichum thermophile. Biotechnol. Lett. 5:265-270.
54. Wood, T.M., C.A. Wilson, and C.S. Stewart (1982) Preparation of the cellulase from the cellulolytic anaerobic rumen bacterium Ruminococcus albus and its release from the bacterial cell wall. Biochem. J. 205:129-137.
55. Wang, D.I.C., G.C. Avgerinos, I. Biocic, S.D. Wang, and H.Y. Fang (1983) Ethanol from cellulosic biomass. Phil. Trans. R. Soc. Lond. B300:323-333.
56. Gritzali, M., and R.D. Brown, Jr. (1979) The cellulase system of Trichoderma: Relationships between extracellular enzymes from induced or cellulose-grown cells. In Hydrolysis of Cellulose: Mechanisms of Enzymatic and Acid Catalysis. Adv. Chem. Ser., R.D. Brown, Jr. and L. Jurasek, eds. American Chemical Society, Washington, D.C., Vol. 181:237-260.
57. Fägerstam, L.G., and L.G. Pettersson (1980) The 1,4-β-glucan cellobiohydrolases of Trichoderma reesei QM9414. A new type of cellulolytic synergism. FEBS Lett. 119:97-100.
58. Kanda, T., I. Noda, K. Wakabayashi, and K. Nisizawa (1983) Transglycosylation activities of exo- and endo- type cellulases from Irpex lacteus (Polyporus tulipiferae). J. Biochem. 93:787-794.

59. Wood, T.M., and S.I. McCrae (1978) The cellulase of Trichoderma koningii. Biochem. J. 171:61–72.

60. Wood, T.M, S.I. McCrae, and C.C. MacFarlane (1980) The isolation, purification and properties of the cellobiohydrolase component of Penicillium funiculosum cellulase. Biochem. J. 189:51–65.

61. Wood, T.M. (1969) The relationship between cellulolytic and pseudo-cellulolytic microoganisms. Biochim. Biophys. Acta 192:531–534.

62. Wood, T.M., and S.I. McCrae (1979) Synergism between enzymes involved in the solubilization of native cellulose. In Hydrolysis of Cellulose: Mechanisms of Enzymatic and Acid Catalysis. Adv. Chem. Ser., R.D. Brown, Jr. and L. Jurasek, eds. American Chemical Society, Washington, D.C., Vol. 181:181–209.

63. Allen, A., and D. Sternberg (1980) β–Glucosidase production by Aspergillus phoenicis in stirred-tank fermentors. Biotechnol. Bioeng. Symp. No. 10, pp. 189–197.

64. Brown, Jr., R.D., M. Gritzali, and W.C. Chirico (1981) Biosynthesis and characteristics of the enzymes comprising the Trichoderma cellulase system. The Ekman Days Symp. III:28–30.

65. Pettersson, L.G., L. Fägerstam, R. Bhikhabhai, and K. Leandoer (1981) The cellulase complex of Trichoderma reesei QM9414. The Ekman Days Symp. III:39–42.

66. Farkas, V., A. Jalanko, and N. Kolarova (1982) Characterization of cellulase complexes from Trichoderma reesei QM9414 and its mutants by means of analytical isoelectrofusing in polyacrylamide gels. Biochim. Biophys. Acta 706:105–110.

67. Labudova, I., and V. Farkas (1983) Multiple enzyme forms in the cellulase system of Trichoderma reesei during its growth on cellulose. Biochim. Biophys. Acta 744:135–140.

68. Lützen, N.W., M.H. Nielsen, K.M. Oxenboell, M. Schülein, and B. Stentebjerg-Olesen (1983) Cellulases and their application in the conversion of lignocellulose to fermentable sugars. Phil. Trans. R. Soc. Lond. B300:283–291.

69. Gum, Jr., E.K., and R.D. Brown, Jr. (1977) Comparison of four purified extracellular 1,4–β–D–glucan cellobiohydrolase enzymes from Trichoderma viride. Biochim. Biophys. Acta 492:225–231.

70. Gritzali, M. (1979) Purification and characterization of an endo-1,4–β–D–glucanase and two exo-1,4–β–D–glucanases from the cellulase system of Trichoderma reesei. Ph.D. dissertation, Virginia Polytechnic Institute and State University, Blacksburg, Virginia.

71. Montenecourt, B.S., and D.E. Eveleigh (1977) Semi-quantitative plate assay for determination of cellulase production by Trichoderma viride. Appl. Environ. Microbiol. 33:178–183.

72. Montenecourt, B.S., and D.E. Eveleigh (1979) Selective screening methods for the isolation of high yielding cellulase mutants of Trichoderma reesei. In Hydrolysis of cellulose: Mechanisms of Enzymatic and Acid Catalysis, R.D. Brown, Jr. and L. Jurasek, eds. Adv. Chem. Ser., American Chemical Society, Washington, Vol. 181:289–301.

73. Montenecourt, B.S., S.M. Cuskey, S.D. Nhlapo, H. Trimiño-Vazquez, and D.E. Eveleigh (1981) Strain development for the production of microbial cellulases. The Ekman Days Symp. III:43-50.
74. Montenecourt, B.S., S.K. Nhlapo, H. Trimiño-Vazquez, S. Cuskey, D.H.J. Schamhart, and D.E. Eveleigh (1981) Regulatory controls in relation to overproduction of fungal cellulases. In Trends in the Biology of Fermentations for Fuels and Chemicals, Basic Life Sciences, A. Hollaender, ed. Plenum Press, New York, Vol. 18, pp. 33-53.
75. Bailey, M.J., and K.M.H. Nevalainen (1981) Induction, isolation and testing of stable Trichoderma reesei mutants with improved production of solubilizing cellulase. Enzyme Microb. Technol. 3:153-157.
76. Beja da Costa, M., and N. Van Nuden (1980) Use of 2-deoxyglucose in the selective isolation of mutants of Trichoderma reesei with enhanced β-glucosidase production. Biotechnol. Bioeng. 22:2429-2432.
77. Kubicek, C.P. (1982) β-Glucosidase excretion by Trichoderma pseudokoningii: Correlation with cell wall bound β-1,3-glucanase activities. Arch. Microbiol. 132:349-354.
78. Kubicek, C.P. (1983) β-Glucosidase excretion in Trichoderma strains with different cell-wall bound β-1,3-glucanase activities. Can. J. Microbiol. 29:163-169.
79. Warczywoda, M., J.P. Vandecasteele, and J. Pourquié (1983) A comparison of genetically improved strains of the cellulolytic fungus Trichoderma reesei. Biotechnol. Lett. 5:243-246.
80. Saddler, J.N. (1982) Screening of highly cellulolytic fungi and the action of their cellulase enzyme systems. Enzyme Microb. Technol. 4:414-418.
81. Gallo, B.J. (1981) Cellulase production by the new hyperproducing strain of Trichoderma reesei MCG80. Natl. Meeting, AIChE., Orlando, Florida.
82. Mishra, S., K.S. Gopalkrishnan, and T.K. Ghose (1982) A constitutively cellulase-producing mutant of Trichoderma reesei. Biotechnol. Bioeng. 24:251-254.
83. Shoemaker, S.P., J.C. Raymond, and R. Bruner (1981) Cellulases: Diversity amongst improved Trichoderma strains. In Trends in the Biology of Fermentations for Fuels and Chemicals. Basic Life Sciences, A. Hollaender, ed., Plenum Press, New York. Vol. 18, pp. 89-109.
84. Zhu, Y.S., Y.Q. Wu, W. Chen, C. Tan, J.H. Gao, J.Y. Fei, and C.N. Shih (1982) Induction and regulation of cellulase synthesis in Trichoderma pseudokoningii mutants EA_3-867 and N_2-78. Enzyme Microb. Technol. 4:3-12.
85. Bissett, F.H. (1979) Analysis of cellulase proteins by high-performance liquid chromatography. J. Chromatography 178:515-523.
86. Ghosh, A., S. Al-Rabiai, B.K. Ghosh, H. Trimiño-Vazquez, D.E. Eveleigh, and B.S. Montenecourt (1982) Increased endoplasmic reticulum content of a mutant of Trichoderma reesei (RUT-C30)

in relation to cellulase synthesis. Enzyme Microb. Technol. 4:110-113.

87. Desrochers, M., L. Jurasek, and M.G. Paige (1981) High production of β-glucosidase in Schizophyllum commune: Isolation of
the enzyme and effect of the culture filtrate on cellulose hydrolysis. Appl. Environ. Microbiol. 41:222-228.

88. Mandels, M., F.W. Parrish, and E.T. Reese (1961) Sophorose as
an inducer of cellulase in Trichoderma viride. J. Bacteriol.
83:400-408.

89. Nisizawa, T., H. Suzuki, M. Nakayama, and K. Nisizawa (1971)
Inductive formation of cellulase by sophorose in Trichoderma
viride. J. Biochem. 70:375-385.

90. Nisizawa, T., H. Suzuki, and K. Nisizawa (1972) Catabolite
repression of cellulase formation in Trichoderma viride. J.
Biochem. 71:999-1007.

91. Gum, Jr., E.K., and R.D. Brown, Jr. (1976) Structural characterization of a glycoprotein cellulase, 1,4-β-D-glucan
cellobiohydrolase C from Trichoderma viride. Biochim. Biophys.
Acta 446:371-386.

92. Hitchner, E.V., and J.M. Leatherwood (1980) Use of a cellu-
lase-derepressed mutant of Cellulomonas in the production of a
single-cell protein product from cellulose. Appl. Environ.
Microbiol. 39:382-386.

93. Miller, T.F., and V.R. Srinivasan (1983) Production of single-
cell protein from cellulose by Aspergillus terreus. Biotechnol. Bioeng. 25:1509-1519.

94. Pamment, N., C.W. Robinson, J. Hilton, and M. Moo-Young (1978)
Solid-state cultivation of Chaetomium cellulolyticum on alkali-
pretreated sawdust. Biotechnol. Bioeng. 20:1735-1744.

95. Takagi, M., S. Abe, S. Suzuki, G.H. Emert, and N. Yata (1978)
Method for production of alcohol directly from cellulose using
cellulase and yeast. In Bioconversion of cellulosic
substances into energy, chemicals and microbial protein, T.K.
Ghose, ed. Symposium Proceedings, Indian Institute of Technology, New Delhi, India, pp. 551-571.

96. Saddler, J.N., C. Hogan, M.K.H. Chan, and G. Louis Seize (1982)
Ethanol fermentation of enzymatically hydrolyzed pretreated
wood fractions using Trichoderma cellulases, Zymomonas mobilis
and Saccharomyces cerevisiae. Can. J. Microbiol. 28:1311-1319.

97. Freer, S.N., and R.W. Detroy (1982) Direct fermentation of
cellodextrins to ethanol by Candida wickerhamii and C. lusi-
taniae. Biotechnol. Lett. 4:453-458.

98. Freer, S.N., and R.W. Detroy (1983) Characterization of cellobiose fermentations to ethanol by yeasts. Biotechnol. Bioeng.
25:541-557.

99. Khan, A.W. (1980) Degradation of cellulose to methane by a
coculture of Acetivibrio cellulolyticus and Methanosarcina
Barkeri. FEMS Microbiol. Lett. 9:233-235.

100. Wolin, M.J., and T.L. Miller (1983) Interactions of microbial
populations in cellulose fermentation. Fed. Proc. 42:109-113.

101. Odom, J.M., and J.D. Wall (1983) Photoproduction of H_2 from cellulose by an anaerobic bacterial coculture. Appl. Environ. Microbiol. 45:1300–1305.
102. Wood, W.A. (1981) Basic biology of microbial fermentation. In Trends in the Biology of Fermentations for Fuels and Chemicals. Basic Life Sciences, A. Hollaender, ed., Plenum Press, New York. Vol. 18, pp. 3–17.
103. Armentrout, R.W., and R.D. Brown, (1981) Molecular cloning of genes for cellobiose utilization and their expression in Escherichia coli. Appl. Environ. Microbiol. 41:1355–1362.
104. Whittle, D.J., D.G. Kolburn, R.A.J. Warren, and R.C. Miller, Jr. (1982) Molecular cloning of a Cellulomonas fimi cellulase gene in Escherichia coli. Gene 17:139–145.
105. Cornet, P., D. Tronik, J. Millet, and J.P. Aubert (1983) Cloning and expression in Escherichia coli of Clostridium thermocellum genes coding for amino acid synthesis and cellulose hydrolysis. FEMS Microbiol. Lett. 16:137–141.
106. Faber, M. (1983) Cornell scientists clone, express cellulase genes in E. coli (meeting report). Biotechnology 1:139.
107. Montenecourt, B.S. (1983) Application of recombinant DNA technology to cellulose hydrolysis (ASM Technology Report). Biotechnology 1:166–167.
108. Gritzali, M. (1980) Biosynthesis of the enzymes of the cellulase system by T. reesei QM9414 in the presence of sophorose. In Biotechnology for the Production of Chemicals and Fuels from Biomass. SERI Workshop Proceedings, Vail, Colorado, pp. 83–90.
109. Mitchell, R.W., B. Hahn-Hägerdal, J.D. Ferchak, and E.K. Pye (1982) Characterization of β-1,4-glucosidase activity in Thermoanaerobacter ethanolicus. Biotechnol. Bioeng. Symp. No. 12, pp. 461–467.
110. Khan, A.W., and W.D. Murray (1982) Single step conversion of cellulose to ethanol by a mesophilic coculture. Biotechnol. Lett. 4:177–180.
111. Mandels, M. (1975) Microbial sources of cellulase. Biotechnol. Bioeng. Symp. No. 5, pp. 81–105.
112. Gallo, B.J., R. Andreotti, C. Roche, D. Ryu, and M. Mandels (1978) Cellulase production by a new mutant strain of Trichoderma reesei MCG 77. Biotechnol. Bioeng. Symp. No. 8, pp. 89–101.
113. Tien, M., and T.K. Kirk (1983) Lignin-degrading enzyme from the hymenomycete Phanerochaete chrysosporium Burds. Science 221:661–663.

PANEL DISCUSSION: COMPARISON OF TRADITIONAL AND GENETIC STRATEGIES

Ross D. Brown, Jr., University of Florida
Joel S. Hirschhorn, Congressional Office of Technology
   Assessment
Hester A. Kobayashi, Standard Oil Company (SOHIO)
Joseph L. McCarthy (Moderator), University of Washington
James W. Patterson, Illinois Institute of Technology
Bruce E. Rittmann, University of Illinois, Champaign
James A. Shapiro, University of Chicago
Oskar Zaborsky, National Science Foundation

J. McCARTHY: I have heard with enormous interest the earlier presentations of this symposium. I think it is important that we consider the following questions: (1) What is the state of the art? (2) What are the needs with respect to pollution? (3) What are the possibilities of using recombinant DNA procedures or other manipulation of genes to improve our capabilities of coping with pollution problems? (4) What are the prospects for research?

J.S. HIRSCHHORN: The Congressional Office of Technology Assessment (OTA) has been working on hazardous waste problems for over three years, and our work is continuing. Our report, "Technologies and Management Strategies for Hazardous Waste Control" (March, 1983; GPO no. 052-003-00901-3), deals with the scientific, technological, and policy aspects of hazardous waste management.

While there are some applications of traditional biological techniques for dilute aqueous waste streams, land treatment of wastes, and cleanup of spills and uncontrolled waste sites, the primary current management option for hazardous wastes (probably at least 80%) is land disposal. Injection wells, various forms of surface impoundments, and landfills are the prevalent methods, in order of use.

Three primary trends will shape the market opportunities for future biological applications:

1) <u>Public Policy</u>. Under both the federal and state programs
for controlling currently generated hazardous wastes (under the pro-
visions of the Federal Resource Conservation and Recovery Act),
there is a clear trend to limit the use of land disposal options by
prohibitions and by more stringent regulations. This is occurring
because of widespread recognition of the very limited ability of
these options to effectively contain wastes and prevent migration of
hazardous substances into the environment. Nevertheless, under the
Superfund program and in private actions for uncontrolled waste
sites, the dominant management options continue to be containment
and land disposal. More permanent solutions involving waste treatment, detoxification, and destruction are likely to become necessary.

Congress is currently considering reauthorization of the Resource Conservation and Recovery Act and in 1984 Congress will re-
consider the Superfund program. The Environmental Protection Agency
(EPA) has not done much to force the use of alternative treatment
technologies and/or to produce less hazardous waste at the source.
Superfund financing now is accomplished through a tax on chemical
petroleum feedstocks. It is possible that Congress will change that
mechanism for financing to a waste end tax, so that every generator
of hazardous waste in the country would be taxed per ton of waste
produced, depending on what the waste is and how it is being managed. Three such bills in Congress could create an economic incentive for waste reduction. Several states have enacted such taxes.

2) <u>Technology</u>. Because of the rapidly growing hazardous waste
management market, there has been extensive development of waste
treatment technologies. About $5 billion is being spent annually to
deal with hazardous waste in the U.S.; that figure will probably
double, perhaps triple, in the next decade in terms of real dollars.
Only a small fraction is now based on biological treatment process.

The OTA report and the report on "Management of Hazardous Industrial Wastes: Research and Development Needs" (March, 1983, National Materials Advisory Board, National Academy of Sciences, Washington, D.C.) both conclude that for every type of hazardous waste
there currently exist alternatives to land disposal, and new and improved options will undoubtedly be developed. Also, new chemical
and thermal on-site treatment approaches are being developed for
dealing with uncontrolled waste sites. Thus, there is and will remain intense competition which biological waste treatment approaches
must meet.

3) <u>Genetic Engineering</u>. The current stage of development of
genetically engineered organisms does not appear to be moving swift-
ly enough, nor does the field appear to be sufficiently closely
linked to process engineering interests in order to capitalize on
the growing market opportunities or to meet the competition. For

example, much of the current work seems to be based on the premise that, for some applications, genetically engineered organisms would be placed directly into the environment to treat and degrade hazardous wastes. Because of public concerns about genetically engineered materials, the fact that no established record of effectiveness and safety exists for them under industrial or field conditions, and the possibilities of unknown and perhaps adverse synergistic effects between such materials and toxic wastes, it would be more prudent to conceive of using closed systems based on traditional unit-processing approaches developed by chemical engineers.

Another problem is that many waste applications require treatment of numerous different toxic chemicals, whereas current biological research and development focuses on treating one chemical with a particular organism. Most thermal and chemical waste treatment approaches have the advantage of acting on virtually all toxic chemicals present in a waste stream or at a site. There are also signs that biological approaches may be unable to reduce concentrations of toxic chemicals to low enough levels; using a final chemical or thermal treatment step might remove any economic advantage for the biological treatment. Broadly speaking, to achieve commercial success there would have to be a very substantial increase in the applied engineering activities associated with development of biological approaches; at the present time these appear to represent a very small part of the effort. Moreover, in examining the entire spectrum of potential applications for genetically engineered materials, it is difficult to see how hazardous waste applications would attract the necessary attention and funding in the rapidly emerging biotechnology industry. If I had to rank the potential applications in terms of attractiveness and likelihood, I would say: 1) source reduction; 2) clean-up of abandoned sites; and 3) end-of-the-pipe treatments.

G.S. OMENN: What sort of responses has OTA received to the hazardous waste report?

J.S. HIRSCHHORN: I think we have had an extremely good reaction. Our job is to present information, analyses, and options for Congress. We hope that the new Resource Conservation and Recovery Act bill will help to strengthen the program administered by EPA.

A major policy option we proposed is the waste end tax. Most decisions in this country are economic decisions. People will "do the right thing" in terms of hazardous waste management if it is determined by the economics. The big problem is preventing the creation of new Superfund sites. There are 16,000 abandoned toxic waste sites known to EPA right now and more are being discovered all the time. Many solid waste sites and municipal landfills now legally receive toxic waste due to various loopholes and exemptions, so the whole hazardous waste problem will probably expand considerably during the next 10 to 20 years.

J.L. MCCARTHY: Do you have any information about the effluent tax system in France under the Agency for the Basin in the Seine and the Rhône?

J.S. HIRSCHHORN: There are some tax approaches in France, Germany, and Japan. Their political and social structures are remarkably different, but all have a lot more direct government activity in waste management than in this country. At the state level, from California, which has the highest waste end tax, there are reports a of one-third reduction in wastes generated after one year of operation of the tax.

R.O. MENDELSOHN: In France there is a set of agencies, called Agencie de Basin, one for each river basin--for example, the Seine. There is a tax based on the levels of several major effluents. The producers pay the tax directly to the Agencie. The Agencie is run by a board which has on it representatives of each industry, the central government of France, the province, and perhaps the cities. These people have the power to disburse the money, to support analytical monitoring, to build pilot plants and treatment plants, and to fund research. It strikes me as being a pretty good device.

A.M. CHAKRABARTY: I completely agree that we need more emphasis on engineering. But the kind of engineering will depend upon the kinds of microorganisms. For example, it would be useful to introduce microorganisms underground for buried wastes in metal drums which are escaping and polluting, and for recovery of oil and minerals. What kinds of microorganisms would be involved, and which technologies? I also agree that, if the laws become more stringent, the chemical engineers would be forced to reduce the amount of toxic wastes that are generated. But it is easier said than done.

J.W. PATTERSON: Right now we have technologies to handle every pollutant. Do not think that we are lacking the technology. What you are proposing to do is to introduce biologically based technology in head-to-head competition with incineration, chemical destruction, physical stabilization, and so forth. You are not proposing to provide a capability that does not now exist. You are proposing to displace an existing technology, and, I will tell you again, economics "rules the roost." Also, the technology must be highly efficient--99.9% or so, to meet the environmental limitations that are imposed on current contaminated environmental sites or a continually generated process stream.

H.A. KOBAYASHI: I don't think that there needs to be a complete displacement of current techniques by biological methods. There is a tremendous economic incentive right now for us to look more at resource recovery and recycling of materials. Many things that we dispose of now might be recovered and used directly, or they might be converted to useful products. We are seeking to combine many techniques--existing techniques, new techniques, physical and chemical techniques, and biological techniques.

B.E. RITTMANN: There is a possible conflict between those who consider themselves to be process engineers and those who consider themselves to be genetic engineers. We need to have cooperation between the two. The process engineer cannot say to the genetic engineer: I have this process and I want an organism exactly like this. A genetic engineer cannot say: I have developed this organism; make a process to fit it. Neither approach will work. You have to have both kinds of people working together, interactively making mistakes (this will be trial and error), and iterating until solutions are devised which are both process feasible and genetically feasible.

J.A. SHAPIRO: If, in 1972, anyone had said that by 1983 we could do what we can do now, people would have thought he was out of his mind. I was one of those people who said it would be 10 to 20 years before any commercial impact of genetic engineering would be felt, but all of a sudden things moved with a speed that no one had anticipated. Somebody studying one of these processes might discover something about these organisms that could make the technology really feasible, in a way current economic and engineering considerations cannot. Perhaps the biotechnology companies are the places where the process-oriented people, the genetic engineers, and the scientists can come together.

R.D. BROWN: I disagree. People who want solutions to problems want solutions to the problems as they see them, when they see them, and on the terms that they see them. If industrial decision makers conclude that something can't be done, very little effort will be put into trying to do it. I think it is best that the question remains open and that no one type of institution is entrusted with the problem. Most of these processes are very complex, and they require multiple enzymes from multiple organisms. I agree with the idea of the cooperative enterprise. The rate-limiting step is going to be communication and cooperation. The rate-limiting element is going to change and the solutions are going to change; no one will simply have the organism for the job or the job for the organism.

H.A. KOBAYASHI: We find working with biotechnology companies very useful in certain cases. However, you must realize that many of the things we do are proprietary. We do not want to expose many of our chemical processes. Even information about the wastes can very easily expose the entire formulation or the technique. Therefore, we, at least in many cases, prefer to work directly with academia either on a somewhat proprietary basis or for basic research.

J. TROVAINE: It was said that we already have existing technologies to deal with any pollutant, and that in order for a biotechnology to be competitive it is going to have to displace existing technology, not provide a brand new solution to problems that do
not already have solutions. That implies a competition that I do
not really think is valid. Let us say that I come up with a bacterium that can degrade a given toxic molecule by 99%, not 99.9999%.
My question, then, is: what about having a combination system where
you first treat biologically and then use an existing incineration
technology or whatever other way you could deal with the given problem? Is that economically feasible?

J.S. HIRSCHHORN: It depends on the situation. Take, for example, the problem of contaminated soil. Right now, the containment
approach is used: put a clay cap on it; build a wall around the
area. If a biological treatment leaves an unacceptably high residual amount, you might still pay the same amount of money for a containment system or for incineration. In the case of processing currently generated waste, you could use incineration and in one shot
get rid of it all. Situations where you could use a series of steps
may be very limited.

J.W. PATTERSON: I do not want to leave the impression that we
are in any way prejudiced against biological systems. Environmental
engineers are the world's greatest users of biological systems. In
total, we have a lot more organisms working for us than all the
graduate and undergraduate microbiology labs in the country; they
work for us every day and we are comfortable with them. Anything
that can be done to improve them is great, perhaps along the lines
mentioned by Dr. Rittmann and Dr. Kobayashi. Organisms have some
great advantages, and they are well established. But whatever you
propose to do to improve them has to work within the existing legal
and financial requirements of pollution control.

J.C. LOPER: Dr. Hirschhorn, perhaps you left too negative an
impression about public acceptance of such microorganisms. I think
that there is going to be so much progress in human-related biotechnology products that there will be quite an awareness of the benefits that this type of technology can bring to human existence. I
think the feeling for biodegradability, since biodegradable detergents were introduced, is very positive. So I think it is not going
to be as difficult as you expressed to get public acceptance for engineered organisms.

J.S. HIRSCHHORN: If I were in the biotechnology business, I
would still go after a closed system, unit operation approach, if I
had the choice early in the game.

A.L. DEMAIN: I see here, as in a number of conferences, a con-
frontation between biologists and engineers. The biologists do not

understand what the engineers do, and the engineers have a hard time understanding what the biologists do. I think the trouble lies in our collective failure to educate bright students in both biology and engineering. I suggest to academicians both in science and in engineering that we should undertake large scale training of bio-chemical engineers; otherwise, these prejudices follow people into industry and into academic life. It is very difficult to get the two groups together, even though there is synergism when they work together.

J.L. MCCARTHY: I certainly agree.

DIVERSE CAPABILITIES OF MICROORGANISMS

INTRODUCTION

Eugene Nester

Department of Microbiology, SC-42
University of Washington
Seattle, Washington 98195

This session, entitled "Diverse Capabilities of Microorganisms," could serve equally well as the opening session or the closing session to the symposium.

The first speaker, Dr. Arnold Demain of the Massachusetts Institute of Technology, will remind you that microorganisms contribute in many significant ways to our quality of life. Arnie will discuss the role that microorganisms play in the making of foods, pharmaceuticals, and in the production of industrial chemicals. The antibiotic era featured an explosion in the number of microbiological products which became available. Very recent advances in molecular genetics are propelling the field into a new growth phase. Dr. Demain brings to this talk a wealth of experience from his industrial work at Merck, Sharp and Dohme, where he was head of the Fermentation Research Group. He is equally knowledgeable in the fields of molecular genetics, biochemistry, and microbiology. He is at home discussing EcoRI, exons and introns, as well as BOD and SCP. I think you will agree, after hearing his talk, that he has the capacity to digest a prodigious amount of basic research material and relate it to its effect on industrial processes.

The second speaker, Dr. Leroy Hood of Cal Tech, will review some of the ingenious and sophisticated techniques of biotechnology that have made the topic of this symposium possible. With the combination of biochemical, genetic, and immunologic techniques that are becoming routine as a result of the efforts of such broadly based scientists as Dr. Hood, we can hope to answer questions that could not even be asked a few short years ago. I believe that his talk will astound you by revealing the ingenuity and power of some techniques that he and his colleagues have pioneered in developing.

275

Our third speaker, Dr. Mary Lidstrom of the University of Washington, Seattle, will consider the challenges that are faced by an investigator attempting to carry out fundamental genetic studies on organisms that refuse to "behave" nicely in the laboratory. Her talk will help to clarify why so many people work on E. coli and so few work on methylotrophs! Nevertheless, it is through the study of these complex organisms using the sophisticated molecular-genetic techniques developed in simpler systems that biotechnology will advance.

CAPABILITIES OF MICROORGANISMS (AND MICROBIOLOGISTS)

Arnold L. Demain

Fermentation Microbiology Laboratory
Massachusetts Institute of Technology
Cambridge, Massachusetts 02139

INTRODUCTION

Up to this point in the conference, I have absorbed several
general impressions from the previous speakers. They involve the
difficulties of studying microbial ecology, the importance of microbial survival, and the promise of microbial genetics in solving some
of the problems of environmental pollution. These bring to mind
several quotations, which I feel are relevant to these topics:

"Ecology is physiology under the worst possible conditions."
-- Thomas D. Brock

"We may rest assured that as green plants and animals disappear
one by one from the face of the globe, some of the fungi will always
be present to dispose of the last remains."
-- B.O. Dodge

"...when you have mutants, you are better off than when you don't."
-- Salvador E. Luria

There has been a virtual revolution in the last ten years in
the application of basic genetics to the solution of practical problems, mainly in medicine. It is generally agreed that we are now in
the "genetic engineering era," propelled by knowledge on the diversity of enzymatic activities, the desirable properties of enzymes as
catalysts, the knowledge of plasmids, phage and transposons, and
their transfer and amplification to yield high degrees of gene dosage. This exciting knowledge has been combined with the long

277

experience of industrial microbiologists in successfully putting
microorganisms and their enzymes to practical use.

   The aim of the present contribution is to describe the broad
array of microbial reactions and the manipulations, both environmental and genetic, that microbiologists have employed to further exploit the activities of microorganisms. The treatment is general,
and not particularly slanted toward environmental pollution, since
other contributors to this volume have much more experience in this
specific area than I. However, I hope it will stimulate thinking on
new approaches toward the utilization of living systems for solutions to environmental problems.

WHY INDUSTRIAL MICROBIOLOGY HAS BEEN SO SUCCESSFUL

   The success of the fermentation industry results from several
important characteristics of microorganisms: (i) a high ratio of
surface area to volume, which facilitates the rapid uptake of nutrients required to support high rates of metabolism and biosynthesis;
(ii) a tremendous variety of reactions which microorganisms are capable of carrying out (this especially applies to secondary metabolism, resulting in a seemingly inexhaustible supply of secondary
metabolites available for commercial exploitation); (iii) a facility
to adapt to a large array of different environments, allowing a culture to be transplanted from nature to the laboratory flask, where
it is capable of growing on inexpensive carbon and nitrogen sources
and producing valuable compounds; (iv) the ease of genetic manipulation, both in vivo and in vitro, to increase production of the products, to modify their structures and activities, and to force them
to make entirely new products; and (v) the ability of microorganisms
to make specific enantiomers, usually the active ones, in cases
where normal chemical synthesis yields a mixture of active and inactive enantiomers.

   This power of the microbial culture in the competitive world of
synthesis can be appreciated by the fact that even simple molecules
of commercial importance, e.g., L-glutamic acid and L-lysine, are
still made by fermentation rather than by chemical synthesis. Although a few products have been temporarily lost to chemical synthesis (e.g., acetone and butanol), it is obvious that most natural
products are still made by fermentation. Despite the efficiency of
the chemical route to riboflavin, production of this compound is
still carried out by fermentation as well as by synthesis; almost-
complete chemical processes to vitamin C and steroids still use microbial bioconversion steps. Most natural products are so complex
and contain so many centers of asymmetry that they probably will
never be made commercially by chemical synthesis.

   Another application of microbial activity is the detoxification
and degradation of sewage and industrial waste. The usefulness of

microorganisms in waste treatment has been recognized since 1914, when the activated-sludge process was first developed. The sludge process depends on a complex population of microorganisms that forms naturally because of each organism's ability to degrade a constituent of the waste material and to coexist with the others in a nutritionally complementary system. The next advance was to enrich the sludge by inoculating it with a desired mixture of microorganisms. Now pure cultures of microorganisms are being made available to degrade specific compounds in industrial waste.

The presence of toxic compounds in the environment is of great concern to all of us. Microorganisms, fortunately, have great abilities to grow on and to degrade synthetic organic chemicals completely to inorganic materials. Pseudomonads are especially active in the degradation of organic compounds. Some species of Pseudomonas are known to utilize over 100 compounds, many of which are quite unusual in structure. Pure cultures of a Pseudomonas sp. can degrade the herbicide 2,4-dichlorophenoxyacetic acid and the chemical intermediate 2,4-dichlorophenol at one-third the rate of glucose catabolism (1). The genetics (2) and biochemistry (3) of many of the dissimilatory pathways are well-known.

Some synthetic compounds in the environment are not completely degraded as sources of carbon for growth but are only bioconverted to other organic compounds; such processes are known as co-metabolism. Even more of a problem are those compounds which are resistant to microbial attack, i.e., recalcitrant molecules (4,5). These include refractory pesticides (e.g., chlorinated hydrocarbon insecticides), polychlorinated biphenyls (PCBs are used for many industrial purposes), synthetic polymers, surfactants (especially alkylbenzene sulfonates with highly branched alkyl moieties), and slow-release nitrogen fertilizers (6).

The combustion of fuels causes serious environmental problems due to sulfur dioxide production from sulfur compounds contained therein. The most noxious of these are the condensed thiaphene type. Recent work has indicated that certain bacteria can remove thiaphenes from crude or heavy oil, partly by assimilation during growth and partly by conversion to water-soluble sulfur compounds (7).

Oil spills (8) and the release of ballast and wash waters from oil tankers (9) are other waste problems that microbiologists are attempting to solve. Microbes are the main degraders of petroleum hydrocarbons in contaminated ecosystems, hydrocarbons being excellent growth substrates for many bacteria and fungi. However, hundreds of different hydrocarbons exist in crude oils and there is no single organism that can degrade all such compounds. Instead, individual microorganisms that consume only individual groups of components of petroleum are usually isolated. Strains of one such species, Pseudomonas putida, carry plasmid genes coding for enzymes that can degrade different components of oil. By plasmid transfer, the capacity to degrade the various components has been combined into one strain. Such a multi-plasmid strain degrades petroleum hydrocarbons faster than any of the original strains (10).

Certain microorganisms are the basis of a metallurgical process that is thought to go back to the Romans: the bacterial leaching of low-grade ores to extract metals from them. Today, copper and uranium are commercially leached by bacteria, mainly members of the genus Thiobacillus. New approaches to such bacterial leaching are also being made. They include the examination of acid- and heat-resistant microorganisms (including fungi) for their extraction abilities, the investigation of the mechanisms underlying the affinity of bacteria for metals, and the genetic manipulation of bacteria to increase their resistance to the toxicity of the metals.

MICROBIAL BIOSYNTHESIS

Microorganisms are important to us for many reasons, but the main one is that they produce things of value to us. These may be very large materials such as proteins, nucleic acids, carbohydrate polymers, or even cells, or they can be smaller molecules which we usually differentiate into metabolites essential for vegetative growth and those inessential, i.e., primary and secondary metabolites, respectively (or as suggested by Martín, general and special metabolites) (J.F. Martín, personal communication).

The most useful proteins are those with enzymatic activity, and many of these are becoming more and more attractive in manufacturing, analytical chemistry, and medicine (Tab. 1). The properties of these proteins that lend themselves to extensive use include their rapidity and efficiency of action at low concentrations and under mild conditions of pH and temperature, their high degree of substrate specificity which decreases production of side-products, their lack of toxicity, and the easy termination of their action by mild treatments. About 200 enzymes are available, but this number only scratches the surface, since about 2,000 enzymes have already been described. Clearly microorganisms are the best source of industrial enzymes, and special strains are used to make each particular enzyme. Reasons for choosing microorganisms over higher plants and animals include the following:

a. Enzyme fermentations are economical on a large scale because of short fermentation cycles and inexpensive media.

b. Screening procedures are simple, and thousands of cultures can be examined in a reasonably short time.

c. Production levels can be increased by thousands-fold via environmental and genetic manipulation.

Table 1.   Some enzymes of present or potential importance.

Aminoacylase	Invertase
Amylase	Lignase
Amyloglucosidase	Lipase
Anticyanase	Lytic enzymes
L-Asparaginase	Microbial rennet
Catalase	Naringinase
Cellulase	Pectinase
Dextranase	Penicillin acylase
"Diagnostic enzymes"	Penicillinase
Esterase-Lipase	Polynucleotide phosphorylase
β-Galactosidase	Protease
Glucanase	Restriction enconuclease
Glucose dehydrogenase	Ribonuclease
Glucose isomerase	Streptokinase-streptodornase
Glucose oxidase	Superoxide dismutase
Glutamic decarboxylase	Uricase
Hemicellulase	Xylanase

d.   Different species produce somewhat different enzymes catalyzing the same reaction, allowing flexibility with respect to desired operating conditions in the reactor. For example, Bacillus
amyloliquefaciens alpha-amylase was used for many years for starch
hydrolysis at temperatures as high as 90°C because of its heat stability. However there was a need for an even more stable enzyme.
In 1972, α-amylase from Bacillus licheniformis was introduced into
commerce - it works at 110°C (11).

In addition to enzymes, bulk cell protein (or even whole cells)
which constitutes what is generally known as single-cell protein or
SCP, is used as a protein source for animals and humans in various
parts of the world. The reason for SCP is clear: in 24 hours a
1,000-pound steer on pasture synthesizes from grass one pound of
protein; 1,000 pounds of soybeans will produce 82 pounds of protein;
in the same period, 1,000 pounds of yeast cells in a fermenter will
synthesize 2,500 pounds of protein, and potentially much more (12).
It has been reported that in 1979, the USSR alone had over 80 factories producing over 1 million tons per year of SCP from agricultural and forest wastes and peat, as animal feed. In England, one
can find food on supermarket shelves containing protein from the
mold Fusarium.

A very useful protein is the delta-endotoxin of Bacillus thur-
ingiensis, used as an insecticide. Amazingly, the protein is produced at such a high level (20-30% of the cell dry weight) that it
crystallizes within the cells (13). Unique microbial proteins still
awaiting application are poly-D-glutamate and poly-L-lysine.

It is quite remarkable that from the same 20 or so amino acids, microorganisms can make beneficial products such as SCP or deadly proteins such as botulinum toxin - a rather convincing demonstration of the importance of amino acid sequence!

At present, nucleic acids are used mainly for research, with the exception of yeast RNA which is hydrolyzed to 5'-mononucleotides used for flavor enhancement.

Microbial polymers such as the polysaccharide xanthan are used for diverse applications, from food thickening to drilling muds in oil fields. The greatest promise for xanthan, however, lies in tertiary recovery of oil, which will become more and more important as the easily recovered oil is depleted. Another polysaccharide, emulsan, is being developed for cleaning out huge oil tankers during their return trip to the oil fields (14). Recently, polyhydroxybutyrate, produced by Alcaligenes eutrophus, has been commercialized as a biodegradable plastic.

Primary metabolites are the small molecules of all living cells that are intermediates or end-products of the pathways of intermediary metabolism, or are used as building blocks for essential macromolecules, or are converted into coenzymes. The most industrially important are the amino acids, nucleotides, vitamins, solvents, and organic acids. They vary in size from hydrogen gas (2 daltons) and methane (16 daltons) to vitamin B_{12} (1355 daltons). It is not unexpected that the amino acids and vitamins are used in nutrition, that ethanol, acetone, and butanol are used as fuel and/or solvents, and that citric and acetic acids are used as acidulants. However, many of these general metabolites are used in novel ways: the sodium salts of glutamic, 5'-inosinic (IMP) and 5'-guanylic acids as flavor enhancers, sodium gluconate as a sequestering agent to prevent the deposition of soap scums on cleaned surfaces, and fumarate in the manufacture of polyester resins.

Microbially produced secondary metabolites are extremely important to our health and nutrition. As a group that includes antibiotics, toxins, alkaloids, and plant growth factors, these special metabolites have tremendous economic importance.

The best known of the secondary metabolites are the antibiotics. About 6,000 antibiotics have been described, two-thirds from actinomycetes alone, and they still are being discovered at a rate of about 300 per year. Some species are remarkable in their ability to produce antibiotics. For example, Streptomyces griseus strains produce over 40 different antibiotics and Bacillus subtilis strains, over 60. One Micromonospora strain can produce 48 aminocyclitol antibiotics. The antibiotics vary in size from small molecules like cycloserine (102 daltons) and bacilysin (270 daltons) to polypeptides such as nisin which contains 34 amino acid residues. They attack virtually every type of microbial activity such as DNA, RNA,

and protein synthesis, membrane function, electron transport, sporulation, germination, and many others.

In nature, secondary metabolites are important for the organisms that produce them, functioning as sex hormones, ionophores,
competitive weapons against other bacteria, fungi, amoebae, insects
and plants, agents of symbiosis, and effectors of differentiation.
Humans have learned to exploit these potent molecules and, today,
secondary metabolites are in commercial or near-commercial use as
pesticides (e.g., kasugamycin, polyoxins), insecticides (<u>Bacillus
thuringiensis</u> crystal), coccidiostats (monensin), ruminant growth
promoters (monensin), anti-helmintic agents (avermectin), plant
growth regulators (gibberellin), immunodepressants for organ trans-
plants (cyclosporin A), anabolic agents in farm animals (zearelanone), glycosidase inhibitors (acarbose), uterocontractants (ergot
alkaloids), and anti-tumor agents (adriamycin). The most remarkable
aspect of this exploitation is that many of the above compounds were
first isolated as toxic antibiotics (e.g, monensin) or mycotoxins
(ergot alkaloids, gibberellin, zearelanone) before they were put to
work for our benefit. Following in their footsteps are a large number of potent secondary metabolites with potent activities which are
under investigation right now. These include herbicides (herbimy-
cins), anti-inflammatory agents (amicomacin A), hypochlesteremic
agents (mevinolin), hyperlipidemic agents (ascofuranone), hypoten-
sive agents (dopastin), vasodilators (WS-1228A and B), complement
inhibitors (K-76 monocarboxylic acid), dextran-sucrase inhibitors
(ribocitrin), immunostimulants (bestatin), carcinogenesis inhibitors
(antipain), elastase inhibitors (elasnin), acid protease inhibitors
(pepstatin) and inhibitors of the angiotensin-converting enzyme
(L-681,176). Indeed, we now appreciate that antibiotic activity is
merely the tip of the iceberg, a mere scratching at the surface of
the potential of microbial activity.

In addition to the multi-reaction sequences of fermentations,
microorganisms are extremely useful in carrying out processes in
which a compound is converted into a structurally related product by
the use of one or a small number of enzymes contained in cells.
Such bioconversions may be carried out with growing cells, resting
cells, spores, or dried cells. One of the earliest bioconversions
was the quantitative conversion of ethanol to vinegar by the acetic
acid bacteria. This group of bacteria is especially useful in carrying out incomplete oxidations of organic compounds and is used
commercially in the oxidation of sorbitol to sorbose, the single
biological step in the otherwise chemical production of vitamin C
(ascorbic acid).

Bioconverting organisms are known for practically all types of
chemical reactions. The conversions are reaction-specific, regio-
specific, and stereospecific, the ultimate in specificity being exemplified by the steroid bioconversions. It is quite remarkable

that before the discovery of the 11 α-hydroxylation of progesterone
by Rhizopus, cortisone was made in 0.16% yield from deoxycholic acid
in a 37 step process, resulting in a cost of $200 per gram. The
bioconversion process reduced the process to 11 steps, made it much
more efficient, and reduced the price almost immediately to $6 per
gram. The last time I checked, cortisone was selling for 68 cents
per gram. This specificity is also exploited in the resolution of
racemic mixtures of enantiomers, especially those of amino acids.
The bioconversion reaction is preferred over a chemical step when a
specific isomer rather than a racemic mixture is desired. Bioconversions are characterized by extremely high yields, i.e., from 90
to 100%. Other attributes include mild reaction conditions and the
coupling of reactions using a microorganism containing several enzymes working in series.

INCREASING THE LEVEL OF BIOSYNTHESIS

     Although microbes are extremely good in presenting us with an
amazing array of products, they are usually "intelligent" enough to
produce them in amounts that they need for their own benefit; thus
they tend not to overproduce their metabolites. The microbiologist,
on the other hand, is not content with such a situation and forces
these organisms into excreting tremendous amounts of these valuable
products. Indeed, the main reason for the use of microorganisms to
produce compounds that can otherwise be isolated from plants and animals or synthesized by chemists is the ease of increasing production by environmental and genetic manipulation. Thousand-fold increases have been recorded for enzymes and small metabolites. Of
course the higher the specific level of production, the simpler is
the job of isolation. Consider the case of Ashbya gossypii which
has been forced into making over 20,000 times more riboflavin than
it needs, or Pseudomonas denitrificans which produces a 100,000-fold
excess of vitamin B_{12}. The original Oxford strain of Penicillium
produced 5 mg of penicillin per liter; today's strains make 30,000
mg/liter, a figure almost as high as the dry weight of the cells in
the fermentor!

     Environmental manipulations have proven to be quite useful for
bringing on enzyme or metabolite overproduction. For example, the
level of leucine biosynthetic enzymes in a single strain of Escherichia coli can be varied over a 3,000-fold range by changing growth
conditions (15). Optimization of fermentation parameters such as
temperature, pH, oxygen transfer, and nutrients is of course extremely important. Enzyme production is often increased by the addition of nonionic surfactants.

     If a process is inducible, inducers can be added. In enzyme
fermentations, these can be substrates, substrate analogues, or
products. Substrate analogues which are not acted upon by the

enzyme ("gratuitous inducers") have been known to increase enzyme production by over 1,000-fold. Usually when an enzyme substrate is also a building block for macromolecule synthesis (e.g., an amino acid) and the product is metabolically dispensible, the product (rather than the substrate) is the inducer. When the substrate is a large molecule, which would not be expected to get into the cell, the inducer is usually a degradative intermediate or product. For example, a potent inducer of cellulase such as sophorose can be made via cellulose degradation by <u>Trichoderma</u> <u>reesei</u>. Cellulases are of potential importance in conversion of wastes (from forest products and other industries, agriculture, and urban areas) to useful products such as fuel ethanol. Also, amylases are often induced by maltose, and lipases by fatty acids. Inducers are known for commercial processes yielding primary or secondary metabolites. They include betaine for vitamin B_{12}, methionine for cephalosporin, and tryptophan for ergot alkaloid production.

Virtually all fermentation processes operate, after the initial growth stage, under conditions of unbalanced growth, and right from the start of any development program, the microbiologist must find the key. The key is often a specific nutrient limitation that restricts growth and brings on product accumulation. Some of these crucial limitations are listed in Tab. 2. In some cases the mechanisms are known. For example, limitation of biotin, glycerol, or oleate in the glutamate fermentation produces a phospholipid-deficient cell membrane allowing the glutamate to exit from the cell,

Table 2. Key nutrient limitations for various fermentations.

Product	Limitation
Glutamic acid	Biotin, glycerol or oleate
Lysine	Threonine
5'-Inosinic Acid (IMP)	Adenine and guanine
Riboflavin	Iron
Citric acid	Iron and manganese
Xanthan	Ammonium
Penicillin	Glucose
Cephalosporin	Glucose
Tetracycline	Phosphate
β-Galactosidase	Glucose
Invertase	Glucose
Protease	Ammonium
Thienamycin	Phosphate
Candicidin	Phosphate
Streptomycin	Phosphate
Tylosin	Glucose and phosphate

thus relieving feedback repression and inhibition. Relief of feedback inhibition and repression is also the mechanism in the lysine
and IMP fermentation. Iron limitation in the citric acid process is
necessary to block the action of aconitase on citrate, iron being
a co-factor for aconitase. The various required limitations of
glucose, ammonium, or phosphate shown in Tab. 2 are necessary to
avoid carbon, nitrogen, or phosphorus nutrient ("catabolite") repression. Achievement of these limitations is carried out in various ways. Auxotrophic mutants are used in the glutamate, lysine,
and IMP fermentations; in citric acid fermentations, the metals are
removed by ion-exchange or by complex formation with potassium fer-
ricyanide. Nutrient repression is avoided by the use of slowly
utilized carbon, nitrogen, or phosphorus sources or by slow-feeding
of the repressive nutrients.

In cases of feedback repression of biosynthetic enzymes by the
product itself, various environmental methods are used including the
addition of a pathway inhibitor, limitation of the growth factor
supply to an auxotrophic mutant, the use of a slowly utilized derivative of the required growth factor, or via the slow growth of
bradytrophic mutants.

Genetic solutions to the problems of feedback regulation, nutrient repression, and the expense of inducer addition have been
quite successful. Constitutive mutations (allowing high production
of a previously inducible enzyme in the absence of inducer or of a
previously repressible enzyme in the presence of repressive nutrients and end-products) and procedures for obtaining such mutants,
are well-known. Such regulatory mutants are often hyper-producers,
i.e., producing even more than the parental culture under the most
favorable conditions known for the parent. For example, Bacillus
licheniformis mutants produce ten times more α-amylase than their
glucose-sensitive parents even in the absence of glucose (16).
Newell and Brill (17), working with Salmonella typhimurium mutants,
found them to produce up to five times more of the glucose-repress-
ible enzymes proline oxidase and Δ'-pyrroline carboxylic acid dehydrogenase than their parent even when glucose was absent. Betz and
colleagues (18) reported on mutants of Pseudomonas aeruginosa which
are resistant to carbon catabolite repression and produce amidase to
a level of 10% of their cell protein. Recently, Schaeffer and
Cooney (19) selected constitutive maltase producers by growing the
inducible parent, Saccharomyces italicus, on the noninducing sugar,
sucrose. The parent has no invertase and thus can only grow on sucrose by producing high levels of maltase which breaks down sucrose
slowly. Not only were the mutants constitutive but they were 2- to
3-fold hyperproducers of maltase.

Regulatory mutants may be selected using antimetabolites, e.g.,
amino acid analogues, for production of amino acids or biosynthetic
enzymes of amino acid pathways; 2-deoxyglucose or D-glucosamine (20)
for carbon source repression; and methylammonium for nitrogen source

repression.   The deoxyglucose technique has been successful in the cases of α–glucosidase, β–glucosidase, α–amylase, cellulase, invertase, and malate dehydrogenase. Methylammonium–resistant mutants have shown resistance to ammonia repression of enzymes including nitrate reductase, nitrite reductase, xanthine dehydrogenase, and urate oxidase. Mutants of Pseudomonas putida resistant to pentafluoromandelate are hyperproducers of mandelate dehydrogenase, an enzyme catabolizing the conversion of mandelate to benzoate (21).

Even more surprising are regulation–reversal mutations. From a parental Bacillus cereus culture requiring starch for β–amylase induction, a 25–fold superior mutant was obtained in which production was repressed, rather than induced, by starch (22). Mutagenesis of a Cellulomonas strain in which β–glucosidase was repressed by glucose yielded a mutant which was a 9–fold hyperproducer and induced by glucose (23). Some methylammonium–resistant mutants yield enzymes whose production is stimulated by ammonia.

In many case, the mechanism by which the enzyme level is increased by genetic manipulation is unknown. Of course, there are many different stages in the biosynthesis of an enzyme where a mutation might increase production (Tab. 3). As shown in Tab. 4, various types of screening and selection procedures have yielded mutants producing increased levels of enzymes.

The influence of gene dosage on enzyme production was indicated quite early during studies designed to yield constitutive mutants from inducible parents. The Escherichia coli mutants of Horiuchi

Table 3.   Possible mechanisms of mutations yielding increased enzyme levels.

1.   Decrease in repressor synthesis by the regulator gene.

2.   Decrease in affinity between repressor and operator gene.

3.   Increase in binding between repressor and inducer.

4.   Increase in affinity between the CRP-cAMP complex and the promotor.

5.   Increase in adenyl cyclase activity.

6.   Decrease in cAMP phosphodiesterase activity.

7.   Increase in affinity between CRP and cAMP.

8.   Increase in affinity between RNA polymerase and the promotor.

9.   Increase in stability of mRNA.

10.   Increase in rate of translation.

11.   Increase in secretion of enzyme.

Screening/Selection Procedure	Enzyme	Organism	Reference
Use of unnatural isomer to satisfy an auxotrophic requirement	D-amino acid oxidase	Escherichia coli	(45)
Resistance to toxic substrate	Catalase	Rhodopseudo-monas spheroides	(46)
Resistance to toxic substrate analogue	Dihydrofolate reductase	Lactobacillus casei	(47)
Resistance to polyene anti-biotic	Protease, alpha-amylase, RNase (all extracellular)	Fusarium sp.	(48)
Resistance to chloramphenicol	Beta-galactosidase, aspartate trans-carbamylase, ornithine trans-carbamylase	Salmonella typhi-murium, E. coli	(49)
Use of substrate as sole nitrogen source	Nicotinamide deamidase	E. coli	(50)
Dependence on enzyme acting in "wrong" direction	Ornithine trans-carbamylase	E. coli	(51)
Auxotrophy	Ribonuclease	Neurospora crassa	(52)
Suppression of auxotrophy	Protease, O-acetylserine-sulfhydrylase	Aspergillus awamori S. typhimurium	(53) (54)
Suppression of hypoproduction	Protease	Bacillus cereus	(55)
Elimination of sporulation	Protease	Bacillus licheni-formis	(56)
	Beta-amylase Phospholipase C	B. cereus Clostridium perfringens	(57) (58)
Sporulation with excess carbon or nitrogen source or both	Protease	Bacillus subtilis, B. cereus	(59-61)
	Levansucrase	B. subtilis	(61)
Increased clear zone around colony	Cellulase, beta-glucosidase	Trichoderma reesei, Cellu-lomonas sp.	(62)
	Protease	B. subtilis, Aspergillus sojae, Asper-gillus nidulans	(63-65)
	Nitrate reductase, xanthine dehydro-genase	A. nidulans	(65)
	Polygalacturonic acid transeliminase	Aeromonas lique-faciens	(66)
Increased product zone around colony	Invertase	Saccharomyces cerevisiae	(67)
	Alpha-amylase Alkaline phospha-tase	B. licheniformis S. cerevisiae, Pseudomonas aeruginosa	(16) (68-69)
	Phospholipase	P. aeruginosa	(69)

←Table 4. Mutations leading to derepression and/or hyper-production
          of enzymes.

et al. (24), isolated in a lactose-limited chemostat and producing
up to 20% of their cellular protein as β-galactosidase, were not
merely constitutives, i.e., they also contained up to four copies of
the constitutive lac operon. Similarly Klebsiella aerogenes mutants
were selected for growth on xylitol, a carbon source not used by the
parent. Continuous culture on xylitol led to strains making so much
ribitol dehydrogenase that the cells could grow even though xylitol
is a poor substrate of ribitol dehydrogenase. The mutant strains
were found to have amplified their ribitol dehydrogenase gene (25).
Since increasing the number of copies of a gene increases production
of its specific enzyme, the ability to do this intentionally is desirable. In microorganisms, an increase in gene copies by genetic
manipulation has been achieved by transferring plasmids (extrachromosomal DNA segments) or by the use of transducing phage. Production of enzymes has been increased many fold by in vivo transfer of
plasmids containing the respective structural genes into recipient
cultures. In a similar way, large increases in production of enzymes have been achieved by using tranducing phage containing the
structural gene coding for these enzymes. Recently the use of in
vitro recombinant DNA techniques has had a major effect on enzyme
production (Tab. 5).

     In increasing the efficiency of bioconversions, it is important
to examine the regulation of enzyme synthesis during growth since
the "quality" of a bioconverting cell population depends on the concentration of enzyme in those cells. Often inducers are useful and
it is imperative to avoid various types of nutrient repression. Mutation can be used to eliminate further catabolism of the desired
product. This has been of great importance in conversions of ster-
ols to steroids by side-chain cleavage and in the biterminal oxidation of n-alkanes to dicarboxylic acids. Recent work in Shanghai
(26) has shown mutation to increase production of C13 dicarboxylic
acids from 10 to 100 g/L. Mutants blocked in degradation of organic
acids can be selected by incubation with a halogenated analogue of
the substrate (27). Lack of the degradative enzyme in the mutant
prevents lethal synthesis of a toxic halogenated intermediate.

     Permeability is often a problem with respect to contact of the
bioconversion substrate with the enzyme in the cell. In certain
processes, Mn^{++} deficiency or addition of surface active agents has
been used to decrease the effect of the permeability barrier. It is
sometimes desirable to grow cells on one substrate and convert a
different substrate; this is known as "co-metabolism." Problems of
product inhibition of bioconversions can be solved by addition of

ion exchange resins or by dialysis culture. Mixed cultures or sequential addition of cells have been used to carry out bioconversions involving several steps in series catalyzed by different cultures.

A recent mixed microbial process in which glucose is converted
to 2-keto-L-gulonic acid by two bacteria (Erwinia sp. and Corynebac-
terium sp.) with an overall molar yield of 85% (28) could have a major effect on commercial production of vitamin C; 2-ketogluconic
acid can be easily converted in a single chemical step to vitamin C.
The problem of insoluble substrates, especially prevalent in the
steroid field, can be resolved by using finely divided suspensions
of substrates, suspensions in surface-active agents such as Tweens,
or soluble complexes or esters of substrates. A remarkable process uses finely powdered solid cortisol (in concentrations up to
500 g/L) Arthrobacter simplex to convert this substrate to crystalline prednisolone in the broth with over a 93% yield (29). Also remarkable is the finding that some bioconversions can be conducted in
completely organic media or in mixtures of organic solvents and water (30-32).

In recent years, there has developed a tremendous interest in
immobilized cells to carry out bioconversion processes. These are
usually much more stable than either free cells or enzymes and more
economical than immobilized enzymes. Processes have been designed

Table 5. Increased enzyme production by recombinant DNA technology.

Enzyme	Vector type	Fold increase	% of soluble protein	% of total protein	Reference
Alpha-amylase	plasmid	5	–	–	(70)
Aspartic beta-semialdehyde dehydrogenase	plasmid	65	–	18-25	(71)
Benzylpenicillin acylase	plasmid	45	–	–	(72)
Delta[1]-pyrroline-5-carboxylate reductase	phage	190	5	–	(73)
DNA ligase	phage	500	–	5	(74)
DNA polymerase I	phage	100	–	–	(75)
Gamma-glutamyl phosphate reductase	plasmid	17	–	–	(76)
Phosphatidylserine synthase	plasmid	15	–	–	(77)
Thymidine phosphorylase	plasmid	100-200	–	–	(78)
Trp operon enzymes	plasmid	50	–	25	(79)
Tryptophan synthetase	plasmid	16	–	–	(80)

using immobilized dead cells, immobilized resting cells, and immobilized growing cells (33). The fantastic stability of some of these
processes is illustrated by the bioconversion in which E. coli immobilized in κ-carrageenan continuously converts ammonium fumarate to
L-aspartic acid with a half-life of 693 days (34). Although immobilized cells are generally regarded as "new biotechnology," the
Schnetzenbach "quick vinegar" process, using microorganisms immobilized as a thin film on wood shavings to convert ethanol to acetic
acid, was developed over 150 years ago (35).

PRODUCT MODIFICATION

     Often, the microbiologist is not satisfied with the product
provided by nature and wants to change it. Why not? After all, the
chemist has been modifying natural products and improving them for
years; we are especially familiar with the success of semisynthetic
antibiotics in the field of chemotherapy. Well, microbiologists
have found that changes can be effected in product structure by either environmental or genetic modifications. The environmental manipulations include "directed biosynthesis" by addition of novel
precursors or by the addition of inhibitors of biosynthesis. New
penicillins, bleomycins, polyoxins, tetracylcines, lincomycins,
streptomycins, and others have been produced by these techniques.
Another environmental method is that of bioconversion of a known antibiotic; this has yielded new macrolides, aminocyclitols, and lincomycins, among others. Genetic manipulations involve the use of
certain types of mutants with or without special supplements. The
most popular method, "mutational biosynthesis," involves feeding to
an idiotrophic mutant an analogue of the antibiotic moiety which it
cannot make. This method has led to the production of new amino
cyclitols, macrolides, and novobiocins. Another procedure is to add
to the medium of an auxotrophic mutant, an analogue of its requirement. Thus, feeding L-S-carboxymethylcysteine to a lys⁻ Cephalo-
sporium acremonium auxotrophic mutant yielded a new penicillin and
feeding ethionine to a met⁻ Penicillium griseofulvum gave a new
griseofulvin. Auxotrophs have also been obtained which produce
new antibiotics without special supplementation; these antibiotics
include derivatives of tetracycline, penicillin N, and cellestice-
tin.

     Another mutant category is that of strains blocked in produc-
tion of the normal antibiotic, but which do not respond to feeding
of the missing moiety, i.e., they are not idiotrophs. They sometimes produce a new antibiotic, often an antibiotically active intermediate or shunt metabolite. These have included cephalosporins,
macrolides, tetracyclines, and rifamycins.

     Finally, there are unblocked mutants which produce a new anti-
biotic alongside the old one; these include a cephalosporin, an an-
thracylcine, and aminocyclitols, among others. Mixtures of mutants,

or the addition of an antibiotic or a mutant accumulation product to
a producer of a different antibiotic, have yielded new tetracyclines,
anthracyclines, and macrolide antibiotics. Recently, genetic recombination of different strains or species have yielded new antibiotics.

Enzymes have also been modified to improve their activities,
such modifications being chemical (e.g., immobilized enzymes) or
genetic. Mutation has yielded enzymes desensitized to feedback inhibition (higher Ki) and with altered pH optima, substrate specificity, V_{max} or K_m values (36,37). Sometimes the new enzyme is actually activated by the effector which was previously an inhibitor.
For example, a phenylalanine-inhibited prephenate dehydratase was
changed into a phenylalanine-activated enzyme (38). Modification of
allosteric inhibition is often selected by resistance to end-product
antimetabolites, or by a double mutation technique, the first to
auxotrophy and the second (suppressor mutation) back to prototrophy.
Such double mutations have resulted in enzymes modified in heat stability, heat activation, substrate affinity, activity, and allosteric inhibition (39). A mutant of Diplococcus pneumoniae resistant to
the folate analogue, amethopterin, and producing 100-fold higher activity of dihydrofolate reducatse, was found to produce a modified
enzyme resistant to inhibition (40). A mutant of Trichoderma
reesei, whose β-glucosidase is less subject to glucose inhibition,
was obtained by plating mutagenized populations on cellulose agar
and screening for increased glucose production around the colony by
a chromogenic method (41).

Mutational modifications of the types discussed above may be
helpful to permit enzymes from microorganisms to function effectively in specific pollution control environments, as described by
Alexander (this volume).

ORGANISM MODIFICATION

In the area of pollution control, efforts are under way to develop new organisms capable of degrading toxic compounds. Here, the
organism itself may be considered the product. Thus, modifying the
product in this case means modifying the organism so that it can degrade a compound not heretofore considered biodegradable. The initial basis for such attempts was the oft-observed phenomenon that
mutational changes in the control mechanisms of enzyme synthesis can
broaden the spectrum of utilizable growth substrates. Then it was
discovered that gene segments coding for degradation of at least two
different hydrocarbons were transposable from their original plasmid
onto other plasmids. These concepts were put to work in attempts to
develop a new organism capable of growth on and degradation of the
nonbiodegradable 2,4,5-trichlorophenoxyacetic acid (2,4,5-T). The
2,4,5-T is a component of the defoliant "Agent Orange", an herbicide, and also a growth regulator for citrus fruit. Chakrabarty and

co-workers (42) inoculated into a chemostat mixtures of organisms from waste dumps together with known bacteria carrying a variety of degradative plasmids. They began the continuous culture process with a low concentration of 2,4,5-T and higher concentrations of plasmid substrates, such as toluene, salicylate, and chlorobenzoate. Later they increased the 2,4,5-T concentration gradually. After about 9 months, they obtained a strain of <u>Psuedomonas</u> <u>cepacia</u> capable of using 2,4,5-T as sole source of carbon and energy, and of degrading 2,4,5-T in soil (43).

From the above case of "laboratory-accelerated evolution," Chakrabarty (44) has postulated a mechanism possibly involved in the natural evolution of organisms degrading xenobiotics such as 2,4-D. In this hypothesis, degradative gene clusters evolve by gene duplication, recombination, and mutation of structural and regulatory genes. These are then assembled, via transposition, on a replicon. Such a replicon later recombines with transfer plasmids to form a transmissable replicon which then passes into other microorganisms accelerating the spread of degradative competence.

The ultimate capability of microbiologists is the creation of new organisms with abilities to produce products completely foreign to their normal activities either in nature or in the test tube. This, of course, has been done many times during the last few years via recombinant DNA technology. Some of the products are shown in Tab. 6. Rather early in this remarkable development, it was realized that the same mg quantities of a mammalian protein such as

Table 6.   Some foreign products made by recombinant microorganisms.

Rabbit hemoglobin
Rat insulin
Human insulin
Human somatostatin
Rat growth hormone
Human growth hormone
Human chorionic somatomammotropin
Mouse beta-endorphin
Human interferon
Core hepatitis B antigen
VP3 antigen of foot and mouth disease
Fowl plaque virus antigen
Urokinase
Calf rennin
Mouse dihydrofolate reductase
Chicken ovalbumin
Human tissue-type plasminogen activator

somatostatin that were produced in a few liters of recombinant Escherichia coli broth previously had to be extracted from the brain
tissue of half a million sheep! Values common in the literature
today are 20 mg of growth hormone or interferon per liter of broth
or one to two percent of total cell protein. It is clear that the
pre-recombinant DNA prices of interferon (20 billion dollars/lb) and
β-endorphin (50 million dollars/lb) and their relative unavailabil-
ity and lack of purity are things of the past due to the capabilities of microbiologists (and microorganisms)!

     The use of recombinant DNA technology may be necessary to de-
velop microorganisms capable of degrading recalcitrant molecules
which cannot be broken down by natural strains or by strains developed by "plasmid-assisted molecular breeding" (Chakrabarty, this
volume). Genetically engineered organisms might also be used in
wastewater treatment. Thus recombinant DNA could conceivably play a
role in future environmental applications, both to reduce bulk
wastes and to inactivate potent chemicals at low concentration in
waters, soils, dumps, or other settings. No doubt there will have
to be careful and constructive meetings of the mind between geneticists and ecologists concerning the release of such in vitro genetically altered organisms into open environments.

ACKNOWLEDGEMENT

     Major funding in my laboratory is provided by the National
Science Foundation.

REFERENCES

1.   Tyler, J., and R.K. Finn (1974) Growth rates of a pseudomonad
     on 2,4-dichlorophenoxyacetic acid and 2,4-dichlorophenol.
     Appl. Microbiol. 28:181-184.
2.   Wheelis, M.L. (1975) The genetics of dissimilatory pathways in
     Pseudomonas. Ann. Rev. Microbiol. 29:505-524.
3.   Gibson, D.T. (1968) Microbial degradation of aromatic com-
     pounds. Science 161:1093-1097.
4.   Alexander, M. (1971) Biochemical ecology of microorganisms.
     Ann. Rev. Microbiol. 25:361-392.
5.   Alexander, M. (1980) Biodegradation of chemicals of environmen-
     tal concern. Science 211:132-138.
6.   Alexander, M. (1973) Nonbiodegradable and other recalcitrant
     molecules. Biotechnol. Bioeng. 15:611-647.
7.   Malik, K.A. (1978) Microbial removal of organic sulfur from
     crude oil and the environment: Some new perspectives. Process
     Biochem. 13(9):10-13.
8.   Bartha, R., and R.M. Atlas (1977) The microbiology of aquatic
     oil spills. Adv. Appl. Microbiol. 22:225-266.

9. Gutnick, D.L., and E. Rosenberg (1977) Oil tankers and pollu-
    tion: a microbiological approach. Ann. Rev. Microbiol.
    31:379-396.
10. Friello, D.A., J.R. Mylroie, and A.M. Chakrabarty (1976) Use of
    genetically engineered multi-plasmid microorganisms for rapid
    degradation of fuel hydrocarbons. In Proc. Int. Biodeg. Symp.
    3rd 1975, J.M. Sharpley and A.M. Kaplan, eds. Applied Science
    Publishers Ltd., London, pp. 205-213.
11. Aunstrup, K. (1979) Production, isolation and economics of ex-
    tracellular enzymes. Appl. Biochem. Bioeng. 2:27-69.
12. Foster, J.W. (1964) Microbes in diplomacy. Grad. J. 6:322-332.
13. Lecadet, M.M., and R. Dedonder (1971) Biogenesis of the
    crystalline inclusion of Bacillus thuringiensis during sporula-
    tion. Eur. J. Biochem. 23:282-294.
14. Gutnick, D.L., E.A. Bayer, C. Rubinowitz, O. Pines, Y. Shabtai,
    S. Goldman, and E. Rosenberg (1981) Emulsan production in
    Acinetobacter RAG-1. In Advances in Biotechnology. Vol. 3.
    Fermentation Products. C. Vezina and K. Singh, eds. Pergamon
    Press, Toronto, pp. 455-459.
15. Davis, M.G., and J.M. Calvo (1977) Relationship between messen-
    ger ribonucleic acid and enzyme levels specified by the leucine
    operon of Escherichia coli K-12. J. Baceteriol. 131:997-1007.
16. Saito, N., and K. Yamamoto (1975) Regulatory factors affecting
    alpha-amylase production in Bacillus licheniformis. J. Bacter-
    iol. 121:848-856.
17. Newell, S.L., and W.J. Brill (1972) Mutants of Salmonella
    typhimurium that are insensitive to catabolite repression of
    proline degradation. J. Bacteriol. 111:375-382.
18. Betz, J.L., P.R. Brown, M.J. Smyth, and P.H. Clarke (1974) Evo-
    lution in action. Nature 247:261-264.
19. Schaeffer, E.J., and C. L. Cooney (1982) Production of maltase
    by wild type and a constitutive mutant of Saccharomyces itali-
    ans. Appl. Environ. Microbiol. 43:75-80.
20. Michels, C.A., and A. Romanowski (1980) Pleiotropic glucose re-
    pression-resistant mutation in Saccharomyces carlsbergensis.
    J. Bacteriol. 143:674-679.
21. Hegeman, G.D., and R.T. Root (1976) The effect of a non-metabo-
    lizable analogue on mandelate catabolism. Arch. Microbiol.
    110:19-25.
22. Shinke, R., K. Aoki, H. Nishira, and S. Yuki (1979) Isolation
    of a rifampicin-resistant, asporogenous mutant from Bacillus
    cereus and its high beta-amylase productivity. J. Ferm.
    Technol. 57:53-55.
23. Haggett, K.D., W.Y. Choi, and N.W. Dunn (1978) Mutants of
    Cellulomonas which produce increased levels of beta-glucosi-
    dase. Eur. J. Appl. Microbiol. Biotechnol. 6:189-191.
24. Horiuchi, T., S. Horiuchi, and A. Novick (1963) The genetic ba-
    sis of hyper-synthesis of beta-galactosidase. Genetics
    48:157-169.
25. Rigby, P.W.J., B.D. Burleigh, and B.S. Hartley (1974) Gene du-

plication in experimental enzyme evolution. *Nature* 251:200–204.

26. Shen, Y.-Q., G.-X. Xia, C.-J. Lou, K.-R. Xu, and R.-S. Jiao (1980) Studies on microbial production of long-chain dicarboxylic acids from n-alkane. 4. Production of long chain dicarboxylic acid by conversion with resting *Candida* yeast cells. *Acta Phytophysiol. Sinica* 6:29–35.

27. Wigmore, G.J., and D.W. Ribbons (1980) p-Cymene pathway in *Pseudomonas putida*: selective enrichment of defective mutants by using halogenated substrate analogs. *J. Bacteriol.* 143:816–824.

28. Sonoyama, T., H. Tani, K. Matsuda, B. Kageyama, M. Tanimoto, K. Kobayashi, S. Yagi, H. Kyotani, and K. Mitsushima (1982) Production of 2-keto-L-gulonic acid from D-glucose by two-stage fermentation. *Appl. Environ. Microbiol.* 43:1064–1069.

29. Kondo, E., and E. Masuo (1961) "Pseudo-crystallofermentation" of steroid: A new process for preparing prednisolone by a microorganism. *J. Gen. Appl. Microbiol.* 7:113–117.

30. Buckland, B.C., P. Dunnill, and M.D. Lilly (1975) The enzymatic transformation of water-insoluble reactants in non-aqueous solvents. Conversion of cholesterol to cholest-4-ene-3-one by a *Nocardia* sp. *Biotechnol. Bioeng.* 17:815–826.

31. Schwartz, R.D., and C.J. McCoy (1977) Epoxidation of 1,7-octadiene by *Pseudomonas oleovorans*: fermentation in the presence of cyclohexane. *Appl. Environ. Microbiol.* 34:47–49.

32. Omata, T., T. Iida, A. Tanaka, and S. Fukui (1979) Transformation of steroids by gel-entrapped *Nocardia rhodocrous* cells in organic solvent. *Eur. J. Appl. Microbiol. Biotechnol.* 8:143–155.

33. Fukui, S., and A. Tanaka (1982) Immobilized microbial cells. *Ann Rev. Microbiol.* 36:145–172.

34. Sato, T., Y. Nishida, T. Tosa, and I. Chibata (1979) Immobilization of *Escherichia coli* cells containing aspartase activity with kappa-carrageenan. Enzymic properties and application for L-aspartic acid production. *Biochim. Biophys. Acta* 570:179–186.

35. Messing, R.A. (1980) Immobilized microbes. *Ann. Rpts. Ferm. Proc.* 4:105–121.

36. Mortlock, R.P. (1982) Metabolic acquisitions through laboratory selection. *Ann. Rev. Microbiol.* 36:259–284.

37. Langridge, J. (1969) Mutations conferring quantitative and qualitative increases in beta-galactosidase activity in *Escherichia coli*. *Molec. Gen. Genet.* 105:74–83.

38. Coats, J.H., and E.W. Nester (1967) Regulation reversal mutation: characterization of end product-activated mutants of *Bacillus subtilis*. *J. Biol. Chem.* 242:4948–4955.

39. Fincham, J.R.S. (1973) Genetic control of enzyme-protein structure and synthesis in fungi. In *Genetics of Industrial Microorganisms: Actinomycetes and Fungi*, Z. Vanek, Z. Hostalek, and J. Cudlin, eds. Academia, Prague, pp. 97–108.

40. Sirotnak, F.M., W.A. Williams, and S.L. Hachtel (1969) In-

creased dihydrofolate reductase synthesis in <u>Diplococcus</u> <u>pneu-</u>
<u>moniae</u> following translatable alteration of the structural
gene. II. Individual and dual-effects on the properties and
rate of synthesis of the enzyme. <u>Genetics</u> 61:313-326.

41. Cuskey, S.M., D.H.J. Schamhart, T. Chase, Jr., B.S. Montenecourt, and D.E. Eveleigh (1980) Screening for beta-glucosidase
mutants of <u>Trichoderma</u> <u>reesei</u> with resistance to end-product
inhibition. <u>Devel. Ind. Micro.</u> 21:471-480.

42. Kellogg, S.T., D.K. Chatterjee, and A.M. Chakrabarty (1981)
Plasmid assisted molecular breeding: new technique for enhanced
biodegradation of persistent toxic chemicals. <u>Science</u>
214:1133-1135.

43. Chatterjee, D.K., J.J. Kilbane, and A.M. Chakrabarty (1982)
Biodegradation of 2,4,5-trichlorophenoxyacetic acid in soil by
a pure culture of <u>Pseudomonas</u> <u>cepacia</u>. <u>Appl. Envir. Microbiol.</u>
44:514-516.

44. Chakrabarty, A.M. (1978) Molecular mechanisms in the biodegradation of environmental pollutants. <u>ASM News</u> 44:687-690.

45. Kuhn, J., and R.L. Somerville (1971) Mutant straints of <u>Escher-</u>
<u>ichia coli</u> K12 that use D-amino acids. <u>Proc. Natl. Acad. Sci.,</u>
<u>USA</u> 68:2484-2487.

46. Clayton, R.K., and C. Smith (1960) <u>Rhodopseudomonas</u> <u>spheroides</u>:
High catalase and blue-green double mutants. <u>Biochem. Biophys.</u>
<u>Res. Commun.</u> 3:143-145.

47. Crusberg, T.C., R. Leary, and R.L. Kisliuk (1970) Properties of
thymidylate synthetase from dichloromethotrexate-resistant <u>Lac-</u>
<u>tobacillus</u> <u>casei</u>. J. Biol. Chem. 245:5292-5296.

48. Nakao, Y., M. Suzuki, M. Kuno, and K. Maejima (1973) Production
of alkaline protease from <u>n</u>-paraffins by a kabicidin resistant
mutant strain of <u>Fusarium</u> sp. <u>Agric. Biol. Chem.</u> 37:1223-1224.

49. Ford, S.R., and R.L. Switzer (1975) Stimulation of derepressed
enzyme synthesis in bacteria by growth on sublethal conentra-
tions of chloramphenicol. <u>Antimicrob. Agents Chemother.</u>
7:555-563.

50. Pardee, A.B., E.J. Benz, Jr., D.A. St. Peter, J.N. Krieger, M.
Meuth, and H.W. Trieshmann, Jr. (1971) Hyperproduction and
purification of nicotinamide deamidase, a micro-constitutive
enzyme of <u>Escherichia</u> <u>coli</u>. J. Biol. Chem. 246:6792-6796.

51. Legrain, C., V. Stalon, N. Glansdorff, D. Gigot, A. Pierard,
and M. Crabeel (1976) Structural and regulatory mutations allowing utilization of citrulline or carbamoylaspartate as a
source of carbamoylphosphate in <u>Escherichia</u> <u>coli</u> K-12. <u>J.</u>
<u>Bacteriol.</u> 128:39-48.

52. Hasunuma, K. (1977) Control of the production of orthophosphate
repressible extracellular enzymes in <u>Neurospora</u> <u>crassa</u>. <u>Molec.</u>
<u>Gen. Genet.</u> 151:5-10.

53. Erokhina, L.I., I.M. Nesterova, and S.P. Istoshina (1976)
Selection of <u>Aspergillus</u> <u>awamori</u>, a producer of acid proteinase, and the role of morphological and biochemical mutants and
prototrophic revertants in the selection of active strains.

Genetika 12:135–141.

54. Borum, P.R., and K.J. Monty (1976) Regulatory mutants and control of cysteine biosynthetic enzymes in Salmonella typhimurium. J. Bacteriol. 125:94–101.

55. Aronson, A.I., N. Angelo, and S.C. Holt (1971) Regulation of extracellular protease production in Bacillus cereus T: characterization of mutants producing altered amounts of protease. J. Bacteriol. 106:1016–1025.

56. Aunstrup, K. (1981) Proteinases. In Economic Microbiology 5. Microbial Enzymes and Bioconversions, A.H. Rose, ed. Academic Press, New York, pp. 49–114.

57. Shinke, R., K. Aoki, H. Nishiva, and S. Yuki (1981) Beta-amylase production by a rifampicin-resistant, asporogenous mutant of Bacillus cereus and its sporogenous revertant. In Advances in Biotechnology 3. Fermentation Products, C. Vezina and K. Singh, eds. Pergamon Press, Toronto, pp. 307–312.

58. Sebold, M., and M. Cassier (1969) Sporulation and toxigenicity in mutant strains of Clostridium perfringens. Spores 4:306–316.

59. Ito, J., and J. Spizizen (1973) Genetic studies of catabolite repression insensitive sporulation mutants of Bacillus subtilis. In Regulation de la Sporulation Microbienne, J.P. Aubert, P. Schaeffer, and J. Szulmjaster, eds. Editions du Centre National de la Recherche Scientifique, Paris, pp. 81–82.

60. Levisohn, S., and A.I. Aronson (1967) Regulation of extracellular protease production in Bacillus cereus. J. Bacteriol. 93:1023–1030.

61. Kunst, F., M. Pascal, J. Lepesant-Kejzlarova, J.-A. Lepesant, A. Billault, and R. Dedonder (1974) Pleiotropic mutations affecting sporulation conditions and the synthesis of extracellular enzymes in Bacillus subtilis 168. Biochimie 56:1481–1489.

62. Nevalainen, K.M.H., E.T. Palva, and M.J. Bailey (1980) A high cellulase-producing mutant strain of Trichoderma reesei. Enz. Microb. Technol. 2:59–60.

63. Higerd, R.B., J.A. Hoch, and J. Spizizen (1972) Hyperprotease-producing mutant of Bacillus subtilis. J. Bacteriol. 112:1026–1028.

64. Nasuno, S., and T. Ohara (1971) Comparison of alkaline proteinase from hyperproductive mutants and parent strain of Aspergillus sojae. Agric. Biol. Chem. 35:836–842.

65. Cohen, B.L. (1972) Ammonium repression of extracellular protease in Aspergillus nidulans. J. Gen. Microbiol. 71:293–299.

66. Hsu, D.J., and R.H. Vaughn (1969) Production and catabolite repression of the constitutive polygalacturonic acid trans-eliminase of Aeromonas liquefaciens. J. Bacteriol. 98:172–181.

67. Montenecourt, B.S., S.-C. Kuo, and J.O. Lampen (1973) Saccharomyces mutants with invertase formation resistant to repression by hexoses. J. Bacteriol. 114:233–238.

68. Schurr, A., and E. Yagil (1971) Regulation and characterization of acid and alkaline phosphatase in yeast. J. Gen. Microbiol. 65:291–303.

69. Gray, G.G., R.M. Berka, and M.L. Vasil (1982) Phospholipase C regulatory mutation of Pseudomonas aeruginosa that results in constitutive synthesis of several phosphate-repressible proteins. J. Bacteriol. 150:1221-1226.

70. Palva, I. (1982) Molecular cloning of alpha-amylase gene from Bacillus amyloliquefaciens and its expression in B. subtilis. Gene 19:81-87.

71. Preiss, J., M. Mazelis, and E. Greenberg (1982) Cloning of the aspartate-beta-semialdehyde dehydrogenase structural gene from Escherichia coli K12. Curr. Microbiol. 7:263-268.

72. Mayer, J., J. Collins, and F. Wagner (1980) Cloning of the penicillin G-acylase gene of Escherichia coli ATCC 11105 on multicopy plasmids. Enz. Eng. 5:61-73.

73. Deutch, A.H., C.J. Smith, K.E. Rushlow, and P.J. Kretschmer (1982) Escherichia coli delta'-pyrroline-5-carboxylate reductase: gene sequence, protein overproduction and purification. Nucl. Acid Res. 10:7701-7714.

74. Panasenko, S.M., J.R. Cameron, R.W. Davis, and I.R. Lehman (1977) Five-hundred-fold overproduction of DNA ligase after induction of a hybrid lambda lysogen constructed in vitro. Science 196:188-189.

75. Kelley, W.S., K. Chalmers, and N.E. Murray (1977) Isolation and characterization of a λpolA transducing phage. Proc. Natl. Acad. Sci., USA 74:5632-5636.

76. Hayzer, D.J., and T. Leisinger (1980) The gene-enzyme relationships of proline biosynthesis in Escherichia coli. J. Gen. Microbiol. 118:287-293.

77. Raetz, C.R.H., T.J. Larson, and W. Dowhan (1977) Gene cloning for the isolation of enzymes of membrane lipid synthesis: Phosphatidylserine synthase overproduction in Escherichia coli. Proc. Natl. Acad. Sci., USA 74:1412-1416.

78. Fischer, M., and S.A. Short (1980) Cloning the Escherichia coli deoxyribonucleoside operon. Abstr. Ann. Mtg. Amer. Soc. Microbiol. 1980:125.

79. Hershfield, V., H.W. Boyer, L. Chow, and D.R. Helinski (1974) Plasmid colE1 as a molecular vehicle for cloning and amplification of DNA. Proc. Natl. Acad. Sci., USA 71:3455-3459.

80. Nagahari, K., T. Tanaka, F. Hishinuma, M. Kuroda, and K. Sakaguchi (1977) Control of tryptophan synthetase amplified by varying the numbers of composite plasmids in Escherichia coli cells. Gene 1:141-152.

TOOLS OF GENETIC MANIPULATION

Leroy E. Hood

Division of Biology
California Institute of Technology
Pasadena, California 91125

In the past ten years several advances in biotechnology have
revolutionized the way fundamental biological problems are approached. I will discuss three of these relatively recently developed disciplines in biotechnology--recombinant DNA, microchemical
instrumentation, and monoclonal antibodies--and I will point out the
striking synergies that arise from their interactions. These synergies will revolutionize biological research in the near future. I
will discuss examples from the health sciences, my area of expertise, yet I suspect many similar applications to your own areas of
interest will come to mind. I will review in general terms the basic approaches underlying the recombinant DNA, the microchemical
instrumentation, and the monoclonal antibody technologies.

DNA and Information Flow

The language of DNA, although simple, is incredibly voluminous
in living organisms. Human cells contain sufficient information to
encode three million different units of information (genes) if, in
fact, all of the DNA information encode different genes. The recombinant DNA technology enables the researcher to isolate a single one
of these three million potential genes and place it in a test tube
to analyze its function and structure.

To grasp the recombinant DNA technology, one must understand
the information flow which goes from the DNA of the chromosomes to
the RNA of the messenger transcripts which are finally translated
into the linear units of amino acid denoted proteins (Fig. 1). It
is in the proteins that the one-dimensional information of the genes
assumes the three-dimensional protein configurations that give our
body shape and function. In a sense the units of information in the
chromosomes, termed genes, constitute a master computer tape which
can be transcribed into a second working computer tape, messenger

301

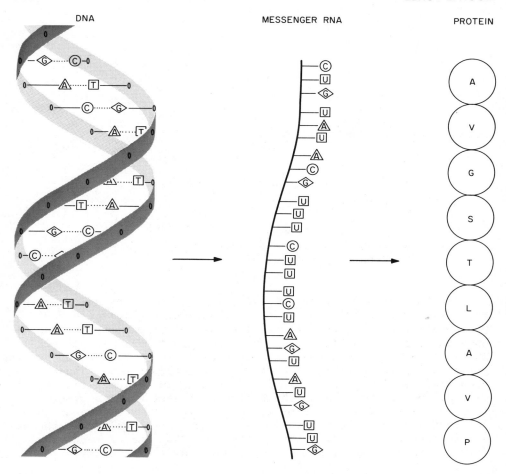

Fig. 1.   A schematic representation of the flow of information from
           DNA to RNA proteins.

RNA, which in turn can be fed into protein synthesizing machinery,
the ribosomes, to make proteins.

     The DNA code is incredibly simple. There are four basic sub-
units, the four different nucleotide bases; they form two pairs: A
subunits with T subunits, and G subunits with C subunits (Fig. 2).
The basic structure of the DNA molecule is two anti-parallel DNA
strands that are hydrogen bonded together through highly specific
complementary interactions of the paired bases. These complementary
interactions confer on DNA its most fundamental property: the property that permits one to carry out recombinant DNA techniques. The
three million potential genes that are contained in human cells are
arranged on 23 different chromosomes. These chromosomes can be

fragmented into three million small fragments and the individual
strands of DNA can be fragmented by a process called denaturation.
The individual DNA strands have the ability to find their original
partner strand and reanneal to one another (Fig. 3). This complementary refolding is dictated by the precise order of the DNA bases.
The specificity of this molecular hybridization is the essence of
the recombinant DNA technology.

Molecular complementarity is the fundamental mechanism by which
information is taken from the genes and read into messenger RNA
transcripts. RNA has four nucleotide bases very similar to their
DNA counterparts. Thus, there is a triplet genetic code dictionary
where three particular DNA or RNA bases encode each amino acid subunit. There are 20 different protein subunits. Thus, given a DNA
sequence, the amino acid subunit sequence can be predicted from the
genetic code dictionary. Conversely, given an amino acid sequence,
the gene sequence can be predicted by reverse translation of the genetic code dictionary. Microchemical instrumentation takes advantage of translation and reverse translation of the genetic code to
generate artificial protein fragments from gene sequences or artificial gene fragments from protein sequences (see Ref. 1 for a concise
review of the properties of DNA and its mode of information expression).

Recombinant DNA Technology

Two distinct types of enzymes, restriction endonucleases and
ligases, have made the recombinant DNA approach possible. The restriction endonucleases cleave double-stranded DNA at particular
base sequences four or six nucleotides in length (Fig. 4). Indeed,
some restriction enzymes cut DNA so that there are complementary or
staggered overlapping ends. This means that any two noncontiguous
DNA fragments may reanneal to one another. Since human chromosomes
are enormously long, containing an average 10^8 nucleotide base pairs
or enough DNA for 10^5 genes, it is important to be able to cleave
DNA into smaller reproducible fragments. The ligase enzyme permits
the joining of DNA fragments in artificial combinations, especially
those with complementary staggered ends (Fig. 4). Thus, DNA molecules can be cleaved into small fragments and joined together in artificial combinations.

The basic strategy in the recombinant DNA technology is to
fragment human DNA with a restriction endonuclease and then to join
all of the individual DNA fragments to plasmids, small circular DNAs
that grow in the bacterium Escherichia coli to produce 50 to several
hundred copies per cell, thus amplifying the human genes by this
same magnitude (Fig. 5). After this procedure, the complex mixture
of E. coli each containing one type of plasmid with a single human
gene is plated out on petri dishes with agar, and various techniques
are used to determine which E. coli has the particular human gene of
interest. Operationally, this means one can produce three million

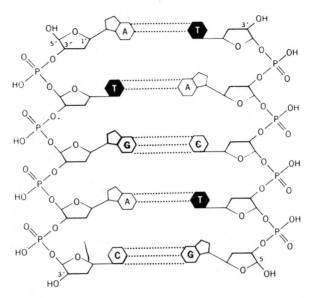

Fig. 2.   Base interactions between the two anti-parallel strands of
            DNA.

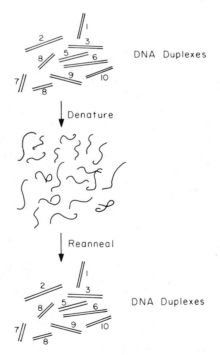

Fig. 3.   The separation or denaturation and specific joining or re-
            naturation of DNA fragments.

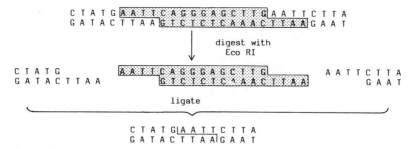

C T A T G [AATTCAGGGAGCTTG] A A T T C T T A
G A T A C T T A A [GTCTCTCAAACTTAA] G A A T

digest with
Eco RI

C T A T G   [AATTCAGGGAGCTTG]   A A T T C T T A
G A T A C T T A A   [GTCTCTCAAACTTAA]   G A A T

ligate

C T A T G|A A T T|C T T A
G A T A C T T A A|G A A T

Fig. 4.   The fragmentation of DNA by restriction enzymes and the
          rejoining of DNA fragments by ligases.

E. coli, each with a different human gene. Operationally, a molecular probe is needed to isolate the appropriate gene. If the desired
gene to be isolated produces lots of messenger RNA and protein, say
globin, it is relatively easy to isolate by conventional techniques
(Fig. 6). The globin gene is termed a frequent messenger gene.

     In contrast, the human gamma-interferon (γ-interferon) gene
produces very little protein and is denoted a rare-message gene.
These genes are very difficult to isolate. Indeed, we have developed at Caltech over the last ten years a microchemical facility to

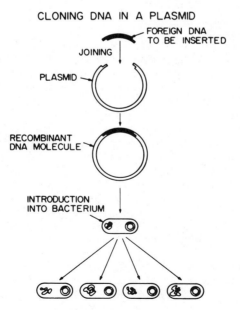

CLONING DNA IN A PLASMID

FOREIGN DNA
TO BE INSERTED

JOINING

PLASMID

RECOMBINANT
DNA MOLECULE

INTRODUCTION
INTO BACTERIUM

Fig. 5.   The insertion of a human DNA fragment into a bacterial
          plasmid. The plasmid infects the bacterium E. coli and is
          amplified.

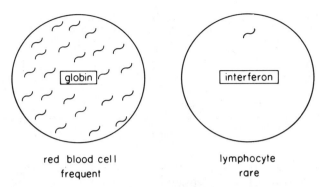

Fig. 6.   Rare-message and frequent-message genes. A rare-message
           gene synthesizes very little mRNA, whereas a frequent-
           message gene synthesizes large quantities of mRNA.

specifically isolate rare-message genes, as I will discuss subsequently. Once any gene has been isolated it is possible after appropriate engineering to place it in bacteria, yeast, or mammalian
cells and produce large quantities of the corresponding protein
(again, Ref. 1 has a concise review of the recombinant DNA techniques).

Caltech Microchemical Facility

     Our initial efforts toward the automated synthesis and sequence
analysis of DNA and proteins were directed at developing a protein
sequenator that was 10,000 times more sensitive than the initial Ed-
man instrument (2-5). A protein sequenator determines the order of
the amino acid subunits in a protein. Subsequently, we have developed or are developing a series of instruments for the automated
manipulation of genes and proteins (Tab. 1).

     Protein sequenator. The protein sequenator is a pair of molec-
ular scissors which allow the scientist to take asymmetric linear
proteins and cleave their amino acids one at a time from one end
of the chain, the N-terminal end. The secrets to our success in
increasing the sensitivity of this instrument were many: we enormously improved the valving system for this sophisticated plumbing
device; we developed a miniaturized reaction chamber (Fig. 7) and a
gas-phase sequencing chemistry to reduce significantly the amount of
protein required for sequencing; we improved the purification procedures for the reagents and solvents of the sequencing chemistry; and
finally we developed a sensitive procedure involving high pressure
liquid chromatography (HPLC) for analyzing the amino acid subunits
(6). With the gas-phase microsequenator, we currently can analyze 5
to 10 picomoles of many polypeptides for 20 residues (this is ~0.1
μg of the model protein, myoglobin). The importance of this increased sensitivity of microsequencing is that we can sequence the

Table 1. Caltech biology microchemical instrumentation facility.

Instrument	Function
Protein Microsequenator	Primary structural analysis (order of amino acids) in proteins and peptides
EOID Mass Spectrometer	High sensitivity analysis of complex mixtures of biochemicals
DNA Synthesizer	Automated synthesis of oligonucleotides (genes)
Peptide Synthesizer	Automated synthesis of peptides and fragments of proteins
Laboratory Computer	Analysis of DNA and protein sequence data

proteins derived from rare-message genes and use the DNA synthesizer to make the corresponding gene fragments by reverse translation using the genetic code dictionary. These gene fragments, then, as we shall see subsequently, allow us to clone the corresponding rare-message gene.

Mass spectrometer. We have worked over the last eight years with the engineers at the Jet Propulsion Laboratory (JPL) in Pasadena to develop a highly sensitive mass spectrometer for analyzing amino acid derivatives at 100- to 1,000-fold greater sensitivity than is possible with the high pressure liquid chromatograph (5). The idea for this instrument emerged from the small and stable mass spectrometer built by JPL and sent to Mars for various analyses. In the last eight years the JPL engineers have (i) developed and automated sample injection system, (ii) developed an electro-optical ion detector, and (iii) designed a data processing system to handle the enormous throughput of information from the detector. The electro-optical detector system is a fixed array of ten thousand electro-optical units per centimeter (Fig. 8). Each unit has the capacity to pick up a single molecular ion and to transmit a signal, after appropriate amplification, through a fibro-optics system into a viticon tube and ultimately into a computer for data analysis.

With this system we have been able to analyze amino acid derivatives at the femtomole level, which is 100- to 1000-fold more sensitive that HPLC analysis. The sample analysis time is approximately five minutes. In the future we envision being able to multiplex several gas-phase sequenators with the mass spectrometer, and, accordingly, have the capacity to analyze 50 to 100 residues a day at subpicomole levels.

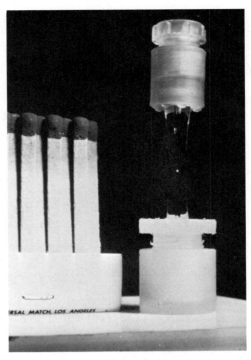

Fig. 7.   An early prototype column for the gas-phase sequenator.
           Protein is affixed to the small bead and the reagents of
           the Edman chemistry are passed over the bead in Argon.
           The cleaved amino acid derivative is eluted from the bead
           in small volume of solvent.

     DNA synthesizer. The automated DNA synthesizer couples the 3'
hydroxyl group of a particular DNA base to an inert matrix, a silica
gel, and then are added in sequential fashion other bases to generate a DNA fragment of appropriate sequence (7) (Fig. 9). The DNA
synthesizer that we have developed at Caltech has several advantageous properties: (i) DNA fragments of 40 to 50 residues can be
synthesized; (ii) it has a cycle time of 10 minutes; and (iii) two,
three, or four different bases can be placed at a single position,
which is important because of the ambiguity of the reverse translation of protein to DNA sequences.

     The DNA synthesizer provides several striking opportunities to
complement the recombinant DNA technology. First, 20 to 30 mer
fragments of a gene can be synthesized in the double-strand form
with complementary single-stranded ends so that they can be joined
together into a complete gene. Dr. Marvin Caruthers has employed
this strategy to synthesize the entire gene for human γ-interferon
in just two months. This gene has approximately 500 base residues.

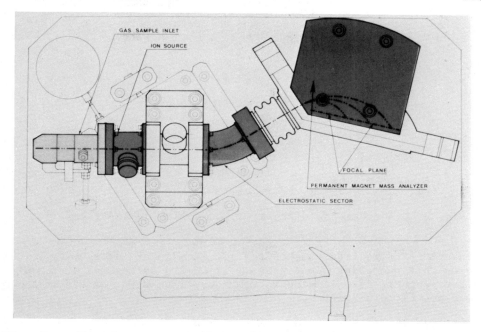

Fig. 8.   The electro-optical ion detector for the mass spectro-
           meter.

Thus, human genes can now be synthesized at will with the possibility of optimizing their coding properties for maximal production in
the appropriate hosts such as E. coli, yeast, or mammalian cells.

    A second possibility is even more exciting. With the protein
microsequenator, the mass spectrometer, and the DNA synthesizer, we
hope in the future to take standard two-dimensional gels, the most
sensitive technique in modern biochemistry for separating complex
mixtures of polypeptides (one dimension separates by protein size
and the second dimension by charge) and use this analytic tool as a
preparative procedure for obtaining sufficient amounts of polypeptides for microsequencing (Fig. 10). Most of the spots in Fig. 10
are present at the picomole level. Accordingly, these individual
spots can be cut from the gel, eluted, and microsequenced. This
amino acid sequence can be reverse translated by the genetic code
dictionary into a DNA sequence (Fig. 11). Then an appropriate DNA
fragment of the gene can be synthesized and used in conjunction with
classic recombinant DNA technology to clone the corresponding gene.
This strategy has been used successfully to clone perhaps twenty or
more rare-message genes very rapidly. In the future, we will be
able to readily clone virtually any gene whose protein product can
be visualized on a two-dimensional gel.

    At Caltech we are now in the process of automating DNA

STEP

1   O~A

2   O~A-T

3   O~A-T-T

4   O~A-T-T-C

5   O~A-T-T-C-A

6   O~A-T-T-C-A-G

7   O~A-T-T-C-A-G-G

8   O~A-T-T-C-A-G-G-C

Fig. 9.   A schematic diagram of the synthetic DNA chemistry.

sequencing and peptide synthesis (5). We also are developing a
device to fingerprint human genes. If we are successful in this
latter venture, it will have a tremendous impact on the diagnosis of
human genetic diseases.

Applications of Biotechnology to Medicine

Human Genetics. Amniocentesis is a procedure to extract fetal
fluids and cells from the amniotic sac. Tests permit the identification of two to three hundred different human genetic diseases by
analyzing either biochemical abnormalities in the fluid or chromosomal abnormalities. But some 2,500 to 3,000 different human genetic diseases have been described clinically.

If one could routinely fingerprint human genes, distinguishing
normal from abnormal genes by differences in restriction fragments,
then it would be possible to think about diagnosing in utero most
different human genetic diseases by amniocentesis, the extraction of
the DNA from fetal cells, and then automated fingerprinting or gene
analysis. Obviously, molecular probes will be required for each
gene to be analyzed. These probes are rapidly becoming available.
We currently have the molecular probes for perhaps 50 different
human genes, and I would guess in the next five years that we will
have the molecular probes for hundreds more. The automated fingerprinting of human genes will revolutionize human genetics.

Cancer. The most dramatic advance in cancer research in the
last ten years is the discovery of oncogenes. Oncogenes are single
genes which upon introduction into normal cells have the ability to
convert them into cancer cells (8). About 18 oncogenes have been
described to date. Each oncogene has its normal counterpart in
every human cell. Thus, molecular biologists are comparing oncogenes with their normal counterparts to identify how they differ in
structure and function. The intriguing question is what does the

Fig. 10.   A two-dimension gel for separating a complex mixture of
           proteins.   The typical protein spot represents about 1
           picomole of polypeptide.

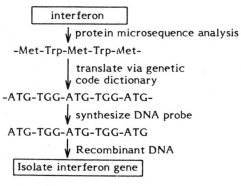

Fig. 11.   The strategy for converting protein sequence into DNA
           fragments and then using these fragments to clone rare-
           message genes.

normal gene ordinarily do, and how is it released from its cellular
control to occasionally become a cancer gene?

Our laboratory has recently identified the function of one
oncogene (9). These studies provide an elegantly simple and com-
pellingly attractive model for a certain subset of cancers. This
cancer gene is virtually identical to one encoding a normal growth
hormone, called platelet-derived growth factor. In this case a ret-
rovirus apparently acquired the normal gene for platelet-derived
growth factor and released it from its normal cellular controls and
placed it under viral control. The idea is that, when this virus
infects appropriate cells, the growth hormone is synthesized and
converts the normal to a neoplastic cell by causing it do divide
repeatedly.

Monoclonal Antibodies and Cancer

The hybridoma technology, a third biotechnology, allows us to
produce homogenous specific antibodies (10). Let me illustrate this
biotechnology by discussing some exciting advances in the therapeutic end of cancer research.

A malignant cell and its normal counterpart are distinguished
from one another by tumor antigens that are present on most tumor
cells, while they are absent in normal cells. A attractive therapeutic strategy for cancer is to synthesize antibodies against tumor
molecules and use these highly specific antibodies to destroy only
the cancer cells. This strategy, termed immunotherapy, has major
limitations. First, the isolation of tumor antigens has been very
difficult. Second, antibodies against many tumor antigens fail to
kill the tumor cells. Indeed, they often "block" the tumor antigens
from the cellular immune response which is generally responsible for
the cellular destruction of cancer cells.

Several advances in immunotherapy have permitted circumvention
of these difficulties. To understand these advances we must discuss
the hybridoma technology. Any foreign material (antigens), when
introduced into the human body, has the ability to make antibodies
that are both highly specific, and, unfortunately, highly heterogeneous; that is, an·immune response generates many different kinds of
molecular antibodies. This heterogeneity is one of the major limitations in the use of antibodies. The development of the monoclonal
antibody or hybridoma technology in 1975 circumvented this difficulty (10) (Fig. 12). In this technique a tumor cell synthesizing one
type of antibody was mutated so that it no longer could synthesize
antibodies. This tumor cell was then fused to a normal antibody-
producing cell to generate a hybrid cell, or hybridoma, which had
two special properties. First, it synthesized the desired homogeneous antibody. Second, it was immortal and could continue to grow
and produce antibody indefinitely. With the hybridoma technique,
researchers have the capacity to make infinite quantities of

homogeneous antibodies of any particular specificity. Let me
discuss two approaches that have employed monoclonal antibodies to
attack the cancer problem.

Immunotoxins. As discussed earlier, antibody molecules often
can interact with cancer cells and fail to kill them. to circumvent
this limitation, toxin molecules, a single one of which has the capacity to kill mammalian cells, may be covalently linked to antibodies specific for tumor cells (Fig. 13). Thus, the antibody
molecule specifically directs the toxin molecule to the cancer cell,
thus killing the tumor cell. In a number of animal model systems,
this approach has been successful. Several serious technical problems remain to be ironed out, but the immunotoxin strategy looks
very promising.

B-cell lymphomas and anti-antibodies. A dramatic experiment by
Dr. Ronald Levy at Stanford has illustrated the possible utility of
anti-antibodies in the therapy of B-cell lymphomas (11). The initial patient treated with this approach had undergone interferon
therapy, chemotherapy, and irradiation, and was in the terminal
stages of his disease with kilogram quantities of tumor. As an alternative approach, Dr. Levy took the B-cell lymphoma cells, which
expressed a unique antibody molecule on their cell surface, and
fused them to mouse myeloma cells that had lost the capacity to express their own antibody molecules (Fig. 14). The resulting hybridoma cell secreted large quantities of antibody molecules from the
patient's tumor cells. These antibody molecules were used to generate a mouse monoclonal antibody directed against the patient's antibody molecule. Large quantities of these mouse monoclonal antibodies were injected into the patient, and in a period of four to six
weeks the disease regressed. Almost two years later, the patient
still appears free of his disease. In some way that we do not

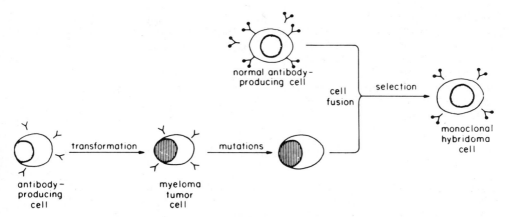

normal antibody-
producing cell

cell
fusion

selection

monoclonal
hybridoma
cell

antibody-
producing
cell

transformation

myeloma
tumor
cell

mutations

Fig. 12.   A diagram of the hybridoma or monoclonal antibody tech-
           nology.

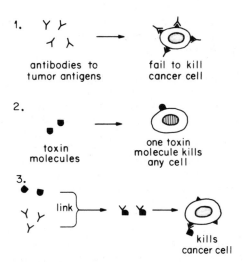

Fig. 13. A model of an immunotoxin, a toxin molecule covalently linked to an antibody molecule.

completely understand, mouse antibodies directed against the human antibodies, which in this case were cancer-specific molecules, had the capacity to destroy the patient's tumor cells. Dr. Levy has gone on to treat several additional patients and is now in the process of evaluating the results. Thus, antibodies may have a variety of different uses in immunotherapy.

Peptide antibodies. One of the most spectacular recent advances in immunology concerns a technique to make antibodies to virtually any part of a protein molecule (12). Antibodies can be raised against peptide fragments 8 to 20 residues in length. Thus, a peptide fragment from a protein molecule is synthesized, coupled to an appropriate carrier molecule, and the complex is then used to raise conventional or monoclonal antibodies (Fig. 15). Generally, the antibodies raised react with the peptide fragment and with the native protein molecule. Antibodies can thus be raised to virtually any portion of a protein molecule. This technique obviously has incredibly significant diagnostic and therapeutic potential. Indeed, this technique has already been employed to generate several vaccines that had not been possible to raise with more conventional approaches.

Replacement Therapy and Genetic Correction

The cloning and expression in bacteria of the genes encoding human growth hormones allows replacement therapy for individuals needing insulin, growth hormones, and a variety of other natural products. The availability of normal human genes also raises the

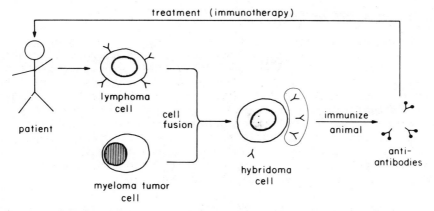

Fig. 14. Immunotherapy for a B-cell lymphona patient (see text).

possibility that good genes can be placed in appropriate human so-
matic cells to correct genetic defects. Just a year ago this possibility appeared very remote because of a variety of technical limitations. However, recent experiments placing foreign genes in embryos suggest that gene transfer experiments may be closer than we
thought. For example, one experiment has placed the gene for rate
growth hormone in mouse embryos (13). Seven of eight of the mice so
treated grew to twice the size of their control littermates. Thus,
the rat hormone gene does get into the mouse embryos and function in
a physiologically relevant manner. In the near future we will be
able to modify many properties in experimental animals and, when appropriate, start considering the application of this technology to
man. This possibility raises a host of social and ethical questions
that will have to be considered by society.

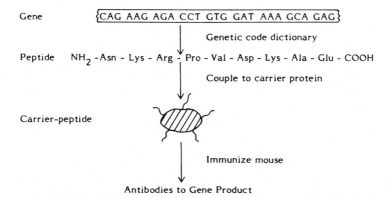

Fig. 15. A model for the generation of peptide antibodies.

Synergy Among the Biotechnologies

The three biotechnologies, recombinant DNA, monoclonal antibodies, and microchemical instrumentation, are enormously synergistic (5) (Fig. 16). Given an incredibly small amount of protein, we
can sequence it; we can synthesize gene fragments by reverse translation of the protein sequence; and we can use recombinant DNA techniques to isolate the corresponding gene. Alternatively, given a
gene sequence, we can, with the peptide synthesizer now being developed at Caltech, synthesize 50 to 60 residue fragments of polypeptide chains. Techniques are being developed to join large peptide
fragments together so that complete protein domains can be synthesized and their functions analyzed in test tubes.

We also can, given the DNA sequence, synthesize after translation with the genetic code dictionary peptide fragments that can be
used to generate monoclonal antibodies against gene products that
have not yet been identified. We can use those antibodies to identify the gene products and determine their functions. Conversely,
given again a particular protein sequence, such as that for human
γ-interferon, we can now synthesize the entire gene and optimize the
structure of that gene so it can be expressed effectively in E.
coli, yeast, or mammalian cells.

These are only a few examples of the synergistic effects of
these three kinds of biotechnologies. These biotechnologies will
not only have a profound effect on the health sciences, but they
will have a profound effect on many different areas including agriculture, energy, fine chemicals, mining, and the topic of this volume. If progress in these biotechnologies continues for the next
ten years as it has for the past ten years, no one will be able to
gauge the rapidly changing shape of the future. The possible future
applications of biotechnology appear virtually unlimited.

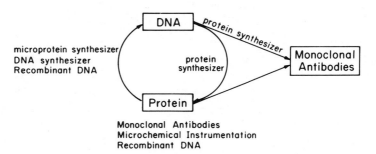

Fig. 16. The synergy of three biotechnologies: recombinant DNA,
         hybridomas, and microchemical instrumentation.

REFERENCES

1. Wood, W.B., J. Wilson, R. Benbow, and L. Hood (1974) <u>Biochemistry: A Problems Approach</u>, 1st Edition. W.A. Benjamin, Inc., Menlo Park, CA (2nd Edition, 1981).
2. Hunkapiller, M.W., and L.E. Hood (1978) Direct microsequence analysis of polypeptides using an improved sequenator, a non-protein carrier (Polybrene), and high pressure liquid chromatography. <u>Biochemistry</u> 17:2124-2133.
3. Henwick, R.M., M.W. Hunkapiller, L.E. Hood, and W.J. Dreyer (1981) <u>J. Biol. Chem.</u> 256:7990-7997.
4. Hunkapiller, M.W., and L.E. Hood (1983) Protein sequence analysis: Automated microsequencing. <u>Science</u> 219:650-659.
5. Hunkapiller, M., S. Kent, M. Caruthers, W. Dreyer, J. Firca, C. Giffin, S. Horvath, T. Hunkapiller, P. Tempst, and L. Hood. A microchemical facility for the analysis and synthesis of genes and proteins. <u>Nature</u> (submitted for publication).
6. Johnson, N.D., M.W. Hunkapiller, and L.E. Hood (1979) Analysis of phenyl-thiohydantoin amino acids by high performance liquid chromatography on DuPont Zorbax cyanopropylsilane columns. <u>Anal. Biochem.</u> 100:335-338.
7. Firca, J., M. Hunkapiller, C. Graham, S. Horvath, M. Caruthers, and L. Hood. An automated DNA synthesizer. (Manuscript in preparation.)
8. Bishop, J.M. (1982) Oncogenes. <u>Sci. Amer.</u> 246:80-92.
9. Doolittle, R.F., M.W. Hunkapiller, L.E. Hood, S.G. Devare, K.C. Robbins, S.A. Aaronson, and H.N. Antoniades (1983) Simian sarcoma virus <u>onc</u> gene, v-<u>sis</u>, is derived from the gene (or genes) encoding a platelet-derived growth factor. <u>Science</u> 221: 275-277.
10. Milstein, C. (1980) Monoclonal antibodies. <u>Sci. Amer.</u> 243: 66-74.
11. Levy, R., and R.A. Miller (1983) Biological and clinical implications of lymphocyte hybridomas: Tumor therapy with monoclonal antibodies. <u>Ann. Rev. Med.</u> 34:107-116.
12. Lerner, R.A. (1982) Tapping the immunological repertoire to produce antibodies of predetermined specificity. <u>Nature</u> 299: 592-596.
13. Palmiter, R.D., R.L. Brinster, R.E. Hammer, M.E. Trumbauer, M.G. Rosenfeld, N.C. Birnberg, and R.M. Evans (1982) Dramatic growth of mice that develop from eggs microinjected with metallothionein-growth hormone fusion genes. <u>Nature</u> 300:611-615.

MANIPULATION OF METHANOTROPHS

Mary E. Lidstrom, Ann E. Wopat, David N. Nunn,
and Aresa E. Toukdarian

Department of Microbiology, SC-42
University of Washington
Seattle, Washington 98195

INTRODUCTION

Recent studies of methane-oxidizing bacteria (methanotrophs)
have demonstrated their ability to oxidize a variety of hydrocarbons
(1). This capability has prompted much study into the possible use
of these bacteria as biocatalysts, and a number of patents have appeared with this goal in mind. Although methanotrophs can clearly
transform a variety of hydrocarbons under laboratory conditions, the
significance of these capabilities in the biosphere is uncertain.
These bacteria are ubiquitous, and if they carry out these oxidations in natural environments they may make significant contribu-
tions to hydrocarbon degradation. In addition, if their unique
capabilities could be harnessed, it is possible they could be used
for developing detoxification processes.

Genetic manipulation will clearly be important in any attempts
to exploit these bacteria. In this chapter, we will describe methanotrophs in the context of hydrocarbon transformation and discuss
this laboratory's efforts to carry out genetic studies in these bacteria.

CHARACTERISTICS OF METHANOTROPHS

Methanotrophs are a restricted group of gram-negative rods,
vibrio, and cocci. The majority of strains that have been isolated
are obligate methanotrophs, unable to grown on any substrate other
than methane, although some strains are capable of growth on methanol. A few strains of methanotrophs capable of growth on multicarbon compounds (facultative methanotrophs) have been reported, but

all of these cultures are either unstable, having been lost in subsequent laboratory culture, or have been shown to be cocultures of
an obligate methanotroph and a heterotroph (10).

Methanotrophs contain an internal membrane system, and can be
divided into two groups on the basis of the membrane pattern.
Type I methanotrophs contain stacks of membranes throughout the cytoplasm, while the Type II strains contain peripheral membrane rings
(18). Although no formal taxonomy exists for methanotrophs, a
scheme has been suggested by Whittenbury and Dalton (18) that includes three Type I groups ("Methylococcus," "Methylobacter," and
"Methylomonas") and two Type II groups ("Methylosinus" and "Methylo-
cystis"). This division into two types is supported by several other parameters, including carbon assimilation pathway, type of resting stage, ability to fix nitrogen, predominant fatty acid chain
length, and mol percent G+C (18). One strain, Methylococcus capsulatus Bath, has characteristics of both types; it has been proposed
that this organism be termed "Type X" (18).

Methanotrophs obtain energy and reducing power by oxidizing
methane to CO_2 via a series of two-electron steps (Fig. 1). Since
the methane mono-oxygenase (MMO) is a mixed function oxidase, it
uses one mole of $NADH_2$ for each mole of methane oxidized. It is not
clear how this $NADH_2$ is provided, but it may be through reversed
electron transport, or one of several NAD-linked dehydrogenases.
Carbon is assimilated at the level of formaldehyde via one of two
unique pathways: the ribulose monophosphate pathway (Type I
strains), or the serine cycle (Type II strains) (1).

Ecological studies of methanotrophs have shown that they are
widespread in nature, and strains have been isolated from a variety
of marine, freshwater, and terrestrial environments (1). In aquatic
environments, they occur at aerobic/anaerobic interfaces, where oxygen and methane are low but detectable. No strains have yet been
isolated that are capable of growth above 55°C. Enumeration of
methanotrophs from natural samples has been difficult due to the low
plating efficiencies of many strains.

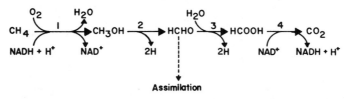

1. Methane monooxygenase   3. Formaldehyde dehydrogenase
2. Methanol dehydrogenase   4. Formate dehydrogenase

Fig. 1.   The oxidation of methane·by methanotrophs (1).

OXIDATION OF HYDROCARBONS BY METHANOTROPHS

Substrate Range

     Although obligate methanotrophs are unable to grow on multicar-
bon compounds, these organisms have been shown to oxidize a wide
variety of hydrocarbons, including straight-chain alkenes and alkanes, and substituted and nonsubstituted aromatics (Tab. 1). The
reactions that have been shown to occur include hydroxylation, epoxidation, and dehalogenation. The products vary with the organism,
and in some cases it is clear that more than one reaction has taken
place. Studies with cell-free extracts and purified MMO from M.
capsulatus Bath have suggested that although the initial attack on
these substrates is carried out by the MMO (4), further oxidations
are apparently catalyzed by other wide-specificity dehydrogenases,
such as the methanol dehydrogenase. These transformations have been
termed "co-metabolism" or "co-oxidation" because they must be supported by the presence of a C-1 substrate, which provides the necessary reducing power.

Possible Environmental Significance

     The oxidative capabilities of these organisms are impressive.
However, the test conditions summarized in Tab. 1 were far from natural, and therefore it is not known whether methanotrophs use these
abilities in nature. The cells used in the tests were resting
cells, grown under optimal conditions, washed and resuspended at
high optical densities (40-60 OD ml^{-1}). Methanotrophs are typically
sensitive to the presence of a variety of multicarbon compounds (5).
Therefore, it is not known whether these bacteria will actually grow
in the presence of hydrocarbon substrates at concentrations sufficient for oxidation. The hydrocarbon substrates were provided at
near saturation concentrations in all cases, and no data are available concerning K_m's for these substrates. However, the K_m's for
methane and ammonia are known, and are separated by over three or-
ders of magnitude [50-60 μM and 87 mM, respectively (3)]. Since the
other substrates show even less structural similarity to methane, it
seems reasonable to expect K_m's on the order of 100 mM for many of
these hydrocarbons. If this were true, methane would be a strong
inhibitor of hydrocarbon oxidation by methanotrophs by virtue of
competitive inhibition, and significant oxidation would not occur at
substrate levels of less than 1 mM.

     Given the present uncertainties of hydrocarbon oxidation by
methanotrophs, it is difficult to speculate on the role of these
bacteria in hydrocarbon degradation in the biosphere. It does seem
likely however, that significant oxidation might occur only under
conditions where low levels of C-1 compounds were continuously supplied in conjunction with relatively high levels of hydrocarbons,
and methanotrophs would probably not be expected to reduce the level

Table 1. The oxidation of compounds by whole cells of methano-
          trophs.

	Products	
Compound	Methylococcus capsulatus	Methylosinus trichosporium
Methane	Methanol	Methanol
Ethane	Ethanol	Acetaldehyde, Acetate, Acetone
Propane	Propanol	
Butane	Butanol	
Hexane	Hexan-1-ol, Hexan-2-ol	
Tetradecane	Tetradecanol	
Hexadecane		Hexadecanol
Ammonia	Nitrite	Nitrite
Ethylene	Ethylene oxide	Ethylene oxide
Propylene	Propylene oxide	Propylene oxide
But-1-ene	1,2-Epoxybutane	
Styrene	Styrene epoxide	Styrene epoxide
Pyridine		Pyridine N-oxide
1-Phenylbutane		Benzoic acid, 4-Phenyl butanoic acid
1-Phenylheptane		1-Hydroxyl-1-phenylheptane, 1-Phenylheptan-7-ol, 1-Oxo-1-phenylheptane, Cinnamic acid, Benzoic acid
m-Chlorotoluene		Benzyl alcohol, Benzyl epoxide, Methyl benzyl alcohol
m-Chlorophenol		Hydroxybenzaldehyde
m-Cresol		Hydroxybenzaldehyde
o-Cresol		5-Methyl-1,3-benzene diol
cis-But-2-ene	cis-2,3-Epoxybutane, cis-2-Buten-1-ol	2,3-Epoxybutane
trans-But-2-ene	trans-2,3-Epoxybutane trans-2-Buten-1-ol	
Butadiene		3,4-Epoxy-1-butene
Cyclohexane	Cyclohexanol	Cyclohexanol, 3-Hydroxycyclohexanone
Cyclohexanol		3-Hydroxycyclohexanone
Benzene	Phenol	Phenol
Phenol	Quinol	Catecol, Quinol
Toluene	Benzyl alcohol, Cresol	Benzoic acid, p-Cresol
Ethylbenzene		Benzoic acid, 2-Phenylethanol, p-Hydroxyethylbenzene, Phenylacetic acid
Isopropylbenzene		p-Hydroxyisopropylbenzene

[1]Adapted from (4,8).

of these compounds below mM concentrations. Certainly, methanotrophs would be involved only in the initial attack of these multicarbon compounds, and mineralization would require the participation
of other bacteria.

Process Considerations

The considerations noted above concerning the role of these
bacteria in nature are important in contemplating the possible use
of methanotrophs in the development of detoxification processes. In
addition, kinetic parameters become significant for process design.
These bacteria grow slowly, with generation times of between 6-30
hr. The rates of hydrocarbon oxidation that have been measured are
likewise relatively low (0.1-20 nmol min^{-1} mg dry weight^{-1}) (1).

Another consideration is the requirement of the MMO for reducing power. In the tests that have been carried out, addition of
formaldehyde or formate was often necessary to detect significant
oxidation, and in other cases the oxidations were apparently supported by endogenous reserves. Any long-term process using activities of the MMO would require an exogenous source of reducing power,
preferably not methane due to substrate competition.

GENETIC STUDIES OF METHANOTROPHS

From the discussion above, it should be clear that although
methanotrophs contain capabilities that are interesting from the
point of view of pollutant detoxification, more studies are necessary to determine their potential in this area. It may well be true
that the utilization of these capabilities will depend upon the genetic manipulation of these organisms. One might envision the alteration of the methanotrophic host itself to provide more favorable
characteristics, or the isolation of the genes necessary for their
oxidative functions, for transfer to more suitable hosts. Our laboratory has developed genetic systems and initiated genetic studies
in methanotrophs, with the goal of studying genetic regulation of a
variety of functions.

Difficulties of Carrying Out Genetics in Methanotrophs

Methanotrophic bacteria are not ideal candidates for genetic
manipulation. Not only do they exhibit slow growth in liquid cultures, they require 2-4 weeks to produce colonies on agar plates.
They also have limited substrate capabilities, with most growing on
no substrate other than methane.

Perhaps the most difficult problem in developing genetics of
methanotrophs concerns mutant isolation. Studies have shown that

a variety of mutagens do not increase the frequency of spontaneous
mutation in methanotrophs (7,20), and it has been postulated that
this might be due to a lack of an SOS repair system. For this reason, mutants for which no direct selection exists are extremely difficult to isolate. Since the spontaneous mutation frequency is on
the order of 10^{-8}, even with the use of enrichment procedures, millions of colonies would have to be screened to detect any mutants.
In addition, these bacteria do not transport well organic compounds
such as amino acids; therefore, it is difficult to obtain auxotrophs. Aside from drug resistant mutants, the only stable mutant
isolated in any obligate methanotroph was a leaky p-aminobenzoic
acid requiring auxotroph of Methylococcus capsulatus, which arose
spontaneously (19).

No reliable gene transfer systems have been reported for methanotrophs. A genetic transformation system was described for M.
capsulatus (19), but it required high DNA concentrations and long
contact times. Some phage have been isolated for methanotrophs
(16), but these have not been tested for transduction. It has been
shown that wide host range conjugative plasmids can be transferred
to methanotrophs (17), but it is not known whether these are capable
of mobilizing chromosomal markers.

Because of the considerations discussed above, we have taken a
recombinant DNA approach to genetic studies in methanotrophs, to by-
pass some of the problems inherent in using classical genetic techniques with these bacteria. We have started this work, first, by
assessing the plasmid content of methanotrophs, and second, by developing a gene transfer system based on recombinant DNA techniques.

Plasmids in Methanotrophs

In order to study the possibility of plasmid-encoded functions
in methanotrophs, we have screened 10 strains for plasmid DNA using
the alkaline lysis technique of Portnoy et al. (12). We were able
to detect plasmids which ranged in size from 27 to 125 megadaltons
(Mdal) in all strains except Methylococcus capsulatus Bath (Tab. 2).
Restriction digest analysis showed that the three plasmids found in
M. trichosporium OB3b were the same as those found in the other two
M. trichosporium strains. However, none of the other plasmids were
similar. This was confirmed by DNA-DNA filter hybridization analysis by the method of Southern (15). Complete homology was detected
between the plasmid DNA from the three M. trichosporium strains, and
a small region of homology was detected between the plasmids from
the Methylosinus species (M. trichosporium and M. sporium). The
function of this region is unknown, but it might reflect common replication regions or other common genes. No other homologous regions
were detected in cross-probing experiments. At present these plasmids are entirely cryptic. If they encoded C-1 specific genes, we
might have expected enough similarity to obtain more hybridization.
They do not appear to encode antibiotic resistance, since all

Table 2.   Plasmids detected in methanotrophs.

Strain	Approximate Size (Mdal)
Type I	
Methylomonas albus BG8	25.6
Methylobacter capsulatus Y	63.2
Methylomonas methanica S1	125
Type X	
Methylococcus capsulatus	none detected
Type II	
Methylosinus trichosporium OB3b	125, 107, 97
Methylosinus trichosporium OB3bH	125, 107, 97
Methylosinus trichosporium OB5b	125, 107, 97
Methylosinus sporium 5	114.4, 72.2
Methylocystis parvus OBBP	125, 107
Methylocystis POC	118, 102, 50

strains were sensitive to 9 different antibiotics tested. However, all ·of these plasmids are relatively large, with coding capacities of from 40 to 200 average-sized proteins of. about 300 amino acids; therefore, it is important to be aware of their existence in carry-ing out genetic studies of these bacteria.

Development of a Gene Transfer System

Since we are interested in cloning specific methanotrophic genes, we have concentrated on developing conjugation systems for gene transfer. We have carried out filter matings using the Inc PI cosmid cloning vector pVK100 (9) (Fig. 2) and have shown that it can be mobilized by the hybrid conjugative plasmid pRK2013 (6) into three different methanotrophs. The frequencies were high for <u>Methylomonas</u> <u>albus</u> and <u>Methylocystis</u> POC (10^{-2}), but much lower for <u>Methylosinus</u> 6 (10^{-8}). In the first two strains, the frequency would be sufficiently high to allow for direct complementation of mutants, while in the <u>Methylosinus</u> strain, the frequency is sufficient only for moving a specific hybrid plasmid into the cells. In all cases, this system will allow us to clone specific genes into pVK100 and maintain them in a variety of methanotrophs. The pVK100 cosmid is capable of carrying DNA fragments of from 15–30 kilobases in size, which will provide a gene mapping tool for complementation analysis.

We have constructed a gene library in pVK100 for the methanotroph, <u>Methylomonas</u> <u>albus</u>, by ligating a size-fractionated <u>HindIII</u> partial digest of chromosomal DNA (fraction greater than 15 kb) into the <u>HindIII</u> site of pVK100, packaging into lambda, and infecting <u>Escherichia</u> <u>coli</u> with the mixture. Pools of over 10,000 clones have been made by washing cells from individual colonies from plates. Random screens have shown a wide variety of insert sizes to be present. We now have the tools to carry out gene transfer in methanotrophs, but we must now have mutants.

<u>Mutagenesis</u>

Any genetic approach to the study of specific functions requires the isolation of mutants. This is particularly difficult in methanotrophs, as outlined earlier. We have attempted to use transposon mutagenesis to facilitate mutant isolation, but have not been successful. We have used a variety of "suicide" vehicles, plasmids that are not stably maintained in the recipient and which also carry transposons. These have included pJB4JI (2), a hybrid Inc PI-mu-Tn5 plasmid, and several Col El plasmids containing Tn5, Tn10, and Tn7. In no case in filter matings could we obtain drug-resistance over

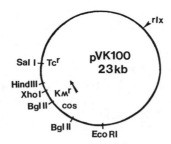

Fig. 2.   The Inc PI cloning vector, pVK100. Tc^r, tetracycline resistance; Km^r, kanamycin resistance; cos, cohesive ends of lambda; rlx, relaxation complex (required for mobilization). Arrow denotes direction of transcription from the kanamycin gene. Gene libraries were constructed at the <u>HindIII</u> site.

the background (spontaneous) frequency, suggesting that the frequency of transfer and/or the frequency of transposition were too low to detect.

We have been more successful in generating transposon mutants by a molecular construction technique. We have constructed a gene library of Methylosinus 6 (M. 6) DNA in pBR325 using HindIII-digested M. 6 chromosomal DNA. Using a heterologous probe from Klebsiella pneumoniae (13) we have isolated a 2.3 kilobase (kb) region of the Methylosinus 6 chromosome that contains a portion of the structural genes for nitrogen fixation. This fragment has been mutagenized in E. coli using a defective lambda-Tn5 phage (11), and each unique transposon insertion has been moved back into the chromosome of M. 6 by the following one-step marker exchange technique. Since the M. 6 fragment was cloned into pBR325, it is unable to replicate in M. 6 but is mobilized into this strain by pRK2013. We mated the Tn-carrying plasmids into M. 6 and selected for the transposon drug marker (Fig. 3). Each of the kanamycin-resistant clones generated in this way was shown to be unable to grow without a source of fixed nitrogen and unable to fix N_2 (reduce acetylene).

In order to assess the molecular events that occurred in the generation of the mutants, chromosomal DNA was isolated from each transposon mutant and Southern blots were probed with Tn5, pBR325, and the 2.3 kb M. 6 nif fragment. These experiments demonstrated that a variety of events had occurred, including true marker exchange (a double-crossover homologous recombination event that resulted in insertion of Tn5 into the chromosome at the same site it existed in the cloned fragment), a single crossover event that inserted the entire hybrid plasmid into the chromosome at the homologous site, and a variety of deletion events that resulted in insertion of partial plasmids. The mutants generated in this way are stable, and have been shown to be missing three nif-specific polypeptides. Our success in this approach suggests that mutants can be generated in this fashion, if a portion of the target genes can be cloned. However, since the molecular events leading to the generation of the mutants tend to be complex, each mutant must be characterized at the molecular level.

An alternative method, the two-step marker exchange (14), involves the use of two incompatible plasmids. This procedure appears to produce a majority of double-crossover events (F. Ausubel, personal communication). However, the drug markers carried by the plasmids available for this procedure are not expressed in M. 6.

SUMMARY

Methanotrophs have interesting properties concerning the oxidation and dehalogenation of both straight-chain and aromatic hydrocarbons. However, the potential of these bacteria in the degradation of these compounds cannot be assessed until more experiment

1. Donor and recipient cultures were mixed together then filtered onto a
   0.45 µm filter.

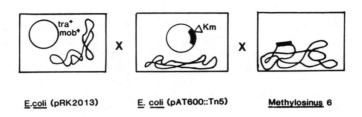

E.coli (pRK2013)   E. coli (pAT600::Tn5)   Methylosinus 6

2. Filters were placed on non–selective medium for 48 hrs to allow for the transfer
   of plasmids.

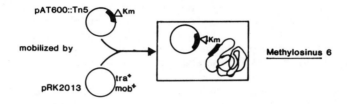

pAT600::Tn5   Methylosinus 6

mobilized by

pRK2013

3. Filters were then transfered to selective medium.

4. After 14–21 days, colonies of Methylosinus 6 appeared on top of the background
   lawn.

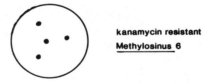

kanamycin resistant
Methylosinus 6

Fig. 3.   One step marker exchange.   tra, transfer functions; mob,
           mobilization functions; Km, kanamycin resistance; heavy
           area represents homologous M. 6 DNA.

experiments are carried out.   It seems likely that genetic capabilities will play a major role in the exploitation of these bacteria.
We have shown that it is possible to use recombinant DNA techniques
to generate mutants and transfer genes in methanotrophic bacteria.

ACKNOWLEDGEMENTS

    This work was supported by grants from the U.S. Department of
Agriculture (#5901-0410-8-0154-0) and the Department of Energy
(#DE-AM06-76RL02225).

REFERENCES

1. Anthony, C. (1982) The Biochemistry of Methylotrophs. London, Academic Press, p. 431.

2. Beringer, J.E., J.L. Beyon, A.V. Buchanan-Wollaston, and A.W.B. Johnson (1978) Transfer of the drug resistance transposon Tn5 to Rhizobium. Nature, London 276:633-634.

3. Dalton, H. (1977) Ammonia oxidation by the methane oxidizing bacterium Methylococcus capsulatus strain Bath. Arch. Microbiol. 114: 273-279.

4. Dalton, H. (1980) Transformations by methane mono-oxygenases. In Hydrocarbons in Biotechnology, D.E.F. Harrison, I.J. Higgins, and R.J. Watkinson, eds. London, Heyden, pp. 85-97.

5. Eccleston, M., and D.P. Kelly (1973) Assimilation and toxicity of some exogenous C_1 compounds, alcohols, sugars and acetate in the methane-oxidizing bacterium Methylococcus capulatus. J. Gen. Microbiol. 75:211-221.

6. Figurski, D., and D.R. Helinski (1979) Replication of an origin-containing derivative of the plasmid RK2 dependent on a plasmid function provided in trans. Proc. Natl. Acad. Sci., USA 76:1648-1652.

7. Harwood, J.H., E. Williams, and B.W. Bainbridge (1972) Mutation of the methane oxidizing bacterium, Methylococcus capsulatus. J. Appl. Bacteriol. 35:99-108.

8. Higgins, I.J., D.J. Best, R.C. Hammond, and D. Scott (1981) Methane-oxidizing microorganisms. Microbiol. Rev. 45:556-590.

9. Knauf, V.C., and E.W. Nester (1982) Wide host range cloning vectors: A cosmid clone bank of Agrobacterium Ti plasmids. Plasmid 8:45-54.

10. Lidstrom-O'Connor, M.E., G.L. Fulton, and A.E. Wopat (1983) Methylobacterium ethanolicum: A syntrophic association of two methylotrophic bacteria. J. Gen. Microbiol. Vol. 129 (in press).

11. Miller, J. (1972) Experiments in Molecular Genetics. Cold Spring Harbor Laboratories, New York, p. 466.

12. Portnoy, D.A., S.L. Moseley, and S. Falkow (1981) Characterization of plasmids and plasmid-associated determinants of Yersinia enterocolitica pathogenesis. Inf. Imm. 31:775-782.

13. Ruvkun, G.B., and F.M. Ausubel (1980) Interspecies homology of nitrogenase genes. Proc. Natl. Acad. Sci., USA 77:191-195.

14. Ruvkun, G.B., and F.M. Ausubel (1981) A general method for site-directed mutagenesis in prokaryotes. Nature, London 289:85-88.

15. Southern, E.M. (1975) Detection of specific sequences among DNA fragments separated by gel electrophoresis. J. Mol. Biol. 98:503-571.

16. Tyutikov, F.M., I.A. Bespalova, B.A. Rebentish, N.N. Aleksandrushkina, and A.S. Krivisky (1980) Bacteriophages of methanotrophic bacteria. J. Bacteriol. 144:375-381.

17. Warner, P.J., I.J. Higgins, and J.W. Drozd (1980) Conjugative transfer of antibiotic resistance to methylotrophic bacteria.

FEMS Microbiol. Lett. 7:181-185.
18. Whittenbury, R., and H. Dalton (1981) The methylotrophic bac-
    teria. In The Prokaryotes, M.P. Starr, H. Stolp, H.G. Truper,
    A. Balows, and H.G. Schlegel, eds. Springer-Verlag, New York,
    Vol. 1, pp. 894-902.
19. Williams, E., and B.W. Bainbridge (1971) Genetic transformation
    in Methylococcus capsulatus. J. Appl. Bact. 34:683-687.
20. Williams, E., M.A. Shimmin, and B.W. Bainbridge (1977) Mutation
    in the obligate methylotrophs Methylococcus capsulatus and
    Methylomonas albus. FEMS Microbiol. Lett. 2:293-296.

PANEL DISCUSSION: EMERGING INDUSTRIAL APPLICATIONS

R. B. Grubbs, Flow Laboratory
Anne Kopecky, Sybron Biochemical
N. Lawrence Ricker (moderator), Univ. of Washington
Kyosti Sarkanen, University of Washington
Stanley A. Sojka, Occidental Chemical Corporation
Burke K. Zimmerman, Cetus Corporation

G.S. OMENN: This panel was organized to allow representatives
of several firms to describe some current, practical applications of
biological methods, including genetic technologies, in control of
hazardous wastes and other pollutants. Our moderator, Dr. Ricker,
is engaged in chemical engineering approaches to wastewater problems. There is a growing relationship between our School of Engineering and the Health Sciences Schools in high-tech applications.
I trust that in the years ahead, both here and elsewhere, there will
be more substantial collaboration across academic fields between
scientists and engineers both in universities and with their counterparts in industry.

N.L. RICKER: Thank you, Gil. First, Dr. Kyosti Sarkanen, Professor of Forest Resources here at the University of Washington,
will address the development of new processes to reduce or eliminate
waste products in the paper and pulp industry.

K. SARKANEN: Based on my experience as a consultant for Crown
Zellerbach Corporation, I would like to present my personal response
to our general question: what place does the emerging biotechnology
have in waste treatment in different areas? My comments will be
directed strictly toward the pulp and paper industry.

Pulp production in the United States is in the order of sixty-
five million tons. We use about 700 pounds of paper and board products per year per capita. Chemical pulp production is dominated by
the kraft process, which uses sodium hydroxide and sodium sulfide to
remove the lignin component from wood materials and to convert it to
pulp fibers.

From one ton of wood, the recovery of fibers is about half a
ton of paper-making fibers. To my surprise, I have found that many
people think that the rest is all waste. In fact, the waste ordinarily is 5%. However, there are accidental spills, which account
for 30 to 40% of the total environmental load from kraft mills.
With improved process control, these spills should become rare.

The unavoidable effluent from a kraft mill comes from the
bleach plant. The dark fibers recovered in chemical pulping contain
4.5% lignin, which has to be removed by bleaching agents (elemental
chlorine, alkali, and chlorine dioxide). Unfortunately, heavily
chlorinated lignin fragments result. Their sodium salts are released into waterways after alkali extraction of the fiber. There
is a great deal of concern about these chlorinated lignins because
they are mutagenic and potentially carcinogenic.

There is a great opportunity for biotechnology in the treatment
of chlorination wastewaters. Quite recently, I visited a new pilot
plant in Finland. The purification process comprises: 1) an anaerobic stage, where a mixed bacteria population removes chlorine from
the aromatic rings; and 2) an aerobic stage, from which the off-gas
contains sulfur compounds. We now have one full scale processing
plant in Finland. The two-stage process is much safer than the normal activated sludge method for the bleach plant effluent.

For the future, it should be feasible to reduce the residual
lignin from 4.5% to approximately 2% of the pulp fibers, which would
eliminate the need for chlorination and alkali treatment. The technology developed first in France, based on alkali and gaseous oxygen
treatment, has been applied in many mills in Sweden, with removal of
approximately half of the residual lignin. Further delignification
can be accomplished with chlorine dioxide, avoiding the hazardous
elemental chlorine step altogether. However, the time span that
will be required in the extremely slow-moving pulp and paper industry is so long that there will be a huge need for biological purification processes for some years at least.

S.A. SOJKA: At Occidental Chemical Corporation, we are applying genetic engineering in pollution control. We are dealing with
very high concentrations of wastes of chlorinated chemical products,
for example, leachates which come from land-fills at Love Canal,
Hyde Park, and other sites. The leachate from these land-fill sites
is complex. There are many compounds. The relative percentages
fluctuate on a daily basis.

The best way that we can characterize these leachates is to
measure the total carbonaceous content. They typically run between
1,000 ppm and 8,000 ppm total organic carbon (TOC), mostly chlorinated aromatic compounds. Hyde Park land-fill site, near Niagara

Falls, was a repository of some 80,000 tons of chlorinated wastes, both solid and liquid.

Part of the mandate in our Environmental Technology Division is to look for new and innovative technologies to meet particular wastewater treatment needs. In late 1979, we asked ourselves whether biodegradation can be used to treat such complex and variable heavily chlorinated wastes. Many wastewater treatment plants in the chemical industry use biodegradation. However, the companies using biodegradation at that time were treating relatively soft wastes with low TOC loadings with very little variability.

We decided to take a chance and embark upon a biological program. The short-term goals were to test conventional types of biological treatment on these complex leachates. The long term goal was to develop microorganisms that could do a better, more finely tuned job for our particular types of wastes. This long term program depends on genetic engineering. Simultaneously, we recognized that there has to be a process technology to use these microbes; otherwise, we would be "inventing half the wheel."

We borrowed an activated sludge wastewater treatment technology from the municipal area. One virtue of this batch mode treatment is that it offers some degree of containment. If you eventually use genetically engineered organisms, you can contain them a lot better than in a typical, continuous flow, activated sludge plant. Furthermore, it combines the three primary roles of a treatment facility--reaction, clarification, and sludge reduction--in the same vessel at the same time.

We started by going to our land-fill sites and taking soil samples. We were able to culture and grow wild-type strains from various land-fills. Much to our surprise at that time, we were able to find microorganisms living in the leachate itself, even though the leachate typically has a pH of 4; there was life in the leachates. The organisms we isolated were all species of Pseudomonas. At the same time, we started up our activated sludge process. We were able to get 80% reduction of TOC merely based on a normal population of activated sludge. When we inoculated these batch reactors with the isolates from the land-fill sites, we observed enhancement in treatability: instead of 80% we got up to 90 to 95% TOC reduction. So the introduction of these bacteria into the activated sludge process was beneficial.

The bacteria came from a land-fill site. I view these land-fill sites as large chemostats. They have been around for twenty years and there has been a process of natural selection as organisms have adapted to their stressful environment. We are now in the throes of operating a pilot plant at the Niagara Falls complex. We are treating not only leachates of various composition, but also our present process water. We have experienced very little difficulty despite the changing characteristics of the feed.

We have tried to improve these wild type strains. We want to do bona fide recombinant DNA experiments on these wild type strains, and we are progressing along those lines. That is one of our long-term goals. Thus far, we have isolated plasmids from the wild type strains; we have restricted them; we are trying to do gene mapping. We are developing a gene bank, and we can attribute certain degradative capabilities towards particular chlorinated aromatic compounds to certain regions of the plasmid. The work is progressing well.

At the moment we are cloning into Escherichia coli and Pseudomonas species with the hope of getting more expression. We want to have control over the rates at which these genetically engineered bacteria will consume the waste, and we want to control the microbes' taste for these organics. We do not yet have any life forms that are better than the wild type isolates.

A. KOPECKY: Several people have used the words "if" or "when" in speculative comments about the efficacy and safety of genetically altered organisms in the field. We have representatives of three companies at this meeting--Sybron Biochemical, Polybac, and Flow Laboratories--each of which has been in the business for between 7 and 10 years of chemical waste treatment with genetically altered organisms.

In our general approach to waste spill or waste treatment sludge systems, we take samples, enrich these samples, and attempt to isolate organisms that will grow on a sole source of carbon, the compounds that need to be degraded. Then we mutagenize the organisms. The object of the mutagenesis is not to grossly alter the natural state of the organism, but to obtain "rate mutations."

Once you have the organism, you have to start thinking along the lines of the industrial application. First, does it really work? You test it on a very limited scale, either in a pilot system in the laboratory or on a limited scale in a given sewage treatment system. You seed the system with the organism, measure reduction of COD or BOD, and, if possible, identify actual reduction of the target chemical. Despite Dr. Alexander's misgivings about the survivability of introduced organisms, we have found that, by going to the source and starting there before we do the mutagenic work, consistently we come out with organisms that show fairly high resistance to metals.

Next, we must address the health and safety problem. We take organisms from the natural environment, but, in the process of altering these organisms by mutagenesis, what is the potential of creating something that might be potentially pathogenic either to

man or plant? At the time that Sybron took on this work we were a
very small group and were not going to take the chance of getting
ourselves stuck with some big lawsuits, so we carefully planned our
strategy. The organism with which the group was working in the initial stages was Pseudomonas aeruginosa. P. aeruginosa is known to
be an opportunistic pathogen. However, if one searches the literature, you find that this particular characteristic is usually associated with the production of toxin A. So the scientists and their
consultants at VPI carried out extensive testing on the amount of
toxin A produced by the series of mutants that had been isolated.

Fortunately, the levels of toxin A were less than 5% of the
levels in hospital isolates which contained the toxin A, and even
lower when compared with most sewage sample isolates. So we felt
relatively safe. At that point, a series of animal studies was set
up with independent laboratories. Some of the exposure methods were
intraperitoneal injections, eye injections, force-feeding, and direct application of the pure cultures onto abraded skin to simulate
burn situations. No significant adverse effects were shown.

Industry will go to extreme means to guarantee the safety of
products. We have got to live on this earth. We do have a responsibility to the public, and we have a responsibility for preventing
any possibilities of legal involvements from claims made against our
company.

Concerning the safety factor, some people seem to want to put
bugs into a system, watch them perpetuate ad infinitum, and continue
that function forevermore. However, we are in the business of selling bugs, so we are quite happy for them to die off!

With regard to rate mutations, I want to discuss the likely
mechanism. When we isolate an organism that shows activity against
a specified compound, we sometimes have obtained as much as a thousand-fold increase in rate, without increase in number of bacteria.
There is no way that this could be due to a chromosomal gene without
getting enhancement in growth of the bug as well. My theory is that
we have isolated one of the large plasmids coding for multiple enzymatic messages. Somehow, our mutational event has released the
plasmid from stringent control. Probably, the plasmid undergoes
rapid replication in the presence of the agent that its enzymes are
going to attack, leaving the bug with very little energy. If the
energy shift is toward making superfluous molecules of DNA relative
to the chromosome, and superfluous enzymes relative to the normal
structural and metabolic enzymes, then the energy shift drains the
organism. So as long as the organism is in the presence of the
agents on which it is working, it literally utilizes the vast majority of its energy to break down these compounds--and, in doing so,
it is weakened. Normal populations existing in a sludge pit, an
aerated lagoon, or a facultative lagoon will quickly out-compete the

organism that we inserted. From our point of view, that is good
because the organism does not persist to potentially do some harm,
and because it sells bugs.

A.L. DEMAIN: I would like to ask a question of Dr. Sojka concerning the residual 5% of substrate that is not attacked. In your
experience, what is the reason for this effect? Is it accumulation
of toxic materials which prevents further degradation? Or are the
reasons kinetic? Depending on the mechanism, might one be able to
reduce that figure down another order of magnitude or more? What is
the effect of a second addition of the inoculum?

S. SOJKA: We have looked at the compounds which remain after
our biotreatment. We view them as being biorecalcitrant, but not
necessarily as toxic. These are perchlorinated molecules of aliphatic type, rather than aromatic type. We have not been able to
biodegrade those types of molecules yet. Our biological treatment
is really a pre-treatment to carbon adsorption. We intend to remove
that residual 5% by passing the effluent through a carbon bed.

In our initial introduction of the inoculant we find that the
organism soon tends to predominate the mixed population of the culture. Therefore, we feel that there is no need for a second inoculation.

J.C. LOPER: I would like to address a point that was raised by
Dr. Sarkanen concerning the toxicity of some of these residues. Our
laboratory has been working on organics of environmental waters,
especially drinking water.

Municipal sludge, as a rule, doesn't generate much mutagenic
activity in Salmonella tests. Industrial waste and mixed indus-
trial/municipal waste typically has a very high mutagenic activity.
Characteristically, that heavy load is not reduced through processing by conventional methods, excluding activated carbon. The mutagens that are known in those systems, if one looks at available
chemical data, often add up to about 5% of the mutagenic activity.
We have not looked at any Hooker systems, as far as I am aware. Do
you monitor biological toxicity? What information do you have about
the impact on biotoxicity from your reduction to 5 to 10% residual?

S.A. SOJKA: We do, indeed, look at toxicity, but from a different point of view. We have an ongoing aquatic toxicology program
where we can, for example, screen leachates before and after
treatment to see whether the treatment has reduced the toxicity.
Through a few types of microorganisms, we use the "Microtox" assay,
which is very quick. We also look at Daphnia magna. We look at
vertebrates, the fathead minnow, for example, so we can make an assessment as to what that treatment technology has done to the toxicity of that particular waste stream. We have not looked at the

microorganism population in the sludge, and we don't know what it is
after it has done its job.

J.C. LOPER: What feeling do you have for the composition of
the material that is being released?

S.A. SOJKA: We know what the chemicals are; they basically are
perchlorinated aliphatic compounds of all types, from C-1 to C-8.

B. ZIMMERMAN: I have been invited as a representative of the
independent biotechnology industry. Perhaps a more appropriate term
would be apologist for the biotechnology industry, in that, were I
to confine my remarks to current activities addressed to pollution
control within the industry, it would be a rather short speech. So
I would like to expand the scope of my remarks to include what the
industry is capable of doing, and what it should be doing.

Degradation of pollutants that already exist in the environment
and degradation of pollutants at the site where they are created or
held prior to release into the environment are two very important
applications of microbiology, including recombinant DNA methods.
There seems to be an underlying assumption that we are going to keep
on with the same old polluting and dirty technologies, and continue
to have to deal with the same molecular garbage that these
industries create. Some of us in the biotechnology industry
question that assumption.

First of all, are there alternative processes or technologies
by which we can create the same products, such as metals and paper
and fuel, but do it in a way that uses less energy and does not create the air, water, and environmental pollutants that the present
technologies do? That is a tall order, but the tremendous capabilities of our technology are likely to yield a "yes" answer for some
or many of these products.

For example, we have heard from Dr. Chakrabarty about the possible use of genetically engineered microbes in the treatment of petroleum, perhaps useful for oil refining. It is possible to solu-
bilize and remove sulfur. Given the prospects for molecular engineering to make lipid soluble enzymes, we should be able to do a
great deal more with biological catalysts in the refining process.

Of course, there are certain intrinsic limitations. In processes that require putting energy into the synthesis of a compound,
nature couples almost all of these enzymes with an energy source
such as NAD or ATP. To develop an industrial process that requires
the generation or the addition of NAD might be prohibitively expensive.

Nevertheless, there are certainly many applications where this
approach is going to be quite productive. Biological fuels such as
ethanol and methane have already been produced. The economics of

petroleum now provide little incentive for providing most of our fuel this way, but there may well come a day when the situation is different.

Another area is the refining of metals. There are bacterial strains that will preferentially accumulate or separate hafnium and zirconium, elements that are important in the semi-conductor industry. At present, it takes a lot of energy and rather complicated processing to separate these materials. It is possible that nature has already solved some of these problems, and with a little help from nature's friends in the biotechnology industry, it could solve a number of additional problems. The food processing industry is already seeing a number of applications from biotechnology, as is wood processing.

What about creating new products, such as biological pesticides? There certainly is interest in the biotechnology industry. Major agricultural chemical producers have invested in some projects to develop biological species-specific pesticides. Dr. Hood described immunotoxins that can deliver any molecule one chooses to any particular cell type. This might be an ideal way to construct a species-specific pesticide. If different species of insects have species-specific antigens on their cell surfaces and if a toxin molecule or the active part of a toxin molecule can be coupled to a monoclonal antibody, we may one day see a whole new class of pesticides that attack only selected target species and nothing else; it should not pollute the environment. There will likely have to be significant molecular refinements based on this principle, especially to ensure delivery of the molecule to the right place within the insect or the plant. This approach could, however, revolutionize the agricultural chemical industry in perhaps a decade or less.

There is some interest in pest-resistant plants, to eliminate the need for pesticides on crops. There are a few naturally occurring genes which, if they were to be introduced into the leaves of important crop plants, could make the leaves unpalatable to the principal insect predators. This is another area which deserves investigation.

Agricultural pollution results from overuse or extensive use of fertilizers in many cases. This is not the typical organic chemical type of pollution. Increased salt concentration in arid soils makes soils incapable of supporting crops. Other difficulties result from overuse of nitrogen. Genetic engineering of soil bacteria and enrichment culture selection of strains of rhizobium or of bacteria that produce plant growth-stimulating substances may be able to increase the productivity of agricultural soils intrinsically, or at least without resorting to extensive chemical applications. To produce the chemicals requires a polluting industry and a lot of energy. It is a chain that goes back through the whole system. Even moderate reductions in the amount of fertilizer needed would have a substantial beneficial effect on the environment.

When you add to current biotechnology techniques the growing interest in molecular engineering, that is, the design of proteins for a particular function and purpose, the possibilities are really endless. There is still much basic research to be done before we will know precisely what polypeptide sequence we have to make for a particular application. But, as we learn more about the folding of proteins and the structural requirements for certain biological and biochemical properties, we should be able to design new products by computer. Then the rest would be a matter of known techniques in polynucleotide synthesis and gene splicing.

Where do we stand in terms of what is really going on in the industry? The fact is that there is really very little incentive within the independent biotechnology companies to explore most of the applications that I have discussed. There is more interest in designing new technologies, but there is almost no interest in dealing with current pollution. There is very little economic incentive for the companies to use their own resources. Most of them are struggling for their identity, their character, and their survival. It is necessary to pick a few targets from which the managers believe the return will be the greatest in the shortest amount of time. The business strategies are debatable, and you will find many different models throughout the industry, but none of them that I know gives a very high priority to pollution control.

The major corporations are not particularly interested in investing in the innovative biotechnology companies to address problems in pollution control. It is not in their interest to do so. The pollution control laws simply do not exert enough pressure on major corporations to stimulate investment in better technologies to control pollution.

There are many of us in the biotechnology industry who would like to work on some of these problems, but there is a scarcity of funds to enable significant exploration of this area. The potential will be realized, but at the present rate, it will take a long time, not to develop the technology itself, but for the incentive to come about for the necessary investment in the development of processes and products which are directly applicable to the alleviation of pollution problems.

R.B. GRUBBS: Instead of talking about what we might be able to do, I would like to talk about what is being done in the area of environmental applications. I will give you a broad overview of what is routine. I will concentrate principally on field work, not on laboratory studies which may or may not some day have commercial reality. Bioaugmentation is already useful in detoxifying many noxious wastes, and it is quite beneficial in alleviating many of the problems associated with traditional wastewater treatment.

As Dr. Zimmerman indicated, everyone wants a clean environment, but there are no incentives to really refine the technology. As long as existing treatments are considered satisfactory, we use them and do not seek better technology.

We have made real progress. We don't have rivers burning anymore; there is fishing again in Lake Erie. Yet, it is not unusual for a publicly owned treatment facility to fail to comply with its design or to face problems of sludge disposal, excessive energy requirements, high maintenance costs, and tricky operational procedures.

Those charged with resolving the problems customarily use only mechanical or chemical solutions. They have known the problems for years and have been able to get by. We have learned, however, that there are many biological techniques that provide additional tools. For example, take sludge disposal. Sludge is mostly water that is either physically or chemically bound to the organic matter that has not been totally biodegraded, and some inorganic matter. If you can improve the organic removal and remove the concomitant bound water, you get rather substantial reductions in the volume of sludge.

At the 1982 Purdue Industrial Waste Conference, Chambers reported the results of a milk packaging facility where significant sludge reductions were achieved by bioaugmentation, the addition of specific mixed cultures. One system employing an oxidation ditch adapted bacterial supplementation to enhance BOD removals. The sludge volume reductions were simply a side benefit. After the program had improved BOD removal, they went off the program to make sure that it was the bioaugmentation that was actually doing the job. Such was the case, as the solid yield per thousand pounds of BOD applied went from 320 pounds during bioaugmentation to 450 afterwards. These results can be described in two ways: as 130 lbs divided by 320, preventing a 40.6% increase in sludge; or 130 divided by 450, a 28.9% decrease in sludge. Either way this a significant decrease in sludge volumes.

The Lincoln Water Pollution Control facility in California, which handles some 1.6 million gallons per day, achieved a 17% reduction in sludge. They went from an average of 128,000 gallons per month to approximately 105,000. Industrial Waste magazine also reported that the Hoover Bearings Facility has obtained denser, more compact sludge from bioaugmentation. Not only can one get rid of the lower sludge bogs, but also organisms can be selected that do not give off the offensive odors. That makes the residual sludge easier to manage and less of a problem to dispose.

Another problem that can be addressed is energy requirements. There have been many reports of the successful use of cultures to control and increase flow in lines. Engineering News Record, for example, last fall reported that New York City has successfully used mixed cultures for treating more than one hundred different sites. Using augers was costing $1,700 per site per year for cleanout; with the bacterial method it cost only $600. If there are fewer restrictions in the pipe, the pumps don't have to work as hard. Cleanouts are very energy intensive, with heavy equipment required.

Energy savings within plants can also be substantial. The Tennessee Valley Authority last year reported that they had conducted studies in both the laboratory and in the field at one of their Columbia, Tennessee facilities, testing mixed bacterial supplements in aerobic digesters. They found that when they went to the large plant, they were able to reduce the energy in the aerobic digester by 75-80%. The bacteria program cost them $3,000 a year, saving $12,000.

Other energy considerations include more efficient anaerobic digester operations. The city of Arvada, Colorado was able to triple production of methane within 60 days of adopting a program. A program in California increased methane production from 6.5 cubic feet to 18.8 cubic feet per pound of volatile solids. This is not too surprising, because methanogenic bacteria do not work directly on the sludge, but rather work on the metabolites of the other organisms that are in the digester.

At the 1982 Water Pollution Control Federation convention in St. Louis, Gosh and Henry of the Institute of Gas Technology, and Feede of the Texas Gas Transmission Company reported that a bacterial additive increased both the methane yields and the gas production rates with a mesophilic anaerobic digester. Under conditions of extreme stress, the methane yield was 50% higher when the digester was being supplemented with specific mixed cultures. There was better reduction of volatile solids and thereby less accumulation of volatile acids.

There have been reports of lowered oxygen requirements. Supplements can be formulated that include facultative anaerobes that will derive their hydrogen ion acceptors from other than dissolved oxygen (DO), so they can go both ways, with lower dissolved oxygen requirements than from obligate aerobes.

Reduction of odors through the control of hydrogen sulfide emissions is widely reported in the literature. It is simple to use cultures that do not give off hydrogen sulfide. Improvements in BOD, COD removals have been widely reported also. Last year Huff and Muchmore reported in the Water Pollution Control Federation Journal that significant improvements in COD removals of a fatty amine production site waste stream could be achieved through the use of specific cultures. The year prior to the bacterial supplementation program had a 68% removal efficiency across their biooxidation system. The first 9 months of 1978, before adopting the bacterial additive program the COD rate had decreased to 63%; they were feeding more chemical "goodies" into the plant.

A 3 month trial program was undertaken in September of 1978. During the trial the COD rates increased to 80%, so they went from

63% up to 80% for the 3 months that the program was under way. They
discontinued the additions and the plant went back to a 50% removal
rate. When they resumed the additions it went back up to a 79%
rate, and they have stayed on the additions since that time.

Similarly, Chambers reported case histories of increasing BOD
rates from an average 87% to 98% removals, and from 91% removal
rates to 98% ± 1%. In addition to improved organica reductions, the
use of bioaugmentation gives more uniform and consistent results.
Industrial Waste magazine showed this to be dramatically true at the
Hoover Bearing facility. During the mild winter months of 1976-77,
weekly BOD effluent values varied quite widely between 2 and
43 mg/l. That is the kind of thing that makes the waste treatment
plant operator wake up in the middle of the night screaming. The
bioaugmentation program was adopted in August of 1978; one of the
most severe winters in Michigan occurred that year, yet the effluent
discharges stayed within the narrower range of 12-20 mg/l. That is
a more consistent result, and an important benefit.

One of the most promising areas is for the pretreatment of sewage in the lines themselves, instead of having a sewage collection
line that acts only as the collector in the working treatment plant.
Through bioaugmentation programs, pretreatment can be carried out
within the lines so that the sewage is prepared for the plant itself. The original work was done in 1972 by the Tahoe City Public
Utility District. They made some other modifications in the sewer
so that it was not quite clear whether it was the bioaugmentation
alone or the other modifications that enabled their regular facility
to perform better.

The following year Lynden Farms, which is a division of Western
Farmers, ran tests in an effort to lower their surcharges. They
were discharging through primary facilities to the sewer system of
the city of Napa, Idaho. While on the bacterial supplementation
program at the Lynden Farm facility, the city's facilities were being monitored. It was found that the BOD being discharged from the
aeration basin of the city was running an average of 50% lower when
Lynden Farms was treating, than during the period when they were
not. Unfortunately, the program was discontinued, even after it was
successful, because the city would give no relief on the surcharges
that were being applied.

The commercial use of bacterial formulations in dealing with
petroleum waste dates back many years. In 1968 when the vessel
Queen Mary was dry-docked to be converted to a museum, oily waters
within the bilges created a serious fire hazard in proximity to the
acetylene torches necessary to cut out some 8,000 tons of machinery.
A commercial bacterial formulation was used, and within 48 hours the
Long Beach fire department was willing to approve the use of torches
to convert the Queen Mary into a museum as planned. Within six
weeks the water within the bilges was so purified that it could be
discharged into the harbor.

In 1969 a series of programs was undertaken at various sites
along the oil fields reaching from Ventura to Santa Maria to clean
up the open field sumps. In one project by the Home State Production Company, 55,566 gallons of hydrocarbon mass were reported to
have been removed in a 62 day period by bioaugmentation. In another
project with Getty Oil that had 3,700 gallons of a heavily tarred
crude, approximately 2,000 gallons were digested and the remainder
was converted to a low viscosity, pumpable crude that could be run
back through the refinery.

With hazardous wastes, uses are being found. Here it is a little more difficult to give case histories with names. Most of the
firms will not allow you to do that. They do not choose to air
their problems in public, and you can understand why, with the risk
of adverse publicity. A classic example is where bioaugmentation
was used to clean up a sump of last resort at one of the major re-
fineries. They had reached the point where "their sump runneth
over." And they were not quite sure what to do with it. My own
firm had had some successful programs at other locations with this
firm. They were able at least to get the sump converted to something of low enough viscosity that it could be pumped and subsequently land-farmed at an approved site. Before that, it was literally too thick to pump, too thin to shovel.

One of the more interesting cases was with the Clearwater,
Florida Gas Division. They had some 610,000 gallons of coal tar
that was left over from the old days of manufacturing producer's
gas. There was a very significant reduction to 80,000 gallons after
8 months. The hydrocarbon remaining was evaluated and found to be
characteristic of a #2 road tar of economic value. More importantly, what remained would no longer be classified as a hazardous
waste. COD of the original tar was 3,800,000 mg per kilogram. This
declined to 1,100,000 after 4 months. The flash point originally
was 85°C. The final flash point exceeded 100°C. Phenol levels
within the bottom tar were originally 1,660 mg/l; after 4 months
this was brought down to 125 mg/l. Two months later the phenol
level of the bottom tar was less than 0.02 mg/l. Oil and grease in
the bottom tar was originally 286,900 mg/l; this was brought down to
5,788 mg/l in 6 months. The cost savings for disposal were very
significant. At a conservative disposal cost of a dollar per gallon, several hundreds of thousands of dollars had been saved. More
importantly, on-site detoxification has defused future ramifications
as well as the inherent dangers in transporting any hazardous waste
from one site to another.

In a similar project in 1978, residues from a pilot coal conversion facility had been collected in ponds and thus posed significant disposal problems. Three ponds were involved. BODs initially were in the order of the 300-495 mg/l, and these were brought
down to the 4 to 8 range. Phenol levels, which were 28-33 mg/l,
were reduced to the .057-.094 mg/l range.

At an aircraft refurbishing plant, treatment of the waste
waters posed major problems. Bioaugmentation in conjunction with
engineering modifications enabled phenol levels to be brought down
from the 700 mg/l level to 1.2 mg/l, when they were detectable.

At one of the Superfund projects, reduction of phenols was
needed. Initial phenol content of the composites from 4 quadrants
of the dump site was 516 mg/l. Within 40 days this was brought down
to 262 mg/l, when winter set in. After warm weather resumed, phenol
content was checked again and found to be below 100 mg/l, indicating
that biodegradation was taking place even during the cold winter
months. This included not only straight chemical phenol, but also
various substituted phenols, including nitrochloro- and alkyl-
phenols.

At another hazardous dump site, one of the emergency response
firms employed bioaugmentation to treat an ethylene glycol situation. Within 5 days, levels of 690 mg/l were being detoxified to
nondetectable levels.

This is just a sample of what can be done. As the poster presentation from Sybron illustrates, that firm has been involved in
similar activities. Polybac has been involved in bringing formaldehyde down from 1,400 ppm to 1 ppm. So there are efforts in progress, but more needs to be done. Conferences such as this one,
where people can be made aware of problems and solutions, are extremely helpful.

M. WATERS: Since you have had this experience, have you encountered any occupational difficulties? And do you use a common
mutagenesis of the microorganisms in the procedure that you use?

R.B. GRUBBS: The case histories that I cited used selected
cultures, and there was no mutagenicity involvement. We've been in
this business since 1962. I know of no health problem that has ever
arisen in that period of time.

M. ALEXANDER: I don't think in 1983 we need to point out that
microorganisms are useful in the control of chemical pollution.
That technology, admittedly at a very primitive stage, was introduced at least a hundred years ago. I think the question is whether
modern technologies, specifically genetic engineering, would be more
useful.

I would like to address a question to Dr. Zimmerman. There
are, of course, major economic problems that prevent some companies
from becoming involved in these technologies. But the heavy chemical industry is strongly committed to pollution control for various
reasons. What opportunities do you see here, not to prevent

pollution, which is what you were addressing, but to control pollution after the pollutant has been created?

B.K. ZIMMERMAN: I think there are a great many opportunities for applying genetic engineering to improve many of the processes discussed here. The difficulty now is finding funding to develop those specific applications. Enrichment cultures and strain improvements have been carried out for 10 years at Cetus for a variety of purposes. Now most of those activities have been cut way back. I would say that, with a few exceptions, most of that work is going to have to be funded by large companies which have a direct interest in controlling pollution.

D. OWINGS: I would like to take a slight exception to your comments. At the present time, Genex is funding its own research in the direct application of enzymes--very often enzymes from genetically engineered sources--with specific applications in various elements of pollution. They are designed for use specifically in the control of slimes in various places and to aid dewatering of sludges. We have started studies in digesters and plant and waste activated sludges using enzymes, some of them from genetically engineered sources, to achieve the same sorts of improvements. We have discussed partnership arrangements with water service companies, and we are developing these products. They are also testing in their labs. These companies would provide the means for commercialization, selling them as service chemicals. So there is some effort by the independent biological firms to bring this sort of activity to commercialization in a very short time frame.

B.K. ZIMMERMAN: My only comment is that as a fraction of the total industrial portfolio, pollution control is a very small element, and perhaps Genex has a major part of that which exists.

N. FRANKEL: Dr. Sojka, how do you implement your research? Are you doing it in house? Did you hire a staff from molecular biology? Or are you funding university studies?

S.A. SOJKA: We have a small in-house staff with expertise in the civil engineering aspects of biological processes. But the genetic engineering efforts are done on the outside at a research institution, and we have contracts at several universities, as well.

N. FRANKEL: Could you state how much this is costing you?

S.A. SOJKA: Since January, 1980, we have spent in the neighborhood of $5 million in our biological program.

M. LEVIN: In terms of cost per ton, can you estimate how much you have saved, or the difference between the method you would have used versus this method?

S.A. SOJKA: We haven't realized any benefits from this program
yet. But we are projecting benefits, because at present we are re-
lying on carbon adsorption as being our best available technology
for treating the wastewaters, and we are spending at the rate of
about $10 million a year on carbon absorption throughout the entire
corporation. So this is an economic incentive for us, to try to
save some money by the alternate technology of biological degradation. The research incentive for us is to lengthen the time that a
carbon bed has to be changed, for example, and that results in a
savings on carbon. We were able to sell this program to management
on a cost reduction basis.

O. ZABORSKY: Dr. Grubbs, could you give us a perspective about
what is happening in other countries in terms of industrial activity? Are your bugs being employed by other people, including industrial concerns in other countries? Is the activity that we are
talking about devoted solely to the U.S., or are other countries
taking note of their waste, using bioaugmentation, or encouraging
programs to get more into genetically engineered bugs?

R.B. GRUBBS: All of the above! Our firm, as are other firms,
is involved in the sale of these products in other countries. A
fair amount of sales is in Europe and in Japan. Japan has been surprisingly slow, although I understand that there is a considerable
interest being shown right now, because Japan has so much emphasis
on microbes for other purposes. It has surprised me that they have
not been quicker in accepting bioaugmentation. But there are active
programs in Europe and in the Asian countries. Many less developed
countries represent some tremendous, untapped potential because they
do not have the economic resources for the construction of some of
the more complicated, larger facilities. Any improvements that less
developed countries can get for better organic removals, control of
malodors, and related needs would be extremely beneficial and cost
effective for them.

A.M. CHAKRABARTY: There is presently some preliminary work being done to establish an international center for genetic engineering and biotechnology to be devoted particularly to the needs of developing countries. The final decision, we hope, will be made in
Madrid in September. Of the proposed work program, pollution control is certainly one of the possibilities.

Many of the items to be addressed are those for which there is
no commercial interest in the developed countries. For example, the
technologies are needed for the development of vaccines for tropical
diseases, foods appropriate to those countries, and control of environmental pollution in areas where pesticides have been misused or
overused and where there are serious contamination problems. These
are all very important areas. This proposed center would be one way

in which such problems could be addressed, with participation of
commercial industry.

A. KOPECKY: We do have worldwide distribution of new technologies. But, in the United States we measure the sewage treatment facilities in a major industry in days' and sometimes weeks' retention
time, whereas in Japan, we are looking at measurements in hourly retention time. Their method of clarifying industrial waste at this
time is mostly by polymer precipitation. The longest retention time
in the sewage treatment plant with which we dealt was eight hours.
We could not handle it in that time, even with super-bugs.

M. ALEXANDER: Might I ask of the several industrial representatives here what specific, rather than general, needs do you think
could be answered by academic researchers in the field of engineering, genetics, ecology, microbiology? Are there specific things
which would help your own programs in the introduction of new- or
even old-fashioned technologies that are modified for current problems?

A. KOPECKY: There is a situation that we have come across that
is very interesting, and that is lignin pollution from kraft mills.
I have personally visited several kraft mills, and these represent
the biggest mess you have ever seen in your life. There are very
good fungi available that will completely degrade the pigments involved in this particular system. The fungus grows at a very low
pH, and the activity of the enzyme is also at a very low pH of about
4 or 5. But if you want to use a fungus, there is no sewage treatment operator who is likely to let you put a fungus in his system.
If researchers could isolate the enzymes and the genes that were
involved in that degradation, and be able to insert them effectively
into bacteria, it would be the greatest gift to the paper industry
other than changing their entire process. The thing that we, as
industry, can contribute to the situation is that we have developed
an extremely inexpensive, mass production method of a long shelf-
life product. Put another way, we are always looking for patents to
buy if they are really good. We have the manufacturing, and that is
the secret of success in mass sales.

We also have the expertise. All three of the groups represented
on this panel have the expertise in the engineering and utilization
of bugs in the field. It is difficult to try to deal directly with
sewage treatment operators who do not comprehend the advantages of
bioaugmentation. We have overcome the communication gap and developed a link, so that the manufacture, sale, and utilization by aug-
mentation of bugs can be implemented by existing industries.

R.B. GRUBBS: One of the real problems facing the environmental
field continues to be cold weather performance. In fact, in many
areas it is just accepted to pollute during the winter, because

there is nothing you can do about it. One of the real problems is
getting the proper settlability of the biomass. All of the thick
textbooks of environmental engineering can be distilled down to one
sentence: Make it sink or make it float. If it does not do either
of those two things, you are in deep trouble. In the wintertime,
many are in deep trouble because they cannot get good settling from
their aeration basins and their secondary clarifiers. This would be
an area of tremendous interest if organisms could be developed to
give excellent settlability while performing in cold weather.

A. KOPECKY: They exist.

R.B. GRUBBS: I know, but there is room for improvement.
Sludge reduction, for example, is a real problem. You solve most of
the other problems, then you contribute to the sludge volumes. It
is like the old saying, "haul it away." We still want to pretend we
can do that kind of thing: don't tell us where, just move it, don't
put it near me. So, we must reduce sludge volumes. We have made
some progress, but many of the solutions face the same limitations
as with the cold weather.

S.A. SOJKA: I think one of the fruitful areas of research
would be looking at reactor design. Basically, we have tanks or
vats. I think there is a lot of room for improving processes by
changing the vat design. I know, for example, in Germany there is a
lot of use of anaerobic digesters that look like an egg-shaped reactor. There is a considerable benefit derived from that simple
change of a reactor design. A lot of it has to do with energy savings in mixing, but there is also an improvement in efficient methane production. We have a long way to go in terms of reactor design. I think anaerobes provide a nice way to get rid of heavily
chlorinated compounds by reductive pathways. The concerns of low
temperature and floc filamentous organisms are real. I think it
would be nice to look at the isomer effects on biodegradation. What
happens if you have a complex organic molecule with various isomers?
Is there a selectivity for those organisms to degrade certain isomers of a specific compound? That would give us molecular information on the destruction of that particular compound.

R.B. GRUBBS: I think all of us could make a very valuable contribution to education. The people who, for so long, had the responsibility for cleaning up the environment knew very little about
microbiology. It is a real dichotomy that the largest user of microbial processes in the world is wastewater treatment, but all the
plants have been designed by people who had little or no understanding of microbiology.

The average member of the public thinks of a wastewater treatment facility something like a "soup" condensation plant or as being
something where sludge is nothing more than instant sewage; "just

add water and stir." That is part of the psychological problems we have. Somehow the public has to be made aware that much can be done to make this planet better. All we are presently doing with waste treatment is what nature is doing. We are just doing it in shorter periods of time and in smaller areas of space. We can inform people this whole world is not falling apart, that we can clean things, and that we have the means available through microbiology.

R. COLWELL: I cannot resist replying, because I find that one of the most difficult problems I have ever faced was trying to get plant operators and municipality officials to understand that micro-biological water purification or sewage treatment is not performed with a few test tube racks. For some reason plant operators are al-ways willing to spend $150,000 for atomic absorption apparatuses and various other kinds of chemical analysis units, but very unwilling to spend the proper money for an autoclave, incubators, and proper microbiological indices measurements.

I volunteered some years ago to do an analysis of all the available data on the Potomac River for the Potomac Basin Commission to report on whether we had improved or regressed in water quality. It was amazing to find out that for several years, over a certain stretch of the river, the NPN counts were precisely the same. I have not since been able to get precisely the same NPNs, although our measurements are very careful. Whoever made the earlier study must have reported what he thought it should be.

Microbiology is very complicated. Somehow it has to be under-stood that, if we are going to genetically engineer these processes, we have got to have the kinds of people and the kinds of expertise that is capable of doing the job.

Let us completely rethink how we handle wastes. Let us forget whether we have tanks and chambers. Let us look at what can be done with a problem such as a great bulk of material that needs to be re-duced to a form that can be safely discharged, if that in fact is one way of doing it, or perhaps completely recycling it. What are the processes that could be applied? Some may be terribly expensive right now, but in a decade they might be relatively cheap. I would like to see some very creative thought put into these problems, rather than just figuring out how to tinker and improve what already exists.

ROUNDTABLE DISCUSSION: DIRECTIONS FOR THE FUTURE

        Martin Alexander, Cornell University
        Rita R. Colwell, University of Maryland
        R. B. Grubbs, Flow Laboratory
        Richard McGinity, Plant Resources Venture Fund
        Robert O. Mendelsohn, University of Washington
        Gilbert S. Omenn (Moderator), University of Washington
        Gordon H. Orians, University of Washington

G.S. OMENN: Developments in genetics and other biological sciences that are highly relevant to the pollution control problem in the long term have come at an astonishing and accelerating pace in the past few years. I doubt that there have been many meetings of microbial ecologists or environmental engineers with as many genetic maps and DNA sequences as we are now seeing. I am confident that future meetings will be even more inclusive of such material, as the power of genetic techniques becomes better recognized. The interactions reflected in this meeting among investigators from different disciplines should lead to cooperative efforts to design bioreactors, to plan changes in wastewater treatment facilities and other kinds of equipment, and, as Rita Colwell urged, to consider new ways of dealing with well-known problems.

I think that the pollution control problem is a tremendous challenge. I was surprised to hear our engineering colleagues state that current techniques are adequate. With at least 16,000 dumps and many other kinds of wastes in our society yet to be managed, we are identifying more pollution of greater diversity. Many of the disposal and encapsulation methods we use at present for persistent chemicals are anything but permanent. Innovative approaches, including biodegradation to less hazardous intermediates or all the way to simple compounds, should be highly valued if they become feasible and affordable approaches.

The recommendations from earlier speakers of some especially promising targets of opportunity warrant emphasis. These include specific well-contained settings and waste streams at the source of

production, the beginning of the effluent trail. One of the most
interesting open field challenges is the very large concentration of
2,4,5-T on certain Air Force bases, as mentioned by Dr. Chakrabarty.
There should be an excellent opportunity for collaborative, open
planning involving the Department of Defense (DOD) and the Air
Force, the Environmental Protection Agency (EPA), and state and
local officials. The organism which has been developed to digest
2,4,5-T could be readily tested at such sites.

With regard to regulation, I have had some experience with regulations as a government official and also as a scientist. I was
surprised to hear several individuals call for regulations from the
EPA that would anticipate future developments in this area, somehow
facilitate them. There is no question that industry and most others
in our society would prefer less uncertainty in planning, especially
in planning long-term development activities and important invest-
ments. I believe industry has experience in these areas which could
be extremely valuable in guiding current deliberations by EPA, and
by state agencies. There is, of course, authority under the Toxic
Substances Control Act (TSCA), Resource Conservation and Recovery
Act, the Clean Water Act, and other statutes to regulate new chemicals, new uses of chemicals, and--according to Anne Hollander of EPA
--chemicals manipulated within organisms. We should emphasize that
EPA has at its disposal a variety of alternative approaches, not
just formal regulations. There is a communication gap of considerable importance in the regulatory domain. Regulators need to realize that their administrative processes and notices of proposed
rulemaking trigger the perception among affected parties that some
fixed rule has been decided upon. I know that Federal Register notices are often intended to stimulate fairly open consideration of
new options, but even I become anxious trying to read Federal Register notices--and trying to read between the lines!

EPA has a good opportunity to cooperate with other federal
agencies and with scientists from all sectors to identify promising
and safe applications of genetically altered organisms. A precedent
for this approach is the work of the Recombinant DNA Advisory Committee in biomedical and agricultural areas, where stepwise development has proved extremely successful, with reassurance about con-
ceivable risks. Advances have been made in developing targets of
opportunity with approved lists of certain kinds of hosts and vectors, and expansion of those lists with increased knowledge.
Advances have come also from defining risk assessment protocols to
address specific scenarios of what might happen with specific hosts
and vectors in a particular environment. That model is made to
order for the admittedly more complicated ecological settings in
which some of these tests might be carried out. The most complicated settings should be dealt with only later, while concentrating
first on point sources, contained dumps, and situations in which a
dump or other facility will be treated by encapsulation or

excavation. At essentially negligible marginal cost, it would be
possible to monitor what happens in experimental manipulations
before the excavated or encapsulated sites are closed off or
disposed of.

We have a broad-based panel covering aspects of economics, the
industrial and commercial side of ecology and microbiology, and risk
assessment. We will start with Robert Mendelsohn, a member of the
University of Washington economics faculty and an innovative environmental economist.

R. MENDELSOHN: I feel like one of the laboratory animals that
was suddenly released into the environment, coming down here from
the economics department. I am a "microeconomist," but I want to
address macro issues in your field from an overall perspective. The
initial insult to the environment is the release of the pollutants.
Then follows dispersion as the pollutant moves through the environment. Various sensitive populations that are exposed to the pollutant have a response to that exposure. Finally, there is a need to
evaluate how serious the responses are in terms of human values.

Pollution control aims to affect this schedule of events so
that final damages are reduced. The reduction of final damages is
the benefit of pollution control. Obviously, the costs of pollution
control are those of the resources utilized to accomplish the control.

Thus far, we have discussed a number of biological procedures
to effect pollution control. They focus primarily on two targets:
controlling the actual emission, mostly by detoxification and controlled environments at the source; and manipulating the dispersion
in the atmosphere, in bodies of water, or in soils.

One of the advantages of a macro perspective is that other possible uses of genetic adaptations become evident. For example, in
the case of heavy metals, possibly we should look for microorganisms
which, rather than resisting heavy metals, actually accumulate them
and die, making it easier to extract the heavy metals from the waste
product. One traditional problem is that the metals get into a food
chain and tend to concentrate there. One possible way to mitigate
this effect is to substitute at certain key links in the food chain
a new organism which does not concentrate the pollutant, so that the
chemical does not move farther along the food chain.

Another approach is to take advantage of the dose/response relationship, looking for new strains of organisms which are no longer
sensitive to the pollutants in the environment. If the full array
of exposed living organisms were more resistant to the pollutants,
the necessity to control the pollutants would be lowered.

   Earlier, Dr. Chakrabarty asked, "If I develop these good
techniques, that clearly do what they are supposed to do in the lab,
why haven't they been adopted?" There are essentially two answers.
One of the problems is that they might not be scientifically effective in the environment. The total effect on the strain, and therefore the total benefits from using the technique, may not warrant
the cost that you would have to spend to engage in the technique.

   Another answer that arises even for techniques which are technically and economically desirable is that existing regulations may
not create the proper incentive to use them. The problem is that
certain kinds of regulations tend not to take advantage of all the
possible ways to control pollution. For example, if a regulation is
oriented toward controlling the insult, perhaps requiring that no
more than one pound of a particular effluent leave the site, then
any technique which is designed to affect any of the later steps is
ruled out as a useful technique. Anything designed to affect dispersion, exposure, or dose response would be useless if the regulation were oriented solely at the emission level. Some kinds of regulations automatically defeat the usefulness of certain techniques.

   Another way that the regulations might inadvertently disqualify
otherwise attractive techniques is that they might just be a little
bit below the level that the technique can be useful. For example,
if the regulation for an emissions control procedure were set so
that the permissible concentration of pollution were just below what
the biological technique could accomplish, then that technique would
be eliminated entirely as a stand-alone pollution control. Perhaps
if the permissible levels were raised slightly, the biological technique could be more effective than any single procedure.

   The final problem to consider is that the benefit/cost analysis, the total impact of these procedures, is not really a very simple analysis. It often involves a lot of complex phenomena. One
good example of how complex the actual cost/benefit analysis might
be is right here in our own Lake Washington. We had a lot of population growth here in the areas around Seattle. The more rural communities dumped their human wastes into Lake Washington. The lake
responded beautifully and started processing them very effectively.
It got rid of a lot of the organic waste. But in the process the
microorganisms grew at very rapid rates, creating conditions that
people found unattractive. One couldn't see very far into the
water, and in the winter the organisms would die and create a bad
odor, especially bothering the people who had bought expensive homes
along the lake. So Seattle launched what has become one of the most
successful water pollution control programs in the country. The
natural system, which was working quite well, was replaced with a
$100 million system which pipes wastes over great distances and
finally processes them with more traditional techniques. Although
the biological system was working fine, society deemed it

undesirable, and spent huge sums of money to replace it. It is not
enough to say that an organism digests certain compounds. There
could be side effects and by-products that nullify the benefits.

G.S. OMENN: Dr. Alexander, in this session it would be especially useful if we could ask you to tell us where you think this
field will be in 5 or 10 years.

M. ALEXANDER: Well, that I won't say! Let me tell you instead
what I think are the needs in the area. The first need I see--and
several people have expressed it in different ways--is, frankly,
dollars. Dollars for _relevant_ research. We can get support, I
think, for basic microbial ecology, and obviously there is a lot of
money in basic molecular genetics. For applied work in this area,
there is very little.

Second, we need to devise meaningful tests to assess effects.
We need to measure whether a particular organism will or will not
affect a particular ecosystem, or particular populations in an ecosystem, without waiting until the ecosystems are deleteriously
affected. We don't want to have a series of guidelines or regulations which seriously deter the research and the economic exploitation of the research. Nevertheless, we have to have meaningful
tests of effects on natural populations, natural communities, and
functions of ecosystems.

Third, we need to know the major chemicals of current concern.
Of EPA's priority water pollutants, we have mentioned only a few and
most of the people who mentioned them did not know that they were on
the priority pollutant list. We have a reasonably long list of
pesticides, many of which are not problems, but some of which are
very severe problems. The TSCA chemical list presently has 55,000
candidates. These should be prime targets of our research.

With regard to the choice of microorganisms, I believe that molecular genetics and genetic engineering need to be developed with
appropriate organisms. Without _Escherichia coli_, we would be no
place in microbial genetics. But _E. coli_ does not inherit the
earth! There are ecological restraints on _E. coli_. We have to look
at microbes which are oligotrophic species, or floc-forming organisms, or species which adhere to surfaces.

Which are the important environments to look at? One can't
study all of the natural ecosystems, and some are much more prone to
having the introduction of microorganisms lead to success. Probably
the managed pollution control system is the best environment. Industries are putting money into this activity, and I think the systems can be modified from the engineering viewpoint, from the microbiological viewpoint, or both.

Finally, in terms of practice, we need to emphasize conventional microbiology and conventional environmental engineering. They
have worked, and probably can be made to work better. We can then
say: Where do these technologies fail? Where will they likely
fail? Such questions will lead us to a series of problems, such as
chemicals at very low concentration or compounds which are apparently co-metabolized in nature, for which we cannot develop a good
treatment system at present. Here is where genetic engineering
should be stressed, but the focus should come from looking in
nature, not just by looking in our scientific journals.

R. COLWELL: Let me first point out where I think some of the
excitement is. I think it's a great time to be a microbial ecologist. First of all we are getting a little--shall I say?--respect,
which we haven't had for decades. We have some tremendous tools.
We have got the computer, data processing, and microcosms and macro-
cosms for study, including our ocean sites. We have the ability to
assemble and reduce tremendous amounts of data for some of the
underlying principles and equations.

Second, we have had fabulous developments in the industry in
fermenters and control mechanisms for large chemostats.

Third, we have this marvelous, new, exciting opportunity to
apply genetic engineering in microbial ecology and ecological processes.

I think where we will need to have a lot of emphasis is on
those organisms that really drive the environment--not E. coli.
When I come to a meeting and hear about the genetics of Beggiatoa
and the physiological processes of vibrio species, Moraxella, and a
few acinetobacter species, then I will know we have really come a
long way. All we have been talking about are what I guess Dr.
Alexander calls "the weeds." In any case, there are few organisms
for which we have a lot of genetic and metabolic information. We
will, I hope, spend a lot of time in the next few years understanding activities of microorganisms under in situ conditions. I would
put less attention on the roster of toxic chemicals. I would probably start with chemostats--though that is neither the only nor the
best way to understand the processes in the environment. We need to
develop systems where we use low temperatures and high pressures if
we are going to simulate environments where we will work in the deep
sea. Some exciting discoveries are coming from the vents and other
undersea areas in terms of salinity, dissolved oxygen, and low concentration of nutrients. We microecologists, along with the engineers and the geneticists, should be developing ways to understand
how these processes function in the natural system, and which organisms carry out the work.

Furthermore, the environment is not uniform. The natural environment is a series of microenvironments. Even in the chemostat, one has microorganisms that are attached to the wall and those that are single cells in the liquid medium. In the natural environment you have surfaces of the animals. In fact, in the deep sea much activity takes place in the gut wall of the deep sea scavenging animal, not in the water column or the sediment. This needs to be understood. We may find new approaches for dealing with some of the problems of waste treatment.

We also should turn ourselves around and look at the waste treatment plant, not as a way of getting rid of things, but as a neat factory, as a source of trace metals that may be of strategic need and value--titanium, vanadium, cobalt, chromium--and possibly down the road, steroids, other metabolic products, and certainly, methane. I understand that a sewage plant blew up in Pennsylvania a year ago, a demonstration that there was an uncontrolled source of fuel that might have been piped out to heat a few homes. In any case, there is the capability of developing an energy source. If we look at it as a processing plant for materials, we might have a whole new perspective.

When we deal with microorganisms that we think we have to add to the environment, such as in an oil spill or a toxic chemical spill, we really have to make it site specific. If you have an oil spill in the Sargasso Sea, it isn't going to do you any good to inoculate organisms that you have developed that have come from, say, soil in Omaha, Nebraska. One must have organisms that function in a Sargasso sea, which has a low temperature, very low nutrient concentration, and high salinity. Or if you are going to deal with an oil spill in Tierra del Fuego, which I had the fun of doing some years ago, you have a really difficult problem, because the ambient temperature, when it is real hot, may be 15 or 16°C, and when it is real cold, is 2 or 3°C. The oil spilled several years ago is still there. If you are going to engineer a mechanism for cleanup there, it is going to have to work at very low temperatures.

What I think microbial ecology will come to, first, is that we will probably build a "synthetic cow." That is, we will take a cow and the organisms in each step of the process of chewing on the hay to whatever comes out the other end in terms of milk, find out what the mixture was that carries out these reactions of cultures, and then be able to understand the processes. I think we will find that there are some exciting products and processes that will come from controlled mixtures of organisms--the co-metabolism that has been mentioned. I suspect that we will have then biologically effective and commercially and economically viable processes for producing compounds that we simply don't dream about at all right now. For example, I understand that palytoxin, which is an enormously complex molecule with nonrepeating subunits, is produced by a bacterium that grows in association with an invertebrate marine animal. How the bacterium puts this all together is a fascinating question. If it is a mixture of products from a single bacterium or a mixture of bacteria, then we may be able to simulate it in a factory.

Finally, I disagree that we have a whole lot of money for basic microbial ecology. It is all well and good to have many of the immediate applications and potential applications of technology in hand, driven by regulatory mechanisms and other kinds of economic incentives. But we have always got to allow room for the introspective thinking and creativity that may provide us with processes that are just curiosities right now but may be an entire new industry in a decade.

G. ORIANS: I must remind you that I am speaking as a vertebrate ecologist. When people talk about floc-forming organisms, I tend to think of a rather different subject! As one who believes that there are risks associated with the development and expansion of technologies, I feel it is incumbent upon us to embark on a program that will at least make some serious effort to minimize the risks while maximizing the benefits that can be had from these technologies.

I would like to make a few comments from my perspective about how one might try conceptually to organize some of the problems and tasks we want to accomplish in an ecological context. That might provide some guidance to the selection of organisms and the kind of experiments that might be performed, both to assess the performance and success of organisms and to minimize the risks that they might pose.

My first suggestion is a way of looking at the target substrates. Materials to be degraded would be classified into two broad categories. One would be the evolutionarily new molecules that did not exist on earth until we started making them. The reason that there is nobody around to detoxify or degrade them is that there has never been a selective advantage in dealing with them before. Many of these molecules, I understand, are not intrinsically difficult to break down in terms of the energy of the bondings. They are simply different from what the organism's machinery deals with. Therefore, engineered organisms are likely to be able to work, ecologically, much more simply on these chemicals than on the second category of molecules. We need to ask: Are we dealing with a new molecule, does it have an intrinsic structure that would make it energetically very expensive to deal with, is the cost/benefit ratio of the organism going to be unfavorable, or is it going to be easy to deal with once we get the right machinery?

The other group of substrates will be the evolutionarily old molecules. We are trying to deal with them in different ways.

Organisms have great difficulty dealing with some of these old molecules. There are very few organisms that degrade lignins and celluloses, and most complicated organisms cannot do it at all without
some help from little ones.

You ask, why do we have forests? In other words, why is it
possible to accumulate these large molecules over decades and cen-
turies in ecosystems? It is not because there has not been a long
evolutionary opportunity for somebody to eat those things. It is
obviously an ecological economics problem, that celluloses are not
basically worth it to most organisms, that you do not get enough out
of dealing with the molecule to make it pay to produce the substances to break it down. You end up in a negative energy balance,
and so the systems operate rather differently. Hence, if we are
trying to devise systems to deal with evolutionarily old molecules,
we are much more likely to require supplements of some sort in the
system to enable the organism to work. The reason that the organisms don't work now is that it is not profitable. We just simply
cannot get the right enzyme and throw it into the environment and
expect it to work. We are going to have to think, why has this not
been a profitable way of making a living out there in the past?
What sort of supplement do we have to provide to the organism to
make it go?

We use just such an approach all the time with domestication.
We selected cows that produced enormous quantities of milk with
respect to any wild cow; however, we have to provide some subsidies.
We know that when you are going to build a cow that is a milk producing machine, you had better also be able to do some other things
for it, because it is not going to manage in certain kinds of environments. For example, they have to be protected against predators,
because they don't run very well. I think some of the same problems
will exist for engineered microorganisms. It may be useful to think
about them and to try to anticipate what the supplements are that
will be needed to make these organisms successful.

The second sort of conceptualization of the problem that I'd
like to deal with, briefly, is to think about the ecological traits
of organisms that would be well-suited to different sorts of situations. For example, in many areas we would like an organism that is
not going to be terribly starvation resistant, so that it is going
to do a job and is going to disappear for us, because that will minimize the risk of having it stay around. There have been particular
spills where you would like to be able to introduce something to reduce concentrations of pollutants, then hope it will die out. If you
have to deal with recurrence, you would be prepared to introduce the
organisms again. We would like to safeguard against unwanted persistence and fear of unexpected effects by building in a destruct
component of the system to be used in those cases where we want to
clean up a particular spill, then have the organisms go away.

There are other environments, such as treatment plants, where it is desirable to have organisms that do persist, because we are going to expose them to the insult repeatedly. The system should be designed accordingly. We may wish to devise organisms that can break down some of the substances but that do not require theses substances as the major energy source. They will obtain their energy needs on something else and therefore will persist even in the absence of the substrate to be degraded. We might wish to build in organisms that have particular scavenging abilities for particular kinds of molecules.

Many sites where we can anticipate repeated exposures are ones, it seems to me, where it should be possible to experiment with low risk, because we can contain the system. We are not going to be dumping organisms out into an open environment and hoping for the best. These will be particular effluent streams out of point sources and in situations where one ought to be able to impose substantial barriers to the escape of the organisms downstream. One can use these effluent streams to test some of our notions about the effectivness of the organisms.

Even in situations where we introduce new organisms into the open environment, it may be possible to take advantage of the natural complex structure of soils, or to induce structures into the system that will tend to impede movement, and we can test how effective those are. We now have a variety of microcosms that have been developed to move from the situation of the very simple laboratory environments of the molecular geneticist to complicated systems without going outside. We ought to make very effective use of these to test the ecological performance of organisms in systems that get somewhat closer to the field sites, without prematurely exposing the environment to unwanted risks. There are some laboratory quasi-field sites such as the ecosystem chambers of the EPA lab in Narragansett, Rhode Island. EPA has constructed a number of model stream channels, where you can simulate movement of water, put a lot of complicated mixtures in, and see how organisms perform. If the organisms turn out to perform in ways you don't want, you have figured it out before they got into a real stream. We should take advantage of these "half-way stations" that can move part way toward the complexities of nature, in which one hopes eventually some of these organisms will be useful, but do so without exposing an environment to risks while we find out how the organisms are going to perform.

R. McGINITY: I appreciate the invitation to offer a few thoughts. There are two reasons why I am here. One is to educate myself to some extent on what is current in biological engineering. The second is to see if there might be situations or products or companies in some phase of evolution that might need financing in order to accelerate progress to a market of some kind.

As far as absorbing some education, I think that was achieved. This conference was very broadening, very enlightening.

However, as far as identifying some opportunities for investment, I am not so sure. That certainly was not the purpose of the meeting, and rightly so. If I would offer a critique, or perhaps propose an item for a subsequent conference, it would be some more attention to strategies for commercializing some of the developments that have been discussed. The potential in the work that is going on and what can be done is amazing. The developments that could flow from this work could easily rival microcircuitry or membrane technology. It would be interesting--perhaps by a case study approach--to show how you actually take the work that is done in the laboratory and package it in such a way so that it is quickly relevant to a group of potential users, not only in dollars and cents, but also in terms of problems solved.

R.B. GRUBBS: I think that what we are really doing is getting to know the organisms better so that we know how to handle them, so that they can do what we want them to do rather than what the organisms will choose, left to their own devices.

I agree with other members of the panel. We need to go beyond thinking in terms of ridding the planet of Frankensteins. Going beyond the scavengers, we can get into biosynthesis, where we are actually converting things to economic value. Then you won't have the problem of sewage treatment plants getting the monies they need to operate properly. An example is the conversion of a hazardous waste into a road tar. That is probably the crudest example, but it shows what can be done. It is going to require some hard work as we learn to be better "microbial psychologists."

G.S. OMENN: Many thanks to all of you for these stimulating remarks. Let us now welcome general comments and questions.

D. VOLK: I would hate to see investigators be involved in the development of systems to attack certain hazardous wastes which, although they are on the list of priority pollutants and on the regulations of state governments as hazardous toxic wastes, do not represent nearly the type of problem or the magnitude of problem that other types of seemingly innocuous pollutants present. For instance, Mr. Grubbs spoke about reducing sludge volumes. In Pennsylvania, probably the largest and stickiest problem we have had over a long time is dealing with disposal or utilization of sewage sludge. If we had less sludge to deal with, it would certainly help our situation, because the main problem is public acceptance. If the volumes were reduced by 20%, I think our problems would be reduced by 50%.

G.S. OMENN: I want to address an undercurrent of unease in
some of these discussions. It was suggested that we need more support for applied research, even at the expense of basic research
support, and it was implied that laboratory scientists should be
challenged to do things for which they have neither interest nor
preparation. Fortunately, this is a diverse and talented society.
We need specialists, and we need people who pursue their own leads
both in basic and applied work. We also need a few people who
understand the linkages and try to make bridges across these difficult problem areas that involve issues far beyond the science.

Scientists have a special role in devising, doing, and evaluating experiments. Regulators, and society in general, expect us to
do so honestly, openly, ingeniously, and effectively. In the areas
that have to do with human health effects and ecological effects, it
is very important that we develop well-defined means of monitoring
and measuring effects. It is important that we share with those who
are interested enough to learn how we do it, how much we know, how
much we don't know, and what we might learn with further effort. We
also can participate, if we wish, as ordinary citizens, in the decision processes necessary for society to make use of certain available technologies.

M. LEVIN: Basically, I think that a strategy to minimize risks
to the public has to be developed through the governmental systems.
Universities may take the lead on research and getting research
funding. And industry may be best at strategies to avoid
governmental regulation!

M. ALEXANDER: One of the problems with toxic wastes—in fact,
all our environmental wastes—is that the group that produces the
waste is not the group that suffers the cost, and the group that
suffers the cost often has no way of communicating just how much it
is affected and how much it would like the other group to stop.
There is a problem with the market economy when it comes to this
kind of contaminant. The only way such a containment will be controlled is by government intervention. However, the government
agency is not always correct, and hopefully, a public forum can make
the system work better. It is important to make sure that government regulations do, in fact, encourage these good techniques that
were not foreseen a year or two ago, and that regulations not seriously deter these new technologies.

G.S. OMENN: In the state of Virginia there is an Environmental
Endowment which was set up with the settlement from the kepone incident and to which there have been a few additions since by court order. The Endowment supports community activities, an environmental
law journal, and a certain amount of field research. There are many
such non-governmental mechanisms which might be developed.

The Federal Government has a mechanism for communication with the broad scientific community in developing agency programs. Several federal agencies have a practice of announcing an "RFA"--not a request for a contract proposal (RFP), but a request for applications (RFA)--indicating an <u>area</u> in which they would like to see some innovative developments. Proposals are solicited around a problem, without designing in advance what the solutions ought to be. Certain parameters, in this case safety, efficiency, and inter-disciplinary and intersectoral cooperation, may be specified. I believe that there are quite a few ways that this area could be stimulated, and that the important criterion of protecting the public health can be maintained front and center.

One small reflection of what can be done is this conference itself. Five different federal agencies, four companies, the University, and Dr. Hollaender's Council for Research Planning in Biological Sciences helped us sponsor this conference.

T. POWLEDGE: I would like to ask Dr. Mendelsohn why you say that only regulation is going to provide incentives. It seems to me that liability and the possibility of lawsuits is a very powerful incentive.

R. MENDELSOHN: That is a good point. If you can prove liability in a court, that often is sufficient incentive for the victim to communicate with the polluter. The problem, of course, is that the courts require strict proof. And strict proof means that you not only have to prove that your damages were directly related to the pollution that you suffered, but that that pollution that you suffered has come from a particular plant. You have to sue only that plant. It turns out that the data generally do not satisfy criteria for strict proof.

D. OWINGS: I want to make some observations. I sense some frustration, particularly among those who are engaged in genetic engineering. We have tools coming along; how are we going to apply them? At Genex, we must decide what projects we fund for internal project development. We try to judge what's going to happen, and then we start eliminating. One of the forms of elimination is, obviously, a concern about regulatory control. For example, when we started working on applications of biotechnology and genetic engineering to waste treatment, we immediately discarded any concept of using an organism to be released into the wild, in part because of the concern about possible governmental controls.

You've got to see a target market big enough that makes it worth the investment. There are some very interesting pollutants. But even at a buck a gallon, which may be the high priced disposal cost of a very bad pollutant, it is going to be a very small volume. Very seldom is it going to be big enough to pay off. The big volume is where there is a lot of sludge being moved about. As noted earlier, if we can cut the water content of the sludge that comes out of Philadelphia by 10%, which is very feasible technically, we are going to save some environmental problems and cut transport costs.

When we do a study project, it costs us, by my calculations, something like $150 a day . The next stage is in the lab, and that is going to cost us $500 a day. If that is going well, we move to the pilot plant, at $2,000 a day. And, if that is going well, we go into commercial production, which at this point in time is costing us $40,000 a day. Study is relatively inexpensive and is what this conference is really about. If we can get the study started--if we get the cases out and discussed--we can then talk about firms to exploit this. If you have a good idea--if you can really degrade something that has a big enough market, it is going to be exploited. Right now we are dealing mostly with concepts.

A.M. CHAKRABARTY: The other side of the coin, of course, is that there are problems which may not be big markets, but which are real problems. I am referring to what happened in Love Canal or Times Beach, and I am sure these two will not be the only ones. In a Congressional hearing, Congressman Gore responded that he agreed with me, and raised the possibility of setting up some specialized cases where guidelines would be relaxed or be applied flexibly.

We haven't really talked about what form of guidelines, if any, should be agreed on that would permit the application of all the genetically or otherwise engineered bacteria for pollution cleanup. Who should be entrusted with the enforcement of the guidelines, and how would one go about applying to the appropriate agency for approval? Also, should there be an upper limit on liability?

G. ORIANS: I would like to pick up Mendelsohn's earlier comment (see Panel Discussion: Comparison of Traditional and Genetic Strategies) about the Agencies des Basins in France, because what is reflected there is a very different philosophy and public policy. There you pay for the privilege of polluting, so to speak. In the United States we have regarded it as bad to pollute; no one has a right to pollute, no matter how much they pay for it. Our regulatory approach not only provides no incentive for the kind of approaches we are suggesting should be developed, but also generates no funds from special taxes that could support the research. As a person who has spent quite a few years on science advisory panels for EPA, it seems to me that some creative use of different regulatory devices could have an enormous influence on incentives and activities.

R. COLWELL: Our colleague from Genex provided an extremely good categorization of roles to be played in this large drama. The high risk creative research that has no immediate payoff should be supported by the National Science Foundation. The ready-to-be-applied research, where you cost out the applications, certainly is the role of industry. In the middle is quasi-industrial research that benefits from a bit of a push in the university research and a bit of a pull by the industry.

M. ALEXANDER: I can not see genetic engineering coming up with a sludgease, or a flocase, or a hog-manurease in the future. These problems need more effort from conventional environmental engineering and microbiologists. There aren not going to be any Nobel Prizes for reducing the quantity of sludge. However, in other areas, as noted, genetic engineering really is promising.

R. McGINITY: On the subject of delivery systems, a model that might be worth considering is the land grant college system. You may not like the hard tomatoes, but the land grant college system is largely responsible for the level of agricultural productivity in the country today.

G.S. OMENN: For those of you who are interested, there was a convocation on "Genetic Engineering of Plants," held on May 23-24, 1983 at the National Academy of Sciences, as part of this ongoing series of conferences about genetic engineering applications. There was substantial participation and discussion of the role of the land grant system and, of course, many other institutions, as well.

P. TAYLOR: I am a former employee of a disposal facility for hazardous wastes. From an industrial standpoint, sticking it in a hole is a much cheaper way of handling hazardous wastes than recycling or reclamation, unless you have a very large volume. That is where the sludges come in. The current technology is filter pressing. If you can come up with a microorganism that can take wastewater in its preliminary stages and turn it into a nonhazardous waste, industry will probably buy that system. The filter press reduces volume by about 20%, yielding a thick cake that is still hazardous under the regulations.

A number of disposal facilities have tried land farming with microorganisms, but have found that it seems to be cheaper just to stick it in a hole. If you can get the price of the microorganism down, I am sure you will be able to sell that technology.

F. TAUB: I am an optimist about the possibility of paying for some of our cleanup operations by producing something that has a high market value.

Sludge is such a bad problem because nobody wants it. Nobody knows how to solve the virus problems, because you cannot afford to heat it to kill the viruses. Nobody seems to want the heavy metals, although they precipitate very readily as sulfides. People do know

how to concentrate the heavy metals, but the methods are not economically feasible.

If you can engineer a bug that will destroy the dioxin contaminant, a lot of the 2,4,5-T that is now stockpiled and that people
are trying to figure out some way to burn would have a market. If
you could figure out a way to economically collect gold and silver
from wastewater, that would help pay for the process of cleaning the
streams.

N. FRANCO: What about research limited partnerships? Are they
salable for something as risky as this, or does it have to be something with a closer payback?

R. McGINITY: They are available, but let the entrepreneur beware and let the buyer, the investor, beware also. It is a potential device, but there are potential pitfalls because the legislation is still pretty new. Also, the partnership will typically
retain some residual rights in whatever technology is developed
which could become a subject of future dispute. Venture capitalists
are much more interested in financing production and energetic marketing of a product that is already developed and for which there is
at least a reasonably clear prospect of a market, than in financing
research.

N. FRANCO: I'd like to make a comment from the demand side of
this market. I'm from the steel industry and we don't go out and
buy something if we don't have to. If you have to drive a nail into
a board, you have to get a hammer, if it's available. What is really happening is that the wood is getting more costly and the hammer
is no good anymore, so we are looking for alternatives.

Earlier in this conference, incineration was mentioned for organic wastes. With the more complex organic wastes, the easiest
thing is to burn them. One of the best and most efficient inciner-
ators is a cement kiln. My company, Bethlehem Steel, is located in
the Lehigh Valley, the "cement belt." I had the brilliant idea of
approaching the cement companies to sell them our coal tar wastes
for incineration. The paint industry earlier sold waste solvents to
a cement company. The state Department of Environmental Resources
allowed the company to run a test burn, which was very successful,
and was approved by the state. Unfortunately, they didn't go
through a public comment procedure and the people who lived in the
town were up in arms about it and have blocked any further incineration. The cement kiln is very efficient as a high temperature incinerator. If you have chlorinated hydrocarbons, you can install a
HCl scrubber with no problem and achieve 99.99% combustion by the
very nature of the process. However, no cement company in the Valley is going to be allowed to burn wastes. The townspeople are preventing it on a technicality that the company has no permit to store

the waste. They have a permit to burn it, but they have none to transport or store it.

Thus, as we see it, the treatment of hazardous organics is going to have to be done on site, and by some new technologies.

T. STODDARD: I want to comment on the reality of some of the problems. In the state of Missouri, there are potentially about 100 different dioxin sites, perhaps 500,000 cubic yards of contaminated soil. The most recent figures I have for incineration are somewhere between $500-$600 per ton for incineration to achieve 99.999% removal of the contaminant dioxin. This excludes the actual movement of the soils to an incinerator facility which could perhaps double that cost. If you are looking at cost, here is economic incentive to encourage basic research and the development of organisms capable of use at very low level concentrations of substrate, or perhaps some other types of genetic manipulation. If you look at the total number of dioxin sites in the country and the availability of treatment technologies, we are looking at hundreds of millions of dollars to clean up our present sites.

G.S. OMENN: Let me thank the panel, every participant, and the dedicated staff for the Conference. This has been a most enjoyable and instructive three days. One of the phrases used in this conference was "enrichment culture." In a way, that term can describe the larger culture in which we operate. We've learned about engineers who are mostly into biologics, and we have learned that the chemists who are genetic engineers would like to make some bridges into these difficult problems. We have tremendously fertile material to share with others and to apply to research in the years ahead.

WASTEWATER TREATMENT WITH BACTERIA ATTACHED TO FIBERS

Robert Clyde

Chemical Engineer
P. O. Box 983
Asheville, North Carolina   28802

Pseudomonas sp. can degrade toluene and several chlorinated compounds. Use of genetic engineering should increase the efficiency of these reactions. It has been found that a dog in Switzerland was able to metabolize 2,3,7,8 dioxin. Most rotary biological contactors are made of plastic, but fibers have much more area. Patent 4,351,905 tells how to attach bacteria to fibers, and a patent soon to be issued explains how to rotate the fibers and get a much faster reaction.

Metals such as uranium, chromium, vanadium, silver, and palladium can also be removed from wastewater with Pseudomonas attached to fibers. Others have used fungi, but bacteria are easier to grow and more amenable to genetic mutation. By increasing the metallothionein or other characteristics, the efficiency can probably be increased further.

Thiobacillus ferrooxidans attached to fibers in a rotary biological contactor can oxidize Fe^2 and make acid mine water in West Virginia easier to neutralize.

In central Florida, 75,000 acres of lakes are used in attempts to settle clay from phosphate mining. Zymomonas mobilis attached to fibers will speed the settling, and this bacterium also converts sugar to alcohol faster than yeast. D. Eveleigh at Rutgers University is using recombinant DNA to enlarge the area of substrate utilization for Zymomonas, which results in less pollution than yeast.

DISSIMILATION OF AROMATIC COMPOUNDS BY RHODOTORULA GRAMINIS

Clyde McNamee, Richard Wattam, Jeannette Flickinger,
David Stewart, and Don R. Durham

Genex Corporation
16020 Industrial Drive
Gaithersburg, Maryland 20877

The yeast Rhodotorula graminis utilizes benzoate, D,L-mandelate, phenylalanine, and salicylate as sole sources of carbon and energy. Pathways for phenylalanine and mandelate catabolism converge at benzoate; growth of R. graminis on phenylalanine, mandelate, and benzoate elicits the synthesis of benzoate-4-hydroxylase, p-hydroxybenzoate-3-hydroxylase, and protocatechuate-3,4-dioxygenase; these enzymes were not detected in crude extracts prepared from salicylate-grown cells. Mutants deficient in either p-hydroxybenzoate-3-hydroxylase or protocatechuate-3,4-dioxygenase were unable to utilize benzoate, phenylalanine, or mandelate; salicylate, however, did support growth. Revertants obtained from either class of mutants resulted in wild-type growth on benzoate, phenylalanine, and mandelate.

These results provide physiological and genetic evidence that mandelate and phenylalanine are metabolized through benzoate to protocatechuate and the β-ketoadipate pathway, whereas salicylate is metabolized by an alternate pathway. Growth of R. graminis on salicylate results in the induction of a soluble, NADPH-dependent salicylate hydroxylase, catechol-1,2-dioxygenase, and muconate lactonizing enzyme. Thus, the available evidence suggests that the metabolism of aromatic compounds by R. graminis appears to be different than those described for the yeasts R. mucilaginosa [Cook and Cain (1974) J. Gen. Microbiol. 85:37] and Trichosporon [Anderson and Dagley (1980) J. Bacteriol. 141-534] in that R. graminis contains ring cleavage enzymes for protocatechuate and catechol and therefore possesses both branches of the β-ketoadipate pathway.

MEMBRANE-ASSOCIATED BENZOATE-4-HYDROXYLASE

FROM RHODOTORULA GRAMINIS

Clyde McNamee and Don R. Durham

Genex Corporation
16020 Industrial Drive
Gaithersburg, Maryland 20877

Growth of the yeast Rhodotorula graminis on benzoate results in the induction of benzoate hydroxylase, p-hydroxybenzoate-3-hydroxylase, protocatechuate-3,4-dioxygenase, and enzymes of the β-ketoadipate pathway. Following subcellular fractionation of crude extracts of benzoate-grown cells, benzoate hydroxylase activity was observed in the particulate (membrane) fraction. Thus, washed membrane preparations, which are devoid of other benzoate-dissimilatory enzymes, were used as a source of partially purified benzoate hydroxylase for further study.

p-Hydroxybenzoate was demonstrated in vitro as the catalysis product of benzoate as determined by high pressure liquid chromatography and thin layer chromatography of reaction mixtures. Benzoate-4-hydroxylase activity was hyperbolic as a function of enzyme concentration (washed membranes) and time, and exhibited a pH optima of 7.6. The enzyme, which apparently does not require divalent cations for activity, utilizes NAD(P)H as a source of reducing equivalents; other potential sources (e.g., tetrahydropterin, tetrahydrofolate, dihydrofolate, dihydroxyfumarate, ascorbate, reduced flavins) were inactive. The Km_s for benzoate and NADPH were calculated as 2.3×10^{-5}M and 2.9×10^{-5}M, respectively.

The particulate nature of benzoate-4-hydroxylase, together with the fact that the enzyme is not pteridinedependent indicates that it is distinct from the isofunctional enzyme described in fungi. Furthermore, to our knowledge, this is the first in vitro demonstration of benzoate-4-hydroxylase activity in yeast.

371

BIODECONTAMINATION OF A FULL-SCALE FORMALDEHYDE SPILL

Layne M. Johnson and Jeffrey M. Thomas

Polybac Corporation
954 Macron Boulevard
Allentown, Pennsylvania   18103

A 21,000 gallon volume of a 50% formaldehyde solution contained in a railroad tank car was inadvertantly spilled over a stone railbed ballast. From this point, the solution flowed into a storm run-off ditch and threatened the water supply of a nearby community. Initially, the spillage was contained, vacuum-pumped, and removed for disposal. Further treatment of the site was accomplished by means of biodecontamination. The formaldehyde solution was sprayed over the ballast and this leachate was allowed to flow into a sealed drainage ditch.

The liquid contents of the ditch were then pumped into a 500 barrel bioreactor. The solution contained in the bioreactor was aerated and a commercial product (HYDROBAC[R] Mutant Bacterial Hydrocarbon Degrader) containing specially adapted and mutated microorganisms was added. Commercial emulsifiers and nitrogen sources were also added to the bioreactor and the mixture was continuously pumped over the ballast, into the ditch and then into the bioreactor for a period of 21 days. The concentration of formaldehyde was reduced from 1400 mg per liter to less than 1 mg per liter within 14 days.

An alternate method to biodecontamination would have been physical removal and placement in a landfill. Such treatment would have dictated that the railbed and the railroad tracks be removed, thereby disrupting rail service. The cost of biodecontamination was approximately 10% of the cost of alternative treatment.

EVOLUTION OF NEW DEGRADATIVE FUNCTIONS FOR HALOGENATED AROMATICS

John J. Kilbane and A. M. Chakrabarty

Dept. of Microbiology
University of Illinois at Chicago
835 South Wolcott
Chicago, Illinois 60612

The Pseudomonas putida plasmid pAC25 specifies an inducible 3-chlorobenzoic acid degradation pathway. 3-iodobenzoic acid is a poor substrate and fails to induce the enzymes of this pathway, even though 3-fluorobenzoic acid and 3-bromobenzoic acid can both serve as inducers and are good substrates. Through chemostatic selection we have isolated a derivative of pAC25 with altered regulation and substrate specificity such that 3-iodobenzoic acid can now serve as a sole carbon and energy source.

The Pseudomonas putida strain RB1 specifies an inducible aniline degradative pathway. Chemostatic selection allowed the isolation of an RB1 derivative that can grow on 3-chloroaniline as its sole source of carbon and energy. The aniline degradative function of RB1 has been cloned on a cosmid vector and has been demonstrated to contain or is adjacent to the cat B gene of P. putida. The 3-chlorobenzoic acid degradative plasmid pAC25 contains a cat B complementing activity that shows no appreciable homology either with the P. putida chromosome nor with the cat B$^+$ aniline$^+$ clone derived from RB1.

BIOLOGICAL DEGRADATION OF POLYCHLORINATED

BIPHENYLS BY MUTANT ORGANISMS

Anne Kopecky

Sybron Biochemical
P. O. Box 808
Salem, Virginia 24153

Arochlor 1260 is one of the most highly chlorinated polychlorinated biphenyls (PCB) known, containing isomers of 5 through 9 chloride groups. Thirty-eight percent and 41% contain 6 and 7 chloride groups, respectively. It is generally considered to be nonbiodegradable.

Researchers at Sybron Biochemical have isolated and mutated a group of organisms that show a high rate of degradative activity toward the Arochlor 1260. Activated sludge containing 100 ppm to 400 ppm of PCBs showed a reduction of undetectable levels using these cultures.

Laboratory experiments were set up to ascertain a quantitative breakdown. Shake tubes were set up containing dilute gross media plus PCBs in buffered salt media. After two weeks the samples were acidified, extracted, and assayed by gas chromotography. Quantitative breakdown is illustrated in a table and by a gas graph tracings.

Ongoing experiments are being run to determine stoichiometric breakdown to carbon dioxide using uniformly labeled C_{14} Arochlor 1254.

Summary: Arochlor 1260 is biodegradable with BI-CHEM 1006 PB. Reduction has been shown in both activated sludge and laboratory tests. Soil treatment methods are presently being developed.

GENE ENGINEERING OF YEAST FOR THE DEGRADATION OF HAZARDOUS WASTES

John C. Loper, Jerry B. Lingrel, Vernon
F. Kalb, and Thomas R. Sutter

Departments of Microbiology
Molecular Genetics and Environmental Health
College of Medicine
University of Cincinnati
Cincinnati, Ohio 45267

We have installed a program to develop cytochrome P-450 systems
in Sacchromyces cerevisiae for the degradation of organic wastes.
Emphasis will be upon polychlorinated aromatic hydrocarbons having
no adjacent carbon atoms free of substitution, including hexachloro-
benzene (HCB), polychlorinated biphenyls, and 2,3,7,8-tetrachlorodi-
benzo-p-dioxin, TCDD. These toxic compounds are persistent in the
environment and are potent inducers of P-450 systems in animal
cells. Both HCB and TCDD can be metabolized by P-450 enzymes to
yield less toxic products. The long range goal is to transfer these
metabolic capacities from animal cells via genetic engineering into
yeast. These yeasts will then be tested for use in polluted mixtures.

Our first goal is to obtain any P-450 gene and study its expression in yeast. For this we have a) demonstrated that in S.
cerevisiae D7 the property for conversion of P-450 to P-420 segre-
gates 2:2; b) prepared genomic libraries of S. cerevisiae and of the
yeast Candida tropicalis, and used complementation by transformation
to search for the P-450 genes lanosterol 14α-demethylase and n-alkane ω-hydroxylase; c) conducted the induction of P-450 by 3-methyl-
clolanthrene and β-naphthoflavone in the chick embryo hepatocyte
cell culture system; d) initiated studies on a cDNA clone of a rate
phenobarbital-induced cytochrome P-450 for expression in yeast.
This latter study is in collaboration with Curt Omiecinski and
Edward Bresnick. (Supported by a grant from U.S. E.P.A.).

MOLECULAR INDUCTION BY PHENOBARBITAL OF

CYTOCHROME P-450 AND EPOXIDE HYDROLASE

Curtis J. Omiecinski[1] and Edward Bresnick[2]

[1]Department of Environmental Health, SC-34
University of Washington
Seattle, Washington 98195

Many xenobiotic chemicals, such as pesticides, drugs, and poly-cyclic hydrocarbons, are bioactivated by the microsomal cytochrome P-450-dependent monooxygenases and epoxide hydrolase to oxygenated intermediates which are often highly electrophilic and capable of binding covalently to cellular macromolecules such as DNA.

We have succeeded in isolating cDNA clones for both epoxide hydrolase and a major phenobarbital-inducible form of cytochrome P-450 by differential screening of a cDNA clone bank of rat hepatic polyA$^+$-RNA from rat liver. However, when similar experiments were performed with the cytochrome P-450 probe, PB-8, a 4 kb species of polyA$^+$-RNA demonstrated extensive homology. Preparations of nuclear RNA were studied and also exhibited a 4 kb species of homologous RNA when probed with the PB-8 clone. Time course experiments indicated that enhanced transcription of nuclear RNA for cytochrome P-450 occurred following phenobarbital administration and was detected as early as 0.5 hr post-injection. Phenobarbital pretreatment also produced increased rates of transcription of epoxide hydrolase RNA.

The isolated cDNA clones should prove useful in elucidating molecular mechanisms that control the genetic expression for these important classes of inducible bioactivation enzymes. (Supported by NIH grant ES 01974 and the Council for Tobacco Research grant 1369).

---

[2]Eppley Institute for Research in Cancer, University of Nebraska
Medical Center, Omaha, Nebraska 68105.

CHEMISTRY AND GENOTOXICITY OF RUNOFFS FROM MODEL COAL PILES

Ralph G. Stahl, Jr.,[1] E. M. Davis,[2] F. E. Arrighi,[2]
T. S. Matney,[2] and J. G. Liehr[2]

[1]School of Fisheries, WH-10
University of Washington
Seattle, Washington 98195

The use of coal for fuel in place of oil and natural gas has been increasing. Typically, coal is stored outdoors in large piles. Rainfall on the coal creates runoffs which may contain materials hazardous to the environment.

To study this hazard, rainfall on model coal piles was simulated, using deionized water and four coals of varying sulfur content. Simulated runoffs were: analyzed for water quality, extracted and then analyzed by capillary GC/MS, and the extracts were tested for mutagenicity with the Ames assay and for clastogenicity with CHO cells.

Runoffs from the high-sulfur coals and the lignite exhibited extremes of pH, conductivity, chemical oxygen demand, and total suspended solids. Most extracts contained at least 10 organic compounds including polycyclic aromatic hydrocarbons. Concentrations were generally less than 50 µg/l. Some of the extracts were weakly mutagenic; S9 decreased this effect. Extracts of runoffs from the high-sulfur coals were clastogenic and cytotoxic; those from the low-sulfur coal and the lignite were less clastogenic but not cytotoxic. Clastogenicity occurred with and without S9.

Our results suggest that runoffs from actual coal piles may be hazardous to adjacent aquatic areas, and may contaminate underground and surface drinking water supplies if not treated sufficiently.

---

[2]The Texas Medical Center, Houston, Texas 77030.

AEROBIC MICROBIAL DEGRADATION OF GLUCOISOSACCHARINIC ACID

Stuart E. Strand,[1] J. Dykes,[1] and V. Chiang[2]

[1]College of Forest Resources, AR-10
University of Washington
Seattle, Washington 98195

α-Glucoisosaccharinic acid (GISA), a major byproduct of kraft paper manufacture, was synthesized from lactose and used as the carbon source for microbial media. Twenty-seven laboratory strains of bacteria were tested and none was capable of growth on GISA. GISA degrading isolates were not found in forest soils. Ten aerobic bacterial strains capable of growth on GISA were isolated from kraft pulp mill environments. Highest growth yields were obtained with _Ancylobacter_ ssp. at pH 7.2 to 9.5. GISA was completely degraded by cultures of an _Ancylobacter_ isolate. _Ancylobacter_ cell suspensions consumed oxygen and produced carbon dioxide in response to GISA addition.

---

[2]Crown Zellerbach, Camas, Washington

PHENOL DEGRADATION IN MICROBIAL FIXED-FILM BIOREACTORS

Gerald W. Strandberg, T. L. Donaldson,
G. S. Shields, and J. D. Hewitt

Chemical Technology Division
Oak Ridge National Laboratory
P. O. Box X
Oak Ridge, Tennessee 37830

This poster presentation will compare results of experiments on the kinetics of phenol degradation by two microbial fixed-film populations with those published in the literature for more conventional aerobic treatment processes. The fixed-film populations, established and maintained in columnar fluidized-bed bioreactors, were initiated with the commercially available dry culture preparations Phenobac[R] (Polybac Corp., Berlin, New Jersey) and Bichem[R] 1001 and 1002 (Sybron Biochemicals, Birmingham, New Jersey). The effect of O_2, temperature, and phenol concentration on the rate of phenol degradation by the fixed-film population in batch reactors and fluidized-bed bioreactors will be discussed.

CONSTRUCTION OF A "GENE LIBRARY" OF <u>PSEUDOMONAS</u> SP. B13 AND

EXPRESSION OF THE 3-CHLOROBENZOATE DEGRADATIVE GENES

Mary-Paz Weisshaar,[1] M. Bagdasarian,[2]
W. Reineke,[1] and F. C. H. Franklin[3]

[1]Institut für Mikrobiologie der
   Universität Göttingen
Grisebachstr. 8
3400 Göttingen
West Germany

To facilitate the genetic analysis and manipulation of the 3-chlorobenzoate degradative functions, it is of interest to clone DNA segments that carry individual genes and blocks of genes that encode parts of or complete catabolic pathways. The construction of "gene banks" will allow the isolation of hybrid plasmids that collectively contain all the endonuclease-generated fragments of the 3-chlorobenzoate degradative plasmid. The pMMB33 cosmid (13.75 kb) we use allows a high expression of the genes from <u>P.sp.B13</u> in <u>E. coli</u> and can be mobilized in <u>Pseudomonas</u>. This poster describes the cloning procedure and the analysis of gene expression.

---

[2]Institut für Molekular Genetik, Berlin.

[3]Biogen, Geneva, Switzerland.

ISOLATION AND CHARACTERIZATION OF TN-5 INDUCED INSERTION MUTANTS IN

THE 3-CHLOROBENZOATE DEGRADATION PATHWAY OF PSEUDOMONAS SP. B13

M. P. Weisshaar[1], A. J. Weightman[2],
W. Reineke[1], and K. N. Timmis[2]

Institut für Mikrobiologie der
  Unversität Göttingen
Grisebachstr. 8
3400 Göttingen
West Germany

Chemical mutagenesis with such chemical substances as EMS (ethyl-methyl-sulfonic acid) and NTG (nitrosoguanidine) has been until now the only way to isolate mutants from p.sp.B13 defective in the 3-chlorobenzoate degradative pathway. This mutagenic technique produces point mutations. Very often multiple mutations are encountered in a single cell. To overcome this problem and get mutants with a more stable pheno- and genotype, it was necessary to develop another mutagenic method for P.sp.B13. Transposonmutagenesis is one of the most powerful techniques available for genetic analysis in bacteria. It also allows mapping of the genes using restriction endonucleases. Transposons such as Tn-7 and Tn-5 previously were used successfully to mutagenize P. putida mt-2 (TOL plasmid) and P. aeruginosa. Tn-5 (encoding kanamycin resistance) is known to insert with a relatively high frequency in the genomes of prokaryotes and eukaryotes independent of the recA function; usually only one Tn-5 element is inserted per genome. It seemed reasonable to try transposon mutagenesis on P.sp.B13 with Tn-5 after Tn-7 and Tn-3 had been used without success.

The vector ColIb drd-1 (so-called suicide transposon donor) was used to introduce the TN-5 into P.sp.B13 after selection on kanamycin. The frequency of insertion was 7×10^{-7} per donor. We

---

[2] Centre Médical Universitaire, Switzerland.

observed 2-3% of mutants defective in the 3-chlorobenzoate pathway. Thus, this method may allow isolation mutants defective in the degradative pathway useful for investigation of the regulation of the pathway and organization of the genes.

POTENTIAL USE OF MICROCOSMS TO ASSESS SURVIVAL, EFFICACY, AND ENVIRONMENTAL SAFETY OF GENETICALLY ENGINEERED MICROORGANISMS

Frieda B. Taub and Andrew C. Kindig

School of Fisheries, WH-10
University of Washington
Seattle, Washington 98195

"Standardized Aquatic Microcosms" for assessing the ecological effects of new chemicals are currently being interlaboratory tested, and could be adapted for use with genetically engineered organisms. They have the potential to evaluate the ability of new microorganisms to survive under conditions of competition and predation, to degrade test substrates in the presence of naturally abundant substrates, to determine pathogenicity to several species of algae and animals, and to disrupt ecological cycles. The 63-day microcosm protocol was developed and tested against a variety of chemicals.

These results suggest that the microcosms can show consistent ecological effects of chemicals on aquatic communities. Because the microcosms are initiated with chemically defined medium and organisms from laboratory cultures, we have hypothesized that the control and treatment behavior should be reproducible between laboratories. Although our past studies have not focused on the non-algal microbial components of the microcosms, it should be possible to enumerate organisms in the same way as in any natural aquatic community.

There are many similarities in evaluating the environmental safety of new chemicals and new organisms. It is feasible to measure acute or chronic effects on numerous organisms that are regarded as representative of taxa, or on important ecological processes. It is difficult to predict ecological effects in the infinite variety of natural environments. It is impossible to ensure that some combination of physical-chemical-biological factors could not occur which would render the new entity unexpectedly dangerous.

CLOSING REMARKS

Gilbert S. Omenn

Dean, Public Health and Community Medicine
University of Washington
Seattle, Washington 98195

We have had a most stimulating and informative meeting. The
quality of research is high, the extent of communication across
fields was encouraging, and the intense discussions and roundtables
yielded these main conclusions:

1) Nature offers remarkable biodegradative capabilities in
certain organisms. Modern genetics can be done with some of these
organisms, and the rates of biodegradation can be enhanced to what
should be useful levels. The ability to dechlorinate highly persis-
tant chlorinated pesticides would be especially desirable.

2) Ecosystems present severe challenges for survival and
effectiveness of genetically engineered or selected organisms, due
to low concentrations of substrate, toxins, predators, physical
barriers, and seasonal or other fluctuations in environmental
conditions.

3) Potential ecological hazards should be minimal so long as
genes are transferred within bacteria or within fungi, as opposed to
moving mammalian genes into plants or bacteria.

4) The best strategy for efficacy and safety is to isolate
organisms from environments of interest--sediments, sludges, dumps,
soils, introduce the plasmid or gene coding for the biodegradative
enzyme(s), and then return the organism to its habitat.

5) We should seek targets of opportunity to test the strains
that are isolated and engineered. The most promising targets are:
   a) point sources of industrial effluents with high concentra-
      tions of specific chemicals;

385

    b) spills of particular chemicals in contained areas;
    c) dump sites being prepared for encapsulation or excavation, in which introduction of organisms and careful monitoring of their effects, survival, and spread can be carried out at minimal marginal costs and with full control of the site;
    d) reduction of volume and bulking characteristics of activated sludge.

6) There was considerable, possibly naive, support for guidelines or regulations to inform and protect industrial and academic developments in this field. The Environmental Protection Agency should be encouraged to help identify and support demonstration projects in the most promising targets of opportunity as an essential preliminary step in devising appropriate guidelines for such work.

7) The marketplace will be a tough test for genetic approaches:
    a) when present methods for pollution control are adequate or are perceived to be adequate, there will be little receptivity for new methods (of any kind);
    b) genetic improvements may best be thought of in concert with existing methods, bridging current practices;
    c) the extent or frequency of the problem must be large enough to warrant upfront investments and marketing efforts;
    d) the regulatory environment must press for control and inactivation of pollutants. A good way to stimulate genetically engineered and other pollution control efforts at point sources would be a shift to a tax on various emissions, rather than on total production.

8) This Conference has demonstrated that specialists in such diverse areas as genetic engineering, microbial ecology, and environmental engineering, and from academic, industrial, nonprofit, and governmental sectors could interact very productively. Our participants disclosed more information from current ecological, engineering, and bioaugmentation work than most of us thought existed at this time. And we all recognized that the pace of technical developments and applications in genetic engineering continues to exceed our expectations.

We look forward to much progress in this challenging field of control of environmental pollutants over the next three to five years.

PARTICIPANTS AND SPEAKERS

Agabian, Nina — Biochemistry, Univ. Washington, Seattle, WA 98195

Alexander, Martin — Agronomy, Cornell University, Itahca, NY 14853

Amiri, Farshad — Environmental Health, Univ. Washington, Seattle, WA 98195

Anderson, Dawn — Microbiology/Immunology, Univ. Washington, Seattle, WA 98195

Bailet, Jeff — Environmental Health, Univ. Washington, Seattle, WA 98195

Ball, Judith A. — Snohomish County Admin. Bldg., Everett, WA 98201

Bang, Greg — Environmental Health, Univ. Washington, Seattle, WA 98195

Barnes, Rob — Pathobiology, Univ. Washington, Seattle, WA 98195

Bechtel, Timothy J. — Scott Paper Co., P.O. Box 925, Everett, WA 98206

Benemann, John R. — Applied Biology, Georgia Inst. of Technology, Atlanta, GA 30332

Boose, David L. — Univ. Pennsylvania, 4214 Walnut St., Philadelphia, PA 19104

Bourquin, Al W. — U.S. EPA, Env. Research, Sabine Island, Gulf Breeze, FL 32561

Breysse, Peter A. — Environmental Health, Univ. Washington, Seattle, WA 98195

Brooks, Ronald E. — General Electric Corp., P. O. Box 8, Bldg. K1, Schenectady, NY 12345

Broomfield, Barbara — Argonne Labs., 9700 S. Cass, Bldg. 362, Argonne, IL 60439

Brown, Kelly — Microbiology, Univ. Washington, Seattle, WA 98195

Brown, Jr., Ross D. — Biochemistry, Univ. Florida, Gainesville, FL 32604

Bryan, Edward H. — National Science Foundation, Civil Eng., Washington, DC 20550

Burnett, Craig — 2852 CES/DEML McClellan Air Force Base, Sacramento, CA 95652

Butz, Robert G. — Velsicol Chemical Corp., 341 East Ohio St., Chicago, IL 60611

Camp, Janice — Environmental Health, Univ. Washington, Seattle, WA 98195

Carberry, Bill — Environmental Health, Univ. Washington, Seattle, WA 98195

Carlson, Curtis A. — Bacteriology, Univ. California, Davis, CA 95616

Case, Joel T. — 500 North St., Blackfoot, ID 83221

Chakrabarty, A. M. — Microbiology, Univ. Illinois Medical Center, Chicago, IL 60612

Chakravarti — INOVA

Chen, Andrew — Genetic Laboratories, CDC, Tucker, GA 30084

Chew, Nancy — U.S. EPA, 1815 Westmoreland Dr., McLean, VA 22101

Clyde, Robert A. — Chemical Engineering, 200 Tunnel Rd., Asheville, NC 28805

Cohn, Daniel H. — Microbiology/Immunology, Univ. Washington, Seattle, WA 98915

Colwell, Rita — Microbiology, Univ. Maryland, College Park, MD 20742

Coppock, Rob — Environment and Society, Univ. Washington, Seattle, WA 98195

Covert, David S. — Environmental Health, Univ. Washington, Seattle, WA 98195

Cox, Evelyn — Environmental Health, Univ. Washington, Seattle, WA 98195

Cunninghan, Virginia — Smith Klein & French Labs., P. O. Box 7929, Philadelphia, PA 19101

Curran, Linda — Battelle, Columbus Labs., 505 King Ave., Columbus, OH 43201

Daigle, Virginia — Environmental Health, Univ. Washington, Seattle, WA 98195

Davis, Mac — Environmental Health, Univ. Washington, Seattle, WA 98195

Demain, Arnold L. — Nutrition/Food Science, Mass. Inst. Tech., Cambridge, MA 02139

Deroos, Roger — Env. Health & Safety, Univ. Washington, Seattle, WA 98195

Dewalle, Foppe B. — Environmental Health, Univ. Washington, Seattle, WA 98195

Drake, J. F. — Biosciences Lab., 3M Center, St. Paul, MN

Drugge, Carl E. — Borden, Inc., 960 Kingsmill Pkwy., Columbus, OH 43229

Durham, Don R. — Genex Corp., 16020 Industrial Dr., Gaithersburg, MD 20877

Eaton, David — Environmental Health, Univ. Washington, Seattle, WA 98195

Edwards, Joe — Boeing Co., P. O. Box 3707, Seattle, WA 98124

Elkin, Samuel	Temple University, 12002 Ferndale St., Philadelphia, PA 19116
Espinoza-Aguirre, Javier	Inst. Invest. Biomedicas, National Univ., Mexico City, Mexico
Farris, Carol A.	U.S. EPA, 401 M St., SW, Washington, DC 20460
Faustman-Watts, Elaine	Environmental Health, Univ. Washington, Seattle, WA 98195
Fleskes, Carol	Water Quality Planning, State of Washington, Olympia, WA 98504
Foght, Julia	Microbiology, Univ. Alberta, Edmonton, Alberta, Canada
Fowle, III, John R.	U.S. EPA, 401 M St., SW, Washington, DC 20460
Franco, Nicholas B.	Bethlehem Steel Corp., Homer Research Lab., Bethlehem, PA 18017
Frazer, Anne Cornish	Microbiology, New York Univ. Medical Center, New York, NY 10016
Furlong, Clement E.	Medical Genetics, Univ. Washington, Seattle, WA 98195
Gapsis, A.	1618A C. De Baca Ln., Santa Fe, NM 87501
Gartland, William	National Institutes of Health, Bldg., 31, Bethesda, MD 20205
Gersberg, Richard M.	Aquagene, Inc., 3831 Front St., San Diego, CA 92103
Giachelli, Cecelia	Pharmacology, Univ. Washington, Seattle, WA 98195
Goldhammer, Alan	Industrial Biotechnology Association, Rockville, MD 20852
Gordon, Milton P.	Microbiology, Univ. Washington, Seattle, WA 98195
Grubbs, B. Jones	Flow Lab., Inc., 828 W. Hillcrest Blvd., Inglewood, CA 90301
Hakulinen, Risto R.	Civil Engineering, Univ. Washington, Seattle, WA 98195
Hilton, Matt	Microbiology, Univ. Washington, Seattle, WA 98195
Hirschhorn, Joel S.	Office of Technology Assessment, Washington, DC 20510
Hisamatsu, T.	Kurita Water Ind., 18321 Southwestern, Gardena, CA 90248
Hollaender, Alexander	Council for Research Plng., 1717 Mass. Ave., Washington, DC 20036
Hollander, Anne	U.S. EPA, 401 M. St., SW, Washington, DC 20460
Hood, Leroy E.	Biology, California Inst. of Tech., Pasadena, CA 91125
Horstman, S. W.	Environmental Health, Univ. Washington, Seattle, WA 98195

Huffman, Gary   Microbiology, Univ. Washington,
                              Seattle, WA 98195
Jackson, Ken   Environmental Health, Univ.
                              Washington, Seattle, WA 98195
Jasper, Paula   Molecular Biology, 9658 24th St.,
                              SW, Seattle, WA 98103
Johnson, Layne   Polybac Corp., 954 Marcon Blvd.,
                              Allentown, PA 18103
Jones, Kim   Env. Health & Safety, Univ.
                              Washington, Seattle, WA 98195
Jurgensen, Shirley   Civil Engineering, Univ.
                              Washington, Seattle, WA 98195
Kalb, Vernon F.   Microbiol., Univ. Cincinnati Coll.
                              of Med., Cincinnati, OH 45267
Kalman, David   Environmental Health, Univ.
                              Washington, Seattle, WA 98195
Kamath, Ajith V.   Biochemistry, Indian Institute of
                              Science, Bangalore, India
Kilbane, John J.   Microbiology, Univ. Illinois,
                              Chicago, IL 60612
Kindig, Andrew   Fisheries, Univ. Washington,
                              Seattle, WA 98195
Kleinman, Goldy D.   Environmental Health, Univ.
                              Washington, Seattle, WA 98195
Kobayashi, Hester   Environmental Testing, Standard
                              Oil Co., Cleveland, OH 44128
Koenig, Jane   Environmental Health, Univ.
                              Washington, Seattle, WA 98195
Kopecky, Anne   Sybron Biochemical, P. O. Box 808,
                              Salem, VA 24153
Kramer, Fran   Argonne National Lab., Bldg. 62,
                              Argonne, IL 60439
Krogh, Joan C.   Boise State Univ., 6717 San
                              Fernando Dr., Boise, ID 83704
Kronstad, Jim   Microbiology, Univ. Washington,
                              Seattle, WA 98195
Kulpa, Charles F.   Microbiology, Univ. Notre Dame,
                              Notre Dame, IN 46556
Kuo, M. J.   Monsanto Co., 800 N. Lindbergh
                              Blvd., St. Louis, MO 63167
Landis, Wayne   Army, Chemical Res. & Dev. Comm.,
                              Aberdeen Proving Ground, MD 21010
Lara, J. C.   Microbiology, Univ. Washington,
                              Seattle, WA 98195
Lawrence, Lynn   Public Health, Univ. Washington,
                              Seattle, WA 98195
Lawrence, Sally   Biotechnology News Watch, 121 N.
                              46th St., Seattle, WA 98103
Lehmicke, Leo   Microbiology, Univ. Washington,
                              Seattle, WA 98195

Levin, Morris	U.S. EPA, Office of Research & Development, Washington, DC 20460
Licht, PE, Louis A.	CH2M Hill, 1600 SW Western Blvd., Corvallis, OR 97339
Lidstrom, Mary E.	Microbiology, Univ. Washington, Seattle, WA 98195
Loper, John C.	Microbiol./Molec. Gen., Univ. Cincinnati, Cincinnati, OH 45267
Lowry, Kim	Environmental Health, Univ. Washington, Seattle, WA 98195
Luchtel, Daniel L.	Environmental Health, Univ. Washington, Seattle, WA 98195
Lukens, Carl	Environmental Health, Univ. Washington, Seattle, WA 98195
Lyon, Steven	San Diego State Univ., 3016 Menlow Ave., San Diego, CA 92105
Ma, Greg	Environmental Health, Univ. Washington, Seattle, WA 98195
McCarthy, Joseph L.	Chem. Eng. & Forest Res., Univ. Washington, Seattle, WA 98195
McGinity, Richard C.	Plant Resources Venture Fund, 175 Federal St., Boston, MA 02110
McNamee, Clyde G.	Genex Corp., 16020 Industrial Dr., Gaithersburg, MD 20877
Mendelsohn, Robert O.	Economics, Univ. Washington, Seattle, WA 98195
Meyers, Richard K.	Petroleum Research, Texaco, Inc., P. O. Box 509, Beacon, NY 12508
Michelson, Karyn D.	Univ. Washington, 4405 Corliss Ave. N., Seattle, WA 98103
Middleton, A. C.	Koppers Co., Inc., 440 College Park Dr., Monroeville, PA 15146
Minnich, Liz	Microbiology, Univ. Washington, Seattle, WA 98195
Mohamed, Mostafa	Pathology, Univ. Washington, Seattle, WA 98195
Monteith, Lee	Environmental Health, Univ. Washington, Seattle, WA 98195
Morgan, James J.	Env. Engineering Science, Cal Tech, Pasadena, CA 91125
Morris, Sharon	Environmental Health, Univ. Washington, Seattle, WA 98195
Munger, Sydney	Environmental Health, Univ. Washington, Seattle, WA 98195
Munson, Ron	Environmental Health, Univ. Washington, Seattle, WA 98195
Murrell, Colin	Microbiology, Univ. Washington, Seattle, WA 98195
Nakamura, Koichi	Kurita Water Industries Ltd., Gardena, CA 90248

Nester, Eugene   Microbiology, Univ. Washington,
                              Seattle, WA 98195
Nielsen, Allen   Conoco, Inc., P. O. Box 1267,
                              Ponca City, OK 74603
Omenn, Gilbert S.   Public Health/Commun. Med., Univ
                              Washington, Seattle, WA 98195
Omiecinski, Curt   Environmental Health, Univ.
                              Washington, Seattle, WA 98195
Orians, Gordon H.   Environmental Studies, Univ.
                              Washington, Seattle, WA 98195
Owings, Don   Genex, 6110 Executive Blvd.,
                              Rockville, MD 20852
Parker, John C.   Microbiology Association, 5221
                              River Rd., Bethesda, MD 20816
Parson, Willie   Microbiology, Evergreen State
                              College, Olympia, WA
Patterson, James W.   Pritzker, Env. Eng., Illinois
                              Inst. Tech., Chicago, IL 60630
Pelroy, Richard A.   Battelle-Northwest Labs. P. O. Box
                              99, Richland, WA 99352
Peterkofsky, Allan   Research, W. R. Grace Co., 7379
                              Rt. 32, Columbia, MD 21044
Pier, Stanley M.   Public Health, Univ. Texas, P. O.
                              Box 20186, Houston, TX 77225
Pirages, Sue Ellen   Office of Technology Assessment,
                              Washington, DC 20510
Popkin, David   4311 Queensbury Rd., Riverdale, MD
                              20737
Powledge, Tabitha M.   Biotechnology, 15 East 26th, New
                              York, NY 10010
Putzrath, Resha   National Academy of Sciences, 2101
                              Constitution, Washington, DC 20418
Rams, Jacqueline M.   Camp, Dresser & McKee, 7630 Little
                              River Tpk., Annandale, VA 22003
Ricker, N. Lawrence   Chemical Engineering, Univ.
                              Washington, Seattle, WA 98195
Riggs, Larry   Genrec, 955 Stannage Ave., Albany,
                              CA 94706
Rittmann, Bruce E.   Civil Engineering, Univ. Illinois,
                              Urbana, Champaign, IL 61801
Rockwell, Chris   Fisheries, Univ. Washington,
                              Seattle, WA 98195
Rogers, John E.   Battelle, Pacific Northwest Labs.,
                              P. O. Box 999, Richland, WA 99352
Rogul, Marvin   Strategic Assessments, U.S. EPA,
                              Rockville, MD 20852
Sample, T. E.   Water Quality Tech, Univ.
                              Washington, Seattle, WA 98195
Sandbeck, Kenneth A.   Microbiology/Immunology, Univ.,
                              Washington, Seattle, WA 98195

Sandhu, S. S.	U.S. EPA, Research Triangle Park, NC 27711
Sarkanen, Kyosti	Forest Res. and Chem. Eng., Univ. Washington, Seattle, WA 98195
Sayler, Gary S.	Microbiology, Univ. Tennessee, Knoxville, TN 37916
Schiewe, Michael H.	U. S. National Marine Fisheries Service, Seattle, WA 98112
Schmitz, Laura	Environmental Health, Univ. Washington, Seattle, WA 98195
Schultz, Cmdr. Warren W.	Biological Sciences, Off. of Naval Research, Arlington, VA 22217
Shapiro, James A.	Microbiology, Cummings Life Sci. Ctr., Chicago, IL 60637
Sharples, Frances	Oak Ridge National Lab., Oak Ridge, TN 37830
Sherris, John C.	Univ. Washington, Seattle, WA 98195
Sibley, Thomas	Radiation Ecol., Fisheries, Univ. Washington, Seattle, WA 98195
Silver, Simon	Biology, Washington Univ., St. Louis, MO 63130
Smart, Charles L.	Toxicology, Mobil Oil Corp., Princeton, NJ 08648
Sojka, Stanley A.	Occidental Chemical Corp., Grand Island, NY 14057
Soule, Oskar	Evergreen State College, Olympia, WA 98505
Spiegel, Michael	Environmental Engineering, 1032 NW 30th, Corvallis, OR 97330
Stahl, Ralph G.	Univ. Texas Sch. of Public Health, P. O. Box 20186, Houston, TX 77025
Steiert, John G.	Univ. Minnesota, Gray Freshwater Biol. Inst., Navarre, MN 55331
Stephens, Richard	Pathobiology, Univ. Washington, Seattle, WA 98195
Stevenson, Donald E.	Toxicology, Shell Development Co., P. O. Box 822, Houston, TX 77001
Stoddart, Cpt. Terry L.	Air Force Engineering Ctr., 5724 Ivy Rd., Panama City, FL 32404
Strand, Stuart	Civil Engineering, Univ. Washington, Seattle, WA 98195
Strandberg, Gerald W.	Oak Ridge National Lab., P. O. Box X, Oak Ridge, TN 37830
Swierzbinski, Joseph E.	Environmental Studies, Univ. Washington, Seattle, WA 98195
Taub, Frieda	Fisheries, Univ. Washington, Seattle, WA 98195
Thomas, Jeffrey M.	Polybac Corp., 2030 Union St., San Francisco, CA 94123

Tomasek, Paul H. — Univ. Minnesota, Gray Freshwater Biol. Inst. Navarre, MN 55392

Toukdarian, Aresa — Microbiology, Univ. Washington, Seattle, WA 98195

Treser, Charles — Environmental Health, Univ. Washington, Seattle, WA 98195

Unger, Leon — Microbiology/Immunology, Univ. Washington, Seattle, WA 98195

Vashon, Robert D. — Environmental Safety, Procter and Gamble Co., Cincinnati, OH 45217

Volk, David — Env. Resources, State of Pennsylvania, Pittsburgh, PA 15222

Waters, Michael D. — U.S. EPA, Genetic Toxicology, Research Triangle Park, NC 27711

Weaver, Craig A. — Microbiology, Univ. Washington, Seattle, WA 98195

Weightman, Andrew — Biochimie Medicale, Univ. Geneve, 1211 Geneve, Switzerland

Weisshaar, Mary-Paz — Inst. Mikrobiologie der Univ. Göttingen, West Germany

Wells, R. Gordon — The Fertilizer Institute, 1015 18th St., NW, Washington, DC 20036

Wetzler, Theodore F. — Environmental Health, Univ. Washington, Seattle, WA 98195

White, James B. — Research Triangle Institute, Research Triangle Park, NC 27711

Whiteley, Helen R. — Microbiology/Immunology, Univ. Washington, Seattle, WA 98195

Whitman, Ira — Princeton Aqua Science, 789 Jersey Ave., New Brunswick, NJ 08902

Williams, Richard T. — 2465 Shadywood Rd., Excelsior, MN 55331

Wilson, Claire M. — Council for Research Plng., 1717 Mass. Ave., Washington, DC 20036

Woods, James — Env. Health, Battelle, 4000 NE 41st St., Seattle, WA 98105

Woods, Sandy — Environmental Eng. & Sci., Univ. Washington, Seattle, WA 98195

Zaborsky, Oskar — National Science Foundation, Chem. & Proc. Eng., Washington, DC 20550

Zimmerman, Burke K. — Cetus Corp., 600 Bancroft Way, Berkeley, CA 92710

INDEX